READING PROBLEMS:
A Multidisciplinary Perspective

100679

Wayne Otto
University of Wisconsin—Madison

Nathaniel A. Peters
Oakland Schools

Charles W. Peters
Oakland Schools

ADDISON-WESLEY PUBLISHING COMPANY

Reading, Massachusetts

Menlo Park, California · London · Amsterdam · Don Mills, Ontario · Sydney

We will always be indebted to our parents—Henry and Edna Otto and William and Muriel Peters—for their inspiration, devotion, and sacrifice without which this book would never have become a reality. To them and to the ideals they represent, we dedicate this book.

Any book is the result of interwoven strands of human efforts. Ours is no different. We would like to acknowledge the support of Oakland Schools, its board of trustees, and its chief administrators—especially Kenneth Brown, superintendent, and David Wells, assistant superintendent.

Preface

The general focus of *Reading Problems: A Multidisciplinary Perspective* is on *reading* disability. Although there is no attempt to deal comprehensively with the full range of *learning* disabilities, the overlap of concerns is fully acknowledged. We have tried to make the coverage palatable and useful to both reading educators and learning disability specialists. More specifically, the focus is on reading disability in the *school setting*. All of the contributors were encouraged to deal not with the esoterica of reading disability, but with rational, realistic approaches to reading problems as they are faced by people in the schools. We believe that school people can deal best with reading problems when they have: (1) a reasonable understanding of the nature of the problem; (2) alternatives for dealing with the problem; and (3) guidelines for getting reading problems in perspective in relation to the total school program. There is no ideal reading program for everybody; but by considering models and alternatives, we can move toward one that is best for each of us.

The first eight chapters of this book provide what we feel is essential background for understanding the diverse causes of reading problems and for seeing them in perspective. Chapter 2, on models of the reading process, deals with normal development in reading. Chapters 3 through 7 deal with different factors in and views of reading disability. Chapter 8 puts it all back together with an interdisciplinary model for dealing with reading problems in the school setting.

Chapters 9 through 18 provide what we feel is essential information for dealing with reading problems at the elementary school, high school, and adult levels. The chapter on media (Chapter 16) is offered because we feel that now is the time to take full advantage of the vast potential of media in dealing with reading problems. The chapter on the reading specialist (Chapter 11) is offered because in our experience the reading specialist often is the catalyst that makes things happen in reading. We do not hesitate to

iii

describe and advocate new roles—e.g., the clinical educator—that we feel are needed and represent advances toward dealing realistically with reading problems. Nevertheless, the overall focus of the second half of the book remains on the *school* and on the *classroom teacher,* because we believe that's where it's at when it comes to dealing with reading problems in a comprehensive way.

Needless to say, we feel that any book that claims to deal definitively with reading problems must have multiple authorship because it must draw from diverse backgrounds of training and experience to be credible. The contributors to this volume are people well qualified for the job. Some are well established and nationally known; others are relative newcomers; but each one is well qualified by training and experience to handle the topic with which he or she is identified. Each contributor is regarded as "authority" for his or her respective chapter(s). That is, contributors were asked *not* to present comprehensive reviews of the literature, exhaustive bibliographies, or a heavily documented treatment of a topic. Instead, each contributor was asked to develop his or her topic in a way that presents a point of view and introduces it to the relatively uninitiate.

The book is intended as an introductory text, to meet the needs of pre-service college students and in-service teachers who are taking their first course in "remedial reading" (or whatever the local euphemism for that area of concern may be). We make no assumptions regarding prior background in dealing with reading problems; the book itself provides whatever background is required to understand the positions and approaches presented. We *do,* of course, assume that the reader has had prior experience and/or training in the *developmental* teaching of reading. This is not your super single volume developmental-corrective-remedial economy special text. We are idealists who are attuned to reality.

Why should you pay any attention to still another "remedial reading" textbook? We submit three main reasons: (1) its breadth of coverage; (2) the credibility it derives from diverse contributors; (3) its timeliness and forward look. The need for a multidisciplinary approach to reading problems is well established and accepted. But it is seldom taken in any definitive sense, because the resource materials come from a variety of sources and they have not been assembled into a single source. This text represents an attempt to do that. Our hope is that the text amounts to a fresh look at a tired old topic at a time when the field is consolidating and looking toward the future.

December 1976   W. O.
N. A. P.
C. W. P.

Contents

Chapter 1

INTRODUCTION

WAYNE OTTO • *University of Wisconsin–Madison*

Our intent in *Reading Problems: A Multidisciplinary Perspective* is to take an interdisciplinary view of reading disability as it is experienced in the schools. Our hope is that this amounts to a fresh new look at a tired old topic. The time is ripe for a new look because the results from the long and costly experiment that was "remedial reading" are now available, and they are unequivocal. The experiment failed. Some of the reasons are examined by Briggs and Coulter in Chapter 11. But even an experiment that fails can provide a basis for moving forward, so long as the positive aspects are recognized and there is an inclination to build on what was learned. That takes perspective, and perspective is what the contributors to this book have to offer.

OVERVIEW OF THE BOOK

The general focus of the book is on *reading* disability. We have not attempted to deal systematically with the full scope of *learning* disabilities, but the overlap of concerns is acknowledged by all of the contributors and explicitly addressed by some. Our goal was to make the coverage palatable and useful to both reading educators and learning disability specialists. The antagonistic relationship that has surfaced between the two groups in some quarters has been nothing but counterproductive. Any sensible moves toward reconciliation can only be viewed as positive.

   The more specific focus of the book is on reading disability in the school setting. We acknowledge that reading problems are school problems. Whether or not such a conclusion is completely justified, the fact is that for the foreseeable future reading problems will continue to exist, and the

1

responsibility for dealing with them will rest with the schools and with the teachers in the schools. School people can best deal with reading problems when they have (1) a reasonable understanding of the nature of the problem, (2) alternatives for dealing with the problem, and (3) guidelines for getting reading problems in perspective in relation to the total school program. There is no ideal reading program for all learners or for all teachers, but the models and alternatives presented in this book can help us move toward what is best for each of us.

The book is intended as an introduction to reading problems and how to deal with them in schools. Although we do not hesitate to describe and/or advocate both traditional and new specialized roles in teaching reading— e.g., the reading specialist, the clinical educator—we emphasize the role of the classroom teacher throughout. The multidisciplinary approach and well-conceived specialized roles promise much in terms of dealing realistically with complex reading problems. But when it comes to dealing systematically and continuously with reading problems, the classroom is where it's at, and the classroom teacher has major responsibility for the action.

The book is a viable text for the first course in "remedial reading" or learning disabilities. As we said earlier, "remedial reading" is an experiment that failed. Nevertheless, the terminology and the course structures of colleges and universities are not likely to change in the near future. The point is that the book could be the introductory text either for preservice college students or in-service teachers or for courses designed to tackle reading problems in a school setting. We make no assumptions about prior background in dealing with reading problems. We have attempted to provide whatever background is required to understand the positions and approaches presented. Alternatives are provided so that the reader is in a position to adapt what is best for a particular situation.

One assumption should be clear. Although this book is an introduction to reading problems and how to deal with them, we assume throughout that the reader has had prior experience and/or training in the *developmental* teaching of reading. Much of what we say in the chapters that follow has to do explicitly with the teaching of reading, but we have not attempted to deal definitively with that topic. Such would be far beyond the scope of a single volume.

OVERVIEW OF THE CHAPTERS

We are convinced that a book that claims to deal definitively with reading problems must have multiple authorship, because it must draw from diverse backgrounds of training and experience to be credible. The contributors to this volume are people well qualified for the job. Each one brings the training and experience required to deal with his or her topic in a sensible, realistic way.

The first eight chapters provide essential background for understanding the diverse causes of reading problems and for seeing them in perspective. Samuels's chapter (Chapter 2), "Theoretical Models of Reading," is not limited to a consideration of problems, but deals instead with the full range of normal reading development. Samuels starts with the assumption that there is "nothing so practical as a good theory," and he says enough to convince most of his readers that what he says is true. The model he presents pays off, because he derives from it a routine for teaching both decoding and comprehension. The inferences are most germane for a text on reading problems, because the routines are likely to be most beneficial with learners to whom the reading process does not come "naturally." Samuels's model takes "reading" apart and then puts it back together. The teacher who learns to do just that is going to be in the best possible position for helping pupils with reading problems.

In Chapter 3, "Reading Problems in Perspective," Satz first underscores the magnitude of the reading problem and then points out the multiple causes for reading problems. He examines early detection and intervention as approaches to dealing with reading problems, and he concludes that early attention is likely to make the most difference. The chapter has much substance, so it is not easy reading. Be prepared for a good cognitive workout. But be assured that the information flow is clear enough to get you to the end with some real understandings.

The purpose of Chapter 4, "A Sociologist Looks at Reading," is to show what sociology has to offer in understanding and dealing with reading problems. Entwisle's most salient point is that the children who learn to read best are the children who *must* learn to read in order to make sense of their lives. Then, having demonstrated that social factors are important to reading, she shows how teachers can alter social structures within their own schools.

Drawing from another discipline, Ozer (Chapter 5, "Assessment of Children with Learning Problems") examines the medical model for diagnosis and seeks modifications that would allow a clearer focus on *treatment*. Ozer's main point is that the goal in diagnosis is to develop a plan for treatment. He speaks for the active involvement of each learner in the plan for treatment. The learner, he says, must realize that to be affected *by* information, the learner must do something *to* it. The role of the teacher, then, is that of consultant, helping the learner to contribute to the solution of the problem.

Medrano's position (Chapter 6, "A Psychiatric Perspective of Reading Disability") is that many learning problems require help from both learning specialists and psychotherapy. His main point is that the disabled learner must accept the *fact* of being disabled and then accept help in dealing with it. Each contributor develops a similar theme, namely, that the disabled learner must become actively involved in the process of overcoming the disability. The implication is that teachers have a greater responsibility than simply to offer quality instruction.

Freeman (Chapter 7) brings the perspective of a speech and hearing specialist to bear as he considers the assessment of oral language as a precursor of reading. In "Language Development," he describes an approach to helping children who have inadeqaute language development and consequent reading problems. A basic point is that the traditional emphasis on teaching *reading* in the schools may cause neglect of problems caused by lack of command of integrative language functions in children who have problems with comprehending, speaking, reading, and writing. Freeman offers suggestions about how professionals, including classroom teachers, can work together to make the most of their personal competencies in helping children develop integrative language skills.

In Chapter 8 ("An Interdisciplinary View of Reading Problems"), N. Peters extends the call for collaborative efforts by professionals, presenting a rationale for the interdisciplinary approach to learning problems. Although the composition of a team, in terms of professional specialties, may vary, the essential requirement is that the team bring to bear the perceptions of varied backgrounds in taking a realistic approach to the diagnosis and facilitation of learning *in the classroom*. The ultimate test of a team's success is its ability to communicate worthwhile information to classroom teachers and parents. Potential contributions of team members with different specialties are discussed. Differences in the composition and functioning of teams at the elementary and secondary school levels are examined in light of the facts in the real world of the schools.

Chapters 9 through 18 provide information for dealing with reading problems at the elementary school, high school, and adult levels. Specific chapters are devoted to the special problems of dealing with high school students and adults with reading problems. Although there is no specific chapter for the elementary school, the younger child is not neglected, for the main line of discussion throughout revolves around the problems associated with breakdowns in the teaching and learning of *developmental* reading.

Chapters 9 and 10 are transitional, moving from a focus on factors associated with reading ability/disability toward a focus on ways and means for tackling reading disability in the schools. In Chapter 9 ("Diagnosis of Reading Problems"), C. Peters presents a model for diagnosis and backs it up with a discussion of specific requirements of a sensible approach to diagnosis. "Show me your reading tests," he says, "and I will tell you your definition of reading." He also says there is a lot more to diagnosis than paper-and-pencil tests; but his point is that the goals of the reading program, not the tests at hand, ought to determine the parameters of diagnosis. Otto's main point in Chapter 10, "Orientation to Remedial Reading," is that successful remedial teaching must transcend the methods, materials, techniques, and organizational schemes that are the raw materials of remedial teaching. The chapter deals more with the how-to-pursue-it than with the how-to-do-it of remedial teaching.

This book is for every teacher who will be faced with the responsibility of tackling reading problems. Yet an entire chapter is devoted to the role and function of the reading specialist. "The Reading Specialist" by Briggs and Coulter (Chapter 11) traces the development of the role of the reading specialist and with sensitivity and empathy puts that role into proper perspective for the present. Classroom teachers, school administrators, and the general public have come, in many instances, to have very unrealistic expectations of the "reading specialist." The perspective is needed. Also needed is a perception of the reading specialist as a catalyst for change. The chapter tells it like it *was* and like it *ought to be!*

C. Peters gets down to specifics in Chapter 12 ("The Comprehension Process") and examines comprehension as the ultimate goal in the complex process of reading. He discusses the important comprehension skills and offers activities for developing them and for developing cognitive strategies. N. Peters continues this discussion in Chapter 13 ("Approaches to Remedial Reading"). The message that comes through most clearly is that effective *remedial* teaching is very highly focused *developmental* teaching. There are no tricks or special techniques for remedial teaching.

Chapters 14 and 15 deal with the special problems of dealing with the reading problems of high school students and adults. In "Problems, Prescriptions, and Possibilities in High School Reading Instruction" (Chapter 14), Singer and Rhodes offer a comprehensive high school program and beef it up with thumbnail sketches of representative high school reading problems and prescriptions for them. The treatment is practical and down to earth, qualities that are absent in too many discussions of high school reading. Kreitlow, in Chapter 15, "Adult Basic Education," points out that this type of education is for adults who either (1) missed out on academic skill development or (2) let their skills deteriorate from little use. His chapter focuses on the special needs of adult basic education students because, as he says, the skill development needs of such adults are not different from the needs of younger learners.

The media explosion of the 1960s produced more than all of the cumulative efforts before that decade. Feldmann's main point in Chapter 16, "Media in Reading Instruction," is that the media culture of today may affect poor readers' school learning in two negative ways: (1) commercial media are more attractive than the usual school media, and (2) little is typically expected of the viewer/listener while he or she is involved with a media presentation. She then goes on, in the bulk of the chapter, to introduce and explain optimal uses of media with poor readers.

Rude's chapter, "Organizing the Reading Program" (Chapter 17), places remedial teaching in the total reading program of the school. The purpose is to take the interdisciplinary model into the classroom. The roles of various school personnel in taking a team approach to tackling reading problems are discussed. Then, in the final chapter ("Improving the Teaching of Reading Through In-service"), Erickson shows how the teaching of reading can be improved through in-service education in reading. The chapter has a dual focus: (1) how to get the process of in-service education going in the schools, and (2) examples of in-service programs designed to help school staffs meet the needs of disabled readers. Erickson's main point is that teachers ought to be true participants, not merely pawns, in in-service programs. When the spirit is willing and the climate is right, in-service education can permit teachers to continue their training and development throughout their careers. In-service education can be a powerful vehicle for keeping reading problems in perspective.

Chapter 2

INTRODUCTION TO
THEORETICAL MODELS OF READING

S. JAY SAMUELS · *University of Minnesota*

The first section of this chapter on theoretical models of reading explains the characteristics of theories, the reasons for their development, and suggestions on how they may be used. The middle section gives an in-depth description of two reading models, and the final section indicates several practical ways in which the reading theories may be used to overcome problems encountered in the classroom. Considering that a substantial number of reading models have been developed, one may wonder why only two are described. A major consideration was that rather than gloss over the surface of a large number of models, I thought it would be more useful to the reader to go into a few models in depth. Another consideration was that the two models described in depth lend themselves to suggestions of ways in which the teaching of reading might be improved. For those who may wish to examine the broad area of theoretical models of reading, refer to the list of suggested readings at the end of this article.

CHARACTERISTICS OF THEORIES

Background

Making order out of apparent chaos: simplifying the complex Many would agree that the world we live in is a pretty complicated place. In order to understand our world, scholars have attempted to find answers to the various questions they have raised. Questions such as "What are the mechanisms of learning and memory?" are so difficult to answer that several scholarly disciplines have been brought to bear on the problem. Psychology, biology, chemistry, and physics each have a somewhat different, but important, contribution to make to a question about the nature of learning and memory.

In some ways our interdisciplinary approach to important problems and questions is reminiscent of the six wise men described in John Saxe's poem "The Blind Men and the Elephant." Curious about the appearance of an elephant that none had ever seen, the six decided to satisfy their curiosity by direct observation and contact with an elephant. The first blind man touched the elephant's sturdy side and likened the elephant to a wall. The second felt the elephant's tusk and thought that the elephant resembled a spear. The third happened to touch the squirming trunk of the elephant and thought the elephant was similar to a snake. The fourth felt about the elephant's knee and said, "Tis clear enough the elephant is very like a tree." The fifth chanced to touch an ear, and to him the elephant was like a fan. The sixth, and last of the blind men, touched the tail and thought that the elephant was very much like a rope. Saxe concluded his poem with this thought:

> And so these men of Indostan
> Disputed loud and long,
> Each in his own opinion
> Exceeding stiff and strong,
> Though each was partly in the right,
> And all were in the wrong!

Limitations to interdisciplinary approaches   This amusing account of the wise men who tried to describe an elephant is somewhat analogous to what happens when different scholarly disciplines approach a problem. We note, first, that each discipline approaches a problem or question from a somewhat different perspective. Consequently, because of differences in approach, method of investigation, and selection of what is to be studied, each discipline arrives at somewhat different answers to the question. Second, just as the blind men described the elephant's leg as a tree and the trunk as a snake, scholars tend to describe the new in terms that are already familiar and known. Thus an element of distortion is brought in. Unfortunately, this distortion is almost a necessary situation, since the only way we can begin to understand that which is new is through our current cognitive structures, understandings, and old labels. Third, since each blind man—or discipline, for that matter—was able to describe only a part of a much larger totality, we get a fragmented picture of the object or phenomenon we are trying to describe. Before we can get a reasonably accurate picture of the phenomenon under investigation, the findings from the several disciplines must be brought together, much like the pieces in a jigsaw puzzle.

This tendency to simplify what is essentially a complex process brings us to the focus of this chapter, which has to do with theoretical models of the reading process. For many centuries now, scholars have tried to bring order out of what appeared, to the uninitiated, to be chaos—to simplify the complex, to explain how various parts of a complicated system interact to work together. This attempt to simplify the complex and to show how components interact in a system is just a part of what is involved in the process of building theoretical models.

How models are commonly used   Although at first it might appear that a topic dealing with theoretical models is far removed from everyday experience, in actuality I am quite sure that each of the readers of this article is familiar with certain aspects of models. What I would like to do here is to remove just a part of the aura and mystique which seems to surround theoretical models by showing how these theoretical models have some degree of overlap with models as they are commonly used. For example, one might ask, "What does an airplane model, an anatomy chart of human skeletal or muscular structure, and a physical map of the world all have in common?" The answer to this question is that all of these models are simplified representations or facsimiles of far more complicated structures. It is important to point out that this is all that is meant by the commonly used term "model." One can even develop a model of a process. For example, teaching is a process that has certain distinct activities, such as goal setting, preassessing, planning, teaching, measuring, and evaluating. It is a simple task, as seen in Fig. 2.1, to draw a flow diagram showing the sequential interrelationship of these activities. Figure 2.1 shows how models are used in everyday life to represent a simplification of either objects or processes. Just as a model may be used in everyday life to represent an object or process in simplified form so that it may be better understood, a model may also be used to represent either an entire theory, or some part of a theory, so that it may be better understood.

Characteristics of a theory   It seems appropriate at this point to describe the characteristics of a theory. A theory generally consists of a set of generalizations, based on scientifically derived findings, which serve as a basis for prediction and hypothesis testing. This definition of "theory" has several important implications. First, it suggests that a theory should attempt to summarize a body of knowledge. The advantage of summarizing a body of knowledge is that the theory subsumes, represents, or incorporates in a simplified form many findings and facts into a few principles or generalizations. Second, the theory will be an important asset in helping us to understand current happenings, events, and processes about us. A third implication is that the theory will enable us to make predictions about future events. Finally, a good theory is not static; rather, it fosters the growth of new

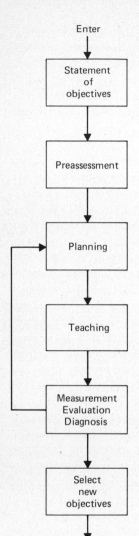

Fig. 2.1. Simplified model of the teaching process, showing components, direction of movement, and feedback loop. This model would be suitable for teaching reading.

knowledge by helping scientists generate testable hypotheses. As new knowledge is accumulated by hypothesis testing, the theory can eventually be modified so as to subsume the new knowledge along with the older findings.

Table 2.1 shows that theory components may be viewed in a time frame of past, present, and future. In addition, a theory can be evaluated in terms of its usefulness. Contrary to popular opinion, there are few intellectual devices so useful as a good theory that permits us to understand events and processes across time boundaries.

Having discussed how models are used in everyday life and described the characteristics of a theory, I should point out that many of my colleagues

Table 2.1. Characteristics of theories in relation to a time frame

Characteristics of theory	Time frame
Summarizes what is known	The past
Aids in understanding ongoing events	The present
Generates predictions and hypotheses	The future

differentiate between models and theories. To some, a "theory" is a set of broad generalizations that can serve as a basis for formulating hypotheses; a "model" is a more precise, and perhaps less comprehensive, statement that leads more readily to hypothesis testing. In this sense, then, models appear to be more precise and testable than theories.

Despite the attempt to differentiate between "theories" and "models," however, one notes in conversing with scholars, as well as in reading their reports, that the distinction between these terms tends to blur and break down, and they are often used interchangeably. For example, when looking under the term "models" in the index of a psychology text, one may be directed to "see theory"; similarly, when looking under "theory," one may be directed to "models." Because of the difficulty in differentiating between these terms, in this chapter the terms "model" and "theory" will be used interchangeably.

Limitations on the usefulness of theories   Theoretical models have been characterized as being capable of summarizing the past, elucidating the present, and predicting the future. Surely we would agree that if a theoretical model can do these things, it is an extraordinarily useful intellectual tool. However, a number of factors may seriously undermine and reduce a theory's usefulness. First, the basic conceptualization may be in error. At one time, for instance, the earth was believed to be the center of the universe. However, in the early 1500s the Polish astronomer Copernicus opposed this view and held that the earth and the other planets move about the sun. Approximately a century later Galileo, an Italian astronomer who was the first to use the telescope, was able to prove the validity of the Copernicus statement and thus destroy the old belief about the centrality of Earth in the universe. Another example of an erroneous basic premise is that at one time the earth was thought to be flat. These two instances of incorrect conceptualizations had serious and practical effects. The first premise, about the centrality of the earth, influenced the way humans thought about themselves in terms of their importance in relationship to the rest of the universe. The second conceptualization, about the shape of the world, influenced the drawing of maps and the willingness to explore beyond those parts of the earth already known.

There are still other ways to reduce the usefulness of a model. As mentioned earlier, a model is a summary, representation, or generalization of a body of knowledge. The generalization or representation may be a verbal description, or it may be in the form of a visual presentation, such as a line drawing. Ideally, the verbal description or visual presentation should be understandable. Unfortunately, some theoretical models of the reading process are either so poorly described or so poorly drawn as to be nearly incomprehensible, even to highly trained psychologists.

An additional weakness of some models is that either because they are not easily comprehended or because they are overly comprehensive in what they are trying to explain, they fail to generate testable hypotheses. This is an important failure for two reasons. First, if we are attempting to predict future events, prediction and hypothesis generation are important to this objective. Second, a theoretical model is a creation of a human mind and subject to error. Once a model has been created, it should be tested in order to ascertain its truthfulness, or validity. The way to do this is through generating hypotheses suggested by the theory and testing them or by positing relationships suggested by the theory and testing them. Without testing the theory, there is no way to judge how good it is. It is through the cyclical process shown in Fig. 2.2 that hypotheses are generated from theory, tested, and the new findings incorporated into a modified theory.

As new information becomes available, the model is modified to include the new findings. Figure 2.3 shows how this process might occur in a model of memory. Figure 2.3(a) suggests that memory has only two components— short-term memory (STM) and long-term memory (LTM). Labels such as "short-term memory" and "long-term memory" are not meant to imply that there are special places in the human brain where these functions occur. Rather, human behavior suggests that there are two very different components to memory. Figure 2.3(a) shows that information entering the system first goes to short-term memory and then on to long-term memory.

Once the information is stored in long-term memory, it may be called on to produce an output. Research on memory indicates that the storage capacity of short-term memory is limited. Only about seven chunks of information can be held conveniently, as many people realize when trying to remember a

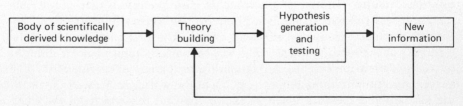

Fig. 2.2. The process of theory building and validation.

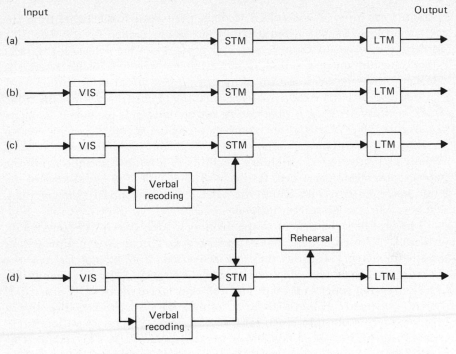

Key:
VIS   Visual Information Store
STM   Short-Term Memory
LTM   Long-Term Memory

Fig. 2.3. Stages of model development as new information becomes available.

new seven-digit telephone number. Another characteristic of short-term memory is that the information it holds does not survive very long. The seven chunks of information are stored for up to 15 seconds. Thus whatever the information in short-term memory, it must be shunted over to long-term memory fairly quickly for it to be stored in a more permanent form. If it is not put in long-term memory before the 15-second period is up, it is lost. The storage capacity of long-term memory is enormous, and the items in its memory are stored for extended periods of time.

Figure 2.3(b) shows a new component to the memory system—visual information store (VIS). When visual information is introduced, information—perhaps in the form of letters—is stored briefly on the retina of the eye, usually for less than one or two seconds. For example, if we have been in a darkened room for a long time and someone flashes a light on and off quickly into our eyes, the glare remains, even though the room is again in darkness. A similar situation exists in night driving. The headlights of an oncoming car blind us for several seconds, even though the lights from the car are no longer present. Similarly, if letters are flashed on a screen very quickly, the image of these letters will remain on the retina for a brief period after the image has disappeared from the screen. This persistence of the light on the letters is a form of memory called visual information store.

One may wonder how visual information in visual information store, which lasts usually for less than one or two seconds, gets to short-term memory. Figure 2.3(c) shows a new component to the memory system—verbal recoding. Experimentation on how letters are memorized indicates that when visually presented letters are shown to adults, it is not the visual form of the letters that tends to get stored. Rather, the adult takes the visual form of the letter and verbally recodes it into the letter name. It is the letter name, then, that gets put into short-term memory.

The final new component to the memory model, shown in Figure 2.3(d), is labeled "rehearsal." The model indicates that items are maintained in short-term memory because they are rehearsed. For example, when the operator gives us a new telephone number, we tend to repeat the number, or rehearse it, in order to prevent loss from short-term memory. Figure 2.3(d) shows the sequence of events to be as follows. (1) Visual information in the form of letters is put into visual information store. (2) The visual letters are recorded—or named—and put into short-term memory. (3) The verbal items in short-term memory are rehearsed and put into long-term memory. (4) The items are stored in long-term memory until the output is desired, at which time they are read out. A summary of the memory characteristics for the several memory systems mentioned is given in Table 2.2.

Table 2.2. Characteristics of visual information store, short-term memory, and long-term memory

Characteristic	Visual information store	Short-term memory	Long-term memory
Capacity	Large	Restricted	Enormous
Longevity	Short—up to one or two seconds	Short—up to 15 seconds	Long
Rate of input	Fast	Fast	Slow
Rate of output availability	Fast	Fast	Slow—learning strategies and memory structure influence availability

MODELS OF READING

Thus far, this chapter has provided background information on theoretical models, what they are, how they are used, and how they are developed. Now we will get directly into some of the actual models of the reading process. We discuss what a model of reading should be able to accomplish, describe several models in detail, and conclude with implications of models for the teaching of reading.

Many kinds of reading, many kinds of models? A model of the reading process should be able to mirror or represent to some degree what goes on when we read. The average reader engages in a wide variety of behaviors when reading. When reading a newspaper, for instance, the reader may look quickly only at headlines and, perhaps, the first paragraph of each article. It is not until the reader finds an article of personal interest that the entire article is read with care. The reader may even read the article several times—the first time rapidly to get a general overview and the second time slowly for details. The reader may even have several reasons for reading the article slowly. One may read slowly in order to comprehend the literal meaning of the passage. Or, one may read slowly in order to comprehend at a higher level of analysis, perhaps to evaluate, criticize, or interpret what an author has said.

Another point to consider is that the beginning reader and the fluent reader are probably using very different strategies for getting meaning from the printed page. The beginning reader is putting a good deal of attention on the printed words, and in the process overlooking meaning. For the beginning reader, the route to meaning is indeed a tortuous one. On the other hand, the fluent reader pays very little attention to the printed words, and for the experienced reader the route to meaning is far more direct and easy. There are times, however, when the fluent reader encounters an unfamiliar word, which may require the laborious decoding characteristic of the beginning reader.

This short description of what readers do—varying reading speed from fast to slow, varying level of comprehension from literal to inferential, varying the strategies for getting meaning—indicates the wide range of variability of reading behavior to be found and to be modeled. Ideally, a reading model should be able to mirror with some degree of accuracy this wide range of reading behaviors. Unfortunately, most reading models make no attempt to represent this variability. Instead, many models would lead one to believe that reading involves but a single process. One model that does make some attempt to show how different strategies or processes may be used is the LaBerge-Samuels model.

The LaBerge-Samuels model of automatic information processing

The LaBerge-Samuels model is an information-processing model. This type of model attempts to identify components in the system, trace the routes that information passes through, and identify changes in the form of the information as it moves from the surface of the page into the deeper semantic-linguistic centers of the brain.

Attention   The very heart of the LaBerge-Samuels model has to do with the role of attention. Attention has two components—internal and external. To the layman, the external aspects of attention are the more familiar. When a classroom teacher says that a student does not pay attention and therefore is not living up to potential, it is external attention that is being described. Other manifestations of external attention have to do with what may be called orienting behavior, or directing one's sensory organs, such as eyes and ears, in such a way as to maximize information input. If an observer can watch the behavior of another, as a teacher often does, and determine whether the other person is paying attention, it is the external aspects of attention to which we are referring.

External attention has important implications for learning in general and for learning to read in particular. First, attention is considered so important to learning that most psychologists would agree that it is a prerequisite and that without attention there can be no learning. Recently, classroom observation has thrown some light on the relationship between external attention and reading. A fairly well-documented finding is that during elementary school years, girls surpass boys in reading achievement. Is this superiority the result of some maturational genetic sex-linked advantage, or is it the result of cultural forces at work in the classroom? Several lines of experimentation suggest that the advantage may be cultural rather than genetic. One line of research shows that when boys are put in booths that resemble an airplane cockpit, they learn more during that reading hour than do the girls. These booths are not only exciting to boys, but also help to focus their attention on the reading by reducing extraneous sources of stimulation. Another line of classroom research found that girls were significantly more attentive during the reading hour than were the boys. These same girls were also superior readers. In this classroom study, taking boys and girls together, as external signs of attention increased, such as looking in books and working on reading assignments, so did the reading scores.

Although such external manifestations of attention form an important aspect of learning, the internal manifestations are even more crucial, and they are the core component of the LaBerge-Samuels model. The internal characteristics of attention are far more difficult to describe than the external characteristics. For example, imagine a laboratory setting in which an experimental subject is given earphones and told that a male voice will be heard in one ear and a female voice in the other. The subject, told to remember the information given by the female voice, has no difficulty performing this task. Even if we increase the difficulty of the task by alternating the ear in which the subject hears the female voice, our subject can successfully direct attention to the appropriate voice. Selecting the appropriate voice to listen to is an example of internal control of attention.

This same ability to process and recall auditory information occurs under natural, real-life situations. Cocktail parties are frequently crowded situations in which many people move about and talk to one another. Imagine talking to a friend in a crowded room at a cocktail party. Both the external and internal components of attention are directed at your friend. Suddenly, from behind, you hear part of an interesting conversation you want to hear more of. Without turning your head away from your friend and without giving any outward signs either to your friend or to the other person behind you, you begin to take in as much from two conversations as you can. At will, you direct and select which conversation you will monitor— first one, then the other—switching your attention back and forth. This ability to take in parts of several conversations by switching attention back and forth and without anyone knowing you are doing so has come to be called the "cocktail party phenomenon."

Internal attention has three characteristics: alertness, selectivity, and limited capacity.

1. *Alertness.* Alertness simply refers to the active attempt to come in contact with sources of information. Alertness can also be thought of in terms of vigilance.

2. *Selective attention.* Our environment is such that at any moment under ordinary circumstances, our sense organs—eyes, ears, nose, skin, tongue— can be bombarded with multiple, competing stimuli. As you read this line, are you aware that the lines above and below are also on your retina? We are generally unaware of this, and the process of selective attention enables us to choose which line we will process. Similarly, when we go to a party there are usually several conversations competing for our attention, yet we are able to select which one we will process at any given moment.

The following example shows how selective attention operates in the visual mode. Below is a passage containing two different ideas—one written in upper-case and the other in lower-case letters. Read only the one in upper-case letters, and be prepared to answer the question at the end.

WHY the YOU purpose SHOULD of GET the THE investigation
SHAFT was A to SHAFT test IS the THE focal MOST attention
EFFICIENT hypothesis WAY this TO hypothesis DELIVER suggests

POWER that FROM when THE a ENGINE picture TO and THE a
REAR word WHEEL are IT presented WILL together NOT the
SPRAY student YOU will WITH focus OIL on NOR that WILL part
IT of BREAK the AS stimulus EASILY which AS most A readily
CHAIN elicits IN a FACT correct A response SHAFT a IS poor AL-
MOST reader INDESTRUCTIBLE finds AND the BECAUSE picture
IT easier IS to ENCLOSED use IN than A the BATH word OF and
OIL attends IT to IS the ALMOST picture SILENT

What are the advantages of a drive shaft?

Most people who read this passage have no difficulty in selecting the
message on which attention was placed. Furthermore, the passage on motorcycle drive shafts was probably read with a high level of literal comprehension.

3. *Limited capacity.* Limited capacity refers to the fact that we can attend
to only one thing at a time. To go back to our cocktail party example, the
person attempting to listen to several conversations was able to process only
one conversation at a time. The individual was able to switch attention back
and forth at will from one conversation to the other, but it was impossible
to simultaneously understand both conversations. Similarly, when reading
the passage about the motorcycle drive shaft, your attention was on that
passage; even though the words from the other message were also on your
retina, the nonattended passage did not get processed.

To summarize, "attention" can be divided into two broad categories, one
having to do with the external and the other with the internal components
of attention. The external aspects of attention are directly observable. For
example, one can note the direction of gaze or where a person is touching.
Generally, external aspects of attention are related to the orientation of one's
sensory organs. The internal aspects of attention—alertness, selectivity, and
limited capacity—are not directly observable. An important concept to remember about attention is that a human is able to attend to and process
only one thing at a time.

Decoding   Internal components of attention are central to the theory of
automatic information processing in reading. It is assumed in the theory, as
well as by many who study the reading process, that getting meaning from
printed words involves a two-step process. First, the printed words must be
decoded. Second, the decoded words must be comprehended. "Decoding" in
relationship to reading means the process of translating printed symbols into
spoken words. It is not necessary for the spoken words to be uttered out loud.
In fact, the "spoken words" could be silently subvocalized.

Comprehension   Although everyone reading this chapter knows what is meant by the word "comprehension," no one at the present time understands *how* we are able to comprehend. If we can characterize the decade of the 1960s as one in which grammatical errors in comprehension were studied, we can say that as we turned the corner into the 1970s, we began the study of semantic factors in comprehension. Numerous scientists from a variety of disciplines are hard at work to discover what processes are involved in deriving meaning from language.

Even though definitive explanations of the mechanisms underlying comprehension are currently unavailable, it seems reasonably clear that attention will be found to be required to process an unfamiliar passage for its meaning. With all the practice one gets at processing for meaning, one may wonder why skill development in this area does not reach the point of automaticity. Granted, when an adult encounters highly familiar words in print, such as "cat," "kitchen," "wheel," or "milk," the meaning of each word is in all probability immediately available without the need of attention. The ability to get the meaning of each word in a sentence, however, is not the same as what is meant by comprehending a sentence. In comprehending a sentence one must be able to interrelate and combine the separate meanings of each of the words. Thus from this point of view, comprehension is a constructive process of synthesis and putting word meanings together in special ways, much like the way individual bricks are combined in the construction of a house. Whereas one may go from print to the meanings of individual words automatically, it is in the act of integrating, relating, and combining these meanings in the unique ways demanded by sentences that is required. Even in passages as simple as "The dog is in the house" or "The grandmother spanked her grandchild," attention will be necessary to determine, for example, the relationship of the dog to the house. Is the dog "on," "in," "under," or "next to" the house? An understanding of the second sentence requires knowledge of what the action is, who the agent is, and who the object of the action is. To understand the relationship of grandmother to grandchild requires complex analysis of such features as how many generations separate the two, and whether there is a direct blood relationship between them.

If even simple sentences require attention in order to determine the relationships that exist among their parts, imagine what happens when more complex sentences are read on more complex topics. Superimpose the added burdens on attention and memory that occur when a poor reader, who is still using attention to get the decoding done, encounters a difficult passage, and there is little wonder that comprehension seems to suffer when a student has difficulty decoding words.

Attention and reading   At any given moment attention can be directed at only a single place. This means that attention can be used on only one process at a time. Getting meaning from the printed symbols on a page is a two-step process involving decoding and then comprehending. In order to comprehend even simple passages, attention is required. The beginning reader, who is at a low level of skill development, must use attention in order to get the decoding done. Herein lies the dilemma facing the beginning reader. If the beginning reader's attention is on decoding, and if attention can be directed at only one process at a time, the comprehension task is not getting done. Since the end product of reading should be comprehension, the beginning reader is faced with a formidable problem.

In many ways the problem facing the beginning reader is similar to the problem facing the beginning driver who is trying to drive a car and comprehend what someone is saying. The beginning driver is putting attention on the mechanical aspects of driving, such as steering, controlling gas, brake, clutch, and gears, signaling turns, and other operations involved in getting to one's destination safely. With attention on the mechanical aspects of driving, the driver finds it difficult to process for meaning any ongoing conversation. However, with continued practice at driving over a considerable length of time, the beginning driver will become a skilled driver. The skilled driver can perform the routine mechanical functions of driving the car with little or no attention. In fact, skilled drivers who regularly retrace the same route time after time often wonder how they arrive at their destination. These skilled drivers are performing the routine, mechanical aspects of driving without attention, and their attention is thus left free to process conversation or to think about private thoughts.

Attention switching in reading   The beginning reader concentrates on decoding rather than on comprehension. This might suggest that the beginning reader cannot comprehend what is on the page, yet we know from both observation and experience that beginning readers *are* able to understand what they read. The question is: How can the beginning reader comprehend when attention is on decoding? The answer was provided by the example of what one does at a cocktail party when one tries to take in several ongoing conversations; one switches attention to the conversation one wishes to process. This is precisely how the beginning reader is able to comprehend—by switching attention back and forth from decoding to comprehension. As many of you know, a beginning reader reads a passage several times. The first time through the passage the student is decoding from symbol to spoken words. This puts a considerable strain on attention and memory systems. After the student has managed to overcome the decoding problem, subsequent readings are for comprehension. This process is shown in Fig. 2.4(a); the student switches attention back and forth from decoding to comprehension.

Although the beginning reader is able to comprehend by switching attention back and forth, the process is slow, laborious, and painful. For those

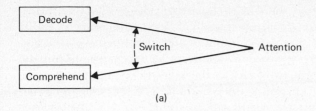

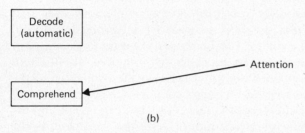

Fig. 2.4. The process of reading development: (a) beginning stages, in which attention switching is required for comprehension; (b) fluent stage, in which decoding is automatic and attention is on comprehension.

who doubt this, can you recall the difficulty you had trying to comprehend a foreign language you had not yet mastered? To assess meaning, you first had to translate the foreign words to English and then comprehend what had been translated.

Thus far, what has been explained is how the beginning reader manages to comprehend by means of attention switching. What is left to explain is how the fluent reader gets the job done.

Attention in fluent reading   I recently asked a skilled typist to type what was printed in a newspaper article. My instructions were that she should strive for accuracy and keep up a modest, steady typing pace. While the typist was at work, I asked her a number of questions, to which she responded appropriately. Our back-and-forth conversation went on without any noticeable decrease in her typing speed. When the typist was finished, we proofed the copy and found it to be virtually free of errors. The typist was thus able to perform both tasks—the typing and engaging in conversation—simultaneously. In a somewhat analogous experimental situation, a skilled piano player was given music she had never seen before and asked to sight-read it. At the same time, a set of earphones was put on the piano player, and she was told that she would hear a voice speaking in a conversational manner and that she was to repeat out loud what she heard. (In a laboratory procedure, repeating out loud what one hears is called shadowing.) In order to be sure that the proper notes were being played and that the correct words were repeated, a tape recorder was set up. Thus the piano player had to perform two tasks at the same time—sight-read unfamiliar music and shadow unfamiliar speech coming in through the headphones. When the procedure was completed, we found that the piano player was able to faithfully perform both tasks simultaneously.

There are certain similarities to be found in the examples of the typist who could simultaneously type and converse and the piano player who could simultaneously sight-read music and shadow speech. Incoming information—both visual and aural—had to be processed. Second, the information that came in by ear for the typist—listening to what I said, processing it, and forming an answer—and by ear for the piano player—listening to a voice present meaningful speech and then repeating it—required attention in order to perform the tasks. A third similarity between the two is that at the beginning stages of skill performance, typing and piano playing require attention. However, as fluency in these tasks developed, both the typist and the pianist were able to perform without attention. Herein lies the answer to the question as to how two tasks can be performed simultaneously, each of which ordinarily requires the services of attention. The answer is simply that as a person develops skill at the task, the skill can be performed without attention. For example, some years ago I visited a friend who was studying to be a surgeon. To practice his surgical knot tying, he had a small board with tiny pegs on it, on which he would hook the threads and tie the knots. In these beginning stages of skill development, while his fingers were slowly working on the knots, his eyes were focused on the fingers to guide the movements. Any attempt on my part to talk was met with my friend's request to hold off on conversation; he said he could not concentrate on knot tying and talk at the same time. It would appear that his attention was being directed at the knot tying, thus preventing my friend from processing conversation. After years of practice on the knot-tying board, my friend was able to tie the knots while he watched television and engaged in conversation. In addition, he performed the knot tying quickly and no longer needed visual guidance. The knot tying was being done with no attention, leaving my friend's attention free to process conversation.

Automaticity   When a task that formerly required attention for its performance can now be performed without attention, the task is being done automatically. Automaticity in information processing, then, simply means that the information is being processed without attention. One way to determine if a process is being done without attention is to give a person two tasks to perform at the same time, each of which requires attention, e.g., requiring a person to simultaneously type a manuscript and answer questions. If the tasks can be performed simultaneously, at least one of them is being done automatically.

With the concept of automaticity in mind, it is now a simple matter to describe how the fluent reader is able to perform the two-step decoding-comprehension process in reading. The decoding is done automatically—with no attention—and attention is thus available for getting meaning from the printed words. This process is shown in Fig. 2.4(b).

There are times, however, when skilled readers turn their attention away from getting meaning from the printed words. One such situation arises when unusual words are encountered, such as foreign words or scientific terminology. Then the reader must put attention on decoding in order to translate these verbal symbols. Another such situation occurs when a skilled reader is proofreading. As most experienced writers know, it is a poor idea to read for meaning while trying to locate errors. Proofreading is done most efficiently when one's attention is directed away from meaning and put on possible errors in the text.

Other components in the LaBerge-Samuels model Most information-processing models indicate the components involved and the direction of flow of the information as it traverses through the system. However, these linear models tend to suggest that there is only one way to process the information. As any skilled reader who has thought about reading processes knows, there are a variety of ways to read. Thus if a theoretical model is to mirror the actual process, it should show the flexibility and variety of processing routes.

1. *Visual memory.* As seen in Fig. 2.5, visual memory (VM) is the first component, or processing stage, in the model. Incoming information from the words in print first strikes the sensory surface of the eye, where detectors process features such as lines, curves, angles, intersections, as well as relational features. For example, what features does one use to recognize the letter "b"?

By analysis, one can separate "b" into a vertical line "l" and a circle "o." But this is entirely unsatisfactory as a method for identifying a letter, because the letters "d," "p," and "g" share these same components. By adding relational features, such as up-down and left-right, to the vertical line and circle, we arrive at a set of features uniquely descriptive of "b"—the circle to the right and at the bottom of the vertical. By contrast, the letter "p" would be described as having the circle to the right and at the top of the vertical. Thus each letter can be described by a set of unique features.

To continue with this explanation of how a perceptual code is learned, as one goes from left to right in the hierarchical model of visual memory, one

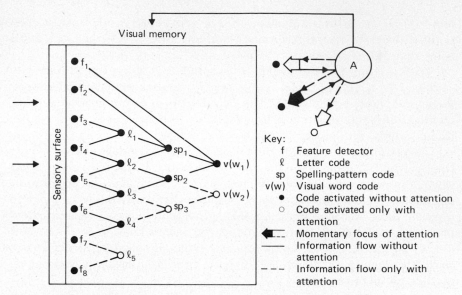

Fig. 2.5. Model of visual memory.

notes that at each higher level of the model, different kinds of information get processed. The model shows how the visual information is analyzed by detectors into features, which at the next level are combined to form letters. At the next level in the model, letter combinations, such as "sh," "th," "bl," "-ing," and "anti-" may be combined to form spelling patterns, and the spelling patterns feed into word codes. The use of the term "codes" in the model means the form in which information is represented. Thus there may be letter codes, spelling pattern codes, and word codes.

There are two additional features in this model of visual memory, labeled f_1 and f_2, which should be expressly pointed out. Unlike the other features that lead into letters, f_1 and f_2 indicate that features other than letters may be used in the identification of a word. For example, word configuration and word length may be used in combination with other sources of textual information in word recognition. Assume that the words we wish to identify are "hippopotamus," "dog," and "cat." Given the following three configurations, it is a simple task to determine which configuration represents each of the three words:

As seen in Fig. 2.5, the various codes are represented by either a filled or empty circle. The empty circle represents a code that is not well learned, and consequently it can be activated only with attention, e.g., codes ℓ_5, sp_3, and $v(w_2)$. The filled circle represents a well-learned code that does not require attention for its activation, e.g., codes ℓ_1, sp_1, $v(w_1)$. These well-learned codes can be processed automatically, with no attention.

2. *Attention.* In Fig. 2.5, the attention center is symbolized by "A" in a circle. Attention is considered essential in the early stages of learning a perceptual code, but is dispensable later on. An individual is free to focus attention at various levels of the visual memory model—on features, letters, spelling patterns, or on whole words. When well-learned codes, symbolized by a filled circle, are activated by stimulation, attention from the attention center is not required for processing. When stimulation to poorly learned codes, symbolized by an empty circle, occurs, attention is required for processing. With continued activation and processing of these poorly learned codes, a person develops a level of skill such that attention will no longer be required for the processing of these codes.

An important distinction to make, not only for theoretical reasons but for practical ones as well, is between accuracy and automaticity. At the accurate levels of skill development, attention is required. When asked if two letters are the same, the student may use attention to scan the features to determine the correct answer. With practice, the student will become automatic and be able to come up with the correct answer without attention. This distinction between accuracy and automaticity holds for perceptual tasks requiring either visual or auditory processing. In most classroom situations the tests that are administered measure response accuracy. Good classroom tests that can measure automatic levels of skill development have not yet been developed.

Before leaving the hierarchical model of visual memory, it would be useful to outline the probable course of learning to identify a letter. This learning is conceptualized as a two-step process. As explained previously, the first task is to analyze and select the relevant features of the letter. To a large extent this task of searching for features is similar to the initial stages in a concept-learning task, in which one must identify the relevant attributes of the concept. Generally, the rate at which children are able to identify the features of letters is quite slow. However, with practice, they develop improved strategies, and the rate at which they can identify these features increases. In order to help children select the appropriate features, it is important to have children make same-different judgments between visually similar letters, e.g., *huvn, mnuv, coeu, klth, xvzw.*

After learning to identify the features of the letters, the student, in the next stage of perceptual learning, must combine these separate features into a single letter code, a process that at first requires attention. With practice the student will unitize these separate features into a single letter code. Skilled readers, for example, see "b" and not "l" plus "o." With extended practice at letter identification, the student's unitization of the features into a letter will occur without attention.

3. *Phonological memory.* Inputs into the phonological memory system come from a variety of sources—visual memory, episodic memory, feedback from semantic memory, and articulatory responses, as well as from direct external acoustic stimulation. Some of these sources of input are shown in Fig. 2.6.

It is assumed that the phonological memory system contains units that are related to acoustic and articulatory inputs. Although acoustic input seems logical enough, one might wonder why there would be articulatory input in a phonological system. In recent years evidence has been gathered to the effect that the kinds of articulatory-muscle responses made in pro-

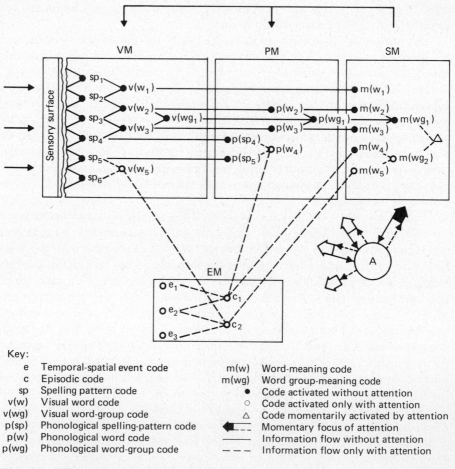

Key:

e	Temporal-spatial event code	m(w)	Word-meaning code
c	Episodic code	m(wg)	Word group-meaning code
sp	Spelling pattern code	●	Code activated without attention
v(w)	Visual word code	○	Code activated only with attention
v(wg)	Visual word-group code	△	Code momentarily activated by attention
p(sp)	Phonological spelling-pattern code	◄---	Momentary focus of attention
p(w)	Phonological word code	———	Information flow without attention
p(wg)	Phonological word-group code	– – –	Information flow only with attention

Fig. 2.6. The LaBerge-Samuels model of automatic information processing in reading, showing feedback loops.

ducing a speech sound may also be involved in perceiving that sound. Thus acoustic input from stimulation external to the individual and articulatory input from stimulation internal to the individual are thought to be part of the phonological memory system.

With the rich variety of inputs flowing into phonological memory, one might be tempted to describe how each of these is organized. However, to do so might seriously reduce the effectiveness of a model by attempting to explain too much or by trying to be overly comprehensive. Therefore, only the organization of acoustic units will be described. The acoustic units in phonological memory are features, phonemes, syllables, and words. These units in phonological memory are counterparts of the features, letters, spelling patterns, and words found in visual memory. Just as the units in visual memory are arranged in a hierarchy, so too are the units in phonological memory.

Acoustic features are represented by contrasts, such as /pa/-/ga/-/ta/. These differences are represented in the place or location where the consonant sound is made. The first sound is made with the lips, the second at the back of the throat, and the third at the roof of the mouth. It is interesting to note that in attempting to describe features we hear, we resort to identifying the place of articulation. Another feature difference is the manner in which the sound is produced. For example, when saying /pa/-/ma/, one observes that both sounds are produced with the lips, but that only in the first sound is the breath expelled. So here the feature contrast is determined not by location of sound production, but by manner of sound production.

The model of visual memory indicates that a letter consists of a set of visual features that uniquely describes it. Similarly, in the model of phonological memory, a phoneme consists of a set of uniquely descriptive acoustic features. A "phoneme" may be thought of as a sound unit that indicates a change in word meaning, such as the difference between /m/, /p/, and /f/ as in man, pan, fan, or the /s/ sound in cat-cats. Each of these phonemes signals a change in word meaning. Despite the enormous variety of words found in the English language, approximately 44 phonemes are sufficient to produce the rich variety of words we use.

4. *Similarities between visual and phonological memory.* We described the hierarchy in visual memory as going from features to letters to spelling patterns, and finally to words. The hierarchy in the phonological memory system is from features to phonemes to syllables, and finally to words. In both the visual and phonological memory systems, it is possible, through the control of selective attention, to work from features up to words or from words down to features. When going from a whole word to features, a decomposition into parts takes place, and teachers often call this process "analysis." For example, when a teacher asks students to listen for the difference between /sat/ and /sad/, the process requires a top-down analysis

from whole into parts. On the other hand, in reading, when a student sounds out a new word letter by letter and blends these sounds to form a word, it is a bottom-up process of synthesizing a word from its parts into a whole word.

5. *Episodic memory.* The episodic memory system is responsible for storing events associated with time, place, and content. When an individual is able to recall the details of an event that occurred some time in the past, it is episodic memory that is being called on. The organization of events in episodic memory might well be in terms of associations among *wh* words, such as *wh*en (time), *wh*ere (place), and *wh*at (content). If the associations among the time, place, and content of an event are weak, one might be able to recall what happened but be unable to recall where or when the event took place. However, if the association among the who, what, and where aspects of an event are strong, the individual should be able to recall all of the details.

Although it is apparent that episodic memory is essential for explaining how we store and recall events, one naturally wonders how episodic memory is used in reading. One notes in Fig. 2.5 that there are solid and dashed lines connecting codes in the model. The solid lines indicate very strong associations. For example, when one hears the word "hard-working," the meaning is immediately available. The link between the sound and meaning of "hard-working" would be represented by a solid line. On the other hand, when one hears the synonyms "diligent" or "sedulous" pronounced, the meanings are not immediately available and would be indicated by a dashed line. In every case the solid lines connect codes that do not require attention for their activation, thus indicating information flow that is direct, fast, and automatic. The dashed lines generally connect codes that are not automatic, thus indicating information flow that is slow, nondirect, and requires attention.

An example of how episodic memory would be used in beginning reading might occur as follows. A young student who has a minor interest in sailboats, but who has been on one several times, may have only slight familiarity with the names and functions of the sails used on boats. A new word, "jib," is visually introduced. The student uses attention to decode the word to its spoken representation. Because the student has only slight familiarity with the term, its meaning is not readily available. The student uses episodic memory to recall how the word was used in describing a sailboat. The search through episodic memory is successful, and the meaning of the word becomes clear. After repeated encounters with the printed word "jib," the student's association to its meaning should be strengthened, and neither episodic memory nor attention would be required to assess the word's meaning. With sufficient practice with the word "jib," the student should have immediate access to the meaning of the word, and episodic memory would no longer be required. According to the model, episodic memory is useful in situations in which word meaning is not directly available from the visual form of a word or from its spoken form. When word meaning is available, episodic memory is bypassed.

6. *Semantic memory*. The final component in the automaticity model is semantic memory. It is here that individual word meanings are produced, and it is also here that the comprehension of written messages occurs. One should recall that earlier in this chapter, we distinguished between the attentional processes involved in getting the meaning of a word and comprehending a written passage. When familiar words are decoded by skilled readers, the word meanings may be assessed automatically, without attention. Comprehension, on the other hand, under most conditions does not occur automatically and therefore requires attention.

In order to get at the underlying meaning in a sentence, attention is used in a number of ways during the comprehension process. It is used to organize the words in a sentence into grammatical units, and it is used to determine the relationships in meanings that exist within and between grammatical units. For example, as verbal concepts, the meanings of "fierce" and of "dog" may exist separately. When, however, the noun phrase "the fierce dog" is encountered, it has one semantic meaning. It is through the services of attention in semantic memory that the blending of these two verbal concepts into one meaning occurs. This example simply illustrates how attention might be used to determine the relationships in meaning within a grammatical unit.

Role of attention in comprehension   Let us now examine how a sentence such as "The fierce dog bit the tall man" is processed for comprehension. Since the focus of this chapter is not on comprehension, the description will be sketchy in the extreme. As shown in Fig. 2.7, when decoding familiar words, a skilled reader assesses the meaning of each word directly, without attention. Attention is used, however, to determine the grammatical units in the sentence. By breaking the sentence into its grammatical units, the reader can determine the agent, the action, and the victim. However, the comprehension process is still not complete. The reader must also decide on the meaning within each grammatical unit and on the meaning for the sentence as a whole. This putting together and combining of meanings is viewed as an active, constructive process that requires attention for its completion.

Optional word-recognition processing strategies   Each of the components of the model of automatic information processing in reading has been described, and we can now describe the various options available for processing a word. Looking at Fig. 2.6, we can trace the information flow for the vari-

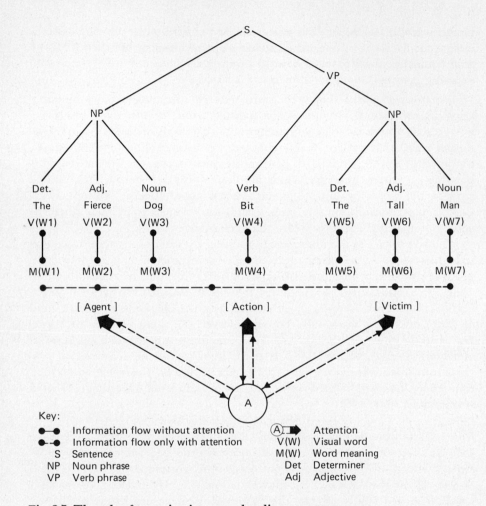

Fig. 2.7. The role of attention in comprehending a sentence.

ous options. (Rather than present the processing options in great detail, I will simply suggest general ways that meaning can be obtained.) These optional strategies start from the top of Fig. 2.6 and proceed downward. Only the symbols in visual memory will be given here. To follow the description below, simply start with visual memory and move along the lines in the figure from left to right.

1. *Option 1.* The visual word $v(w_1)$ is automatically decoded, and the word meaning is available automatically. This would occur when a skilled reader reads a common word, like "dog" or "car."

2. *Option 2.* The visual word $v(w_2)$ is automatically decoded. In turn the

phonological code for the word is activated automatically, which in turn automatically activates the word meaning. This would occur when a skilled reader encounters a common word, but subvocalizes it.

3. *Option 3.* Two different visual words $v(wg_1)$, such as "ice" "cream" or "hop" "scotch," are decoded as a word group automatically. In turn the phonological code for the word group is activated automatically. Next, the meaning of the word group is made available automatically in semantic memory.

4. *Option 4.* A visual word, such as "digraph," is coded automatically into two spelling patterns—"di" and "graph." This is represented in Fig. 2.6 as sp_4 and sp_5. Next, the phonological code for these spelling patterns is activated automatically. However, from this point on, attention is used to blend the two spelling patterns into one word, to excite the episodic code, and the meaning code for the word. This course of events would occur with a skilled reader who has no difficulty with decoding, but who is somewhat uncertain about the technical definition of the word "digraph."

5. *Option 5.* A highly unfamiliar visual word is coded with attention into $v(w_5)$. Attention is used to activate the episodic code, the phonological code, and the meaning code. This sequence of events might occur with a foreign name that is too difficult to pronounce easily.

Feedback from semantic memory   Before leaving the model of automatic information processing, one should take note of the arrow leading from semantic memory to visual and to phonological memory (see Fig. 2.6). This arrow is an indicator of an important function and represents a marked departure in the automaticity model from typical information processing models. These models represent a straight flow of information from input to output; the automaticity model, however, has feedback loops, since what happens in semantic memory may influence processes that occur earlier. For example, let us assume that a skilled reader is reading a manuscript for meaning. Since both the words and the content of the manuscript are familiar, the processing option taken is such that information flow goes from visual memory directly to semantic memory, bypassing phonological memory. At a certain point, the content becomes unfamiliar and more difficult, and the reader has difficulty with comprehension. Now, the reader changes the processing strategy and begins to subvocalize the words, as is common when the reading task increases in difficulty. The information flow now is from visual memory to phonological memory and then to semantic memory.

As another example to illustrate how semantic memory may influence the other components in the model, let us assume that a reader is processing words at the word level in visual memory. Encountering a highly unusual word, the reader drops down to a lower processing level in visual memory—

to the letter pattern or to the letter level—and blends the sounds together in phonological memory.

Hypothesis/test model of reading

Of the large variety of reading models that have been developed, the hypothesis/test model of word recognition is perhaps the most widely known. Although the automaticity and the hypothesis/test models are presented as two distinct models, they are not mutually exclusive, and in fact it will be shown that the automaticity model can include the processes described by the hypothesis/test model.

Word recognition as a constructive act   Before embarking on a formal description of the hypothesis/test model of reading, a few words of introduction to the model are in order. First, according to the hypothesis/test model, word recognition is a constructive type of activity in which the output may be greater than and different from the input. Although this last statement may at first seem surprising, it actually reflects experiences all of us have shared. For example, political cartoons are based on the idea that each individual can be represented in drawing by a few features that are most characteristic and that uniquely depict that individual. From these few features in the cartoon, we recognize and are able to construct the person represented. In this sense, then, recognition of an entire person is constructed from a few features drawn in the cartoon.

In order to appreciate the notion of word recognition as a constructive act, one must contrast this model with other notions of reading, in which the output is considered to be essentially the same as the input. For example, when given the visual word f-a-m-i-l-i-a-r, the reader is supposed to decode each of the letters to a sound representation, blend the sounds together, and then match the phonological word to some word in memory. According to this view, input and output are essentially the same. Models of reading that postulate this view are no longer taken seriously. If you can recognize a person in any of the following ways—by silhouette, by the way the person walks, by voice alone—you are engaging in recognition as a constructive act. From just a part, you are recognizing the whole person. Of course, you may be wrong in your recognition response. If the penalty for an incorrect recognition is low, you are willing to risk making a recognition response with only a little bit of available information. On the other hand, if the consequences for making false recognition are serious, you may want a great deal more information before risking a recognition response.

Another important feature of the hypothesis/test model is that just as the text brings something to the reader, the reader brings a great deal to the text, namely, the knowledge, experiences, and attitudes gathered over time.

When the information contained in the text matches the knowledge and experiences of the reader, the act of comprehending the text should be simplified. Thus we see that reading is a constructive, active process in which the reader brings to bear on the text an accumulation of skills, attitudes, and knowledge.

More specifically, word recognition can be described as a four-step process. The goal of the process is to recognize the word represented by the line in the sentence: "Father cut the green _____."

1. *Using information.* Information contained in a sample of text is read. For example, the text contains the following words: "Father cut the green _____." The reader reads this.

2. *Generating hypothesis.* Using the information contained in the passage, the reader generates one or more hypotheses of what the missing word might be. Given the context ("Father cut the green _____."), the reader might predict that "grass," "emerald," or "wood" was represented by the line.

3. *Testing hypothesis.* The usual way to test a hypothesis or prediction is to get information and to determine how closely the information matches the prediction. In this case, the information is contained in the letters of the word. The reader identified the letters "gr." These letters match those in one of the predicted words, "grass."

4. *Accepting or rejecting the hypothesis.* Since the information contained in the letters "gr" matches one of the predicted words ("grass"), the reader accepts the hypothesis.

Note that the reader did not have to visually discriminate all of the letters in the word, but instead constructed the entire word on the basis of minimal visual information. If none of the letters in the word had matched the predicted words, the reader would have had to take in more visual information in order to recognize the word. Assume, for example, that the target word was "hedge." In order to recognize this word, the reader would have had to process more visual information than was necessary for one of the predicted words.

When a word can be constructed from little visual information, it should take less time. Conversely, when more visual information is required, it should take additional time to recognize a word.

Although this brief sketch describes the process of word recognition in terms of the hypothesis/test model, several additional comments are worth making. Earlier, it was stated that the automaticity model can include within its conceptualization the hypothesis/test model. Let us explore how this would be done.

There are times when we read when our familiarity with and knowledge of the text are so great that we can easily anticipate or predict what words

will follow, as in "red, white, and _____" or "fourscore and seven years
_____." When we encounter such "easy" sentences, the level at which we
visually process words (whether it is at the level of letters, whole words, or—
if we have enough confidence in our prediction—not at all), is very different
from when we encounter an entirely new idea expressed in a style that is
difficult to understand. Thus our knowledge and comprehension of the text
influence the level of visual processing. This is exactly what was said about
the automaticity model, namely, that the feedback loop from semantic
memory influences the level of visual processing in visual memory.

Criticism of the hypothesis/test model   The description of the model suggested that specific words are predicted or hypothesized. It is highly probable that in actual reading, this does not happen at all, at least not at the
fairly high rates of speed at which fluent readers must recognize words.
Rather, the model may very well describe the process of word recognition
for the less than fluent reader, who has a much slower reading rate.

The four-stage process of word recognition in the hypothesis/test model
takes time to execute. It takes time to generate a hypothesis, time to test the
hypothesis, and time to evaluate the hypothesis in terms of whether it should
be accepted or rejected. The fluent reader can probably recognize a word in
isolation faster than the time it takes to go through this entire hypothesis/
test process. But, the critics will charge, is there not evidence to show that
it takes longer to recognize a word flashed by itself—SNOW—than one in
context, as in WHITE SNOW? These studies of flashed-word recognition
have a major flaw in the procedure and are not good analogues of what goes
on in real reading. In the studies done with flashed words, the experimental
subject has a lot of time to think about the word that was flashed. In real
reading, the person does not have time to stop after each word and think
about it.

Modifying the hypothesis/test model   A small but important modification
in the hypothesis/test procedure allows us to overcome the criticism that
the model probably does not predict specific words. The pace at which we
read is too fast for that. If you doubt this, the next time you attend a lecture, attempt to predict what the speaker will say. You will find that you
can shadow the speech—perhaps a syllable or two behind the speaker—but
you will not be able to predict, as described in the hypothesis/test procedure.

The essential modification I am suggesting for the hypothesis/test model
of recognition is that we predict meaning and not particular words. For
example, assume that in the passage you are reading, the man being described is a gardener and the passage is about the man's work. The sentence
states: "Father cut the green _____." If one reads words such as "grass"

or "hedge," they make sense in terms of the meaning of the passage. On the other hand, if one reads words such as "emerald" or "glass," they do not make sense, and the reader may have to go back to the word again in order to make sure that it was correctly recognized.

According to the modification I am suggesting in the hypothesis/test model, in which we anticipate meaning and not particular words, the actual stages might be as follows:

1. *Information use.* Information in the text is read.

2. *Expectations are generated at the meaning level.* From the sample of text that has been read, the reader generates general expectations at the level of meaning. In other words, as we read, we may attempt to anticipate what ideas or thoughts might logically follow. Many of us are familiar with this attempt to anticipate ideas. Everyone has undoubtedly had the experience of trying to explain something to another person, only to be interrupted by the other person, who tries to complete the thought for us. Similarly, as readers, we are forming general expectations of what the writer of the text may be attempting to state.

3. *Word recognition.* Numerous sources of information converge to aid in word recognition. The word itself contains some sources of information, e.g., spelling rules, word length, and word contour. Words are spelled and pronounced according to rules, and skilled readers and even many beginning readers know these rules. Given the following letters, for example, the reader can generate many words starting with those letters: b_____, c_____, or br_____, ch_____. Spelling rules, word length, and contour information may all converge to aid in recognition, as in:

b▢ versus br▢ or c▢ versus ch▢.

Other sources of information that aid in recognition are contained outside the word itself, and these may simply be thought of as context aids. For example:

The baseball player hit the ball with the b▢.
The mouse ate the ch▢.

Depending on the reader's skill, the expense of making an incorrect recognition, and the amount of information found within and outside the word, the reader "recognizes" the word, using as little visual information from the word itself as is possible.

4. *Accept/reject the word recognition.* If the word recognized makes sense in terms of anticipated meaning, the word is accepted. On the other hand,

if the word does not make sense, the reader may be forced to gather more visual information until an appropriate recognition is made. Reading regressions, in which the reader must go back to an earlier part of the text, often take place when the reader realizes that there is a mismatch between what is being read and what makes sense.

IMPLICATIONS OF THEORETICAL MODELS OF READING FOR DIAGNOSIS OF READING PROBLEMS AND INSTRUCTION

Implications of the automaticity model

Earlier, it was said that there is nothing so practical as a good theory. In this, the final section, a few of the practical implications of the reading models presented will be explored.

The automaticity theory helps to diagnose certain kinds of common reading problems. Some teachers have observed that students may be able to recognize words accurately but not be able to comprehend with ease. Teachers call this problem "barking at print." Automaticity theory would suggest that one possible reason for the student's problem is that the decoding is requiring attention. Since a person's attention cannot be on comprehension and decoding simultaneously, the act of decoding is interfering with comprehension.

Another common problem one can observe occurs when skilled readers, often college students, claim that even though they read the text with care, they cannot remember what was read. Because the students are skilled readers, the actual decoding of the words on the page can take place without attention. Thus attention is free to be directed elsewhere. Instead of focusing attention on deriving meaning from the text and understanding and recalling the author's viewpoints, the students' attention wanders elsewhere, on matters entirely unrelated to the text. Thus the students decode the text but are thinking about that Saturday night date or misunderstandings with roommates.

These problems require quite different remedies. For students whose attention is on decoding rather than on comprehension, one solution is to give them a text that is easier to read. Another solution is to suggest that they read the text several times until the meaning becomes clear. This practice is often followed in beginning stages of reading. The first time or two, students read the text, emphasizing decoding. Once they are able to decode the words, the students switch their attention to meaning. A third solution is for the teacher to realize that more than accuracy is needed for students to become skilled readers. One must go beyond accuracy to automaticity. In human activities that require high levels of proficiency and skill, a considerable amount of time must be spent in practicing the skills leading to mastery. Only by spending a great deal of time in actual reading will the student develop beyond the level of mere accuracy. This practice may be on important subskills in reading, but it must also include time spent on reading easy and interesting meaningful material. At one time teachers felt guilty about having students spend time on a task at which the students had exhibited some minimal level of proficiency. What the teachers were afraid of was being accused of giving the students "busy work" assignments. Teachers should realize that to go beyond accuracy to automaticity in reading requires practice. So what may appear to be "busy work" to some is actually "automaticity training" to others. Time spent in reading simple meaningful material, however, is a good way to give the student the practice necessary for building the necessary skills for automatic decoding.

For students who are skilled readers but have poor recall, it is often helpful to explain that the poor recall is due not to a memory deficit, but to lack of attention directed on processing the text. Although the mere understanding of the nature of the problem is often helpful to the student, additional aid is frequently needed. To help students focus attention on text meaning, they should be taught how to engage in self-testing. Asking "What ideas were expressed on this page?" at the end of each page helps students in the areas of comprehension and recall.

The last suggestion grows directly out of automaticity theory. An interesting question is what can be learned about how to teach reading from areas of human performance requiring extraordinary high levels, e.g., music and sports. Both of these areas have similarities in training methods which differ from those generally used in reading. For example, let us compare the teaching of reading and music.

In music, the teacher may assign one or two pieces of music and tell the beginning student to practice these pieces for a week. The student's goal is to play the pieces accurately and with fluency. Thus the student practices the same pieces over and over, trying to reduce errors and to blend the notes into a smooth rendition. A somewhat different situation exists in beginning reading. Although the goals in both music and reading are accuracy and fluency, the beginning reader is seldom encouraged to read and reread a passage until these goals are achieved. Instead, teachers tend to move many students too rapidly through the pages in the reading text before any degree of mastery has been reached.

For several years we have been using a technique we call "the method of repeated readings" with enough improvement in students' comprehension and reading speed to justify suggesting it here. It is not a total method, but is used in conjunction with whatever the ongoing reading method happens to be. Of course, many teachers will probably want to alter this method of repeated readings somewhat to fit particular classroom needs.

1. Have the student select a short reading selection that is neither so hard that the student cannot read any of the words nor so easy that the student can read it with high accuracy and speed. The selection can be as short as 50 words or as long as 500 words, depending on the skill of the reader.

2. In addition to the reading selection, you will need a chart for recording word-recognition errors and speed, as well as a stopwatch.

3. The student reads the selection out loud to a helper—a teacher, teacher aide, parent, or student tutor. The helper counts the number of errors and records the time in seconds. These data on errors and speed are put on the chart for each testing.

4. The student sits down again and rereads the selection until called to read again by the helper. It may be necessary to write the words the student cannot read on a sheet of paper and have the student study these words in addition to rereading the selection.

5. The testing-rereading cycle is repeated until the student can read the selection with some degree of fluency. It is *not* important to eliminate all word-recognition errors, but it is important to have the student read the selection with fluency. When this goal is reached, a new selection is chosen and the process is repeated. The charts provide feedback to the student to indicate rate of progress.

A useful modification of this technique is to have the helper dictate the story onto a tape recorder. While listening to the story on the tape recorder, the student is silently reading along. Then, as soon as possible, the student practices rereading the story silently without the tape recorder. Thus there is a progression from reading with auditory support to reading without support. The practice is continued until the student can orally read the selection with fluency.

Implications of the hypothesis/test model

In discussing the theory underlying the hypothesis/test model, it was stated that reading is a constructive act and that fluent readers can recognize a word using only some of the letter cues in the word. Many beginning readers have not learned the word-recognition strategies underlying the hypothesis/test model, and the following method suggests a way to teach this strategy. Three experimental studies using normal and disabled students indicated significant improvement in word recognition and comprehension. The four steps in the procedures are: (1) using information from the passage; (2) making a prediction; (3) comparing the printed word to the predicted word; and (4) accepting or rejecting the prediction. Each of the four stages in the hypothesis/test strategy represents a skill that can be learned. The recommended procedure is to begin training at the oral-language level, train to mastery at this level, and then introduce the same skill visually.

The seven component skills derived from the model are as follows:

1. Training on the ability to say a word given an initial sound. Student is given drills of the following nature:

Stimulus: Teacher says, "Tell me a word starting with the sound /p/."

Response: Student gives a word starting with that sound. Any word starting with the sound is acceptable.

Training in this skill is easily accomplished by giving students a few minutes daily practice in a small-group setting.

2. Training on the ability to determine the beginning letter of a spoken word. Student is given drills of the following nature:

Stimulus: Teacher asks, "What is the first letter in the word 'girl'?"

Response: Student gives the name of the initial letter in "girl," i.e., "g."

This skill is easily taught by giving students a few minutes of practice daily.

3. Training on the ability to visually recognize the initial letter of a word presented orally. Student is given drill of the following nature:

Stimulus: Teacher says, "What is the first letter in the word 'boy'?" Then the teacher shows a card with the letters "b," "c," "t," "r" printed on it.

Response: Student points to the letter "b."

This skill can be taught in large groups by duplicating answer sheets having numbered arrays of letters to go with the word for that number. Teacher says, "The first word is 'boy.' Circle the first letter of the word boy."

4. Training on the ability to use auditory context to predict words that could logically follow. Student is given a drill of the following nature:

Stimulus: Teacher says, "My mother sleeps on her _____."

Response: Student predicts the missing word. Any word that makes sense is acceptable.

5. Training on the ability to use auditory context to predict word(s) that could logically follow in a sentence, hearing just the initial sound of the word. Student is given drill of the following nature:

Stimulus: Teacher says, "The cat ran after the /m/ _____."

Response: Student predicts what the missing word might be. The words must begin with the /m/ sound and make sense in the context.

Skills 4 and 5 can be taught in a large group in an enjoyable way by reading a short story to the class and having the students fill in some of the words. The teacher may or may not pronounce the initial sound, depending on which skill is being stressed; or, the two conditions can be mixed together, particularly when the students have nearly mastered the skills.

6. Training on the ability to use visual context to predict word(s) that would logically follow in a sentence, without seeing the initial letter of the word. Student is given drill of the following nature:

Stimulus: Experimenter shows the following in printed form: "The children open the _____."

Response: Subject is asked to read and predict the word in the blank. Any word that makes sense is acceptable.

7. Training on the ability to use visual context to predict word(s) that could logically follow in a sentence, when given the initial letter of the target word. Student is given drill of the following nature:

Stimulus: Experimenter shows the following in printed form: "The girl ate the b_____."

Response: Subject is asked to read this and predict the word in the blank. Any word beginning with "b" that makes sense is acceptable.

Extensive practice on skills 6 and 7 can be given by duplicating passages at the students' reading level, but deleting some of the words. If skill 6 is being taught, simply leave blanks of uniform length to indicate a missing word. When teaching skill 7, print the beginning letter (or letters if a blend or digraph). Oral reading of the passage in a group situation gives each child limited practice. Additional practice can be accomplished by suggesting that the student take the sheet home and read it to a parent or sibling. Teacher aides and student aides can also be used to provide additional practice.

In closing this chapter, I am reminded of the story about the college student who went home from school and was asked, "What did you study this quarter?" The student replied that he studied theoretical models of reading. "And what did you learn about theoretical models?" the student was asked. "More than I ever wanted to know," he replied. My hope is that this has not been the case for you.

SUGGESTED READINGS

Davis, Fredrick B. *The Literature of Research in Reading with an Emphasis on Models,* East Brunswick, N.J.: Iris Corporation, 1971.

Gibson, E. J., and H. Levin *The Psychology of Reading,* Cambridge, Mass.: M.I.T. Press, 1975.

LaBerge, D., and S. J. Samuels "Toward a Theory of Automatic Information Processing in Reading," *Cognitive Psychology,* 6 (1974): 293–323.

Singer, H., and R. Ruddell *Theoretical Models and Processes in Reading,* Newark, Del.: International Reading Association, 1970.

Smith, Frank *Understanding Reading,* New York: Holt, Rinehart and Winston, 1971.

Chapter 3

READING PROBLEMS IN PERSPECTIVE

PAUL SATZ · *University of Florida*

INTRODUCTION

The purpose of this chapter[1] is to provide a broad, critical sketch of major trends and developments in the area of childhood learning disorders. Although this area comprises only one part of the broader area of childhood mental illness and behavior disorders, as defined by the current NIMH Task Force, the incidence and shattering effects of these disorders may well represent one of the major child and adult mental health problems today. In fact, the scope and magnitude of learning disorders are so pervasive that they are observed, in varying degrees, throughout the whole range of childhood mental health disorders, including the psychoses. Studies have now shown that learning disorders that persist into late childhood and adolescence generally lead to serious emotional and behavioral disturbances that threaten the educational and social fabrics of our society (Eisenberg, 1966; Gates, 1968; Kline, 1972). Learning disorders, for example, now represent the major single cause of school dropouts in our educational system (Silberman, 1964). They also represent one of the major problems observed in referrals to clinics and juvenile courts (Critchley, 1968; Meerlo, 1962; Mendelson, Johnson, and Stewart, 1971; Schmideberg, 1949; Wright, 1974).

It has been shown that many of the aggressive, antisocial disturbances associated with learning disability, particularly in adolescence, may precede the development of schizophrenia in the adult (Menkes, Rowe, and Menkes, 1967; Robins, 1966). More striking, however, is the relationship between reading failure and criminal behavior. In a recent study, Wright concluded as follows (1974, p. 4).

The Crime Study Commission in this report will attempt to go one step further in the search for the cause of crime by postulating a theory, which simply stated, will argue that, reading failure is the single most significant factor in those forms of delinquency which can be described as anti-socially aggressive. If we believe that a significant amount of crime is committed by individuals who began their antisocial behavior as school dropouts and who graduated from juvenile delinquents to youthful offenders to adult criminals, then this theory, if proven, becomes a vitally important indicator for crime prevention.

To illustrate the magnitude of this problem—which encompasses educational, social, economic, and psychiatric institutions—I will present some of the findings reported by the recent HEW National Advisory Committee on Learning Problems. These findings, summarized by Kline (1972, p. 16), pertain to only one category of learning disorders—reading.[2]

(1) Fifteen percent of the children in our schools have severe reading disabilities. This represents an incidence of approximately eight million school children in the United States. (2) The enrollment in the primary and secondary grades of our public schools is 51,500,000. The average annual cost per child is $696.00. If one child in twenty (five percent) is not promoted, the national loss expressed in economic terms alone is $1.7 billion. (3) Children of adequate intelligence but retarded in reading often perform adequately in nonreading school work during the early grades. However, as the years of reading failure build up feelings of inadequacy and dissatisfaction with school, these students' overall academic work is severely affected. (4) A follow-up study shows that sixth-grade underachievers continue to be underachievers in the ninth grade, with a resulting tendency to drop out. (5) The American Association of Junior Colleges has estimated that from one-third to one-half of their new students have significant reading problems and that 20 percent of their new students in the most disadvantaged areas are unable to profit from their present remedial programs, so severe is their handicap. (6) Every year some 700,000 children drop out of public school. (7) Sixty percent of the enrollees in the Job Corps Urban Centers have less than a sixth-grade reading ability, and about twenty percent of them read below the third-grade level. (8) Seventy-five percent of juvenile delinquents are significantly retarded in reading. The 1968 cost for detention of a juvenile delinquent in a federal institution was $6935 per year. (9) The retention of reading underachievers costs the nation's public education system in excess of one billion dollars every year. (10) Unless the causes of failure are determined and specific remedial instruction is provided, a child profits little from repeating the same grade. (Recently, I saw a little boy who had repeated grade 1 and was now repeating grade 2 for the third time. Despite an IQ of 118, he was still

unable to read from a preprimer, and he knew nothing about phonics.) (11) The present state of affairs is such that there can be no assurance that a diagnostic study will be accurate or that remedial instruction will be sufficient to meet a child's needs. Unfortunately, today's situation opens the way to exploitation and to well-meaning but ineffective effort.

These incidence figures provide an instructive but sobering assessment of the problem. But how about the causes which may underlie the problem? Unfortunately, it is at this juncture that matters become more complex, if not obtuse. The HEW report laid much of the blame on the educational system, concluding that the nation's effort to teach reading is mostly an ill-defined, directionless, uncoordinated "patchwork" affair lacking urgency. Similar extreme conclusions were voiced recently by Kline (1972) and Furth (1972), suggesting that ineffective teaching and poor methodology probably account for the majority of reading and learning disabilities in our schools. And then we have the "armchair" speculations of respected authorities now suggesting that emotional factors represent the *major* causal factor in learning disabilities (Bettelheim, 1972)—a conclusion that is dramatically at variance with current knowledge (Ames, 1968; de Hirsch, Jansky, and Langford, 1966; Eisenberg, 1966; Gates, 1968; Kline, 1972). Such a conclusion perniciously puts the responsibility and blame on the handicapped child by reference to intrinsic motivational factors.

A review of the current literature, however, indicates that the search for a single primary cause of reading and learning disorders is not likely to be productive in this decade, if ever. In fact, the available evidence points to multiple precursors and/or determinants, including genetic defects (Critchley, 1968; Kline and Kline, 1975; Owen, Adams, Forrest, and Fisher, 1968; Silver, 1971), prenatal and perinatal complications (Davie, Butler, and Goldstein, 1972; de Hirsch, Jansky, and Langford, 1966; Eisenberg, 1966; Paine, 1968; Smith, Flick, Ferriss, and Sellmann, 1972), postnatal brain trauma and infection (Clements, 1966; Eisenberg, 1966), cultural deprivation (Bloom, 1964; Davie *et al.*, 1972; Eisenberg, 1966), inadequate teaching (Furth, 1972; Kline, 1972), sensory defects (Eisenberg, 1966), intellectual retardation (Eisenberg, 1966; Myklebust, 1968), emotional problems (Bettelheim, 1972), and complexities in our English orthography (Makita, 1970; Rozin, Poritsky, and Sotsky, 1971).

THE CLASSIFICATION PROBLEM

This confusing set of interrelationships—particularly between learning disorders and biological, educational, socioeconomic, and psychological variables—has long presented a problem at the most basic level of science, namely, nosology. Unfortunately, the problem still exists, despite repeated attempts to formulate a valid and reliable classification of learning disorders

(Chalfont and Scheffelin, 1969; Clements, 1966; Waites, 1968). In fact, this problem presents, in my judgment, one of the major and persistent hurdles to progress in the area of childhood learning disorders. On what basis, for example, could children with learning disabilities be differentiated? Historically, the method of classification has been based on the criterion of major handicap, which essentially reduces to the principle of homogeneity by exclusion (Myklebust, 1968; Strauss and Lehtinen, 1947). That is, a learning disability was (and continues to be) defined as a major handicap when the behavioral signs (achievement criterion) occurred in the *absence* of other major handicaps, e.g., intellectual retardation, sensory impairment (vision/hearing), and gross neurological damage (Clements, 1966; Critchley, 1968). Some authors have further restricted this diagnostic classification by excluding other major handicaps, e.g., sociocultural deprivation (Eisenberg, 1966; Waites, 1968) and emotional problems (Myklebust, 1968).

Most authors now concur that the major handicap in childhood learning disability is primarily a behavioral or achievement criterion which may be specific, e.g., reading or auditory decoding, etc., or general, e.g., perception, language, and/or conceptualization. This vote of unanimity, however, should hardly be surprising or enlightening. The coexistence of other "major" handicaps would have contraindicated, by definition, a specific learning disability! However, more serious problems exist with these terminological ploys, which continue to obscure and muddle the waters. First, if one uses the principle of exclusion to define childhood learning disability, one must include a number of other specific childhood disorders which are *similarly defined,* e.g., psychoneurological learning disability (Myklebust, 1968), educational handicapped (Owen, 1968), central processing dysfunctions (Chalfont *et al.,* 1969), minimal brain dysfunction (Clements, 1966), specific dyslexia (de Hirsch, Jansky, and Langford, 1966), specific devlopmental dyslexia (Critchley, 1968; Waites, 1968), specific reading disability (Money, 1962), primary reading retardation (Rabinovitch, de Jong, Ingram, and Withey, 1954), and strephosymbolia (Orton, 1937). The major handicap in each of these disorders is an achievement, e.g., learning, or behavioral, e.g., perceptual-conceptual-linguistic-mnemonic, criterion that occurs in the *absence* of other major handicaps, e.g., intellectual retardation, sensory impairment, gross brain injury, socioeconomic deprivation, and/or emotional instability.

Second, it should be apparent that several of these excluded major handicaps (biological, socioeconomic, psychological) have already been identified as precursors or determinants of childhood learning disorders. If so, why attempt to exclude them in the diagnostic classification of learning disability? One obvious explanation is the need to classify on the basis of the criterion that makes for the greatest homogeneity in the subpopulation (Myklebust, 1968). Thus by classifying on the basis of major handicap, one is able to define a smaller, and presumably less heterogeneous, diagnostic group. An equally plausible, but more invidious, explanation is that the *major* handicap, e.g., achievement criterion, occurs in the presence of *minor* handicaps, e.g., biological, socioeconomic, psychological, which are implicitly assumed to be casually or etiologically related to the major handicap. As such, these minor handicaps, e.g., neurological deviation, are treated loosely as independent variables and/or hypothetical constructs, which are often not accessible to observation or direct measurement. The two most striking examples involve cases of "suspected central nervous system deviation," i.e., minor sign, or "constitutional-genetic anomaly," i.e., unobservable event postulated to underlie the disorder. This latter point illustrates the third major criticism of current methods of terminology and nomenclature in this area—that the disorder(s) or diagnostic classification(s) is frequently defined not only on the major and observable handicap, but also on the minor handicap (inferred) or the unobservable handicap (hypothetical construct) postulated to underlie the disorder.

This additional inference muddles, if not violates, the attempt to formulate a diagnostic system on observable events. Behavioral signs or symptoms (major handicap) are immediately *confounded* with inferred or unobservable causal events (minor handicaps or hypothetical constructs). Consequently, the diagnosis of minimal brain dysfunction (MBD) is based on the major handicap (learning or behavioral disability), which is observable, and the minor signs (usually hyperactivity or perceptual dysfunction), which are postulated to represent deviations in central nervous system function (Clements, 1966). This process smacks of the old psychiatric model in which symptoms, etiology, and prognosis were all derived from the diagnostic label. A review of current research in learning disabilities reflects a curious disregard of this diagnostic inferential problem. For example, in his Phase I NINDS review, Clements (1966) acknowledged the purist point of view by stating that the term "minimal brain dysfunction (MBD)" most often represents an unproven presumptive diagnosis. However, he quickly dismissed this issue in favor of the pragmatic view. He says:

> With our limited validated knowledge concerning relationships between brain and behavior, we must accept certain categories of deviant behavior, developmental dyscrasias, learning disabilities, and visual-motor perceptual irregularities as *valid indices* of brain dysfunctioning. They represent neurologic signs of a most meaningful kind, and reflect disorganized central nervous system (CNS) functioning at the highest level ... We cannot afford the luxury of waiting until causes can be unquestionably established by techniques yet to be developed. (pp. 6–7)

In my opinion, this type of viewpoint has unfortunately influenced a less rigorous and more soft-headed pragmatic approach to research in learning disabilities. More specifically, it has given implicit consent, if not license, to less sophisticated investigators and clinicians to confound the diagnosis, i.e., achievement criterion, with unwarranted etiological speculations.[3] As pointed out, the diagnosis of MBD is usually based on the major handicap (learning disability), which is observable, and the minor signs (usually motor incoordination, distractibility, or perceptual difficulty), which are postulated to represent deviations in CNS function (Clements, 1966). The problem is that each of the minor signs could also be explained on the basis of non-biological factors, e.g., developmental, psychological, or sociocultural. Visual-perceptual and perceptual-motor organization is less well integrated in developmentally younger normal children, in disabled readers (usually younger), in less intelligent children, and in culturally-deprived children (Ames, 1968; Benton, 1962; Eisenberg, 1966; Satz and Van Nostrand, 1972; Snyder and Pope, 1972).

Similarly, gross and fine-motor organization has been shown to be less well integrated in emotionally disturbed children without evidence of CNS dysfunction (Paine, 1968) and in culturally deprived families in which the father is absent (Willerman, 1972). The role of childrearing practices is particularly evident in this regard. Sollenberger (1968), for example, has observed no evidence of hyperactivity/impulsiveness in Chinese-American children living in New York. A similar observation was reported recently for children from mainland China (V. Douglas, personal communication). Apparently the family cohesiveness and structure in these families provides a measure of external control which may facilitate the development of internal cognitive controls over motor behavior. In a similar vein, data from the Fels Institute for longitudinal research have recently shown that parental and environmental forces also exert a major effect on the long-term prognosis of hyperactive children. Parental and environmental forces were shown to be selectively negative for male in contrast to female hyperactive children throughout childhood and adolescence (Battle and Lacey, 1972).[4] Also, the high incidence of hyperactive/impulsive behavior in lower-class children who came from broken homes has already been well documented (Davie et al., 1972; Robins, 1966).

It should be emphasized that these studies do not discredit the influence of CNS mechanisms in the etiology of these behavioral disorders; they merely indicate that hyperactive behavior can be strongly influenced or modified by environmental factors, particularly within the family. This latter finding, which concerns the important interaction between biology and environment, may well account for the controversy in classifying these behavioral disorders (Kenny et al., 1972). In fact, this study concluded that "hyperactivity is an ill-defined and inconstant phenomenon commonly associated with organic and/or developmental defects coupled with unfavorable environmental influences" (p. 407).

Equally abusive is the tendency to postulate an underlying genetic defect (unobservable event) in the diagnostic formulation of specific developmental dyslexia (Critchley, 1968; Waites, 1968). Once again, the diagnosis is based on the major handicap (reading achievement) in the absence of other observable major handicaps, e.g., intellectual retardation, gross brain injury, sensory defects.[5] Yet the diagnostic label is muddled with surplus meaning attesting to the basic, though unobservable, event postulated to underlie the disorder. Does this mean, therefore, that other disorders of reading which are similarly defined in the absence of other major handicaps, e.g., strephosymbolia, specific reading disability, dyslexia, primary reading retardation, educationally handicapped, etc., also have the same underlying unobservable defect? If so, why use different diagnostic terms? If not, how can a distinction be justified on the basis of an unknown and unproved etiology?[6]

In contemporary medicine, a disease entity like cancer is defined on the basis of systematic and observable symptoms which can be related to microscopic changes in the molecular or biochemical structure of the organism. Although medicine has identified numerous types and classifications of cancer cells and has speculated on many of the biologic mechanisms that may trigger the disease, the underlying causes, when unknown, are not invoked to justify the diagnosis.

This later comment brings us back to one of the major criticisms of current progress in childhood learning disorders. We still lack an objective framework in which to classify and differentiate the numerous types of learning deficiency. The major obstacle clearly concerns the tendency to *confound* classification (major observable handicap) with etiology, in which the "causal" event is loosely inferred from other minor signs (often behavior) or is based on unobservable inner events which may or may not exist. Although some advocates of the etiology position may dispute the gravity of this point by admitting the possibility of *other* causally inferred mechanisms in the same disorder (e.g., Clements, 1966; Critchley, 1968; Myklebust, 1968), the same error is committed by reference to unknown events in the formulation of the disorder. Moreover, the inferential nature of the diagnosis connotes a certain level of scientific credibility, which may differentially affect the child's school placement, treatment/remediation, and psychological development.

DEFINITIONS OF A LEARNING DISABILITY

Consider, for the moment, the following list of conflicting definitions of learning disability, which was compiled by the recent NINDS Task Force (Chalfont and Scheffelin, 1969, pp. 147–148):

A learning disability refers to a retardation, disorder, or delayed development in one or more of the processes of speech, language, reading, spelling, writing, or arithmetic resulting from a possible cerebral dysfunction and/or emotional or behavioral disturbance and not from mental retardation, sensory deprivation, or cultural or instructional factors. (Kirk, 1962, p. 261)

We use the term "psychoneurological learning disorders" to include deficits in learning, at any age, which are caused by deviations in the central nervous system and which are not due to mental deficiency, sensory impairment, or psychogenecity. The etiology might be disease and accidents, or it might be developmental. (Myklebust, 1963, p. 27)

Children who have learning disorders are those who manifest an educationally significant descrepancy between their estimated intellectual potential and the actual level of performance related to basic disorders in the learning processes, which may or may not be accompanied by demonstrable central nervous system dysfunction, and which are not secondary to generalized disturbance or sensory loss. (Bateman, 1965, p. 220)

The term "minimal brain dysfunction syndrome" refers ... to children of near average, or above average general intelligence with certain learning or behavioral disabilities ranging from mild to severe, which are associated with deviations of function of the central nervous system. These deviations may manifest themselves by various combinations of impairment in perception, conceptualization, language, memory, and control of attention, impulse, or motor function.

Similar symptoms may or may not complicate the problems of children with cerebral palsy, epilepsy, mental retardation, blindness, or deafness.

These aberrations may arise from genetic variations, biochemical irregularities, perinatal brain insults or other illness or injuries sustained during the year which are critical for the development and maturation of the central nervous system, or from unknown causes. (Clements, 1966, pp. 9–10)

A child with learning disabilities is one with significant intradevelopmental discrepancies in central-motor, central-perceptual, or central-cognitive processes which lead to failure in behavioral reactions in language, reading, writing, spelling, arithmetic, and/or content subjects. (Kass, 1966)

A learning disability refers to a specific retardation or disorder in one or more of the processes of speech, language, perception, behavior, reading, spelling, or arithmetic. (Kirk, 1966, pp. 1–2)

A child with learning disabilities is one with adequate mental abilities, sensory processes and emotional stability who has a limited number of specific deficits in perceptive, integrative, or expressive processes which severely impair learning efficiency. This includes children who have central nervous system dysfunction which is expressed primarily in impaired learning efficiency. (National Council on Exceptional Children, 1967)

Children with special learning disabilities exhibit a disorder in one or more of the basic psychological processes involved in understanding or in using spoken or written languages. These may be manifested in disorders of listening, thinking, talking, reading, writing, spelling, or arithmetic. They include conditions which have been referred to as perceptual handicaps, brain injury, minimal brain dysfunction, dyslexia, developmental aphasia, etc. They do not include learning problems which are due primarily to visual hearing or motor handicaps, to mental retardation, emotional disturbance or to environmental disadvantage. (National Advisory Committee on Handicapped Children, 1968)

A perusal of the definitions reveals that reading disorders—complex in their own right—are lumped together with problems of speech, language, perception, cognition, memory, spelling, and writing. Furthermore, most authors imply that abnormalities in CNS organization may underlie the disorders, i.e., by inference, and some explicitly infer an underlying CNS defect (e.g., Clements, 1966; Myklebust, 1963).[7] Three authors explicitly exclude sociocultural deprivation as a factor in these disorders (Clements, 1966; Kirk, 1962; National Advisory Committee on Handicapped Children, 1968); the remaining authors omit reference to this factor and thereby obscure the problem of definition/classification. Similarly, three authors exclude psychogenetic-emotional problems as a factor in learning disability (Myklebust, 1963; National Advisory Committee on Handicapped Children, 1968; National Council on Exceptional Children, 1967), whereas the remaining authors omit reference to this factor or postulate it as a primary determinant (Kirk, 1962). The only acceptable points of agreement in the preceding definitions concern the identification of the major handicap in terms of a behavioral-achievement criterion (reading, writing, spelling, speech, language, memory, and perception) in the absence of mental retardation or gross sensory damage. The unacceptable points of agreement concern the explicit or implicit references to unobservable and unspecifiable CNS events which are confounded with the diagnosis. Moreover, most of these inferences are based on behaviors which could also be explained on a nonbiological basis.

I would like to propose that we put an immediate stop to this inferential-etiological approach in the diagnosis of childhood learning problems and concentrate on a classification schema based on the major observable achievement handicap, i.e., behavioral criterion. Agreement should then be reached on specifying those variables or factors to be considered in defining the disorder, e.g., average-above average intelligence, freedom from gross sensory and neurological damage. Children with emotional-behavioral problems should probably not be excluded because of the disproportionate increase in these problems in disabled learners over time (Critchley, 1968; Eisenberg, 1966; Gates, 1968; Kline, 1972; Meerlo, 1962; Schmideberg, 1949). Similarly, children from disadvantaged backgrounds, who nevertheless have at least average intelligence, should likewise *not* be excluded from this category, particularly in view of the high inverse relationship between socioeconomic level and learning disability (Bloom, 1964; Davie *et al.*, 1972; Eisenberg, 1966). However, learning-disabled children who are disadvantaged and intellectually below average should probably be excluded from these specific learning disability groups.

There are several advantages to this classification schema. First, it is descriptive and as such avoids reference to confounding explanatory inferences on etiology (hypothetical constructs). Second, it operationally specifies those variables which must be present to define the disorder. Third, it focuses on achievement-oriented behaviors, i.e., major handicap, that are measurable, which in turn allow one to pinpoint or specify the type of special handicap, e.g., reading, writing, arithmetic, perception, speech, etc. Consequently, the presence of a learning problem (achievement criterion) associated with hyperactivity or perceptual difficulty (minor signs) in a child who is not retarded or sensorially impaired should justify a descriptive diagnosis of specific learning disability associated with hyperactivity—but nothing more! However, to infer that the underlying defect is in the brain—which would follow with our current explanatory labels (minimal brain dysfunction or otherwise)—can serve only to retard scientific knowledge *and* the child! Why, for example, should our diagnosis be confounded at this time with inferences about unknown CNS events (usually pernicious), when the behaviors on which they are based would permit equally persuasive nonbiological assumptions? At present, both types of explanatory inferences should be removed from our diagnostic classifications pending further longitudinal and cross-sectional research.

What is desperately needed is a focus on matters of first-order relevance, i.e., an objective and descriptive classification of learning disorders that can later be investigated on an explanatory, or second-order, level. This subsequent level of relevance involves the relationship(s), if any, between the behavioral-achievement criterion, i.e., learning handicap, and a range of other variables, including prenatal, perinatal, and postnatal status (e.g., trauma/infection), developmental milestones, familial-constitutional characteristics, sociocultural factors, and the like. The research strategy should provide a framework in which to determine whether differences in the achievement criterion, e.g., reading skill, vary as a function of differences in those biological, psychological, and sociocultural variables that have already been linked, in part, with childhood learning problems. At present there is no available evidence to ascertain whether the degree of reading handicap or its natural history, for example, varies as a function of birth status, e.g., prematurity, trauma, infection, or even of socioeconomic level. Nor do we know whether the severity and prognosis of children with specific reading disability are quantitatively or qualitatively different in children whose parents were similarly handicapped in reading. If such differences could be demonstrated, attempts could be made to refine our diagnostic categories at more than a descriptive level.

EARLY DETECTION: THE NEED FOR LONGITUDINAL FOLLOW-UP RESEARCH

Answers to these questions are going to depend on more ambitious cross-sectional and longitudinal studies. Attempts must be made to determine the relationships, if any, between the achievement criterion and the antecedent factors (independent variables) just discussed. However, unless these retrospective studies are subsequently phased into prospective studies, our understanding of learning disabilities will continue to be obscured by speculation and opinion. A review of the current literature reveals a pitifully small number of natural-history or longitudinal studies in this area. This state of affairs exists despite the repeated recommendations of experts (Critchley, 1968; Money, 1962; Sontag, 1971). According to Sontag (1971, p. 1001):

> The longitudinal approach is, then, essential in studies of prediction over time, individual differences and their etiology, and individual developmental pattern. It is essential for the evaluation of motivational or educational intervention programs as well as the transience or stability of particular characteristics. To determine the effects of the use of growth hormone in children with growth defect problems, it is obvious that repeated time-spaced measurements are essential to measure growth responses. The current rash of intervention programs and enrichment programs in underprivileged groups, mentally defective groups, and so forth, can only be evaluated by longitudinal methods.

The application of longitudinal research in the area of learning disorders is absolutely essential for moving to explanations of second-order relevance. This research, moreover, need not involve a "womb-to-tomb" approach. The nature of the design should depend on the hypotheses or questions being asked.

There are two general problem areas that need immediate investigation —the detection, or prediction, problem and the natural-history, or prognosis, problem. The prediction problem is uniquely relevant in that it attempts to find functional relationships between independent variables sampled much earlier in the child's life, e.g., biological, sociocultural, developmental-psychological, and criterion variables sampled ontogenetically later, e.g., developmental or achievement behaviors. Much of the infrequent earlier work was specifically addressed to relationships between birth-history data and *early* postnatal development (Gallagher and Bradley, 1972). Seldom were these relationships extended to later periods including the early preschool years (achievement criteria). More recently there has been increased interest in the more applied aspects of early detection. This research has focused on the predictive classification of performance measures taken usually at preschool (K or Gl) against the criterion of achievement measures one to three years later.

These two types of longitudinal designs—one sampled initially around birth, the other initially during preschool—have yielded uniformly discouraging results vis-à-vis predictive classification (Gallagher and Bradley, 1972). Although functional relationships have generally been observed between the prior independent variables and the subsequent criterion variables, the predictive power has been poor. This is particularly true of the more recent early detection studies, which are specifically addressed to the prediction of future criterion group membership, i.e., high or low risk.

According to a recent review by Gallagher and Bradley (1972), the early identification of developmental difficulties has been discouraging regardless of the area involved, e.g., hearing, vision, central procession (Apgars, mild mental retardation), learning disability, emotional disturbances, and speech difficulties. The fields of "identification audiometry" and learning disorders were particularly vulnerable to criticism on the basis of low validity (high false positive and negative signs), poor methodology, and the lack of theoretical constructs. This state of affairs is most unfortunate, considering the vast expenditures of time and money already given to this area, the admitted relevance of the problem, and yet the limited available knowledge.[8] Most authorities in the field of learning disorders would now agree that a valid early-detection or warning system is vital for the success of treatment and/or prognosis (Ames, 1968; Critchley, 1968; Eisenberg, 1966; Keeney and Keeney, 1968; Kline, 1972; Money, 1962). Satz and Friel (1973) have stated that early intervention should be vigorously pursued, but only when based on a valid early-warning or detection procedure. The potential advantage of early detection is that intervention can be started before the child begins formal learning or reading—at a time when his or her central nervous system may be more plastic and responsive to change—and at a time when he or she is more likely free of the frustrations and emotional turmoil associated with repeated academic failure.

The explicit need to begin identification and remediation as early as possible is strengthened by the recent survey by Keeney and Keeney (1968) on treatment. It was shown that "when the diagnosis of dyslexia was made in the first two grades of school nearly 82 percent of the students could be brought up to their normal classroom work, while only 46 percent of the dyslexic problems identified in the third grade were remediated and only 10 to 15 percent of those observed in grades five to seven could be helped when the diagnosis of learning problems was made at those grade levels" (Strag, 1972, p. 52).

These percentages are compatible with the opinions of several other investigators who have suggested that the effects of remediation are proportionately decreased when initiated in late childhood (de Hirsch, 1968; Lenneberg, 1967). Unfortunately, there is a dearth of supporting data, other than opinion, to substantiate the Keeney report. The problem is due largely to the paucity of research on natural history and prognosis of learning disorders, with or without treatment, in the literature.

On the other hand, it has been suggested from infrahuman studies that the child may be more sensitive to environmental stimulation, e.g., remedial intervention, when the brain is maturing and when behavior is less differentiated (Caldwell, 1968). Bloom (1964) has shown that variations in the environment have their greatest quantitative effect on a characteristic, e.g., speech, during its most rapid period of change—ages 2–10—and the least effect during the least rapid period of change—ages 11–15. Infrahuman studies also suggest that organization can be strongly modified only when active processes of organization are under way and that when facilitated, they progressively inhibit attempts at reorganization (Scott, 1968).

These studies clearly justify the need for more research on early detection. Vigorous efforts at this level can provide additional payoff with respect to theory. The reason is that theory requires a framework in which to conceptualize the precursors or antecedents of learning disorders that may be more temporally or closely related to the underlying biological and environmental causes.

The preceding theoretical rationale reflects some of the basic assumptions that underlie all behavioral research (Lindgren and Byrne, 1971, pp. 18–19):

1. All behavior is caused; that is, it is determined by and is the necessary consequence of antecedent events.

2. The causes of behavior are multiple.

3. The causal factors leading to the variance in the behavior being studied must be identified if valid principles or generalizations are to be developed.

4. The principles or generalizations that govern causal factors or account for variations in behavior are simpler than the original data on which they are based.

THE NEED FOR LONGITUDINAL FOLLOW-UP RESEARCH   55

5. The test of whether principles or generalizations are valid is whether they can be used to predict behavior.

A theory that purports to identify these precursors must postulate or attempt to explain the functional relationships between developmental competencies or environmental advantages at an earlier period, e.g., prereading, and the later acquisition of a separate criterion phenomenon, e.g., reading rate or comprehension. Such a theory must also attempt to explain why many children, for example, with reading disability are handicapped on a number of developmental skills not directly related to the reading process, e.g., right-left confusion, visual-perceptual difficulty, perceptual-motor disturbance, verbal nonfluency.

This phenomenon can be explained only if one has a knowledge that covers the fields of developmental and educational psychology, neuropsychology and pediatric neurology, and psychiatry. This requirement might explain why so few attempts have yet been made to account for these associated developmental handicaps in specific reading disability (Satz and Van Nostrand, 1973). Any breakthroughs in the area of learning disorders will have to integrate developmental concepts into current theory. Such integration has been reported recently in the works of de Hirsch and associates (1966, 1968) and Satz and associates (1970, 1971, 1972, 1974, 1975). Shipe and Mierzitis (1968) point out that the concept of special learning disabilities carries with it three developmental assumptions: (1) such disabilities are rooted in the child's early development; (2) these antecedents can be defined and measured empirically; and (3) the condition can be altered by educational intervention. Similar suggestions are also voiced by Frank (1969) in his review of the evaluation of emotional disorders in children.

The preceding discussion has attempted to focus briefly on a number of problems that are retarding progress in the field of learning disorders. The problem of diagnosis and classification is extremely important. Similarly, there is a need for more and better longitudinal research. However, good longitudinal research in this area must be tied to some theoretical framework that is testable and that incorporates basic developmental concepts.

A review of the literature indicates that progress in theory development in learning disorders has lagged considerably. By contrast, empirical studies have abounded, often with woefully inadequate methodology and with little regard or patience for longitudinal research. The mystique of "quick and dirty" studies prevails amidst a plethora of often irrelevant and unexplained relationships between variables. Moreover, the diagnostic criterion variables are all too often invested with surplus meanings attesting to unknown or inferred etiologies. The area of learning disabilities is truly a controversial and muddled domain.

EARLY DETECTION STUDIES: A REVIEW

The need for a valid early-warning or detection system exists and is applauded by most authorities. It is recognized that validation of these predictive measures would provide further information on the "precursors" of specific learning disability, which may shed further light on how environmental experience and biology act together to create differences among children in mental ability and rate of progress in school. Yet when one examines the literature on early detection, one finds a persistent disregard of sampling problems, test construction and selection, multivariate-classification, statistical decision theory (e.g., detection signs, base rates, conditional probabilities, and the like), and developmental theory. Virtually all of the studies have been based on small samples and have included male/female and black/white subjects. This procedure seems senseless in view of the high attrition rates reported over time and the fact that these disorders are known to be sex-linked, with the disadvantage being disproportionately in favor of boys (Bentzen, 1963; Critchley, 1968; Eisenberg, 1966; Naeye *et al.*, 1971). Consider, for example, the longitudinal study by Galante, Flye, and Stephens (1972), which sampled an entire kindergarten class (N = 114) in 1961 and followed them for seven years! When the criterion measures were assessed in 1968, only 71 children remained in the sample, and of that number 6 boys and 1 girl were classified as learning-disabled. On the basis of only seven Ss, the authors concluded that no single causative factor emerged, although an accumulation of minor deficits appeared in all of the severe underachievers. This type of study, unfortunately, provides little insight into the antecedents of learning disability. No information was given for selection of the test battery (empirical), valid and false positive rates were not reported, and a univariate model was used, with no attempt to secure cross-validation data. Many of these criticisms could also be leveled at the recent longitudinal predictive studies of Silberberg, Silberberg, and Iversen (1972), Evans and Bangs (1972), Eaves, Kendall, and Crichton (1972), Haring and Ridgeway (1967), Feriden and Jacobson (1970), and Weiner and Wepman (1971).

The Haring and Ridgeway study (1967) is particularly vulnerable to criticism, although the researchers did sample a large group of kindergarten children identified by teachers as high-risk learning problems (N = 1200). Instead of trying to validate their large predictive test battery against a later and independent criterion, they merely looked for unique patterns within their "assumed" high-risk children. Not surprisingly, they found none. In a critical review of this study, Gallagher and Bradley stated that "it would be similar to grouping all children who are sick. They would fail to yield distinctive illness patterns because the distinctiveness of individual illnesses would be swamped in the general pool of 'sickness' " (1972, p. 108).

The current practice in longitudinal predictive research is to identify children who are "assumed" to be potential high-risk learning causalities during kindergarten (based on parental or teacher judgments) and then to sample a much smaller, extreme, subgroup from this pool for investigation ($N \leqslant 40$). These methodological short-cuts may provide some information on the valid positive detection signs, but they surely bias an adequate analysis of the false positive detection signs. Furthermore, these studies are extremely vulnerable to the base-rate problem (Meehl and Rosen, 1955; Satz, Fennell, and Reilly, 1970; Satz and Friel, 1973). Also, what conclusions are permissible when the final criterion group is based on a sample of 10 to 20 underachievers one to three years later?

One of the landmark studies in this area was conducted by de Hirsch, Jansky, and Langford (1966). The authors followed more than 100 children from kindergarten to the end of grade 2, when criterion assessments were made on reading, writing, and spelling (behavioral achievement criteria). This study is also one of the better conceptual approaches to predicting reading disability in that the design and selection of tests ($N = 37$) were based on reasonably sound developmental and neurological theory, i.e., the maturation-lag hypothesis. The weaknesses of the study were again associated with the small sample size ($N = 106$), the inclusion of both males and females, the large number of low-income children from different races, the utilization of univariate rather than multivariate methods of analysis and classification, no consideration of base rate, no determination of valid positive and negative detection signs, no factor analysis of the test battery, and no cross-validation of the predictive index.

These criticisms probably limit many of the interesting extrapolations made by the authors (1966, 1968). In fact, many of the basic conclusions derived from this study—which are quoted widely—are based on only eight failing readers who emerged at the end of grade 2! These eight children, however, were severely handicapped; they all scored zero on the Gray Oral Reading Test and revealed a wide range of perceptual, cognitive, speech, and language difficulties. Six of the eight were boys and three were Negroes.

Despite these criticisms, the de Hirsch project must be applauded for its heuristic value. This timely and valuable study has focused attention on the relevant early-detection problem. In fact, some of preceding problems were corrected in a later study by these authors (Jansky and de Hirsch, 1972). The project included a much larger sample of children ($N = 508$) who were tested with many of the same tests during spring of their kindergarten year. The sample was drawn from five public schools in two districts in New York City. Forty-two percent of the children were black, and 54 percent were boys. Two years later reading measures were obtained on 79 percent of the remaining sample to evaluate the predictive accuracy of the kindergarten tests. The results were encouraging; approximately 75 percent of the failing readers were detected (valid positives), and only 25 percent were missed (false negatives). However, approximately 20–25 percent of the average readers were incorrectly classified as high risk (false positives). The best predictors were letter naming, picture naming, Gates word matching, Bender Gestalt copying, and Binet sentence memory. It should be apparent, therefore, that the high predictive accuracy was facilitated in part by the use of tests that assessed aspects of the reading process as early as kindergarten. That is, independence between the predictors and reading-criterion outcomes was not obtained.

This problem, however, is not as serious as the failure to utilize computer-generated cutting lines for the predictions and the failure to cross-validate the predictions on a separate group of children two or more years later. The literature on early detection reveals a virtual disregard of this crucial validity issue. The Jansky and de Hirsh study (1972) also revealed that 41 percent of the black girls and a staggering 63 percent of the black boys were failing readers at the end of grade 2. This finding, although important, suggests that the early-detection outcomes were based largely on culturally deprived children and not on cases of specific reading or learning disability. Similar general criticisms could be leveled at the early-identification research of Silver and Hagin (1964) concerning their innovative SEARCH battery. In other words, more basic research is still needed on larger samples of children followed for much longer periods of time before early attempts at intervention are implemented. The risk of misclassification, particularly for false positives, is too costly in human terms should intervention programs be established for predicted high-risk children (false positives) who would have turned out to be average readers in later years without such help. Thus the admitted need for valid early detection, before the child begins reading, should be balanced by judicious concern for the risks of misclassification for all children.

One solution to this problem would be to sample a *total* population of kindergarten children, preferably white boys (because of their greater risk for *specific* reading disorders in later years) and to follow them longitudinally, within a natural-history framework, for several years in order to more fully evaluate the detection and outcome problems. Such a design, moreover, should include a separate cross-validation group of white boys who are tested at the beginning of grade K (a year later) and followed for the same number of years for comparison purposes.

The longitudinal project being carried out by the author and associates represents a beginning effort in this direction (Satz and Friel, 1973, 1974; Satz, Friel, and Goebel, 1975; Satz, Friel, and Rudegeair, 1974, 1976). The project, now in its sixth year, has three primary objectives: (1) to test a theory (Satz and Van Nostrand, 1973) that purports to identify the predictive antecedents (precursors) of specific reading disability several years *before* the disorder is clinically present; (2) to evaluate the mechanism (brain maturation lag) presumed to underlie and influence later developmental changes (developmental lag) in this disorder; and (3) to determine differential prognosis, if any, in these children (dyslexic) as compared to other groups of failing readers.

The project to date has focused largely on the first objective, i.e., early detection. The results have shown that the battery of developmental and neuropsychological tests administered at the beginning of grade K (1970) has continued to forecast reading-achievement levels at both extremes of the reading distribution, i.e., severely disabled and superior readers, in later years (grades 2–5), regardless of the types of reading measures employed, the length of time involved between test and criterion evaluation, and the intervention efforts implemented *independently* within the schools! These follow-up studies, which are based on 95 percent of the original population, have also shown that a few of these tests have consistently ranked highest in terms of predictive accuracy across criterion probe years. Each of these tests (finger localization, recognition-discrimination, and alphabet recitation) are postulated to represent measures of early developing skills which are in rapid ascendancy during the "five-seven" age shift (Kagan) and which are felt to be crucial to the early phases of reading (Satz and Van Nostrand, 1973). In other words, the high predictive accuracy of these measures suggests that they may be assessing a general level of immaturity or developmental unreadiness in the five-year-old child who is destined to become a failing reader. If true, the results would be compatible with theories postulating a developmental or maturation lag in those high-risk children (Critchley, 1968; de Hirsch and Jansky, 1966; Jansky, 1975; Money, 1962, 1966; Silver and Hagin, 1964). The results, however, tell us nothing about the mechanisms (causes) postulated to underlie these behavioral precursors or antecedents. They merely represent phenotypic expressions of more basic mechanisms, e.g., brain maturation lag, which at the present time cannot be observed. Although it was stated earlier that the test of whether principles or generalizations are valid is usefulness in predicting behavior (Lindgren and Byrne, 1971), it is felt that the present generalizations are based on more complex behavioral phenomena, i.e., precursors, which may have their own temporal precursors and underlying causes. Hence, the present formulation concerning a brain maturation lag (hypothetical construct) must be viewed with caution as an explanation concerning etiology. However, the results do lend more support to its behavioral counterpart, namely, developmental lag.

Additional support for the predictive validity of this early-detection battery has been reported in two recent cross-validation studies (Satz and Friel, 1976; Satz, Friel, and Rudegeair, 1976). If these results could be replicated on much larger samples of children by other investigators, educators could begin to focus on new intervention approaches that might, for example, attempt to facilitate the acquisition of those developmental skills shown to forecast later problems in reading and writing. This type of prevention offers a new set of challenges, because it focuses on early remediation before the child begins formal reading.

SOME EARLY DETECTION AND INTERVENTION STUDIES

The integration of early *detection* and *intervention* represents, in my opinion, a need of the highest priority. "It should not be forgotten," state Gallagher and Bradley (1972, p. 118), "that better service to children—the solution of their problems, not merely their identification—is a matter of public priority. Unless we can do substantially better in providing treatment services, such as early childhood developmental clinics to back up early identification of developmental problems, the screening efforts described here do not really amount to more than an academic interest."

Unfortunately, I fear that my pleas for joint early detection and intervention research will fall to deaf ears or to soft-headed emulation. For example, a recent study by Silberberg *et al.* (1972) attempted to investigate this problem in a follow-through design. Because a number of investigators have already demonstrated the predictive validity of letter and number recognition on later reading proficiency, the authors attempted to accelerate this prereading skill in an experimental group of "normal" kindergarten children and to determine the short-term (three months) and long-term (one year) effects of this training (two months) on reading achievement at the end of grade 1. The results were both instructive and misleading. The effects of training on this prereading skill persisted for short-term intervals (three months), but not for long-term intervals. This should prove instructive, if not sobering, to the vast majority of reading and educational specialists who are evaluating treatment effects for only short-term intervals. This focus on short-term effects, without any longitudinal follow-through, is certain to limit progress in the area of remediation.

The misleading finding concerns the conclusion "that accelerated training in reading readiness does not affect subsequent ability to read, but rather affects only the scores achieved on the reading readiness tests administered upon completion of the training period" (Silberberg *et al.,* 1972, p. 259). In other words, the authors immediately generalized from the results on alphabet and number recognition and concluded that "one may even question the value of formalized training in other reading readiness activities as well" (p. 255). This conclusion, although typical of much of the research in learning disorders, is both reckless and unjustified. The reason is that letter and number recognition is only one of many reading readiness skills, and its predictive correlation with reading achievement has never been high to begin with. In fact, Silberberg *et al.* reported a coefficient of approximately 0.65

(male and female), which would account for only about 43 percent of the variance. This would leave most of the variance unaccounted for, which in retrospect should have precluded the use of the letter and number recognition as a training skill, if not a predictive skill.

Somewhat similar problems were recently reported in another study, which attempted to combine the development of a preschool predictive instrument with the effects of a replicable preschool training program on later academic school achievement (Evans and Bangs, 1972). Once again, the conclusions were both instructive and misleading. It was instructive to note that the majority of those "high-risk" children who were enrolled in the language and learning program for two years prior to kindergarten were performing at grade level when followed up several years later. This was not true for the majority of those "high-risk" children who either dropped out of the program or were placed in no-treatment control groups. At one level, these results are encouraging for the value of early intervention.

However, the results were quite misleading with respect to how the "high-risk" children were identified. Apparently, both parental referral and scores on the screening battery were used to identify high- and low-risk groups. Yet inspection of the predictive classification outcomes revealed a high number of false positives in the high-risk no-treatment group (18 percent) and a high false negative rate in the low-risk no-treatment group (25 percent). The danger here is that treatment was initiated for the other groups before the predictive validity of the tests was established and cross-validated—and perhaps on many children who may not have been high-risk to begin with! Moreover, the identification of children was vaguely confounded with parental referral plus test results, with no explanation as to how the smaller final sample was selected.

These criticisms are meant to be constructive in that both studies represent radical departures from previous intervention studies, with an attempt to combine early detection with intervention and follow-up evaluation. For this reason they should be applauded. However, the scope of this type of research is so broad that the occurrence of design and procedural errors could vitiate the conclusions reached. The major problem is that early intervention should be based on evidence of early valid detection. One should not be instituting intervention or learning-readiness programs on the basis of developmental measures that lack predictive validation and cross-validation. If this caution is not heeded, vast resources will be committed to training skills that are irrelevant and/or training children who do not need such help. One must also consider the negative aspects of false labeling on a normal child during these formative preschool years.

The problem of training on irrelevant skills is most vividly illustrated in the area of perceptual-motor programs. A review of this literature, which is much larger than the longitudinal research, reveals a hopelessly confusing set of results. An excellent recent review by Hammill (1972) concluded that "little correlation existed between measures of visual perceptions and tests of reading comprehension and that training visual perceptual skills, using currently available programs, has no positive effect on reading and possibly none on visual preception" (p. 552). This position is also shared by two other recent reviews on the subject (Mann, 1970; Sullivan, 1972). Mann (1970) took particular aim at current concepts of perception and concluded that there is neither an adequate definition of perception nor an adequate neuro-physiologic theory to explain it. Yet most treatment centers for learning disorders have access to a wide grab-bag of visual-perceptual programs—the Frostig-Horne, the Kephart, the Fitzhugh Plus, and the Winter Haven, to name but a few. Perceptual training, according to Mann (1970), is now big business and "is very much a part, if not the cornerstone, of today's modern orthopedegogy" (p. 30). Countless numbers of disabled learners are placed in these training programs, often without regard to age and whether or not they have any "perceptual" or visual-motor handicap. As long as the child enters with a diagnosis of dyslexia, minimal brain dysfunction, or specific learning disability, the special educator (or teacher aide) often assumes that this problem exists or is etiologically related to the problem. Again we find the problem of diagnosis, with all of its aforementioned confusion, repre-senting the basis for treatment.

Why, one might ask, do these training programs persist in the face of negligible results on reading achievement? One partial answer is the avail-ability and professional marketing of these program kits. Another answer is that *some* children seem to benefit from this training; Sullivan (1972) and Hammill (1972) report positive gains in approximately 30 to 40 percent of the studies. Another explanation is the frequently reported relationship between learning disorders (including reading) and perceptual difficulties (Benton, 1962; Silver and Hagin, 1964). According to Mann (1970, p. 36):

A large proportion of handicapped children and poor learners certainly have difficulties in drawing, produce rotations in copying designs, create fragmented or bizarre human figures, are ineffectual at visual articula-tion, scanning and fixation, show reversals in reading, manifest clumsi-ness and poor orientation, have difficulties in catching and throwing balls, have problems in extended visual perception. . . . Can these ob-servable and confirmable "facts" be disregarded in the training of such children? The answer assuredly is "no." But neither should the co-existence of defects be interpreted as forming a causal relationship, or the existence of perceptual defects blind us to the fact that in addition to them, a handicapped child usually presents a variety of other deficits in other behavioral systems, e.g., language, affect.

The preceding comments on perceptual training again highlight the need for theories in cognitive-perceptual development to account for these observed relationships between reading disability and perceptual organization. Why, for example, do some disabled learners manifest this problem, whereas others do not? Why do some of these children benefit from perceptual-motor programs, whereas others do not? In what way is the process of learning to read dependent, if at all, on perceptual operations? Are these operations more crucial to the early versus later phases of reading acquisition? Only recently have some of these questions been asked, although some of the basic research was conducted years ago in the laboratories of Gibson (1968) and Pick and Pick (1970).[9]

The recent theory of Satz and associates (1970, 1973) represents an attempt to explain the perceptual handicaps in reading disability as a function of maturation, or chronological age. The theory postulates that perceptual difficulties are more likely to be observed during those years (four to eight) in which perception is under primary development. Consequently, if a lag in maturation is assumed to underlie these disorders, delays in perceptual development should be observed primarily in younger rather than older handicapped readers. The theory states that with maturation, the child tends to "catch up" or overcome earlier developmental handicaps, but may now lag in those skills having a later or slower rate of development, e.g., language and formal operations. The theory is compatible with developmental positions that postulate that the child goes through consecutive stages of thought during childhood, each of which incorporates the processes of the preceding stage into a core complex and hierarchically integrated form of adaption (Bruner, 1968; Piaget, 1926). Although preliminary supporting evidence has been reported for these developmental hypotheses (Satz and Friel, 1974; Satz, Friel, and Rudegeair, 1974; Satz and Van Nostrand, 1972), major evaluation must rest on the results of longer periods of follow-through, preferably until adolescence (this research is now in its sixth year of study, with the children in grade 5).

The reason for this digression is to point out that sound developmental and neurological theory is essential, whether one is talking about causality, precursors, nature of the disorder, treatment, or prognosis. With respect to remediation, there must be a rationale for the type of intervention program, and outcome should be evaluated against the framework of natural history and prognosis of these disorders. It may be that disabled learners who have benefited from perceptual-motor training may have been younger children, or they may have had more difficulties in perceptual organization or both. No one has yet attempted to make this distinction. Furthermore, most of the intervention studies have been carried out on chronologically older children, who may already have overcome their earlier perceptual handicaps.

Attention to these developmental and theoretical issues may help to resolve some of the tediously repetitious controversies on perceptual training. I doubt, however, that it will quell the opposition of those who eschew any consideration of perceptual factors in reading acquisition. They state that if reading is the goal, instruction in reading is preferable to training in perception (Bibace, 1969; Cohen, 1969; Hammill, 1972; Pennypacker, 1972). According to Cohen (p. 13), "the best way to teach reading is to teach letters and sounds and do it well." On the basis of available evidence, this position is reasonably tenable, but it provides no theoretical rationale as to how to deal with the early-detection problem. If children can be validly detected before they begin formal reading, we should attempt to intervene on those potentially high-risk children. The evidence suggests that intervention at this preschool phase, e.g., kindergarten, may be both more optimal and effective. If so, why wait and decrease the chances of success? Moreover, waiting until the child begins to manifest the problem introduces so many of the secondary problems already discussed.

SUMMARY AND RECOMMENDATIONS

This chapter has attempted to focus briefly on a number of problems that continue to retard progress in the area of reading and learning disabilities. The following section presents a brief summary and set of recomendations that I feel might help to resolve some of these persistent problems.

1. I would like to see a major commitment, preferably by the National Institutes of Health, to support vigorously a program of *prophylaxis* in the area of learning disorders. This could easily be accomplished via contract and/or competitive peer-review research. Enough time has been spent, much of it wastefully, in pursuit of the fragmented problem. Children with learning disabilities have often been studied too late in their development, without recourse to direct information on their earlier developmental history (prenatal, perinatal, and postnatal), including preschool, with only occasional and subjective information on familial factors, e.g., reading. Moreover, the children have often been subjected to the markedly variable competence-sophistication of the experts, who may have labeled them anything from "retarded" to "brain-damaged" to "emotionally disturbed," even with the same presenting behaviors, and placed them in a specialized treatment program consistent or not with the diagnosis. Seldom, moreover, has the treatment been evaluated with respect to efficacy or long-term prognosis. Too often, these children, and their parents, have endured the consequences of this dubious "state of the art."

   The incidence of learning disorders is not decreasing; in fact, it may be increasing (Kline, 1972). Moreover, the effectiveness of current remediation or intervention programs is quite variable, if not discouraging, particularly in the area of perceptual-motor training. Seldom are follow-up evaluations made, and when reported they reveal an attenuation or reversal compared with short-term gains. Indeed, a review of the more recent follow-up studies on learning disorders (including hyperactivity) continue to report persistent residual problems in a number of areas (perceptual, mnemonic, cognitive, linguistic, motor), *including* severe emotional, behavioral, and antisocial disturbances (de Hirsch, 1968; Jonsson, Mendelson, Johnson, and Steward, 1971; Menkes, Rowe, and Menkes, 1967; Silver and Hagin, 1964; Stewart, Pitts, and Craig, 1966; Weiss *et al.*, 1972). The tragedy is that most of the children in these follow-up studies have been recipients (short and long term) of drug and behavioral teaching programs in the past. More sobering are the results on the effectiveness of special education classes in Denmark (Jansen *et al.*, 1970). Formal introduction of these programs was initiated in the 1930s as a preventive measure. The authors reported that although 15 percent of all Danish school children will, at some time during their schooling, have been placed in these remedial programs, it has not helped to reduce the increasing needs for this instruction over time.

These facts, while disquieting, should instruct us to the urgent need for early detection and intervention, but within a longitudinal context that affords an evaluation of both short- and long-term gains (one to five years). I would recommend immediate support for those projects devoted to early detection and cross-validation, preferably on larger samples than presently exist. This strategy would perforce delay some of the early-intervention studies proposed.

2. More basic longitudinal research is needed to pin down the much earlier effects of environmental deprivation and birth-history complications on the rate and growth of cognitive and motor skills during infancy and childhood. We must attempt to understand how environmental experience and biology act together to create differences among children in mental ability and rate of progress in school. These questions can be studied only by systematic longitudinal research. Failure to do this will only maintain our current ignorance on the effects of cultural and environmental deprivation on hyperactivity and related disorders of learning. Moreover, it will retard progress in the development of a descriptive and explanatory diagnostic classification of learning disorders.

Two recent longitudinal projects have made substantial contributions to this area. The study by Davie, Butler, and Goldstein (1972) identified every child born within a seven-day period in England, Scotland, and Wales in 1958 (N = 1600) and reexamined a subgroup of them at the age of seven. The results again confirm the debilitating effects of socioeconomic deprivation and birth complications on early school achievement. Prematurity was also shown to be disproportionately higher in those children who were failing in reading, writing, and spelling at the age of seven.

The study by Smith *et al.* (1972) utilized a sequential series of multi-variate analyses to predict developmental-psychological competence at age seven from prenatal, perinatal, and postnatal data derived from the Collaborative Child Development Study (Charity Hospital, New Orleans). Although predictions were made on only extreme criterion subgroups ("normal" and "abnormal"), the results were extremely accurate and showed that the primary predictive variance was accounted for by the prenatal and perinatal measures. The authors presented no theoretical interpretation of the results; however, the fact that all of the children were black, and primarily disadvantaged, suggests that neurological status before or during the first neonatal year may substantially forecast extremes in developmental competence seven years later.

The study by Davie and associates (1972) again highlights the relationship between environmental deprivation and later school achievement. The application of multivariate-predictive analyses to these data would help to tease out the effects (additive or interactive) of environmental and biologic factors in later school achievement. A more basic question, however, is whether the retarding effects of environmental restriction are reversible during infancy or childhood. If so, it would provide further support for much earlier intervention, particularly for those deprived children who are more likely to be at risk in later years. The recent longitudinal research programs of Kagan (1973), Robinson and Robinson (1971), and Van de Riet (1972) have demonstrated that retardation in cognitive and motor skills can be reversed in children who have experienced prolonged periods of deprivation. In fact, Van de Riet showed that significantly greater gains in intelligence occurred in children who were placed in experimental training programs at younger ages (four to five versus six to seven). This finding again suggests that reversibility may be inversely correlated with age.

3. A new descriptive classification of learning disorders is needed that precludes reference to unknown or inferred etiologies. Considerable attention was given to this problem in the earlier section of this chapter. It was shown that current terminology is so loose and replete with surplus meaning that different diagnostic labels could be inferred from the same behavioral performance with different explanatory implications.

4. More theoretical formulations are needed that incorporate developmental and neurological concepts, but that generate testable hypotheses. Past research has focused too often on isolated functional relationships between variables that provide few insights into the nature of learning disability. More conceptual frameworks are needed to prevent needlessly repetitious "shotgun" or single-variable approaches. There have been too many "quick and dirty" studies, and they tell us little about why "Johnnie" can't read or learn efficiently.

5. We need more research on the natural history of learning disorders, which again requires the use of longitudinal designs. The relationship between antisocial behavior, e.g., juvenile delinquency, and reading disorders in adolescence (Critchley, 1968; Johnson, 1967; Meerlo, 1962; Schmideberg, 1949; Wright, 1974) should alert us to the tragic consequences that may result when intervention programs are not provided or have failed. If these adolescent children had been followed in earlier years, preferably from birth, it may have been possible to determine whether certain biological and/or environmental factors may decrease the chances of remediation—particularly if started too late in the child's development. It would be interesting to know whether some of these more refractory cases have selective physical abnormalities (Waldrop and Goering, 1971) that might forecast schizophrenic disorders in late adolescence.

6. Finally, the support and resources of the National Institutes of Health are vitally needed to provide the intellectual framework in which to carry out these objectives. Longitudinal research, in particular, requires more support, over longer periods of time, than do other types of research. But the payoffs are potentially greater. Many of the longitudinal studies reviewed in this chapter were supported from such funds. However, to accomplish these objectives, major commitments must be made by the National Institutes of Health to support this type of research, regardless of the political or economic climate of our country. If not, our children will suffer, and as they do, so will our nation.

NOTES

1. The major part of this chapter was originally presented to the Research Task Force of the National Institute of Mental Health, Section on Child Mental Illness and Behavior Disorders, under the title "Learning Disorders and the Remediation of Learning Disorders." This chapter was also supported in part by funds from the National Institutes of Health (NS 08208 & MH 19415).

2. Disorders of reading, however, may well represent the major source of learning problems in Western culture. Inspection of subject characteristics in learning disability studies usually reveals a disproportionate number of children with reading, spelling, and writing problems (e.g., Myklebust, 1968; Owen, 1968; Satz and Friel, 1973). This may be due to the complex range of skills which subserve the processes of reading and writing (e.g., perceptual-motor, conceptual, linguistic, mnemonic), plus the fact that these processes represent the major sources of instruction (learning) and evaluation (achievement) in our schools today.

3. The International Study Group on Child Neurology (MacKieth and Bax, 1963) concluded that the term "minimal brain dysfunction" should be discarded on the basis of its terminological looseness. The authors stated: "It became clear that this term has, for most people, the anatomical and aetiological implications that there has been an episode of injury and that this has produced an anatomical change. Yet

closer examination makes it clear that evidence of anatomical damage is usually absent, that evidence or history of an injuring process is often absent, and that disorder of function is the evidence for applying the diagnostic label of minimal brain dysfunction."

4. The fact that the incidence for males is disproportionately higher than for females in disorders of reading, learning, and motility (Bentzen, 1963) further underscores the need to determine the role and interaction of both environmental *and* biological variables in these disorders. Recent evidence has strongly suggested such an interaction (Bentzen, 1963; Davie *et al.*, 1972); yet self-appointed experts, particularly in the educational domains (Cohen, 1972; Furth, 1972; Gordon, 1972) continue to adopt a rigid environmental posture that defiantly rejects or minimizes the role of biological variables. This position unfortunately continues to obscure, if not retard, progress in the area of childhood learning disability (see later sections for a discussion of these problems).

5. Some authors even exclude cultural and emotional handicaps (Eisenberg, 1966).

6. The author does not intend to dismiss those studies that have reported familial occurrence of reading deficiency in *some* reading-disabled children (Owens *et al.*, 1968; Silver, 1971) or the high concordance rates for reading disability in monozygotic twins (Hallgren, 1950; Norrie, 1954). The point is that the concordance rates are based on small samples, and familial incidence of a given behavior does not necessarily mean that the abnormality is genetically determined. Instead of investing the term "reading disability" with unproven etiological meaning, investigators should begin to identify those children who have a positive family history of reading deficiency and determine whether this concordance trait (phenotype) differentially affects the nature of the disorder (e.g., developmental skills) and its prognosis over time. Not one study has yet been addressed to this question. In fact, only one study has yet even attempted to measure the self-reports of reading deficiency in the parents (Owen, Adams, Forrest, and Fisher, 1968).

7. However, the same behaviors that are used to invoke a CNS defect by one author may be used by another to invoke a developmental (Satz and Van Nostrand, 1972) or sociocultural lag (Bloom, 1964). More often the bases for these inferences are left unexplained.

8. My impression, though admittedly subjective, is that much of the early detection research has been funded largely through the various Title III and VI state educational programs—and often without any central coordination. Consequently, much duplication and needless repetition of inadequate designs have resulted in studies which have lacked theoretical substance and sufficient intervals between assessment and criterion evaluation.

9. This again points out the frequent communication gap between laboratory and applied research. In fact, few of the basic journals in developmental psychology are currently reporting data that have even an indirect relationship to the area of learning disorders. I refer in particular to *Child Development,* which in the past two years has published only a scattering of research relevant to this area. This comment reminds me of Sontag's (1971) recommendation for longitudinal research. He pointed out the irony that journals such as *Child Development* and *Child Development Monographs,* which had been created for the publication of longitudinal and interdisciplinary research, have for long periods "carried almost none of either" (p. 990).

REFERENCES

Ames, L. B. "Learning Disabilities: The Developmental Point of View," in H. R. Myklebust, ed., *Progress in Learning Disabilities: Vol. One,* New York and London: Grune & Stratton, 1968, pp. 39–74.

Bateman, B. "An Educator's View of a Diagnostic Approach to Learning Disorders," *Learning Disorders, Vol. I,* Seattle, Washington: Seattle Seguin School, 1965.

Battle, E. S., and B. Lacey "A Context for Hyperactivity in Children over Time," *Child Development* **43** (1972): 757–773.

Benton, A. L. "Dyslexia in Relation to Form Perception and Directional Sense," in J. Money, Ed., *Reading Disability: Progress and Research Needs in Dyslexia,* Baltimore: Johns Hopkins Press, 1962, pp. 81–102.

Bentzen, F. "Sex Ratios in Learning and Behavior Disorders," *American Journal of Orthopsychiatry* **23** (1963): 92–98.

Bettleheim, B. "Bringing Up Children," *Ladies Home Journal,* June 1972.

Bibace, R. "Relationships between Perceptual and Conceptual Cognitive Process," *Journal of Learning Disabilities* **2** (1969): 17–19.

Bloom, S. *Stability and Change in Human Characteristics,* New York: Wiley, 1964.

Bruner, J. S. "The Course of Cognitive Growth," in N. S. Endler, L. R. Boulter, and H. Osser, eds., *Contemporary Issues in Developmental Psychology,* New York: Holt, Rinehart and Winston, 1968, pp. 476–494.

Caldwell, B. M. "The Usefulness of the Critical Period Hypothesis in the Study of Filiative Behavior," in Endler, Boulter, and Osser, *op. cit.,* pp. 213–223.

Chalfont, J. C., and M. A. Scheffelin *Central Processing Dysfunctions in Children: A Review of Research,* U.S. Department of Health, Education and Welfare, NINDS Monograph No. 9, 1969.

Clements, S. D. (Project Director) *Task Force I: Minimal Brain Dysfunction in Children,* U.S. Department of Health, Education and Welfare, National Institute of Neurological Disease and Blindness, Monograph No. 3, 1966, pp. 9–10.

Cohen, S. A. "Studies of Visual Perception and Reading in Disadvantaged Children," *Journal of Learning Disabilities* **2** (1969): 498–507.

Cohen, S. A. "The Adolescents with Learning Problems: How Long Must They Wait? Critique," *Journal of Learning Disabilities* **5** (1972): 275–276.

Critchley, M. "Dysgraphia and Other Anomalies of Written Speech," *The Pediatric Clinics of North America* **15** (1968): 639–650.

Davie, R., N. Butler, and H. Goldstein *From Birth to Seven,* London: Longman, 1972.

de Hirsch, K. "Specific Dyslexia or Strephosymbolia," in G. Natchez, Ed., *Children with Reading Problems: Classic and Contemporary Issues in Reading Disability,* New York: Basic Books, 1968, pp. 97–113.

de Hirsch, K., J. Jansky, and W. S. Langford *Predicting Reading Failure,* New York: Harper & Row, 1966.

Eaves, L. C., D. C. Kendall, and J. U. Crichton "The Early Detection of Minimal Brain Dysfunction, *Journal of Learning Disabilities* **5** (1972): 454–462.

Eisenberg, L. "The Epidemiology of Reading Retardation and a Program for Preventive Intervention," In J. Money, Ed., *The Disabled Reader: Education of the Dyslexic Child,* Baltimore: Johns Hopkins University Press, 1966, pp. 3–20.

Evans, J. S., and T. Bangs "Effects of Preschool Language Training on Later Academic Achievement of Children with Language and Learning Disability: A Descriptive Analysis," *Journal of Learning Disabilities* **5** (1972): 585–592.

Feriden, W. E., and S. Jacobson "Early Identification of Learning Disabilities," *Journal of Learning Disabilities* 3 (1970): 589–593.

Frank, G. H. "Psychiatric Diagnosis: A Review of Research," *Journal of General Psychology* 81 (1969): 157–176.

Furth, H. G. "Symposium on Current Operation, Remediation and Evaluation: Dallas, Texas. Meeting Report," *Journal of Learning Disabilities* 5 (1972): 650–652.

Galante, M. B., M. E. Flye, and L. S. Stephens "Cumulative Minor Deficits: A Longitudinal Study of the Relation of Physical Factors to School Achievement," *Journal of Learning Disabilities* 5 (1972): 75–80.

Gallagher, J. J., and R. H. Bradley "Early Identification of Developmental Difficulties," in I. J. Gordon, Ed., *Early Childhood Education,* Chicago: University of Chicago Press, 1972, pp. 87–122.

Gates, A. I. "The Role of Personality Maladjustment in Reading Disability," in Natchez, *op. cit.,* pp. 80–86.

Gibson, E. J. "Learning to Read," in Endler, Boulter, and Osser, *op. cit.,* pp. 291–303.

Gordon, I. J. "On Early Learning: The Modifiability of Human Potential," in P. Satz and J. J. Ross, eds., *The Disabled Learner: Early Detection and Intervention,* Rotterdam, The Netherlands: Rotterdam University Press, 1972, pp. 3–27.

Hallgren, B. "Specific Dyslexia," *Acta Psychiatrica et Neurologica Copenhagen,* 1950, Supplement 65, pp. 1–287.

Hammill, D. "Training Visual Perceptual Processes," *Journal of Learning Disabilities* 5 (1972): 552–559.

Haring, N. G., and R. W. Ridgeway "Early Identification of Children with Learning Disabilities," *Exceptional Children* 33 (1967): 387–395.

Jansen, M., J. Ahm, P. E. Jensen, and A. Leerskov "Is Special Education Necessary? Can this Program Possibly Be Reduced?" *Journal of Learning Disabilities* 3 (1970): 434–439.

Jansky, J., and K. de Hirsch *Preventing Reading Failure,* New York: Harper & Row, 1972.

Jonsson, G. "Delinquent Boys, Their Parents and Grandparents," *Acta Psychiatrica Scandinavica,* 1967, Supplementum 195.

Kagan, J. "The Deprived Child: Doomed to Be Retarded? *Los Angeles Times,* February 25, 1973.

Kass, C. "Conference on Learning Disabilities," Lawrence, Kansas, November 1966.

Keeney, A. H., and V. T. Keeney *Dyslexia, Diagnosis and Treatment of Reading Disorders,* St. Louis: Mosby, 1968.

Kenny, T. J., et al. "Characteristics of Children Referred because of Hyperactivity," in *Annual Progress in Child Psychiatry and Child Development,* ed. S. Chess and S. Thomas, New York: Brunner/Mazel, 1972.

Kirk, S. A. *Educating Exceptional Children,* Boston: Houghton Mifflin, 1962.

Kirk, S. A. *The Diagnosis and Remediation of Psycholinguistic Abilities,* Urbana: University of Illinois, Institute for Research on Exceptional Children, 1966, pp. 1–2.

Kline, C. L. "The Adolescents with Learning Problems: How Long Must They Wait?" *Journal of Learning Disabilities* 5 (1972): 262–271.

Kline, C. L., and C. L. Kline "Follow-up Study of 216 Dyslexic Children," *Bulletin of the Orton Society* 25 (1975): 127–144.

Lenneberg, E. H. *Biological Foundations of Language,* New York: Wiley, 1967.

Lingren, H. C., and D. Byrne *Psychology: An Introduction to a Behavioral Science,* New York: Wiley, 1971.

MacKieth, R. C., and M. C. O. Bax "Foreword: Minimal Brain Damage—A Concept Discarded," in *Minimal Cerebral Dysfunction,* London: National Spastics Society Medical Education, Little Club Clinics in Developmental Medicine, No. 10, 1963.

Makita, K. "The Rarity of Reading Disability in Japanese Children," *American Journal of Orthopsychiatry* **40** (1970): 599–614.

Mann, L. "Perceptual Training: Misdirections and Redirections," *American Journal of Orthopsychiatry* **40** (1970): 30–38.

Meehl, P. E., and A. Rosen "Antecedent Probability and the Efficiency of Psychometric Signs, Patterns or Cutting Scores," *Psychological Bulletin* **52** (1952): 194–216.

Meerlo, J. A. "Reading Block and Television Apathy: An Alarm for Parent," *Mental Hygiene,* October 1962.

Mendelson, W., N. Johnson, and M. A. Stewart "Hyperactive Children as Teenagers: A Follow-up Study," *Journal of Nervous and Mental Disease* **153,** 4 (1971): 273–279.

Menkes, M. M., J. S. Rowe, and J. H. Menkes "A Twenty-Five Year Follow-up on the Hyperkinetic Child with Minimal Brain Dysfunction," *Pediatrics* **39** (1967): 393–399.

Money, J., ed. *Reading Disability: Progress and Research Needs in Dyslexia,* Baltimore: Johns Hopkins Press, 1962.

Myklebust, H. R. "Psychoneurological Learning Disorders in Children," in S. A. Kirk and W. Becker, eds., *Conference on Children with Minimal Brain Impairment,* Urbana: University of Illinois, 1963, p. 27.

Myklebust, H. R., ed. *Progress in Learning Disabilities, op. cit.*

Naeye, R. L., et al. "Neonatal Mortality, the Male Disadvantage," *Pediatrics* **48** (1971): 902–906.

National Advisory Committee on Handicapped Children "Special Education for Handicapped Children, Toward Fulfillment of the Nation's Commitment," First Annual Report, January 31, 1968.

National Council on Exceptional Children Learning Disabilities Division Formulational Meeting, St. Louis, Missouri, April 1967.

Norrie, E. "Ordblindhedens," in K. Hermann, ed., *Reading Disability,* Springfield, Ill.: Charles C. Thomas, 1959.

Orton, S. T. *Reading, Writing and Speech Problems in Children,* New York: Norton, 1937.

Owen, F. W. "Learning Disability—A Familial Study," *Bulletin of the Orton Society* **18** (1968): 33–39.

Owen, F. W., et al. "Learning Disabilities in Children: Sibling Studies," *Bulletin of the Orton Society* **18** (1968): 33–62.

Paine, R. S. "Syndromes of 'Minimal Cerebral Damage,'" *Pediatric Clinics of North America* **15** (1968): 779–802.

Pennypacker, H. S. "Precision Teaching: Effective Strategies and Tactics for Intervention on Behalf of the Disabled Learner," in P. Satz and J. J. Ross, eds., *The Disabled Learner: Early Detection and Intervention,* Rotterdam, The Netherlands: Rotterdam University Press, 1972, pp. 243–265.

Piaget, J. *Judgment and Reasoning in the Child,* New York: Harcourt and Brace, 1926.

Pick, H. L., and A. D. Pick "Sensory and Perceptual Development," in P. H. Mussen, ed., *Carmichael's Manual of Child Psychology,* New York: Wiley, 1970, pp. 773–847.

Rabinovitch, R. Σ. et al. "A Research Approach to Reading Retardation," *Association for Research in Nervous and Mental Diseases* 34 (1954): 363–396.

Robins, L. N. *Deviant Children Grown Up,* Baltimore: Williams & Wilkins, 1966.

Robinson, H. B., and N. M. Robinson "Longitudinal Development of Very Young Children in a Comprehensive Day Care Program: The First Two Years," *Child Development* 42 (1971): 1673–1683.

Rozin, P., S. Poritsky, and R. Sotsky "American Children with Reading Problems Can Easily Learn to Read English Represented by Chinese Characters," *Science* 171 (1971): 1264–1267.

Satz, P., E. Fennell, and C. Reilly "The Predictive Validity of Six Neurodiagnostic Tests: A Decision Theory Analysis," *Journal of Consulting and Clinical Psychology* 34 (1970): 375–381.

Satz, P., and J. Friel "Some Predictive Antecedents of Specific Learning Disability: A Preliminary One- and Two-Year Follow-up," Rochester, New York, Academy of Aphasia, October 16, 1972*a*.

Satz, P., and J. Friel "Some Predictive Antecedents of Specific Learning Disability: A Preliminary One-Year Follow-up," in P. Satz and J. J. Ross, eds., *The Disabled Learner: Early Detection and Intervention,* Rotterdam, The Netherlands: Rotterdam University Press, 1972*b*, pp. 79–98.

Satz, P., and J. Friel "Some Predictive Antecedents of Specific Reading Disability: A Preliminary Two-Year Follow-up," *Journal of Learning Disabilities* 7 (1974): 437–444.

Satz, P., J. Friel, and R. Goebel "Some Predictive Antecedents of Specific Reading Disability: A Three-Year Follow-up," *Bulletin of the Orton Society* 25 (1975): 91–110.

Satz, P., J. Friel, and F. Rudegeair "Some Predictive Antecedents of Specific Reading Disability: A Two-, Three- and Four-Year Follow-up," in J. T. Guthrie, ed., *Aspects of Reading Acquisition,* Baltimore: Johns Hopkins Press, 1976.

Satz, P., J. Friel, and F. Rudegeair "Differential Changes in the Acquisition of Developmental Skills in Children Who Later Become Dyslexic: A Three-Year Follow-up," in D. Stein, J. Rosen, and N. Butters, eds., *Plasticity and Recovery of Function in the Central Nervous System,* New York: Academic Press, 1974, pp. 175–202.

Satz, P., D. Rardin, and J. Ross "An Evaluation of a Theory of Specific Developmental Dyslexia," *Child Development* 42 (1971): 2009–2021.

Satz, P., and S. Sparrow "Specific Developmental Dyslexia: A Theoretical Reformulation," in D. J. Bakker and P. Satz, eds., *Specific Reading Disability: Advances in Theory and Method,* Rotterdam, The Netherlands: Rotterdam University Press, 1970, pp. 17–39.

Satz, P., and G. K. Van Nostrand "Developmental Dyslexia: An Evaluation of a Theory," in P. Satz and J. Ross, eds., *The Disabled Learner: Early Detection and Intervention,* Rotterdam, The Netherlands: Rotterdam University Press, 1972, pp. 121–148.

Scott, J. P. "Critical Periods in Behavioral Development," in Endler, Boulter, and Osser, *op. cit.,* pp. 213–223.

Schmideberg, M. *Searchlights on Delinquency,* New York: International University Press, 1949, pp. 174–189.

Shipe, D., and S. Mierzitis "A Pilot Study in the Diagnosis and Remediation of

Special Learning Disabilities in Preschool Children," *Journal of Learning Disabilities* 2 (1969): 579–592.

Silberg, N. E., M. C. Silberberg, and I. A. Iversen "The Effects of Kindergarten Instruction in Alphabet and Numbers on First Grade Reading," *Journal of Learning Disabilities* 5 (1972): 254–261.

Silbermann, C. *Crisis in Black and White,* New York: Random House, 1964.

Silver, A. A., and R. A. Hagin "Specific Reading Disability: Follow-up Studies, *American Journal of Orthopsychiatry* 34 (1964), 95–102.

Silver, L. B. "Familial Patterns in Children with Neurologically-Based Learning Disabilities," *Journal of Learning Disabilities* 4 (1971): 349–358.

Smith, A. C., et al. "Prediction of Developmental Outcome at Seven Years from Perinatal and Postnatal Events," *Child Development* 43 (1972): 495–507.

Snyder, R., and P. Pope "Auditory and Visual Inadequacies in Maturation at the First Grade Level," *Journal of Learning Disabilities* 5 (1972): 40–45.

Sollenberger, R. T. *Journal of Social Psychology* 74 (1968): 13.

Sontag, L. W. "The History of Longitudinal Research: Implications for the Future," *Child Development* 42 (1971): 987–1002.

Strag, G. A. "Comparative Behavioral Ratings of Parents with Severe Mentally Retarded, Special Learning Disability, and Normal Children," *Journal of Learning Disabilities* 5 (1972): 52–56.

Strauss, A. A., and L. Lehtinen *Psychopathology and Education of the Brain Injured Child,* New York and London: Grune and Stratton, 1947.

Sullivan, J. "The Effects of Kephart's Perceptual Motor-Training on a Reading Clinic Sample," *Journal of Learning Disabilities* 5 (1972): 32–38.

Van de Riet, V. "The Culturally Deprived Child: A Sequential Learning Approach," in Satz and Ross, *op. cit.,* pp. 209–223.

Waites, L. (Recording Secretary) *Report of the Proceedings of the World Federation of Neurology: Research Group on Developmental Dyslexia and World Illiteracy* 22 (1968).

Waldrop, M. F., and J. D. Goering "Hyperactivity and Minor Physical Anomalies in Elementary School Children," *American Journal of Orthopsychiatry* 41 (1971): 602–607.

Weiner, P. S., and J. M. Wepman "The Relationship of Early Perceptual Level Functioning to Later School Achievements in Black Disadvantaged Children," Department of Health, Education and Welfare, Division of Research and Demonstration Grants, Social and Rehabilitation Service, 1971.

Weiss, G., et al. "Studies on the Hyperactive Child: Five Year Follow-up," in *Annual Progress in Child Psychiatry and Child Development, op. cit.*

Willerman, L. "Social Aspects of Minimal Brain Dysfunction," *Annals of the New York Academy of Sciences,* 1972.

Wright, P. W. "Reading Problems and Delinquency," paper presented at the World Congress on Dyslexia, Mayo Clinic, 1974.

Chapter 4

A SOCIOLOGIST
LOOKS AT READING

DORIS R. ENTWISLE • *The Johns Hopkins University*

Sociologists have paid curiously little attention to language. Educational sociologists, when they have studied language, have tended to focus on teenagers or adults and on how the amount of schooling (or social class) is related to language use. They have paid scant attention to reading or to any other specific subject. One might therefore think that the discipline of sociology has little to say about the acquisition of reading skills or about early reading achievement. That is certainly true in a superficial sense; there is not much written by sociologists about reading per se or even much written by sociologists about young children. On the other hand, some extremely important notions can be drawn from the field of sociology that have *direct* application to the teaching of reading and to the acquisition of reading skills. These notions are, to name just a few, the influence of society on language learning, the social nature of rewards, the influence of significant others on performance—in other words, most of what is known about social-class differences or social stratification as it relates to educational attainment. Accordingly, this chapter will take as its purpose the examination of reading from a sociological perspective.

SOCIOLOGICAL DEVELOPMENT AND CULTURE

Human beings are the consequence of generations upon generations of biological evolution. The human body has truly marvelous structures for transmitting, receiving, and processing written and spoken symbols. This biological legacy is hard to overrate. Yet human beings are also heirs to social evolution and are now just as dependent on efficient social mechanisms

Preparation of this chapter was facilitated by N.I.E. Grant No. NIE-G-74-0029 entitled "A Longitudinal Study of How Children (Black, White, Low SES, Middle SES) Develop Expectations for Their Own Performance" and by NIMH Grant No. MH12525-05 entitled "Research Training in Developmental Sociology."

which have evolved over the centuries as they are on a suitable gene pool. Bruner (1966) reminds us of this. If a culture is to survive, each generation must learn the culture's symbol systems. A society may perish because its culture, including its technology, is maladaptive, but a society may also perish because it cannot *transmit* its culture. A society's mechanisms for transmitting its culture are therefore as vital as what is transmitted.

A fundamental dimension of culture and of culture transmission is written language. Every known society has developed a spoken language. Written language is not universal, however. The cognitive complexity of written language may be appreciated from the fact that apparently the alphabet was invented only once, an enormous achievement. Its invention, furthermore, freed human beings from immediate experience and thereby greatly facilitated the transmission of culture. By writing down a recipe, for example, or by drawing a map, one individual can easily preserve information for use in the future and/or put that information into a form that makes it easy to transmit to other persons. A textbook is thus much more efficient than a lecturer.

Cultures with written language are enormously favored for survival. Cultures with efficient educational systems are favored even more. The enormous advantages the United States holds over any developing nation is measured not only in resources or technology, but also in the productive potential that the United States can readily develop in each new generation.

Language learning

Every normal child learns to speak his or her native tongue without specific teaching. Children learn to speak the language they hear spoken by persons to whom they are tied in social networks. It is taken for granted that children in France learn French as a first language, whereas those in Great Britain learn English. What is less obvious is that *social* boundaries also control the learning of language.

Every known society is divided into social layers. Some persons enjoy higher status than others. In a highly industrialized and complex society like our own, where there are diverse ethnic and racial groups as well as an elaborate division of labor, the stratification process is carried to an extreme. There are upper-class whites and upper-class blacks, for instance, and subtle variations in status within each group. There are also persons of both races who are in the middle, lower down, or at the very bottom of the social ladder. Most persons, of course, fall in the middle layers.

Persons within a society's stratification system may have only a fuzzy recognition, if any, of status boundaries or how one crosses the boundaries. Language, however, signals status powerfully even for persons who are not consciously aware of the fact. Teachers can easily judge a child's social status, for example, from his or her speech. Department store clerks can quickly decide which customers are likely to be financially well off, even from telephone conversations.

Differences in speech come about partly because verbal interaction between persons in different social layers is restricted. Blue-collar families act in a way to insulate themselves from contacts with middle-class persons and act so as to increase contact with their own kind. Cohen and Hodges's (1963) research shows that blue-collar workers avoid becoming involved in verbal interchanges with middle-class persons. Probably in every country, but certainly in the United States and Canada, there are consistent and systematic differences between the speech of middle-class persons and those persons below them in the stratification system. In the United States persons of middle-class status, or higher, comprise roughly 30 percent of the population.

Social class and language

The middle-class child learns a somewhat different language from the ghetto child—vocabulary, phonology, and syntax are all modified to some degree. Put simply, the words a child uses, how they are uttered, and how they are strung together reflect social boundaries. Perhaps more important, the middle-class child learns to use language *as an instrument,* differently from the ghetto child. The child uses it differently in interacting with other persons or in reacting to the environment. The middle-class child learns to respond to "suggestions" and to use language itself as a primary means of solving problems.

The ghetto child is likely not to be well tutored in uses of language for interacting with persons outside his or her own social group or for solving certain kinds of problems. Ghetto parents do not use language very productively for these purposes either (see Cohen and Hodges, 1963). They also are not very good at using language to teach their children how to deal with the world (Hess and Shipman, 1965).

To comment on these matters a bit further, a major language difference associated with social class, and probably one important for children learning to read, is how free speech is from its immediate context. How readily can speech be understood without other clues, such as who is speaking or where? Middle-class speech in the United States tends to be more context-free than blue-collar speech. The middle-class teenager who does not acknowledge a gift from grandmother will get a parental admonition: "It is easier to give graciously, you know, than it is to receive graciously." By this the parent reminds the teenager of a *general* class of behaviors involving donors and recipients and the kinds of social actions that accompany the passage of goods between the two. The context is very general. The parent also allows the teenager to save face and lessens the negative impact of the words by the phrase "you know." The parent's words also suggest indirectly that some further action involving a suitable acknowledgement is required in this specific case, without giving the teenager a direct command or telling the teenager exactly what to do. Middle-class teenagers, furthermore, have been socialized so that the parent's approach works—the teenager is likely to act on the "suggestion."

A working-class parent, dealing with a similar situation, might say: "You got that present from Grandma? Next time you see her, say something." This message presumes a specific social context involving a specific person and outlines a narrow class of actions to take place at a specific time. It gives no hint of a more general context for social action. The point as far as this chapter is concerned is that the middle-class child is more likely to be exposed to speech that is abstract—speech that must be understood outside a particular social context and speech that takes into account alternative modes of action and alternative contexts. Middle-class speech is also likely to have so-called mitigating forms—speakers "suggest" instead of "command," "remind" instead of "order." Children who are used to receiving such "suggestions," though, know that no equivocation is implied! Verbal signals can be very subtle. If the middle-class mother clears her throat at the dinner table, she may be signaling that someone is not using the proper cutlery (see Berko-Gleason, 1973). Middle-class children are attuned to such signals.

All of these features of middle-class speech can be readily related to reading. Most of them should *facilitate* learning to read. Reading is likely to be free of specific social context. The symbols to be decoded in reading from the printed page are, more often than not, totally free of context— they are usually not related to the persons who happen to be present when the child is reading. Reading successfully requires that the learner be ready to try different alternatives, different decoding strategies. The person I read to today may be the same one I read to yesterday, but only by paying attention to all the cues in this sentence up to now will a correct rendition of "read" be made by the reader. The reader may need to try different interpretations until he or she hits on the one that makes the most sense. By using more abstract language and allowing more alternative courses of action, the middle-class parent encourages styles of thought that probably aid in reading acquisition.

Cognitive style and social class

Actually very little is known *specifically* about how social class influences the process of learning to read. I want to make several kinds of observations, however, in addition to those made above about sociolinguistic customs and context dependence as related to social class. I see numerous examples of research on child-rearing practices that affect particular cognitive skills of children, skills which may help or hinder these children as they start to learn to read. The list of these skills given here is not intended to be exhaustive; rather, the intent is to point up some specific components of socialization practices—how children are reared—that could be important for learning to read and to sensitize teachers to observing similar things.

I have seen few reports of differences in visual perception associated with social class, other than those concerned with visual defects and disease. Insofar as anyone knows, the development of letter perception as studied by Gibson and her associates (see Gibson, 1969) is the same across subcultural groups or social-class levels, although this may warrant some checking. Differences in auditory perception associated with social class have been reported, but these differences are difficult to interpret. They probably do not mean that children of one group have basically different hearing capacity from children of another group. Baratz's (1969) work shows that errors black children make in repeating standard English sentences are related to the differences between black nonstandard speech and standard English (third-person singular verb inflections, "he go," and the like). Children who speak only standard English make comparable errors in repeating black nonstandard English sentences read to them. Ability to make certain auditory discriminations likely depends on the kinds of discriminations one is *used* to making. People hear things that are important for signaling meanings. They do not hear things unrelated to meaning. Testing a student on discriminations outside his or her normal dialect may result in an unfair competence assessment. It seems to me that any basic differences in children's visual or auditory acuity are superficial or directly attributable to social factors. In other words, children have the same biological endowments in terms of sight and hearing.

Child-rearing practices have other characteristics also associated with social class which could be of enormous importance for reading. Diffuse affective factors, such as self-confidence, feelings of ability to control the environment, and hope in the future, must shape cognitive development. Social and ethnic groups differ greatly in how confident they are of extracting benefits—economic or educational—from their surroundings. These groups also differ in how responsible they personally feel for success or failure. Middle-class persons are likely to interpret events as caused by themselves; blue-collar persons see fate or luck as the cause of what happens to them.

Other affective factors, such as whether material rewards are more or less attractive than verbal rewards, whether the child can work now for rewards in the future (delay gratification), whether the child has feelings of hostility toward adults, are also important because they govern the sources of motivation. The promise of some free time or a piece of candy may persuade lower-class children to practice spelling, whereas the teacher's smile or the hope of a good mark in a month or two may not. Even such small things as the tone of voice used to deliver instructions has a differential effect —positive intonations are reported to work best in giving lower-class kindergarten children instructions, whereas middle-class children respond similarly to positive, neutral, or a negative tone (Kashinsky and Wiener, 1969).

The child's feelings of control and generalized expectation for success may be especially important in reading, a task that continues for years. Research on this topic is not as tidy as a superficial look at the literature might suggest, however. Most of the studies of control beliefs do not take IQ into account, for example.

The relation between control beliefs and achievement—children who see themselves in control of what happens to them do better schoolwork (Coleman, 1966)—could easily represent a relation between control beliefs and IQ. It is not surprising that children with higher IQ's should feel themselves in more solid command of their own destinies, irrespective of social class. Brighter children probably are better *able* to control what happens to them. Thus although control beliefs differ by social class, it is hard to know exactly what brings the difference about—whether IQ or social class or some combination of the two.

There are apparently large social-class and ethnic differences in problem-solving strategies. Can the child think up and test out several different possible solutions to a problem? Can the child endure the waiting while checking various solutions? Can the child put into words the crucial elements of a problem? Can the child remain happy despite the uncertainty that many problems create? In several studies of verbal interaction between mothers and their children as the mothers attempted to guide their children in solving problems, middle-class mothers took more actions than did lower-class mothers to help their children become successful problem solvers (see Bee *et al.*, 1969; Hess and Shipman, 1965). The middle-class mother allows her child to work at his or her own pace, offering general structuring suggestions on how to search for a problem's solution and telling the child what he or she is doing that is *correct*. The lower-class mother, by contrast, makes more controlling and disapproving comments; she makes more highly specific suggestions that do not emphasize basic problem-solving strategies.

The task of learning to read is in many ways a learning of effective problem-solving strategies. The problem is to decode written symbols. Social-class differences in the way problems are seen and structured, therefore, could bear heavily on reading success. The child must learn how to decode messages. If, first of all, the child *expects* success and also has the intent of persisting until successful, no one would doubt that his or her chances of success are improved. In decoding a message, the child makes use of many kinds of cues—semantic, contextual, grammatical, sociolinguistic—so that it is profitable to think up and try out various hypotheses about the message. If one set of cues seems to be in conflict with another set, the child may wish to revise the hypothesis about the message. When the situation is structured as "this message is more likely to be right than another one" and when the child can tolerate uncertainty while testing out different ideas, the child's chances of reading the "correct" message are improved. At least when the child is cognitively attuned to uncertainty, she or he comes to the classroom with the expectation that alternative behaviors are "good" and not "wrong."

Taking this evidence altogether, what one sees is greater cognitive flexibility in the middle-class child. Concentrating on details when necessary, the middle-class child tries and retries solutions until a satisfactory and integrative solution is found. This is exactly what reading requires.

CAUSES OF SOCIAL-CLASS DIFFERENCES

Speech and child-rearing differences associated with socioeconomic position, like those described, may explain in large part why children from lower-class homes perform more poorly on measures of reading competence than do children from more favored backgrounds, even when the children are of the same IQ. Strong group differences do exist. It is important to remember, however, that *individual* differences within groups are large, and some children from low-income homes will show accelerated progress in reading. In fact, because middle-class children are in the minority in the country taken as a whole, there are probably as many or more blue-collar and lower-class children with high potential as there are middle-class children. Teachers should bear this in mind.

What actually causes differences among children? Social class does not *cause* differences; rather, it is *associated* with differences. The social influence of the family seems to outweigh the influence of the school in causing differences among children. Reviewing the progress of preschoolers enrolled in several types of enrichment programs, Bronfenbrenner (1974) found that parents' influence was prepotent. Programs aimed at parents were somewhat effective in improving children's performance. Programs in which only the curriculum or the school facilities were altered had disappointing outcomes. Other evidence that the family is relatively more influential is found in the Coleman (1966) report. Family background characteristics turned out to be relatively more important than school characteristics in forecasting achievement, in that report. Schools vary tremendously in the resources and talents they command, but differences in achievement between schools are usually small compared to differences between students from different home backgrounds. Although studies like the Coleman report focus on overall achievement rather than on reading itself, reading is such a large component in overall achievement that no doubt findings for reading parallel those for achievement more generally.

Causes of differences early in school

What families do to cause children to differ in ability to learn to read is far from clear; in fact, almost nothing is known about it. We do know that differences appear very early, so what families do early in life must be important.

The author and her associates have been engaged in a large study of children in two schools whose social-class backgrounds differ markedly (see Entwisle, 1976; Entwisle and Hayduk, 1976). Children in these two schools are, fortunately, not much different in IQ. They have been under study from the time they started school (entering first grade) to see how they progressed in learning to read. Some of them now have been followed for three years.

All of the children—whether middle-class or blue-collar—*expected* to do well in reading when they started school. A very large majority of children in both schools expected an A or a B in reading on their first report card. Rather surprisingly, the children who were less favored economically and socially had higher expectations than the middle-class children. Socioeconomic status, in other words, was inversely related to how well the child thought he or she would perform in reading after the time of entering school. Almost all of the working-class children expected an A in reading on their first report card.

Parents' influence

As part of the same study, parents told their expectations for their children —they guessed what their children would get in reading on the first report card. Middle-class parents were guarded but essentially correct. They were right more often than not in guessing what mark their children would get in reading on the first report card. When they were wrong, the estimate tended to be on the low side. A parent was more likely to guess "B" and the child to get an "A" than the reverse, for instance. Middle-class parents' guesses were strongly related to the child's IQ, even though the parent did not know the child's actual IQ.

Working-class parents, by contrast, tended to guess too high. Middle-class parents had a realistic idea of what their children's actual performance was likely to be. Guesses of working-class parents about how their children would perform in reading on the first report card were more likely to be wrong than right. The working-class parent expected his or her child to get a B, but very few children did as well as this on the first report card.

The data so far available, although limited, shed some interesting light on how social-class differences may originate. Middle-class parents have a realistic idea of their children's actual ability. They create a psychological situation that favors happy consequences for the children. The middle-class parent's expectations, being correct, are likely to be met; or, if they are not met, the child tends to exceed them. The middle-class parent is therefore likely to be pleased with the child's first report card. The child either does as the parent expects or happily surprises the parent.

The working-class parent, on the other hand, is likely to be displeased, for the child does not live up to parental expectations. The parent may disguise this disappointment (actually, we do not know whether or not this happens), but children are extraordinarily perceptive. One would guess that the child is aware of the parent's disappointment.

Given this background, it is hardly surprising to find that middle-class parents have more influence on their children than working-class parents have on theirs. The research shows that what middle-class parents expect leads children's marks in reading to rise or to fall. Parents are more influential than any other factor studied so far in this research on what affects first-grade reading success in middle-class children.

Peer influence

Middle-class classmates apparently have negligible influence on a first grader's reading performance. The opposite prevailed in the working-class school. There parents exerted negligible influence, whereas peers were influential in first grade. The researchers will continue to study the relative influence of parents and peers.

This research, far from complete, also must be taken as suggestive because it is limited to two schools—one middle class the other working class. What is true for these schools may or may not hold in other schools. On the other hand, the research shows that the ideas children have about themselves and what their parents and/or peers *think* about them actually affect what they do, even in first grade.

The research indicates that working-class children themselves *do not* think they will do poorly in reading beforehand, a finding that may surprise some readers. In the past, people have often assumed that the less advantaged child had a low or negative self-image, without actually checking the assumption. Our work so far suggests that it would be a mistake to try to strengthen the working-class child's self-image in first grade with the hope of boosting reading achievement. Those children might learn to read better if their hopes were *not* so unrealistically high to start with. More modest hopes would lead to more reinforcement, i.e., more positive rewards associated with learning. Wildly high hopes cannot help but lead to frustration

and disappointment. Children's natural inclination in the face of disappointment is to deny or withdraw, both actions which undercut learning. How
best to cope with too high hopes remains to be determined. Teachers of
children from different social groups work with very different kinds of individuals, though, and the same measures or procedures that work well in
teaching one group to read may be ill-suited for teaching another group.

SOME SUGGESTIONS FOR TEACHING

During the latter half of the 1960s considerable work in sociolinguistics (how
speech and language development are affected by social factors) assumed that
linguistic development was fairly complete by the time a child was five years
old. Now it is becoming clear that considerable further development occurs
after that age. This makes sense, because we know that certain mental abilities flower at later ages, and no doubt general cognitive development either
precedes or accompanies language development. The age ranges from 5 to 7
and from 12 to 14 are important transition points in cognitive development
and probably also in language development (Palermo and Molfese, 1972).

Evidence also is mounting that certain language skills develop earlier in
some social groups than in others. For example, working-class whites or
black children show considerable improvement in the repetition of sentences
with simple grammatical structures over the first three grades of school
(Frasure and Entwisle, 1973). The same kind of improvement has also been
observed for rural white children over the early school years (Weener, 1971).
The point is that the level of language or speech development for various
children is probably not the same at the time most children start school.
Some children could probably profit from specific kinds of language training or drills linked to reading, but the kind of supplementary training
needed is not the same from group to group. There has been little effort so
far to gear language-training programs to needs of specific social groups. I
think work along these lines would bear fruit.

Linguistics and dialect

The "Great Society" programs of the 1960s stimulated the field of applied
linguistics, especially in relation to school achievement. There are striking
dialect differences in various parts of the United States. Prior to 1960 dialect
was by and large ignored. Teachers did not understand very well what dialects actually were or how to deal with them. Now many inner-city teachers
realize that "two cent" (no plural inflection) is not an "error," but rather a
consistent grammatical feature of the nonstandard dialect spoken by some
blacks. Teachers now see "two cent" as a variant form rather than as a
grammatical blunder. Research on dialect has had good consequences for

teachers because it has increased their awareness of cultural and ethnic differences.

What other implications does dialect have beyond the teacher's appreciation of it? Clearly, if a child speaks one dialect and must learn to read from primers written in a different dialect, the task is harder than that of a child whose spoken language matches that of the printed page. But more is at stake here than reading per se, else the solution would be simply to have primers in dialect. The child must eventually become fluent in the majority dialect, the so-called network, or standard, English.

I feel, and many others agree, that if the child learns to read a dialect and secondarily is taught reading in standard English, learning to read may be made harder altogether than if the child began using standard English materials. The child has to learn to read twice, in a manner of speaking. Dialect-speaking children usually understand standard English in its spoken form, and in my opinion it is better to start with materials in standard English and work on these (more on the reasons later).

The number of dialects is also a problem. At least seven major dialects are spoken in the United States. To take account of all of these dialects would require the development of reading materials and training of teachers in several dialects. Such an undertaking is formidable, if not impossible. The mobility of persons within our society calls into question how useful it would be to emphasize different dialects. The person raised in Appalachia is likely to end up in Richmond, Baltimore, or Philadelphia. Most important in my thinking as I recommend beginning in standard English, however, is the fact that linguistic differences are probably not very important compared to social differences.

Bilingual experiments

Two experiments in Montreal by Wallace Lambert and his associates (1969, 1970) began bilingual training in kindergarten and continued it during the early grades. Briefly, Canadian Anglophone children were placed in kindergartens where French was spoken almost exclusively. Then, throughout the first and second grades these children received all of their school instruction in French. (English continued as their "home" language.)

In evaluations to date, the program has shown up astoundingly well. Children from the two independent experiments show a high level of skill in receptive and productive aspects of French, a good command of English, and a high level of skill in nonlanguage subjects, e.g., mathematics, taught through the "foreign" language only. Comparisons hold up against a French control class in the same district.

These bilingual experiments seem to parallel the experiences of many children in the United States from homes where a black dialect or another language, e.g., Spanish or Navajo, is spoken and who then enter schools where standard English is spoken. Such children begin kindergarten and hear "standard English." They then start first grade, where they receive instruction in school subjects in "standard English." They thus continue in a dialect (language) at home and hear a different dialect (language) during school hours. Why is the outcome of this experience of American children, which often leads to poor reading achievement, so different from the outcome of the bilingual experiments with Montreal children? Offhand, it would seem to be much easier to learn a slightly modified version of a language one already speaks rather than a "foreign" language with a new vocabulary and a different grammar.

The answer, I think, lies in the social context. In Montreal there is recognition by the students, teachers, parents, and the community of the explicit task being undertaken. The task is clearly defined—to learn a second language—and it is undertaken with great community enthusiasm and social support. In the United States, by contrast, until recently there has *not* been explicit recognition of the existence of minority dialects; rather, there has been pressure against recognizing black speech or other dialects. Schools have been slow to realize that a new dialect (standard English) may need to be acquired by minority-group children.

Also, in Montreal the social-reward system of the peer group and of the home is probably not changed by the speaking of French during school hours. In fact, learning and speaking French may lead to increases in social rewards. The Montreal parents are very proud of their bilingual children. On the other hand, in the United States minority-group children often have majority-group teachers, and in most places where students and teachers are of different social classes, students belong to the group of lower status. The social rewards are reduced.

Even more important, the speaking of standard English by members of lower socioeconomic groups in the United States may be severely punished by both the family and the peer group. Economic insecurity and life-style produce great press toward group solidarity in the lower class. Such people look to their neighbors and friends in time of need and spend proportionately much more leisure time with them (Cohen and Hodges, 1963). A threat exists, therefore, for the person who symbolically relinquishes membership in the group by taking up the speech style of another group. A dialect-speaking child who returns home with a different speech style may risk ostracism by the family.

The success of the bilingual program in Montreal and the lack of success generally with children who speak minority dialects in the United States suggest that the social context of language acquisition is the key. It is probably more important to alter the social context than to pay a lot of attention to linguistic matters. Learning about linguistic differences may help teachers create a more harmonious social context, and that, rather than linguistics per se, may explain the payoff from knowledge about linguistics. My recommendation to teachers is to be sensitive to how the child's linguistic characteristics affect his or her social situation.

Peer tutoring

Peer tutoring, with older students instructing beginning students, shows great promise, in my opinion. Significant gains occur for both groups, but especially for the older pupils (Hill, 1975). I have personally observed black fourth-grade boys successfully and enthusiastically teaching black first-grade boys on a one-to-one basis. What does this accomplish?

First, and perhaps most important, it causes the older children to review and to drill repetitively on basic skills under conditions in which the social structure leads to rewards, not punishment. If fourth graders were asked to drill *themselves* on low-level skills, they would: (1) be socially isolated while they were drilling; (2) have difficulty seeing progress; (3) no doubt interpret the drill as nonrewarding or even punishing; and (4) probably not spend time on the parts of the task most in need of drill. When the same fourth graders teach first graders, the social situation defines the fourth graders as competent. They see themselves selected not because they need drill, but because they are "good" at the activity in question. The first graders' misapprehensions or weaknesses, furthermore, are likely to be the very ones the fourth graders also find troubling. The fourth graders, when challenged under conditions of high expectations by others and of strong social support, will be more likely to perform at a high level. Even though the subject matter is below their grade level, they can give it their full attention under highly satisfying conditions. It would be hard to imagine more propitious circumstances for remedial instruction.

What of the younger children? Will they benefit also? Their academic profit is less from the tutoring activity than the tutors' profit. For boys, however, there may be subtle advantages in having male role models in the largely female authority system of the elementary school. In any case, tutoring would likely take only 20 to 30 minutes per day and would provide variation and novelty in the instructional program. In practical terms a tutoring session could provide a welcome change in pace for first-grade boys, especially the low achievers who have short attention spans.

SUMMARY

Reading cannot be viewed apart from total language development. What is germane for overall language development has to be germane for reading. It is easy to underrate the most obvious fact of all: children readily learn language when they interact with other people where meaning is important —where the functions of language in the life of the speaker are significant. We see proficient readers in those groups for which reading has importance —middle-class groups. The children who learn to read best are those who need to read in order to make sense of their lives. If reading does not trigger the child's imagination or curiosity, the child will not be enthusiastic about it. These motivations run deep; they are not aroused by surface features, such as pictures in texts or themes about minority-group characters. If schools draw from the symbolic world of the middle class, the non-middle-class child gropes around in a foreign symbol system, one that does not link to his or her outside world. The basic requirement for language learning— relevance—is violated.

Differences in reading educability exist. The causes are debatable. I suspect, however, that *social* factors are the important ones for reading. Teachers can design programs within their own schools to alter social structures. Some of the suggestions in this chapter may help in such efforts. We badly need educational programs in which social structures are altered.

REFERENCES

Baratz, J. "A Bi-dialectical Task for Determining Language Proficiency in Economically Disadvantaged Negro Children," *Child Development* 40 (1969): 899–902.

Bee, H. L., et al. "Social Class Differences in Maternal Teaching Strategies and Speech Patterns," *Developmental Psychology* 1 (1969): 726–734.

Berko-Gleason, J. "Code-Switching in Children's Language," in T. Moore, ed., *Cognitive Development and the Acquisition of Language,* New York: Academic Press, 1973, pp. 159–168.

Bronfenbrenner, U. *A Report on Longitudinal Evaluations of Preschool Programs,* D.H.E.W. Publication No. (OHD) 74–25, Ithaca, N.Y.: Cornell University, 1974.

Bruner, J. S., R. R. Oliver, and P. M. Greenfield *Studies in Cognitive Growth,* New York: Wiley, 1966.

Cohen, A. K., and H. M. Hodges "Characteristics of the Lower-Blue-Collar Class," *Social Problems* 10 (1963): 303–334.

Coleman, J. S. *Equality of Educational Opportunity,* Washington, D.C.: Office of Education, 1966.

Entwisle, D. R. "Young Children's Expectations for Reading," in *Aspects of Reading Acquisition: Proceedings of the Fifth Blumberg Symposium,* Baltimore: Johns Hopkins Press, 1976.

Entwisle, D. R., and L. Hayduk *Too Great Expectations,* forthcoming monograph, 1976.

Frasure, N., and D. R. Entwisle "Semantic and Syntactic Development in Children," *Developmental Psychology* 9 (1973): 236–245.

Gibson, E. J. *Principles of Perceptual Learning and Development,* New York: Appleton-Century-Crofts, 1969.

Hess, R. D., and V. Shipman "Early Experience and Socialization to Cognitive Modes in Children," *Child Development* 36 (1965): 869–886.

Hill, P. T. "Interim Report No. 1, Compensatory Education Study," Washington, D.C.: National Institute of Education, August 1975.

Kashinsky, M., and M. Wiener "Tone in Communication and the Performance of Children from Two Socioeconomic Groups," *Child Development* **40** (1969): 1193–1202.

Lambert, W. E., and J. MacNamara "Some Cognitive Consequences of Following a First-Grade Curriculum in a Second Language," *Journal of Educational Psychology* **60** (1969): 86–96.

Lambert, W. E., M. Just, and N. Segalowitz "Some Cognitive Consequences of Following the Curricula of the Early School Grades in a Foreign Language," in J. E. Alatis, ed., *21st Annual Roundtable*. Washington, D.C.: Georgetown University Press, 1970, pp. 229–279.

Palermo, D. S., and D. L. Molfese "Language Acquisition from Ages Five Onward," *Psychological Bulletin* **78** (1972): 409–428.

Weener, P. "Language Structure and Free Recall of Verbal Messages by Children," *Developmental Psychology* **5** (1971): 237–243.

Chapter 5

ASSESSMENT OF CHILDREN WITH LEARNING PROBLEMS: A CHILD DEVELOPMENT APPROACH

MARK N. OZER • *George Washington University School of Health and Allied Sciences*

INTRODUCTION

The issue of diagnosis of reading problems has been considered as part of an approach to the broader area of learning problems in children. The first section of this chapter deals with the concept of diagnosis as has evolved in neurology and, by extension, in psychology and education. The product of such assessment is the answer to certain questions. The process of such assessment is based on certain assumptions about how the nervous system works—a particular model. It is suggested that the model to be used be brought up to date and be more related to the actual process of learning. The process of assessment may then sample the way the brain really works, and the product would be a plan for treatment. An example is then provided of a way to do assessment that is a sampling of the learning process. The assessment not only samples the way a child learns something, but also provides an interactive experience in which the child increasingly knows the ways he or she may learn and is a model of the process of child development. This principle of interactive assessment is then applied to some specific issues in the area of reading problems.

DIAGNOSIS IN A "DISEASE" MODEL

Diagnosis in medicine has meant the systematic collection of data to be used as a basis for making decisions for treatment. Diagnosis therefore has as its *product* a number of answers that may then lead to a plan for treatment. The patient's symptoms or complaints and the findings on examination are analyzed to answer the following questions:

1. Is disease present?
2. Where in the body is the disease?
3. What caused the disease?

Neurology as a branch of medicine asks these same questions about the nervous system. A history of the illness is taken; motor and sensory, as well as mental, functions of the nervous system are tested to find patterns of loss that are associated with disease in the brain, spinal cord, muscles etc. (Bender, 1967). The first question, as to whether physical disease is present, is then answered, depending on the particular pattern of loss of function. The characteristics of such patterns also help indicate *where* in the nervous system the problem exists, so that it may be removed. For example, weakness and loss of sensitivity to pain on the left side of the body are associated with disease on the opposite side of the brain. The causes of such difficulties may vary, but the approach works well when the brain tumor or clot can be removed and the patient recovers. In looking at disease in this way, the disorder in function is presumed due to some cause foreign to the person (Reise, 1950). It is particularly useful in adult neurology and in relation to the treatment by surgery of physical problems of the nervous system. We may call this entire approach the neurological disease diagnostic model.

The diagnostic approaches to *developmental* problems started historically with "cerebral palsy." There were frequently actual physical changes in the brain or spinal cord that one could see on examination after the patient's death or on special X-rays. Such physical changes were not different in kind from the physical changes that occur with other diseases of the nervous system. Therefore, the same kinds of questions were asked. However, we are not dealing with the same kind of problem.

The cause of the "cerebral palsy" that we see in the patient had its effect some time in the past, and the child is developing so as to compensate for some of the handicaps. The third question, as to cause, seems less important than in the case of neurological disease. Whether there was not enough oxygen at birth or some other injury or infection in the past does not affect what needs to be done now. The second question, as to *where* the damage is, also seems less relevant, since we are not going to remove any part of the brain, as we would in the treatment of a tumor or some other cause of neurological disease (Crothers and Paine, 1959).

Some of the questions that have been asked about brain disease are not really useful questions, but we have continued to ask them in the area of developmental problems. Their lack of relevance seems particularly obvious when the concepts of "cerebral palsy" were applied to what was felt at first to be lesser degrees of brain damage, then brain dysfunction when no physical damage could be seen, then learning disabilities of which reading disabilities form a part (Paine *et al.,* 1968).

Assessment in the fields of psychology and education has remained concerned with the same questions that have been successfully asked about disease in the nervous system. An issue that still concerns many diagnosticians is the question of whether "disease" is present in the child. The question is asked in terms of the degree of deviation from the norms established for children of that age. The cut-off points vary, but generally one becomes concerned if the child is more than one standard deviation from the average for that age. One aspect of diagnosis that has remained active in the disease model is the early identification of those children whose function is deviant on some standardized instrument (Frankenburg and Dodds, 1967). This is also the basis for many of the assessment techniques developed more specifically for educational problems, such as the Developmental Test of Visual Perception (Frostig, 1964), etc.

The second question that has been asked in the diagnosis of neurological disease, *where* the problem is, is also asked in the area of developmental problems. The distribution of strengths and weaknesses in the various subtests of the Illinois Test of Psycholinguistic Abilities (ITPA), for example, is used to analyze the function of the individual. The concept is similar to the examination of the various functions of the body or nervous system to help determine where one should probe with X-ray, for example, preparatory to surgery.

Considerable effort is also devoted to relating such patterns of deviance to some specific causal event in the past in an attempt to answer the third question, as to underlying cause. Categories in use at this time include the various types of "brain injured," "emotionally disturbed," "culturally deprived," etc. Criteria have been established for defining such categories, but it is the rule, rather than the exception, for any particular child to qualify for several categories or none.

The presumption in developmental or learning problems has been that a diagnosis had been made if these three basic questions had been answered. However, it is important to recall that the goal in diagnosis is a plan for treatment. A plan for treatment for the person with neurological disease does arise with the use of these questions. It is suggested that a plan for treatment in the area of child development requires different questions from those asked in the past. It would also be helpful to consider what in the past have been the bases for how the brain had been thought to work. Such ways of thinking have affected the way the assessment has been carried out. It is necessary to look at the assumptions on which we have worked in order to see when other approaches may be more appropriate in the future.

DIAGNOSIS IN AN EDUCATIONAL MODEL

The traditional ways for assessment of developmental problems in education and psychology have asked the same questions that were asked in the study of the patient with neurological disease. The *products* were thus the same, although the needs may have been different. It is important to look as well at the *process,* or techniques, of the examination.

The assessment techniques are an outgrowth of the way it was felt that the nervous system works. A way of thinking about the brain was conceptualized by Hughlings Jackson, a British neurologist, about one hundred years ago. He chose to consider that the brain acts like a reflex arc. That is, the brain receives sensory inputs, e.g., through vision, sounds, touch, and pain, and then responds with motor outputs. Thus the brain may be considered as a sort of switchboard. Jackson deliberately chose to ignore the "state of mind" of the person being examined. Specifically excluded from consideration was the way the person felt about what was going on and how the examiner felt as well. Jackson called the brain a "sensory-motor machine." The examination procedures were based on the premise that one could measure objective functions in an objective fashion. It must be emphasized that Jackson chose this model of the way the brain works deliberately, because he wished to study physical disease in the nervous system (Englehardt, 1975).

Many, if not all, of the testing procedures in psychology and education have taken these same assumptions about how the brain works. The testing procedures are standardized in that the examiner is required to ask the questions in a specified way. The conditions for testing are thus not varied in terms of the way the child may be approached, other than what may be necessary to keep the child working so that one may get a valid score describing his or her performance. The objective is to measure how the person does, so that the performance may be compared to the norms established for that age group on that test. The product sought is a score, or measure, of the person. The basic assumption is that one is measuring some objective function that would have predictive value for other functions in life, such as the ability to do schoolwork. Tests in this model, such as the Stanford-Binet and the Wechsler tests, have been used for placement of children for the past 50 years on a large scale. They have come under increasing attack as to their appropriateness for educational planning for individual children in terms of both the tasks and the process of examination (Bersoff, 1973).

There had been a deliberate attempt to assess brain function as objectively as possible. The examination was viewed as noninteractive, with both the examiner and the person being examined unaware of what each was contributing to the situation. Yet the reflex model of the brain as a "sensory-motor" machine unaffected by the examination had been known for some time to be incorrect. Sherrington had shown in 1966 that the same stimulus applied to the same place in the nervous system had different effects at different times. Reflect action at any one point in time and place is the outcome of interaction of that stimulus with the remainder of the organism. "Each reflex must be considered the functional expression not of a single level (of the nervous system) but of the whole . . . [and] according to a given situation, the past and future of the organism" (Sherrington, 1906). How, then, could this finding be applied to the examination process?

The nervous system is not just a passive receiver of sensory inputs. If you touch a person, he or she may not feel it, because physical disease of the nervous system prevents that feeling. In addition, the touch may be unnoticed because something else is going on that is more important to the person. This is a common occurrence in the classroom; the child has not heard what is being said because of a distraction—something else is going on in the immediate environment.

In studies with children as well as with some adults, touch was simultaneously applied to the face and hand. Under these circumstances, the stimulus to the hand was ignored, and the patient pointed to the face alone when asked where he had been touched. When, however, touch was applied only to the hands, it was noticed. One explanation for this phenomenon was that the face has more sensory endings and is more sensitive. The important point of this face-hand test is that the presence of competing stimuli affects the degree to which an input is received and responded to (Bender, Fink, and Green, 1951).

The general level of awareness also affects how well and how strongly a motor response is carried out. Patients were studied both before and after they had been given a drug that caused sleepiness. Before receiving the drug, the patient had no weakness of the legs. When sleepy, however, the patient was now found to have weakness of the right leg, whereas the left leg was not affected (Teng and Bender, 1955).

These procedures have become part of the way a neurologist might examine function. They helped to make the examination more sensitive in picking up the presences and location of disease in the nervous system. What do these approaches contribute to our thinking about the way the nervous system works? They began to get people thinking that we are not measuring something fixed and unchanging. If we vary the conditions of testing, we change what we find. It is well known that the time of day, the different examiners, and many other factors change the results we get. Where does this leave our model of the nervous system as a "sensory-motor" machine whose objective functions are to be measured objectively? Where does this leave the traditional psychological and educational tests built on this same model of the nervous system?

Traditional testing had attempted to do away with bias by using a standardized, fixed way of carrying out the tests. I suggest that all testing is an interaction between the people involved and that all testing is affected by the characteristics of those people. Instead of thinking that we can do away with such bias, why not be aware of what we are doing? We can then be explicit in the way we change the presentation and feedback so that the patient will be able to give the correct response.

A change had occurred in the thinking of those studying brain function. One could begin to look for what one needed to do to bring about change in the way the organism functioned. The examination of brain function did not have as its only product a measure of whether the person could or could not do something. Within the limits of the time available, one could explore what would make it possible for the person to carry out the task at issue.

A newer model of the nervous system was the basis for this approach. This model looked at the activities of the person as a result of not only what was in him or her, but also what was in the environment in the person of the examiner. This newer model emphasizes function rather than the physical structure of the nervous system alone. Function may change, whereas damage to the structure may be considered as more fixed and unchanging. There is a physical structure through which the sensory inputs and the motor responses are mediated. However, there was no longer the sense that the brain just sits there and is somehow unaffected by what is being done. Indeed, the whole basis of education is that change can occur and obviously does occur. Thus developmental problems cannot be approached in the same way as neurological disease.

An early application of this newer model was to measure what was required for a child to identify touch on the hand as well as on the face. Could one make the examination of brain function reflect this process of change? This phenomenon was felt to be of particular interest because of teachers' concern with the "distractible" child. A series of cues were provided. The measure was of the number and type of cue required before the child could identify touch on the hand in the presence of the competing, presumably stronger, stimulus to the face (Ozer, 1967). Motor function could also be measured in this fashion. The initial presentation might involve both verbal instructions and visual demonstration. If this was not successful, additional cues were provided by actually moving the child through the activity and then, if necessary, breaking the task into segments. The child's score reflected what was necessary in order to accomplish the task at issue. Positive feedback as to results was also provided (Ozer, 1968). The thinking at the basis of this examination procedure was that if the assessment of brain function is to be made relevant to educational needs, it should sample the educational process it is trying to predict.

Psychoeducational approaches in this newer model include the use of minisituations. Measurement of the child's behavior takes place during actual learning of material that directly relates to classroom functions. Thus if the child is having difficulties in reading, one samples a reading task rather than tasks such as used on intelligence tests. An examination of how the child learns new material goes on with self-conscious awareness on the part of the examiner of what changes need to be made to reach a particular end-point. Suggestions are then made to the teacher on the basis of the actual sampling done. Exploration goes on with emphasis on some of the character of the feedback provided (Bijou and Peterson, 1971), as well as on the stimulus conditions (Bijou and Baer, 1965).

It has been suggested that the questions asked in the diagnosis of neurological disease are not sufficient for the developmental problems of children. The treatment of these problems is educational. What questions, then, might be asked so as to develop a plan for treatment of an educational nature? The products might usefully be the answers to the following questions.

1. What does the child now do successfully; where do you start?

2. What are the goals?

3. What works in accomplishing these goals?

The process of assessment is a sampling of what works. Thus there has been a change in both the *product* and the *process* of diagnosis, with the examiner now an active participant.

DIAGNOSIS IN A "CHILD DEVELOPMENT" MODEL

Considerable movement has had to occur in the way one thinks about assessment. Change had already occurred in the *product*. A plan that was appropriate for the treatment of physical disease of the nervous system was recognized as inappropriate for developmental problems. An educational plan must ask different questions. The *process* of assessment has also changed in relation to a different model of the way the brain works, one in which the individual is affected by what goes on in the environment. The assessment is therefore a short-term exploration of what works in a relevant area of concern. Assessment has become a replica of the teaching that will go on over the longer term in the classroom. The examiner functions like a teacher, but is more self-consciously aware of what is going on.

Unfortunately, the term "trial teaching" reflects the limitations of the model so far described. Emphasis is on the examiner's awareness. However, what is or should be going on is not merely trial teaching, but also learning. An important ingredient must be made more explicit in our model of the brain and in the psychoeducational procedures. That ingredient is the clarity with which the other member of the interaction—the student—participates.

The teacher must be aware of the child, whose performance determines what is to be done to modify the conditions appropriately so as to find out what works. The teacher learns what works by taking an active role in varying the situation. In a similar fashion, the child must learn rather than be taught. In order for learning to go on, the child must be aware of what he or she is doing in the interaction. To the extent that such awareness is present, one is replicating the learning process.

Sherrington had described the response of the organism to be more than the outcome of the stimuli provided by the examiner. The same stimulus applied to the same place had different effects when applied at different times. The stimulus had not changed; the intensity of electrical charge remained the same, and it was applied to the same place in the nervous system. The effects or results had changed because the organism was different. The person had changed, and the person is an integral part of the interaction. When various cues were provided on the face-hand test, the child began to notice the touch on the hand as well as on the face. When moved through the motor activity, the child was now able to carry it out, whereas earlier he or she was not able to do so when only told or shown. The child had changed. Is this change only a passive one?

The model of the nervous system needs to be expanded beyond the concept that it is affected by what is going on around it. The nervous system is a functional instrument for the self-realization and self-preservation of the organism. At any one time, the person attempts to compensate for an injury in order to maintain function as an integrated whole. The symptoms we see are the more or less effective attempts to compensate. An injury to the left side of the brain frequently changes the language skills of the patient. In studies of patients with this sort of injury, a series of questions was asked. When the questions related to the situation at the time of injury or to the disability that resulted, the patient's language became confused. When these same patients were asked other questions that did not relate to the injury, there was no language confusion. In other words, questions had different effects, depending on what they meant to the person (Weinstein *et al.*, 1966).

An individual is considered to be in dynamic mutual interaction with the environment. This is true in terms of both energy and information. When the organism takes in food (energy), it is changed by means of digestion, and the resulting energy becomes part of the organism. "Assimilation" is the term given to the action by which the food is broken down so that it may eventually become part of the person. The organism, by having done something to that food and made it part of itself, has changed. It is now different from having received that energy. "Accommodation" is the term given to what happens to the person. Both processes go on. One cannot have assimilation without accommodation. The person, in order to be affected *by* the food, must have done something *to* it.

Learning has been viewed as a dynamic interaction in terms of information. According to Piaget (Furth, 1969), the information taken in is broken down, or digested. It is assimilated. The information has been changed, as has the person, by having now made that information part of himself or herself. The person, in order to be affected *by* the information, must have done some active thing *to* it. I further suggest that the person, in this case the child, be brought to self-conscious awareness that that indeed is going on. To the degree that awareness occurs, a process of child development is also going on.

The examiner must be aware of what he or she is doing in relation to the conditions for presentation (stimuli) so as to modify those conditions in some orderly way. In order to do so, the teacher must also get some response from the child as a basis for deciding whether a modification is necessary. Is the child doing the task correctly or not? This response by the child serves as "feedback" to the teacher. In order for the teacher to function, the child must be part of the interaction. An exchange of information must occur. Just as the teacher serves as feedback to the child, so too the child must receive a response—whether or not he or she was correct—from the teacher. Thus the teacher's response serves as feedback to the child. This type of feedback is called feedback about results.

A requirement of the learning situation, regardless of the task, is this aspect of feedback. Variation can be made within the diagnostic procedure to explore combinations of social praise along with tangible rewards, e.g., tokens, as well as the frequency or schedule with which they might be optimally provided (Bijou and Warren, 1969). Suggestions to the teacher are then based on the actual experience on the task the child is having difficulty with. These suggestions obviously have implications for the teacher's use of this concept of feedback to other tasks. The crucial ingredient has not yet been specified. That ingredient is the child's explicit awareness that receiving such feedback is important because it serves as direct input in establishing both the type and frequency of the feedback of results.

The goal of an assessment procedure differs somewhat from that of an ordinary teaching exercise. It is an active exploration of what works in learning not only this specific short-term task, but also other tasks both in the classroom and elsewhere. The product therefore includes awareness on the part of the examiner of how one may most effectively vary the presentation conditions. Such presentation conditions have general applicability and are merely exemplified in the process of learning this specific task. Just as in terms of the feedback about results, awareness must be shared with the child as to what works in terms of the presentation conditions. The examiner learns what works by actively manipulating the options. Similarly, for the child to learn what works, she or he must have the experience of actively participating in manipulating those options.

Feedback of results on the task at issue is necessary but not sufficient. It is also necessary to learn what worked in accomplishing the task so that one can do so again elsewhere. The teacher needs to provide feedback to the child as to what worked. The teacher needs to provide *informational* feedback as well as feedback of results. For such informational feedback to become part of the child, he or she must have done something with it, e.g., used it and seen that it worked. The child must therefore receive a response not only in relation to the specific idea but also for the activity of having requested it. For example, a boy is able to carry out a motor task when he is moved through it. He is told that "moving through it" worked. The next time he is unable to follow the verbal instructions, he is asked: "Would it help if I move you through it? You say 'move me through.' " Perhaps he is now able to verbalize his request. If he does so, the comment would be, "Thank you for telling me to move you through it. Let's try it." When he gets the task done, he is told, "What worked was you telling me to move you through it. That was a good job."

There are thus three aspects to feedback that should go on during the assessment in order to have both the child and the examiner learn what works. Feedback of results (FR) is related to the performance on the task used as the context. There should be some success on the task, or at least on some portion of it. The task might be to decode a word, add a series of numbers, tie shoelaces, etc. In the context of learning that task, the child also learns some things that work. In order to make this aspect explicit, the examiner provides informational feedback (FI). What worked, for example, might be showing as well as telling, doing one part at a time. What worked might also include the frequency and type of reward. The third aspect is the opportunity for the child to participate in the interaction, or what might be termed feedback about participation (FP).

Learning occurs for the child to the degree that she or he is a participant in the interaction. It occurs in relation to learning "what works" to the degree that the child participates in stating what works, seeing it put in action, and receiving feedback as to the idea the child contributed. The degree of such participation may be described in terms of the level or stage analogous to the stages of child development.

The development of the individual may be considered as an increase in the degree of organization as a functional adaptive system (Connolly, 1972). "Adaptation" includes the ability both to act on (assimilate) and to be affected by (accommodate) things, people, and information. The term offers an opportunity to look at both aspects and to determine the degree to which each is going on as a measure of the degree of mutuality in the interaction (Land, 1973).

The newborn infant has little mutual interaction with the environment, but rather is optimally given a great deal of both physical and interpersonal nurture. There are many stimuli in the environment as yet unorganized by the infant. Gradually the child begins to take increasing power and to grow in the process of affecting the environment. The child's awareness of having impact comes from the feedback of those around him or her. Deprived of such feedback, the child's growth is limited. One major step in growth is the development of language, which gives the child a means of organizing stimuli by putting names or categories to things. The child can now assimilate many more stimuli and internalize them. He or she may interact more effectively with people, now having a more finely tuned instrument by which to make his or her wants known. The child's rate of development is enhanced to the degree to which he or she is able to affect and be affected by the environment through the use of language.

In replication of this process of child development, the learning process as carried out during the diagnostic assessment also has stages of mutuality of interaction. In the first stage, the child merely acquiesces nonverbally to what is being done to him or her. The child can exert power by refusing, but does not yet have the use of the verbal "handles" by which to make wishes known and therefore take increased power and responsibility. The child is told (fed) what is being done, in preparation for later being able to take a more active role. The ratio of mutuality in the interaction may be estimated as 20% by the child and 80% by the adult.

Next, the child verbalizes what he or she has been fed, by echoing or parroting the words. This is a major step in development because the child has participated in an active way. The words now come from both the child and the adult. The ratio of mutuality in the interaction may be estimated as 40% by the child and 60% by the adult.

In the third stage, the child has now used the verbal "handles" and has the opportunity to select what he or she wishes to say from the options made available by the adult. The options are limited, but the child has the freedom of choice within those options. The ratio of mutuality may be estimated as 60% for the child and 40% for the adult.

The next stage is when the adult merely asks, "What may work?" and the child freely offers a suggestion. The responsibility is moved overwhelmingly to the child. The ratio of the interaction may be estimated as 80% by the child; 20% by the adult. Full responsibility would be the independent application of the ideas elsewhere.

Although various intermediate stages may be described, the issue is that the process of learning what works is developmental. To the extent that the child participates, to that extent does it become part of himself or herself. It is the awareness of the objective of such participation by both the adult and the child that has been made explicit and the heretofore missing ingredient in our thinking.

THE CHILD DEVELOPMENT OBSERVATION

A protocol called the Child Development Observation (CDO) has been designed as an interactive process during which various problem-solving strategies are explored with the child in the context of learning something (Ozer and Richardson, 1972). The person interacting with the child affects the child's performance by changing in various ways the techniques for both presentation and feedback. Both the child and the examiner become aware to varying degrees as to what is working. The process by which awareness comes about is through self-conscious use. The child experiences these various approaches and takes increasing responsibility in defining what is to be done. The child becomes explicitly aware of what is working by seeing it put into effect by the adult at the child's request. One product of such an interaction is a feeling of success in accomplishing something. A more important product is a set of statements, or "handles," that may be used elsewhere in modifying the conditions for presentation and feedback so that success may be achieved in a more general sense. The learning of such coping techniques may be expected to go on to the extent that the process is a clearly reciprocal one in which the child's input is shown to affect the adult.

This approach differs from the traditional test in that it samples a process of change rather than a static measure of some objective function. For example, on a test such as the ITPA, one may determine that the child has an "auditory sequencing" problem. One has not sampled the conditions under which the child may be able to learn a telephone number. This approach differs from the usual diagnostic teaching in that it incorporates a concern for the child experiencing the learning process. The product of the interaction is an experience for both people. The complexity of the experience, the clarity of the experience, and the depth of the experience will vary with the developmental stage of those involved. One does not merely sample development, one enhances it.

There are three objectives to be stated in carrying out this interaction.

1. What are the characteristics and objectives of the context task?
2. How many "handles" is the child to learn to use?
3. What level of development is there to be in the use of these "handles"?

The choice of situation or task to be used as the context for interaction can be based on several criteria. Initially, a set of predetermined prototype tasks was designed for the young school-age child, e.g., identifying "right" and "left" labels on body parts, following more complex two-part instructions, connecting circles in the presence of competing visual and verbal distractions (Ozer and Richardson, 1974). These tasks offered an opportunity to explore a number of strategies for modifying conditions for presentation and feedback. In extending the principles to a range of needs and ages, it became evident that the specific characteristics of the tasks are less important. Tasks for preschool children have included buttoning or zippering a coat and tying laces. Tasks for hearing-impaired children have included spelling a word in sign language.

The choice of task is actually limited only by the flexibility of the examiner. The only criterion that must be considered is that the task should be short (10–15 min) and that it can be modified so that success can occur. In many settings, it has been possible to identify an appropriate situation by collaborating with the parents, teacher, or child, thus ensuring that the situation used as a context has some relevance to their concerns.

The strategies for presentation and feedback that may be explored are also potentially large in number. Categories have been established in order to arrive at some clarity for communication. One may vary presentation conditions (stimuli) in terms of *time, channel,* and degree of *focusing.* Similarly, one may categorize the feedback aspects in terms of *quality, intensity,* and degree of *sharing.*

One way to affect the conditions is through the use of *time.* One may repeat something and then repeat it more slowly. One may segment the task and do one part at a time. One may accentuate the order or sequence across time. One may choose to do the first part at the beginning, or one may start with the part already known. One may do the last part of the task first, in order to see the results immediately. One may emphasize the duration of time available. Examples of verbal "handles" include the following:

"Please repeat what you said."

"Please give me one part at a time."

"How much time do I have to do it in?"

"Please tell me what needs to be done first, second, third."

These are but illustrations of the way we all use time. The child learns that these are usable statements. There is no inference from this particular situation that the child is a person who benefits only from affecting the time parameter. These ideas are options that have been illustrated in the context of the specific situation. Other situations may require these ideas as well as others.

Another way to affect the conditions is to use various *channels* of input. The most obvious ones are auditory-verbal, visual-demonstration, and kinesthetic-movement. The most efficient technique in terms of cost is to be able to tell the child what to do. However, it is not always the most effective technique. Obviously, demonstration is frequently necessary and actual participation even more effective, although increasingly more costly in terms of individual attention. Examples of the "handles" that we all use include the following:

"Please show me what you mean."

"Please do it with me so I can get the feel of it."

Again, no inference need be made that this child is an "auditory" or "visual" or "kinesthetic" learner. Each "handle" works at various times and in various situations. The aim is for the child to become more aware of the options. If one channel of input does not work, another or combinations of channels may be tried.

The third major way to affect conditions for presentation is by varying the degree of *focus*. Focusing deals with the degree to which something stands out. It relates to the relationship between figure and ground at any given time. One may make something stand out by making it larger, more colorful, louder, move, etc., or by reducing the number of items on a page, by coming closer, etc. One may accentuate direction by drawing arrows. One may accentuate boundaries by drawing a line or map. Examples of the "handles" we all use for focusing include the following:

"Could you speak louder?"

"Could I shut off the TV so that I can hear you better?"

Again, no inference need be made that these techniques are unique and useful only for the "distractable" child. We are all distractable in various situations. We have learned that there are things that we can do when we are distracted. When we apply these techniques, we are no longer distracted. These are options for us to use that may also be used by the child.

In this fashion, the diagnostic assessment is an exploration of what works. The time is not spent on tests to determine whether the child has a problem in "visual perception," for example. If the child has difficulty with letter reversals, the examiner may explore the value of segmenting the letter and accentuating the order of the parts for the "b" and "d" and having the child write it. Other combinations of strategies may work as well. The issue is for the examiner to be aware of what options are being tried and to communicate what they are so that the teacher, and the child, may use them. The options must be relatively simple and easily described so that they may be used in real life. The categories of *time, channel* and degree of *focusing* are means of organizing a large number of options.

Similarly, one may explore the feedback conditions that may work. The category of the *quality* of feedback includes the various types of feedback described earlier, including feedback as to results (FR). Differential feedback is provided, depending on performance. The term "good" may be used to exemplify affirmative social feedback as to results. The term "OK" may be used to exemplify less affirmative feedback when the results are not correct. The statement "OK" on the part of the examiner leads into a question of what may work to enable the child to succeed more completely. Affirmation also goes on of the information offered as to how the task may be done more successfully (FI). "I'm glad you asked me to repeat it again more slowly. Let's try that." That statement also includes affirmation of the fact that the child contributed to the solution (FP) as well as the specific idea.

Affirmative feedback increases the likelihood that the behavior will recur; it tends to build the person up. Negating feedback, such as "No, that's wrong," tends to tear the person down. However, affirmative feedback as to results is not sufficient. It does not tell the person how he or she may do it again. Affirmation of the ideas used and the degree of participation provided gives the person a greater awareness of the ideas so as they can be used elsewhere.

In general, the more difficulty the child has, the more *intense* the affirmation should be when the child accomplishes something or contributes to the solution. The intensity of the feedback needs to be stronger, more frequent, more immediate when getting started. The child gradually might then be able to make such statements as:

"I need you to tell me how I'm doing more often at the start."

"Let me check it out."

The third aspect of feedback is the degree of *sharing*. The examiner, aware of the objective of increasing the sharing of ideas, provides affirmation of the degree of contribution. The child's awareness of this issue might be illustrated by a statement such as:

"I don't understand. Will you help me?"

"It would help me if you show me."

With some children, the objectives for the interaction might emphasize the awareness of the techniques for presentation and the development of a vocabulary for affecting those conditions. With other children, the objectives for the interaction might emphasize a greater awareness of the interpersonal aspects with the development of a vocabulary for doing so. In all instances, both aspects of vocabulary are necessary, although the emphasis may vary. On an initial assessment, for example, one may want the child to be able to make only *one* statement as to presentation and *one* statement as to feedback. For both aspects, the statement made may be at the "select" level.

A system has been designed by which this sort of assessment is made part of the child's life at home and at school (Ozer and Dworkin, 1974). The teacher and parent, as well as the child, are asked to begin to identify their areas of concern; this provides the context for the interaction during the diagnostic session. The Child Development Observation is carried out in the presence of the teacher and parent. The perceptions by the significant adults in the child's life as to what they noticed that worked during the CDO are used as the basis for making suggestions for the home and classroom. Everyone present is asked to consider goals to be met before the next interaction with the diagnostician. A plan that incorporates both the goals stated and the techniques noticed is devised. Follow-up is provided to those involved to explore again what worked in their hands and the degree to which the goals were met. New goals are set for the future. The objective of this "Collaborative Service System" is to transmit to the child and the adults a planning process. The child who is having learning problems becomes the context for additional learning of a process by which other children may be helped. This system carries out on a larger scale what goes on during the Child Development Observation, in which the task at issue becomes the context for exploring what may work in other settings.

A new model of diagnostic assessment has been designed in relation to the child with developmental problems. This model views diagnosis as an ongoing process. Plans are made in accordance with the awareness and concerns of those who will implement such plans. Plans are revised in accordance with changing needs. Moreover, learning continues of the process of planning how learning may go on. One does not merely sample the process of development; one enhances it by illustrating it in a more self-conscious way.

APPLICATION OF THE "CHILD DEVELOPMENT" MODEL TO READING PROBLEMS

The assessment has been viewed as a sampling of the process of child development. The process of development is enhanced by a greater awareness by the child of how to take increasing responsibility for his or her learning. The role of the diagnostician—whether an educational specialist or classroom teacher—is that of a consultant, helping the child to contribute to the solution of a problem.

In applying this approach to the assessment of problems in reading, we will take several common areas of concern, as defined by Wilson (1967). For example, a child reverses words or letters in oral reading in the classroom. The diagnostician has defined the problem in consultation with the teacher, who describes her concern in terms of her own experience. The diagnostician helps the teacher to specify her concern more clearly. What specific types of words seem to cause difficulty? In this way, the context for the diagnostic interaction is established. What might we try to accomplish in the interaction? What classroom materials might we use? How well should we expect the child to do? By asking such questions, the consultant is attempting to get the teacher to go through the process of developing an educational plan.

The assessment process would sample the conditions under which such reversals might be diminished. The task might be to differentiate "big" from "dig." What strategies might be used? Of the categories described earlier, *focusing* might be useful. One could enhance the relevant parameter, namely, where the circle at the base of the letter is situated. One could make it more colorful or larger. One might also choose to *segment* the letter, i.e., break it up into parts. The segmentation might clarify the distinction between the line and circle that comprise the two letters. In addition to this visual *channel,* one might also sound the two letters and write them. One might similarly explore what feedback conditions might be effective. What would be appropriate rewards, how frequently should they be given, etc.? How many of these strategies should the child be able to learn by the end of this particular interaction and at what level of awareness? The objective at the end of the session might be for the child to be able to have stated freely, after having been shown, that it worked to segment the letter and to know when he or she is correct and for such feedback to be very frequent at the start.

The teacher might usefully be present at this interaction. What is being illustrated is more than a way of working only with this child's particular problem. Probably other children share this problem. More important, what is being illustrated is a way by which the children might be helped to become more aware of the ways in which they learn. The diagnostician with an ongoing role might successively increase the awareness of what works with this child at subsequent interactions. In addition, there must be some provision for the teacher to learn from the observation of the way the diagnostician works, but the emphasis should be on the child as the prime client.

The teacher might notice that another child loses his or her place in reading. The assessment process would sample the conditions under which one may keep one's place. One strategy that may work here is *focusing.* Would it help to define the place in reading more clearly, perhaps crayoning where one starts on the page? Having the child keep in place with a finger or a ruler or using a "window" are all focusing techniques. How many techniques do we want the child to take away from the interaction and at what level of awareness?

There has been no attempt to explore in any exhaustive way the strategies that may be used with the variety of reading problems. In the instances cited, the exploration is of what works. The specific techniques of focusing, for example, will vary with the task. What is to be made explicit is the compensating strategy that helps to overcome the difficulty. The child is made aware of what is being used and has the opportunity to use that strategy and to take increasing responsibility in doing so. Such awareness is enhanced by having the child verbalize the strategy. When encouraged to verbalize the strategy during the interaction, the child begins to make such statements in other settings as well. A program is set up by which at successive interactions with the teacher or specialist, the child begins to use an increasing number of problem-solving techniques.

What is being learned is not only the successful accomplishment of a particular task, but also a set of compensating strategies by which to approach problems. The problem-solving process is an interactive one between the child and the adult. The child's particular difficulties are but the context in which he or she takes responsibility for learning. Other kinds of problems will undoubtedly appear at other times for which solutions will need to be found. It is the process of exploring some solutions in interaction with an adult that is being modeled. Such a model is the essence of a person seeing himself or herself as an active participant in development. To the extent that the assessment process has contributed to such development, it is not merely diagnostic, but also an integral part of treatment.

REFERENCES

Bender, M. B. *The Approach to Diagnosis in Modern Neurology,* New York: Grune and Stratton, 1967, pp. 4–7.

Bender, M. B., M. Fink, and M. Green "Patterns in Perception on Simultaneous Tests of the Face and Hand," *Arch. Neurol. and Psychiatry* **66** (1951): 355–362.

Bersoff, D. N. "Silk Purses into Sows' Ears," *Am. Psychol.* **28** (1973): 892–898.

Bijou, S. W., and D. M. Baer "Contributions from a Functional Analysis," in L. P. Lipset and C. C. Spiker, eds., *Advances in Child Development,* 1965, 211–231.

Bijou, S. W., and R. F. Peterson "Psychological Assessment in Children: A Functional Analysis," in P. McReynolds, ed., *Advances in Psychological Assessment,* Vol. II, Palo Alto, Calif.: Science and Behavior Books, 1971, pp. 63–78.

Bijou, S. W., and S. A. Warren "Objective Observations in Field Situations for Clinical Assessment," *Memorial Volume to Harvey Digman,* ed. E. E. Meyers and G. Tayan, Berkeley: University of California Press, 1969.

Connolly, K. "Learning and the Concept of Critical Periods in Infancy," *Devel. Med. Child Neurol.,* **14** (1972): 705–714.

Crothers, B., and R. S. Paine *The Natural History of Cerebral Palsy,* Cambridge, Mass.: Harvard University Press, 1959.

Englehardt, H. T. "John Hughlings Jackson and the Mind-Body Relationship," *Bull. Hist. Med.* **49** (1975): 137–141.

Frankenburg, W., and J. Dodds "The Denver Developmental Screening Test," *Journal of Pediat.* **71** (1967): 181.

Furth, H. G. *Piaget and Knowledge,* Englewood Cliffs, N.J.: Prentice-Hall, 1969, pp. 175–177.

Land, G. L. *Grow or Die,* New York: Random House, 1973.

Ozer, M. N. "The Face-Hand Test in Children: Directions and Scoring," *Clin. Proceed. Childrens Hosp. D.C.* **23** (1967): 305–308.

Ozer, M. N. "The Neurological Evaluation of School Age Children," *Journal of Learn. Disab.* **1** (1968): 84–86.

Ozer, M. N., and N. E. Dworkin "The Assessment of Children with Learning Problems: An In-Service Teacher Training Program," *Journal of Learn. Disab.* **7** (1974): 539–574.

Ozer, M. N., and H. B. Richardson "Diagnostic Evaluation of Children with Learning Problems: A Communication Process," *Journal of Childhood Education* **48** (1972): 244–247.

Ozer, M. N., and H. B. Richardson "Diagnostic Evaluation of Children with Learning Problems: A Process Approach," *Journal of Learn. Disab.* **8** (1974): 88–92.

Paine, R. S., J. S. Werry, and H. C. Quay "A Study of Minimal Cerebral Dysfunction," *Develop. Med. Child Neurol.* **10** (1968): 505–510.

Reise, W. *Principles of Neurology: In Light of History and Their Present Use,* New York: Nervous and Mental Dis. Monogr., 1950, pp. 3–13.

Sherrington, C. *The Integrative Action of the Nervous System,* New Haven and London: Yale University Press, 1906.

Teng, P., and M. B. Bender "Effect of Barbiturates on Latent Motor Deficits," *Neurology* **5** (1955): 777–786.

Weinstein, E. A., et al. "Meaning in Jargon Aphasia," *Cortex* **2** (1966): 165–187.

Wilson, R. M. *Diagnostic and Remedial Reading,* Columbus, Ohio: Charles E. Merrill, 1967.

Chapter 6

A PSYCHIATRIC PERSPECTIVE
OF READING DISABILITY

PETER P. MEDRANO

Oakland County Community Mental Health Board, Pontiac, Michigan

During the past decade marked interest has been shown in the subject of reading disability, and within the public schools recognition and acceptance of this disorder have increased. Despite these apparent advances, however, the assumption often exists that reading disabilities must be profound and severe in order to be defined as such; consequently, the milder forms of this disorder are frequently overlooked. Nevertheless, the children who exhibit such minor deficiencies often seem to react with greater emotional manifestations than those who are more severely handicapped. They sense and resent their difficulties and fail to comprehend their inability to compete with classmates who, no more intelligent than themselves, nonetheless lack their reading problems.

School personnel often refer to the psychiatrist students whose underachievement is associated with disruptive behavior and disinterest in academic work. Learning disabilities, particularly those involving reading, are still a big puzzle to many educators and mental health professionals. The tendency to think of the underachieving child as "lazy" or "unwilling to try" is still prevalent. Whenever a youngster claims to hate teachers or schoolwork or to find the whole idea of education "stupid," the clinician should first consider the possibility that the child has an academic problem. It is not unusual for a clinician to concentrate entirely on the emotional problems of an underachiever and fail to inquire about the child's learning skills. In many cases, just such an inquiry might provide a clue to the youngster's resistance and negative attitude toward school-related activities.

Sometimes professionals are guilty of hasty observations and recommendations. For example, the teacher who finds a student negative or unresponsive to his or her teaching methods may assume that the student's basic problem is an emotional one. When such problems do arise, the psychiatrist is often called on to make a differential diagnosis. A differential diagnosis must be made between an emotional disorder with a superimposed learning problem and an academic problem with a superimposed emotional disorder. A shy, timid child may have difficulty reading in front of the class for fear of making mistakes. The child may nervously mispronounce words and hurry through sentences in order to complete the assigned reading task. This child's poor performance might lead to the conclusion, by academic standards, that he or she is an underachiever. On the other hand, a difficult, unruly student's disruptive behavior could be an open expression of the frustration related to a concealed learning disorder. Mental retardation and organic disorders are also diagnostic considerations that should be kept in mind, since these two conditions may manifest themselves in the form of a learning disorder.

The private practitioner sees only a small segment of those experiencing learning difficulties; the community has to deal with these problems on a much larger scale. Communities, after all, reflect the attitudes of the people who compose them. The policies of schools, and even of entire school districts, regarding learning disorders can be affected by individual attitudes or misunderstanding. For example, the confusion of learning dysfunction with "laziness" has far-reaching consequences for the child. The high incidence of children with learning disorders who have been placed in classes for the emotionally disturbed is only one example of what can result from the lack of appropriate knowledge of the problem. It is for this reason that the trend toward cooperation between community mental health services and the schools in the treatment of children with learning disorders associated with emotional problems must be supported. Instead of concentrating their attention on exclusive modes of treatment, the two types of agencies must unite to develop entire programs for dealing with a wider range of disabilities.

HISTORICAL OVERVIEW

Several theories have been formulated to explain learning disorders. These theories have ranged from genetic and constitutional to social and experiential determinants. They have all been considered at different times very important etiological factors. This chapter will focus on the attempts that have been made to relate reading problems to specific causes. The theories reviewed in the following pages represent the efforts made by different schools of thought to understand and explain reading disorders. The concepts considered in this chapter are: the learning-block concept, negative-oppositional attitude toward learning, overpassive behavior, primary reading disability, chronic emotional disorders, sociocultural and emotional deprivations, and hyperactivity. Each of these concepts remains popular in some circles, in spite of the accumulated evidence which points to multiple etiological factors and not necessarily to an exclusive determinant.

Learning block

Individuals attempting to resolve painful emotional problems frequently utilize blocking as a defense mechanism to keep pain and distress out of the reach of consciousness. Until recently, it was believed that a child's failure to learn to read could be due to the existence of such a block (Gardner and Sperry, 1974; Josselyn, 1969). The supposed block was thought to consist of unconscious, unresolved conflicts which impeded the development of learning skills. Psychotherapy designed to remove the block was often recommended; once the emotional block was removed, it was believed, the youngster would be able to continue his or her education without further problems.

The blocking concept proved confusing and disturbing, however, to parents, who were told that their child would eventually outgrow this condition and continue to progress at a normal educational rate. But parents often failed to see the expected improvement take place. Another, related, aspect is the concern some parents have about the quality of teaching their children receive in the lower grades. They fear that children who have been exposed to rigid, harsh, critical, or punitive teaching methods may develop a keen sense of failure, with subsequent resistance to learning. Kindergarten and first-grade teachers are, therefore, usually blamed for academic problems that surface later on. Advances in the field of learning disorders have questioned the validity of the learning-block theory, but nevertheless remnants of this idea are still found occasionally.

Negative-oppositional attitude

Children rebelling against parental demands or reacting to their own fears of failure sometimes develop a negative, oppositional attitude toward learning, particularly toward reading. Such children generally have difficulty verbalizing their feelings; characteristically, they are either openly defiant and aggressive or outwardly apathetic while inwardly hostile (Gardner and Sperry, 1974). Their negative attitude toward learning can be understood in terms of the personality-development process. The individual passes through different stages in the development of his or her personality. Occasionally, however, that development is either arrested or slowed—temporarily or permanently—through traumatic emotional experiences. In some individuals the degree of regression or arrest can be quite profound, reaching down to very primitive and immature levels of personality development. The result is a negative attitude, resistance to emotional growth, and a defective capacity for interpersonal relationships. The negative-oppositional factor stresses the ability of these variables to obstruct the learning drive and to lessen academic motivation.

A seven-year-old girl developed elective mutism; she wouldn't communicate at all with the teacher and only very little with peers, and any attempt to teach her how to read was met with open negativism. Not surprisingly her overall academic performance was very much affected. Therapy revealed a strong tendency to control and manipulate adults. As she learned through psychotherapy to feel more comfortable around adults, she was able to accept their help, and her academic work improved.

Overpassive behavior

Hostile aggressive tendencies are generally viewed as instinctive drives found in all individuals. The fact that they are present at a very early age suggests that their manifestations are most varied and complex. It is through a maturational process that individuals learn to deal with and handle the hostile aggressive feelings in a sociable and acceptable fashion. The approach that each person uses to handle these impulses will determine to a great extent his or her personality and social adjustment.

The belief that reading is an active and aggressive act has been viewed by some as a factor to explain reading problems in passive-dependent individuals (Gardner and Sperry, 1974; Josselyn, 1969). Reports sometimes summarize the basic problem as follows: "The child lacks the necessary drive to successfully complete a designated reading task." It is known that the reading process demands a child's assertiveness, self-confidence, and a fair degree of frustration tolerance; it is thought that an insecure, self-conscious, and overly dependent child may find the task more difficult. Conversely, an individual who has improved his or her sense of self-worth and thus becomes more actively engaged in the learning process could be expected to show a corresponding improvement in learning skills, especially those pertaining to reading.

Primary reading disability

This concept was introduced in the late 1950s (Rabinovitch, 1959). It was based on the finding that many children with reading disability exhibited functional lags in the visual, auditory, motor, conceptual, and perceptual areas. On examination, however, these children showed no evidence of gross neurological abnormality. The reading disability was explained in terms of marked developmental lag affecting the language area. The primary functional disability was seen as being independent from, although connected to, the secondary emotional problems that learning-disabled children develop.

This theory has been widely questioned, but it has definite merits. It points to basic academic deficiencies which have long gone unrecognized. Furthermore, by directing the educator's attention to specific remedial measures, it has resulted in the development of more practical, rounded programs for the treatment of learning disorders.

Chronic emotional disorders

Educators have observed that the symptoms of chronic emotional illnesses may have a negative functional impact. One of the functions affected by such disorders is reading; the protracted nature of the chronic disorders and their debilitating effect may well interfere with the acquisition of the necessary reading skills. Three specific psychopathologic disturbances can be distinguished: the chronic neurosis, deep-seated depression, and psychosis. In cases of neurosis, there is a waste of emotional energy, which affects mental concentration, attention, and the individual's ability to handle abstract, symbolic material. At the same time, a depletion of psychic energy, as is found in cases of depression, creates an impoverished emotional and mental condition which will turn any learning situation into an ordeal. The depressed youngster is generally without the necessary interest, motivation, and involvement in the learning process. When reading, for example, he or she will quickly give up when a new word appears, lacking sufficient energy to overcome the frustration that accompanies any learning experience. Psychosis can be a devastating condition that impairs the individual at all levels—mental, emotional, and physical. The degree of reading impairment can be related to the age of the subject at the onset of psychosis; if the child is affected during the early, formative years of childhood, the damage to learning abilities will be correspondingly more severe. Although some psychotic children may demonstrate superior mechanical reading skills, their comprehension and use of the reading material are, for the most part, defective.

Sociocultural and emotional deprivation

A child deprived of adequate stimulation in his or her early, formative years may exhibit learning problems, including reading disability, later on (Richardson, 1973; Wolff, 1970). Maternal deprivation, particularly due to lack of appropriate mothering or emotional conflicts in relationships between mother and child, can result in developmental lag affecting physical, mental, emotional, perceptual-cognitive, and language function (Yarrow, 1972). The degree of disability can be commensurated in terms of the severity and duration of the condition.

The effects of deprivation and institutionalization in children have been widely described in the literature (Spitz, Bowlby, etc.). These children have been found to be aggressive, diffused, lacking in appropriate guilt feelings, destructive, and unable to establish close and meaningful personal relationships. In academic settings these children seem to have poor attention span, low concentration power, minimal frustration tolerance, and little academic motivation.

Another consideration related to this topic is the educational background of the parents, which usually is closely related to their social status and often accounts for the differences in academic expectations (Yarrow, 1972). Children who have been socially and economically deprived may not have had the appropriate intellectual and academic exposure; or, their parents may have failed to provide support and encouragement to stimulate their interest in school-related matters. On the other hand, a child raised in a family that places a high value on education will find much support and intellectual stimulation within the home.

Hyperactivity

The hyperactive syndrome is a behavior disorder found in a relatively high percentage of the school population (Thompson, 1974; Werry, 1969). Currently, educators equate this condition with learning disorders; the medical profession refers to it as M.B.D., or minimal brain dysfunction. Overactive behavior, poor attention span, impulsivity, distractibility, and the presence of so-called soft neurological signs are all symptoms of this condition. Some hyperactive children experience difficulty in analyzing and integrating sounds and symbols and in comprehending and retaining reading material. Their frustration tolerance and ability to concentrate are low; they find it very difficult to sit still, and they are sometimes overaggressive and disruptive. Such children quickly come to the attention of teachers and school administrators as potential discipline problems, and for this reason their reading problems are often overlooked entirely or considered as secondary or of lesser importance.

A great deal of information about the hyperactive syndrome has been accumulated, particularly during the past ten years (Gross and Wilson, 1974; Thompson, 1974; Werry, 1969). The concept of minimal brain dysfunction has been challenged because of the inconsistency and diffuseness of the neurological findings. However, recent studies have demonstrated a relationship between neurological deficiencies and cognitive-perceptual problems (Gross and Wilson, 1974; Sechzar, Faro, and Windle, 1974). It is important to identify children with this particular condition, because it requires a much more specific form of treatment, especially when medication is prescribed.

CLINICAL SYMPTOMS

The clinical symptoms found in learning-disabled children are manifested by coping mechanisms which commonly reflect long-standing frustrations and academic failure. These symptoms appear in clusters, and their manifestations vary from child to child. The following sections identify more commonly found symptoms and comment on their significance and treatment implications for those attempting to work with learning-disabled children. Among the myriad of symptoms, some of the most characteristic and frequent ones are underachievement, denial, low self-esteem, depression, anxiety, self-doubt, hostility, and overaggressiveness.

Underachievement

Academic underachievement is undoubtedly of primary importance. A youngster who fails to work up to potential arouses concern among teachers and parents alike. Such a child may appear oblivious to the poor grades received or unaware of having academic problems. Quite often, the underachiever is perceived as being lazy or unwilling to work. However, at a deeper level this child is concerned about his or her low performance, but is also cognizant that good grades or improved academic standing does not materialize as a result of his or her best efforts. The child's self-comparison with peers is unfavorable, and despite secret competition with them, the child realizes that lack of success represents limited academic skill.

Denial

Denial, or the "I can do it if I want to" syndrome, is a psychological defense mechanism used to ward off the pain and misery experienced under stress. Children with reading problems may attempt in a variety of ways to cover up or deny the existence of those problems. For example, when asked about school, the youngster will usually reply that things there are alright and might even volunteer the information that his or her favorite subject is reading.

Another example of good coping strategy related to this defense mechanism is a child who, when asked to explain or tell about what he or she has just read, will contrive a story that may or may not be related to the story in the book. This same child may attempt to cover over the reading material with his or her hands or head, so that an observer will not notice the child's "mistakes."

Many of the students who exhibit this syndrome are of average or above average intelligence. Although cognizant of their limitations, they are unwilling to accept them, and they frequently assume a self-sufficient, over-confident attitude. Inwardly, however, they shrink when called on to perform, because they know that they will be unable to perform up to expectation.

Avoidance

Avoidance is a condition frequently manifested by withdrawal or apathetic behavior. The underachiever gradually withdraws from the teacher, educational opportunities, and ultimately anything having to do with reading. By avoiding the area of stress, the child hopes to conceal an academic handicap (Gardner and Sperry, 1974). The avoidance mechanism can be related to the denial syndrome described above; however, the youngster showing avoidance refuses to engage in academic activities and claims that he or she either doesn't like or need to learn how to read. As a result, the child becomes unavailable whenever reading tasks are given.

Low self-esteem and depression

A child who has been subjected to continual academic stress and who continues to fail tends to have a low self-opinion. Although depression as an emotional condition has for some time been studied and delineated in adults, it has been argued that children do not experience this condition, but rather show symptoms equivalent to those of a depressive condition. However, recent observations have shown that children do indeed manifest symptoms of depression (Gardner and Sperry, 1974; Glasser, 1968). Feelings of inadequacy, low self-esteem, and an anticipation of failure are characteristic symptoms in children who become discouraged by their lack of achievement. Such children see themselves as being "different"; they fail to measure up to the standards of their parents and teachers, or even to their own. Not infrequently they manifest a negative self-image, calling themselves "dumb," "stupid," etc. Children suffering from depression are generally tense and irritable, especially in competitive situations; internally, they develop a self-defeating, "what's the use?" attitude. Compounding this problem, some parents, especially those with high educational expectations, may put pressure on an underachiever or react to her or his scholastic failure in a punitive manner. Such tactics generally exacerbate the situation rather than ameliorate it. Let us consider an example.

Bob's father was a factory worker who had great scholastic aspirations for his children. As a young man, he had had one plan—to go to college—but his plan was interrupted by premature marriage. Thus when Bob demonstrated academic difficulties, his father was disappointed and impatient. Bob felt largely responsible for his father's ill feelings, but nonetheless quite helpless and discouraged. It was only after his father understood and accepted Bob's academic limitations that a more sensible approach to his problem was developed.

Anxiety

Anxiety is intimately related to academic stress and to the insecure feelings underachievers experience in the learning situation. The majority of reading-disabled children who are aware of their academic limitations become very anxious. Such students are never quite sure of their ability to perform; whenever they are asked to read either individually to the teacher or in groups, they become nervous and tense. They are afraid of making mistakes and of being reprimanded; yet while sensitive to criticism, they are also eager for praise and success. Clinically they seem to be restless; usually they "try too hard." Children suffering from anxiety invest tremendous amounts of energy in performing what might be considered rather simple academic tasks, and at the end of such an ordeal they may appear physically exhausted. Sometimes anxious children are considered to be perfectionists. It takes them a long time to complete a task, they use heavy pressure lines in drawing and writing, and they use the eraser copiously at the first sign of a mistake. Basically they find it difficult to please themselves and need a great deal of reassurance.

Self-doubt

Self-doubt and feelings of uncertainty are two symptoms sometimes difficult to ascertain, but nevertheless very important to identify. They seem to derive from the children's past experience, which has taught them that they are likely to make mistakes. Therefore, it is not easy for them to feel comfortable when dealing with new reading material or performing in a group situation. It appears they are continually expecting someone to correct them or to point out their mistakes. Their general decision-making and judgmental capacities may also be affected, making them resentful of anyone who might place them in positions of self-doubt and uncertainty.

Overaggressiveness

As a means of compensating for feelings of inadequacy, a reading-disabled child may become hostile and overaggressive, refusing to allow anyone to refer to the disability or to criticize. Often such youngsters stand out among their peers for their toughness and readiness to fight. Delinquent behavior, when present, may stem from deep feelings of inadequacy and awareness of academic failure. As their attention drifts away from the classroom, such children fantasize retaliation and in their idle moments may construct situations that will provide them with a sense of accomplishment—however socially unacceptable such situations may be. Antisocial behavior can be interpreted as a manifestation of the anger and frustration experienced by the underachiever when surrounded by others who fail to understand or accept his or her limitations.

TREATMENT

Treatment for children who exhibit emotional disorder is essentially a team approach; teacher, psychiatrist, reading specialist, and parents all work together with the learning-disabled child. Obviously, the most important aspect of this approach is the establishment of a comprehensive remedial program geared first to assess the degree of disability and second to delineate the kind of curriculum that will help to correct it. Usually the youngster is referred to individual or group tutoring or to a learning center, where treatment is at the child's current level of functioning.

It is important that the tutor be a learning specialist with experience in dealing specifically with reading disability. Classroom teachers may help children presenting a mild disorder by providing extra assistance and coaching, but children with serious reading disabilities should be referred to someone highly trained in this field.

Psychotherapy is geared to deal with the emotional problems that stem from learning disorders. One major task in therapy is to help the youngster accept his or her learning problem and to accept needed help in coping with it. It is only when the child is willing to accept such help that things can begin to change.

In order to reach this point of acceptance, the therapist must deal with the feelings of inadequacy, frustration, and insecurity that the child has developed over the years. If a child's learning disability results in serious behavioral problems at home and in the classroom, it is important that the therapist work in conjunction with both school and parents, stressing the need for support of the child and understanding of his or her limitations. Open communication among all participants is imperative, as the child will tend to manipulate both school and parents; although desirous of improvement, the child may unconsciously resist change and cling to former behavior patterns.

The use of medication might be indicated if there is a rather serious hyperactive behavioral disorder. It has been observed that amphetamine-related drugs increase the attention span and concentration of such children and diminish their impulsivity (Douglas, 1974; Gross and Wilson, 1974). Medication must be used judiciously, however. There has been a tendency on the part of educators to request physicians to prescribe medication for hyperactive children and a corresponding tendency for physicians to go along with these requests without first conducting an accurate and extensive evaluation of the child's condition. Such an evaluation should always be performed, and only if the syndrome is well defined should medication be prescribed.

An important phase of drug treatment is the establishment of a good follow-up program, which should consist of monitoring the effects and side-effects of the medication. Parents and school teachers should be impressed with the idea that medication is a convenient tool in the overall treatment and not a substitute for a comprehensive treatment approach. Medication is not recommended for children who merely seem to be restless or somewhat disorganized.

The following case study illustrates in a practical sense many of the theoretical considerations discussed thus far. The sequence from diagnosis to treatment also offers an example of the procedure that could be followed in dealing with cases of reading problems associated with emotional conflicts.

John A. is eight years old and in the third grade. He began his education in a parochial school, but was transferred to a public school shortly before his referral to the psychiatrist. The school psychologist referred John because he was experiencing academic difficulties which seemed to stem from an underlying emotional problem. John's difficulties lay in the areas of reading, writing, and spelling; he had no problems with math. His reading skills were below grade level, and he exhibited a marked tendency to give up when he encountered too many new words. Clinical interviews and further testing showed him to be very constricted, insecure, and inhibited. In general, he displayed considerable uncertainty and a lack of self-confidence in the academic area. These findings indicated that rather than John's academic difficulty being caused by an emotional problem, the reverse might be true. The primary problem was apparently academic; John was suffering from a mild form of learning disorder, which in turn produced a noticeable emotional reaction. He became tense and inhibited in the classroom, both fearful of failure and anxious to achieve. Rather than make a mistake, he quickly gave up the attempt to master new words. This behavior was attributed to a lack of motivation and effort on John's part; he just "wasn't trying." Yet the evaluation showed that John was trying very hard indeed—so hard, in fact, that it was affecting his emotional state. John's emotional problems did not seem to warrant the use of medication or placement in a class for the emotionally disturbed. Instead, he was referred to the school learning center for remedial reading. John responded favorably to this approach; as he made academic progress, he showed greater acceptance of his own limitations, his self-confidence increased, and his overall motivation was enhanced.

PROGNOSIS

In terms of the prognosis, it is important to determine the severity of the disorder. There are many different levels of dysfunction which will eventually need some type of treatment. A child with a severe reading problem will require a very intensive remedial program of indeterminate length. Tutoring or modifying the general program should meet the needs of children whose reading disorders are only mild, however.

The age of the child at the time of diagnosis is another important factor. Satz, in Chapter 3 of this book, describes such an identification process. A youngster who is diagnosed and treated at an early age usually finds it easier to accept his or her problem and is more receptive whenever help is offered. The student who reaches high school with a marked reading retardation is headed for a variety of academic, social, and emotional problems. Sometimes a reading-disabled child exhibits an emotional reaction disproportionate to the degree of disability. A youngster whose learning disorder is only mild could show an overwhelming, disruptive response, whereas one whose disability is more severe might react with resignation and make a reasonable adjustment by accepting his or her handicap.

The child's academic motivation must be preserved at all costs; once it is lost, the child encounters numerous problems and becomes alienated from any available help. Hence it is vitally important that the people involved in helping the learning-disabled child be well trained and experienced in such work. Because the problems encountered demand special attention on the part of school personnel, it is particularly important to continually reassess the quality of existing reading programs. Specific recommendations for improving reading programs are dealt with in depth in other chapters.

In summary, prognosis in a case of learning disability depends on several factors. Promptness of diagnosis and the degree of disability are basic considerations. Understanding and acceptance, combined with the opportunity to learn in a warm, supportive educational setting have great therapeutic significance. The youngster will respond to such treatment with deep feelings of gratitude and genuine motivation. Finally, the people who work with learning-disabled children should have experience in dealing with both academic and psychological problems, so that they can offer attractive, exciting alternatives to children who feel defeated and, in many ways, helpless.

BIBLIOGRAPHY

Douglas, V. I. "Sustained Attention and Impulsivity Control: Implication for the Handicapped Child," in *Psychology and the Handicapped Child,* Washington: Department of Health, Education, and Welfare, Office of Education, 1974.
Freeberg N., and D. Payne "Parental Influence or Cognitive Development in Early

Childhood: A Review," in *Annual Progress in Child Psychiatry and Child Development,* ed. S. Chess and A. Thomas, New York: Brunner/Mazel, 1972, pp. 166–189.

Gardner, G. E., and B. M. Sperry "Learning Disabilities and School Phobia," *American Handbook of Psychiatry,* Vol. II, ed. Arieti Silvano, New York: Basic Books, 1974, pp. 116–129.

Glasser, V. "Masked Depression in Children and Adolescents," in *Annual Progress in Child Psychiatry and Child Development, op. cit.,* 1968, pp. 345–355.

Gross, M. B., and L. W. Wilson *Minimal Brain Dysfunction,* New York: Brunner/ Mazel, 1974.

Josselyn, I. "Passivity," in *Progress in Child Psychiatry and Child Development, op. cit.,* 1969, pp. 468–484.

Rabinovitch, R. B. "Reading and Learning Disabilities," *American Handbook of Psychiatry, op. cit.,* Vol. I, 1959, pp. 857–869.

Richardson, S. A. "Psychosocial Factors Contributing to Deprivation in Child Development," in *Children with Learning Problems,* ed. Selma G. Sapir and Ann C. Nitzburg, New York: Brunner/Mazel, 1973.

Sechzar, J. A., M. D. Faro, and F. W. Windle "Studies of Monkeys Asphyxiated at Birth: Implications for Minimal Cerebral Dysfunction," in *Progress in Child Psychiatry and Child Development, op. cit.,* 1974, pp. 228–248.

Thompson, L. J. "Learning Disabilities: An Overview," in *Progress in Child Psychiatry and Child Development, op. cit.,* 1974, pp. 166–181.

Werry, J. S. "Developmental Hyperactivity," in *Progress in Child Psychiatry and Child Development, op. cit.,* 1969, pp. 485–505.

Wolff, D. H. "Critical Periods in Human Cognition Development," *Hospital Practice Journal* 5 (Nov. 1970): 77–87.

Yarrow, L. J. "Maternal Deprivation," in *The Child, His Psychological and Cultural Development,* Vol. I, ed. A. Friedman and H. Kaplan, 1972, pp. 221–230.

Chapter 7

THE ASSESSMENT OF ORAL LANGUAGE
AS A PRECURSOR OF READING

GERALD G. FREEMAN

Oakland Schools Speech and Hearing Clinic, Pontiac, Michigan

INTRODUCTION

Educators have long recognized that language arts programs should promote the development of verbal comprehension, oral expression, reading, and writing as progressive linguistic skills. However, observations of common educational practices reveal that early elementary curricula usually place immediate emphasis on teaching reading. It is assumed that children will have mastered verbal comprehension and oral expression prior to entering school.

Fortunately, most children do understand and speak their native language by the time they reach school age. However, when a child demonstrates difficulties in comprehending spoken language, speaking, reading, or writing, the integrative aspects of these linguistic modes tend to be overlooked. The responsibility for the management of the problem is delegated to a specialist—speech pathologist or reading expert—depending on the predominant symptom. Frequently, neither of these specialists has a well-founded appreciation for the interrelatedness of language functions.

More recently, speech pathologists and reading specialists have recognized overlapping areas of roles and responsibilities in the delivery of services to children who have difficulty learning to read. This circumstance has resulted from an expanded awareness that reading is dependent on language (Kavanaugh, 1968; Venezky, 1968); primary language skills are prerequisite to literacy. As such, it follows that some cases of reading failure actually reflect inadequate mastery of verbal comprehension and oral expression (Rees, 1974; Stark, 1975). The development of such skills becomes an initial goal of remediation, a task that requires a combination of professional competencies.

In addition, the literature regarding learning disabilities in children has stressed that difficulties demonstrated by a child in comprehending spoken language, speaking, reading, or writing sometimes involve more than a circumscribed problem. For example, Johnson and Mykelbust (1967) view some reading problems as secondary to central auditory disturbances. Remedial management of such problems requires a cross-disciplinary approach.

In light of these considerations, it is the purpose of this chapter to discuss a clinical-educational approach for children who demonstrate inadequate language development and consequent reading problems. (For further discussion of the clinical educator, see Chapters 8 and 13.) Because of the complexities involved in language acquisition and the substantial literature devoted to it, no attempt will be made to summarize pertinent theories, philosophies, or scientific findings on which this approach is based. (For such discussions see Bloom, 1970; Brown, 1973; Piaget, 1955.) Rather, a scheme for the evaluation of primary language skills, as precursors of reading, will be presented as a means for collecting and interpreting data which may be utilized to implement remedial language programs.

DEFINITION OF LANGUAGE

Because of its focus on the vocal system as a means of communication, the definition of language presented by Carrow (1972, p. 54) represents an appropriate point of departure.

> Language may be functionally defined as an arbitrary system comprised of sets of vocal symbols which represent a conceptual system used by man to communicate. This linguistic code is expressed orally in speech and graphically in writing. Essential to language is the relationship between the two systems, linguistic and conceptual.

This definition provides a practical structure for the analysis of a child's primary language skills—encoding and decoding phonological, semantic, and syntactic components of language—the first step of a remedial program. It indicates the need for attention to a child's vocal utterances, as well as to the conceptual system represented by such utterances. It implies the need for attention to: (1) linguistic components, (2) linguistic processes, and (3) the referential system represented by observable language behavior.

EVALUATION OF THE LINGUISTIC CODE

There is no single test or instrument that measures primary linguistic skills. As a result, it is necessary to use a variety of tests and techniques—formal

Table 7.1. Scheme for organization of linguistic evaluative data

	Process	
Linguistic components	*Encoding*	*Decoding*
Phonological	A	B
Semantic	C	D
Syntactic	E	F

and informal—to assess the components of a child's language behavior. Even this method falls short of providing a measure of total language function. However, it enables the evaluator to identify some of a child's linguistic strengths and weaknesses.

Regardless of the specific tests or techniques used, it is necessary to organize them into a manageable and useful scheme. Lerea (1958) suggested the design for such a scheme when he recommended adaptation of the linguists' system of analyzing languages to clinical-educational practices. He challenged speech pathologists to move beyond their primary concern for the phonological aspects of language toward a broader assessment which includes measurement of a child's ability to comprehend and express vocabulary and syntax.

A useful model for the initial linguistic assessment, therefore, involves attention to the phonological, semantic, and syntactic components of language, with regard to the processes of decoding and encoding, as shown in Table 7.1. The organization of data into the six designated cells permits the evaluator to (1) look at various dimensions of the symptomatic behavior, (2) establish baseline behaviors for linguistic components, and (3) analyze component-process relationships inherent in linguistic tasks.

When reviewed systematically at given time intervals, this plan provides a suitable means for obtaining a series of descriptions of language behavior in which temporal changes may be noted (Freeman, 1971). In addition, as new tests and standards of measurement become available, they may be substituted for old ones, or added, within the same fundamental scheme. For example, the recent techniques described by Lee (1966) for developmental sentence analysis or those proposed by Carrow (1974) for assessment of elicited language provide information which can be readily organized within this framework.

UTILIZATION OF STANDARDIZED TESTS

A number of tests have been developed to assess linguistic functions. Some provide data which clearly fall into a single component-process cell of the model, such as A or D. Others have been designed with decoding and encoding counterparts; thus the same instrument may be used to serve a dual purpose (cells E and F). A third group provides information which crosses cell boundaries. The appendix to this chapter provides examples of such tests organized according to the modular cell for which each provides data.

For example, the Peabody Picture Vocabulary Test (Dunn, 1965) requires a child to select one of four pictures on the basis of its name. Its results clearly fall within the semantic/decoding (cell D) modular component. The Northwestern Syntax Screening Test (Lee, 1971) similarly demands picture selection on the basis of a stimulus sentence—syntactic/decoding (cell F)—then superimposes the task of expression by asking the child to repeat sentences regarding specified pictures—syntactic/encoding (cell E). The Action-Agent Test (Gesell, 1940) elicits responses to "What-plus-action" questions, such as, "What flies?" It requires syntactic decoding, though elicits encoded behavior which may be used for evaluating the phonological, semantic, and syntactic components of a child's language.

The selection and use of specific tests depends on the training, experience, and competence of the evaluator. With the exception of the assessment of phonological decoding—usually regarded as the sole territorial right of speech pathologists—most language tests have been designed for use by various professional workers, including psychologists, reading specialists, and speech pathologists. Test users should be aware of their limitations as well as their value in determining remedial strategies. (For further discussion of establishing criteria for test selection, see Chapter 9.)

First, although one objective in administering language tests is to establish skill-related baselines of behavior, at times the child with a language problem responds to formally presented stimuli in a manner unanticipated by the test's author(s). In such instances, the evaluator may find it necessary to utilize the testing procedure as a means of gathering informal rather than formal data. Although deviations from established procedures of administration prevent standardized scoring, they often provide essential information for program planning. The evaluator is encouraged, therefore, to record all of a child's actual responses to tests rather than merely designating whether or not a specific response is correct. These observations, along with available test results, then may be collated and discussed within the model presented in this chapter.

For example, during administration of the Peabody Picture Vocabulary Test, a child may ignore the evaluator's request to point to the stimulus pictures and instead name all of the pictures on a page. Under such circumstances, the evaluator should avoid being bound by the test form and should record all of the child's verbal output. These data may prove more useful as a basis of analysis and assessment of the child's encoded linguistic skills at each level than those that would have been collected to evaluate semantic decoding through the standardized procedure.

A second concern regarding formal language tests relates to their validity. Because of the complexities and integrative aspects of language, frequently it is impossible to test a circumscribed linguistic component, even though the title of a test reflects the intent to do so. For example, tests of auditory discrimination clearly fall, on the surface, into the phonological/decoding cell of the model. Such tests, however, generally involve a child's differentiating between two rhyming words or syllables with a single phonemic variant. The child is asked to indicate whether or not the stimuli are the same. Although differentiating the phonemic structure of the words is requisite to a correct response, other variables that may affect performance include the child's auditory acuity, auditory memory, and understanding of the concepts of "same" and "different." The fact that a child fails to perform at age-level expectations on such a test is important, though in itself may not reflect specific difficulties in auditory discrimination or indicate the need for a program of language remediation that stresses improved auditory discriminative abilities.

On the other hand, a child's responses to test tasks designed for other purposes may be highly indicative of an auditory discrimination problem. For example, experience has demonstrated that it is not uncommon for children with language problems to demonstrate such tendencies on the Action-Agent Test. Typically, when asked, "What melts?" they reply "Cows" (milks) and in response to, "What aches?" they reply "Chickens" (eggs). Undoubtedly, a single response of this nature is relatively insignificant. However, if a child demonstrates similar behaviors throughout an evaluative session, the data collected informally may be as credible, if not more so, than those collected through the use of standardized procedures designed to measure specific linguistic behaviors.

A third problem in the use of formal measures relates to artifacts in the testing situation. The limited sample of language behavior that is observed and recorded in a single evaluative session rarely reflects a child's typical and varied daily linguistic performance. The variability among evaluators who administer tests is difficult to control, despite standardized procedures. The population of children on whom normative data for a test were collected may be biased with respect to a specific child. In addition, with children who have suspected language problems, it is essential to establish that they understand the directions of each task. When they do not, the evaluator risks recording responses that are unrelated to the situation.

For example, the Wepman Auditory Discrimination Test (1958) requires subjects to indicate whether or not two stimulus words are the same; during administration of this test, I have found that some children initially respond on the basis of their understanding of the vocabulary. Others seem to respond hastily or through inattention. In these or similar circumstances, it is an injustice to a child to suggest that the skills demanded by the test have been measured.

A fourth concern regarding standardized tests relates to the recent tendency of school personnel to rely on them to demonstrate professional accountability. A pretest-intervention-posttest model is used to measure a student's progress. Although this procedure may appear logical, in some instances, particularly as applied to children with language problems, it may only reflect that a child has been taught to perform the tasks on a test rather than to internalize or generalize linguistic principles. The effectiveness of a language-intervention program should depend more on recorded observations of children's linguistic performances in natural communicative situations than on their programmed responses to specific test stimuli.

For example, a five-year-old child with whom I recently had contact demonstrated a delay in language secondary to a neurological and intellectual delay of 12 to 18 months. Inasmuch as the child experienced difficulty in comprehending the concepts of "the same" and "not the same," a program of remediation was instituted to enable her to do so. Briefly, the program involved the child's following directions to identify one of three objects that was not the same as the others. After the child had learned to accomplish this task with a variety of objects, the evaluator administered the Columbia Mental Maturity Scale (1972). This instrument, with a format similar to the program of remediation, requires the subject to identify a single stimulus picture that differs from the foils. On this instrument the child's performance exceeded age-level expectations. Yet in the classroom or other situations, she was unable to generalize her understanding of "the same" and "not the same"; she remained perplexed when these concepts were presented out of the specific context in which she had learned to use them. Regardless of her test performance, the remedial objective was not completely achieved.

Despite these limitations, standardized tests provide an important means of gathering data. Depending on the circumstances in which they are used and the evaluators who use them, standardized tests may provide information regarding a child's levels of observable linguistic performance and indicate areas which should be probed further through diagnostic teaching. They may provide baseline information or a corpus of informal observations which may be used in the organization and implementation of programs of remediation. In perspective, though, the data which they yield reflect the symbolic representations of a conceptual or referential system, about which additional insights are necessary.

EVALUATION OF THE CONCEPTUAL SYSTEM

The most prominent feature of a clinical-educational approach to children with language problems involves the ongoing assessment of their language-related processes. In this regard an initial procedural model may be derived from learning theorists, who have stated that sensory-motor experiences and perceptions of these experiences are contingencies to concept development and that many words come to stand for or name concepts that have been learned preverbally (Carroll, 1964; Richardson, 1967). Briefly, the basic processes involved in language development are reception, perception, conceptualization, and verbalization. As a result, the management strategies for children with language disorders depend on specific behavioral signs that are suggestive of dysfunction in one or several of these processes.

The process of reception refers to sensory intactness. As related to language development, evaluations in this area most obviously focus on a child's auditory and visual acuity and should include immediate screening assessments of hearing and vision. In addition, however, informal observations in this area often provide information regarding the primary modes of input which may be utilized most effectively with specific children. Through diagnostic teaching the evaluator should attempt to probe the types of approaches—visual, auditory, tactile, multisensory—through which each child seems to learn best. This information is used to guide the predominant style of presentation of remedial procedures.

Perception, as used in this context, refers to distinguishing the finite physical characteristics or attributes of stimuli. A child who capably sees three shapes, for example, still may have difficulty distinguishing their specific forms. Although the child's visual acuity, or reception, is intact, his or her sensory perceptual skills are inadequate. Similarly, a child's hearing acuity may be sufficiently sensitive to detect two sounds of equal intensity, though she or he may experience difficulty distinguishing between them.

In a pragmatic, clinical-educational sense, the process of conceptualization involves the ability to group stimuli according to the similarities of their properties or attributes. It involves sensing an object, distinguishing its attributes, and categorizing it according to societal practices. For example, given two containers of equal size and shape—one styrofoam and one clear plastic—a person automatically classifies the former as a cup and the latter as a glass.

Verbalization refers to the assignment of labels to concepts. In the previous example, it involves learning to say the actual words, "cup" and "glass," when faced with these two objects.

The interrelationships among these processes have been summarized by Chappell (1976). He states that children's knowledge of the physical world continually changes as they gain an increasing repertoire of the attributes that are specific to certain objects and that may be general to many. He describes the learning process as involving a gradual attainment of equivalence between an appreciation of concepts—their full meanings—and the assignment of accepted labels to them.

Despite these interrelationships, it is practical to evaluate children with language problems in terms of the predominance of processing difficulties which they demonstrate. In other words, a language impairment is viewed and analyzed as a manifestation of difficulties in reception, perception, conceptualization, verbalization, or any combination of these. It is postulated that such difficulties have interfered with language learning and that remedial procedures should be directed toward them.

THE REMEDIAL APPROACH

Whereas the evaluation of the linguistic system provides data to substantiate levels of observable language performance, the assessment of the conceptual system provides insights regarding process disturbances that are reflected in this performance. The beginning point in language training, therefore, focuses on the identification of a child's specific assets and liabilities in the processes related to language learning; the clinical-educational approach then utilizes the observed assets within these areas to teach skills in areas of apparent deficiency.

The key features of this approach may be stated as follows: sensory-motor, perceptual, conceptual, and verbal skills are taught in accord with the child's functional level in each of the areas. The development of concepts precedes active efforts to elicit appropriate verbal responses. If sensory-motor deprivation is apparent, basic training is begun in this area, utilizing techniques that span the contributions of Montessori (1965) and Kephart (1960); if sensory-perceptual development is delayed, the specific techniques used may include those of Strauss and Lehtinen (1947), Frostig (1964), or those suggested by Zigmond and Cicci (1968).

The essential aspect of this program is not the test or series of items used to evaluate specific language-related areas, but the time invested in organizing responses—whether they are elicited through the use of formal test items or by other means—in terms of their possible relationships to language processes. Such organization facilitates the operation of at least four general principles through all aspects of a child's program: (1) attention is paid to the language-related processes, (2) the child's assets are utilized, (3) the progression is from concrete to abstract—from experience to the words, (4) remediation is tailored to each child in terms of the behavioral deviations demonstrated relative to disturbances in language-related processes.

For example, if sensory-perceptual dysfunctions seem to be interfering with a young child's age-appropriate concept development, the remedial program begins at this level, proceeds to concept development, and eventually stresses verbalization. Specifically, it seems reasonable to assume that a child who sees, but has difficulty distinguishing between, a circle and a square will not develop appropriate understanding of their labels or the ability to express these labels meaningfully. This child's program of remediation, therefore, progresses from concrete experiences with circles and squares—

utilizing this child's sensory strengths—through matching, sorting, identifying, and naming. Such a progression considers the child's current level of success and attempts to reach the desired behavior in incremental units rather than to provide the means for eliciting rote verbal behavior.

A quite different example involves young children who demonstrate rich concept development, but fail to verbalize in accord with expectations. Such children frequently respond through gestures and pantomime, coupled with inadequate use of vocabulary and syntax. In these instances, the initial remedial program might stress verbalization, without specific attention to perceptual or conceptual skills. If such needs later are indicated, the program may be altered accordingly.

Although the desired end result is verbalization, the attainment of this result does not always begin with a program designed to elicit verbal responses, either of a socially meaningful or structurally significant nature. Rather, an effort is made to begin at the functional linguistic or prelinguistic level of each child, to provide each with success experiences at that level, and to lead each to the desired behavior in an orderly progressive manner.

APPLICATIONS TO READING FAILURES

The relevance of this discussion to children whose ostensible problem is reading failure lies in the fact that in some instances these problems stem from primary language disorders. Although the number of such cases has not been substantiated on a national basis, Kirk and Elkins (1975) report that the academic problems of 29 percent of the children enrolled in demonstration centers for learning-disabled youngsters were attributed to language disorders. If one adheres to the developmental progression of linguistic skills —verbal comprehension, verbal expression, reading, and writing—it seems reasonable to assume that remediation for these children should emphasize the primary linguistic skills—understanding spoken language and expression —prior to reading.

It is the contention of this discussion that reading specialists work with some children whose reading failures are secondary to primary language disturbances. Yet the methods employed by these specialists to promote reading skills sometimes fail to address the children's underlying linguistic deficiencies. For this reason, all children with reading problems should undergo the previously described types of formal and informal assessments. The evaluative results, then, can be utilized to plan and implement remedial programs in terms of each child's linguistic needs.

For example, as Yoder (1974)* has indicated, the comprehension and use

---

* D. Yoder, personal communication, February 8, 1974.

of *wh* questions (what, who, where, whose, etc.) implies knowledge of the concepts represented by the interrogative words, as well as understanding of the structures that must be used to respond appropriately to them. Specifically, the concept of time underlies comprehension of the word "when"; the response to a "when" question demands understanding of adverbial, prepositional phrase, and tense structures. Similarly, a "where" question demands understanding of spatial concepts, as well as those related to adverbial and prepositional phrase structures.

The child who demonstrates difficulties with "wh" words at the auditory-verbal level has little foundation to cope with them successfully during reading. This child may be experiencing problems with the syntax or may be deficient in understanding the concepts represented by the interrogative words. In the first case, a remedial program might take the form of the developmental syntax approach described by Lee (1974). In the second case, a program of conceptual development might be instituted. The point is that such factors should be differentiated through evaluation so that the remedial programs instituted promote the development of the primary auditory-verbal skills on which reading is based.

Similarly, other aspects of a child's inability to read and comprehend may relate to primary linguistic problems. Does a child's inability to cope with plural forms reflect an inadequate concept of number, morphological rules, or syntax, or a deviation from standard articulatory practices? Does a demonstrated difficulty with tense forms suggest inadequate concepts of time? The remedial specialist must probe to find the answers to such questions and organize programs in response to them. Otherwise, the foundations for progressive linguistic skill development—reading and writing—may be weakened.

REMEDIAL PRINCIPLES

As indicated throughout this discussion, a remedial language program is based on evaluative findings and impressions. These data, in the context of an educational setting, should identify a child's linguistic capabilities and weaknesses. They should constitute an assessment of needs on which program planning and implementation can be based. The diagnostic procedure as described, therefore, is organized to determine what the child can do rather than to investigate the etiologic underpinnings of the observable behavioral deviations.

That is not to say that diagnostic protocols designed to identify the etiologic bases of language problems should not be followed. On the contrary, such investigations are essential for at least three reasons: (1) parents want to know why their children demonstrate language problems, and it is the responsibility of professional workers to help them find the answers, (2) the need for intervention of a medical and/or social-emotional nature may be indicated and should be instituted as part of the total remedial program, and (3) from an academic standpoint it is helpful to establish relationships between known conditions and observable behaviors. Indeed, a multidisciplinary etiologically based study of a child with a language problem is essential, though it must be placed into a perspective of educational value.

Rarely do etiologic-based findings provide direction for planning and implementing programs for children with language disorders. First, these findings tend to categorize children into diagnostic classifications (learning-disabled, mentally retarded, emotionally impaired, mildly brain damaged, etc.) which in themselves sometimes fail to denote the causes of the problem. For example, the designation of a language disorder as secondary to a learning disability of mental retardation qualifies one descriptive term with another; it does not indicate the etiologic bases of the alleged primary condition (the learning disability or mental retardation).

Second, such classifications do not define the unique linguistic needs of the children within each category. They imply an in-group homogeneity of needs rather than a highly individualized, personalized program of language development for each child. Yet regardless of the classificatory designation— mentally retarded, mildly brain damaged, learning-disabled, emotionally disturbed—the language needs of a group are as specific and different as each of the children within it.

Because of these circumstances, the emphasis of the clinical-educational evaluation should be based on a broader behavioristic viewpoint. It should stress description rather than classification—what the child *does* over what he or she *is*. It should indicate how the language problem at once reflects and inflects learning.

A clinical-educational approach, furthermore, views remediation as a process of continuing evaluation. It establishes the success level of a child relative to a specific linguistic skill, identifies the target behavior, outlines an incremental plan to facilitate the development of this behavior, and modifies the plan to meet the changing needs of the child. It progresses from the gross to the fine, from the concrete to the abstract. As Wallace and Kauffman (1973) suggest, remedial instruction is precisely organized in a sequential manner to insure that one skill is based on another and that each progressively leads to the established goal.

A major problem encountered in programs of diagnostic teaching involves the unwillingness or inability of educators to present tasks at a level sufficiently low to insure consistent success on the part of the child. Even if the target behavior is clearly identified and progressive steps have been outlined to achieve it, there seems to be a tendency for educators to provide remedial stimulation several levels above the child's capabilities. This approach encourages the child to leap from an observable level of performance to a superficial display of the desired behavior instead of reaching the goal in incremental units. Its outcomes include rote counting instead of the development of number concepts, programed answers to questions that are not understood, or mouthing words on a page instead of reading.

An illustration of exemplary diagnostic teaching should clarify the application of these principles. It involves the case of a six-year-old child who experienced decoding difficulties related to an apparent auditory sequencing problem. Although the child was able to comprehend and follow single stage directions, he became confused when faced with double or triple stage instructions unless they were provided one segment at a time. For example, if told, "Fold your paper," he would do so. However, if told, "Fold your paper and print your name on top," he became perplexed unless the total direction was divided into its three stages, each offered one at a time (fold your paper—show me the top—print your name there). To complicate the issue, the child's defensive reactions led him to begin to follow most directions before they had been completed; he seemed to fear that if he did not react immediately, he would fail totally. As a result, in the process of completing the first stage, he seemed to miss subsequent stages and looked around to see what others were doing, sometimes creating a disturbance.

On the basis of initial evaluative procedures, it was determined that a major goal for this child should be to enable him to follow three stage directions. Diagnostic probing revealed that he consistently experienced success when faced with a single verbal or nonverbal stimulus. He was unable to repeat a sequence of two or three nonverbal sounds, such as tapping, as he immediately reacted to the first before the entire stimulus series had been completed.

As a result, the following progressive objectives were organized to achieve the target behavior: (1) stepping over one to four two-by-four boards (placed railroad-track style) in response to one to four handclaps, waiting for the entire stimulus before starting; (2) dropping one to four blocks into a container under the same circumstances; (3) identifying one to four noisemakers in the sequence in which they were presented; (4) following single stage directions with familiar materials; (5) following one to three stage directions with familiar materials; (6) following single stage directions of any sort.

This plan illustrates a progression that moves in incremental units from the child's level of success to the desired behavior. It provides success experiences and learning opportunities at each level by breaking the desired skill into successive subskills. It moves from the gross to the fine, from the concrete to the abstract. It was tailored to the needs of the child and reflects creativity in diagnostic teaching and remedial skill development.

INTERDISCIPLINARY ASPECTS OF
LANGUAGE REMEDIATION

As services in schools have increased in number and sophistication, a wider range of educational personnel has become involved in the identification, evaluation, and program planning for children with language disorders. Rarely is the educational management of these children limited to the service of a single discipline. Instead, an interdisciplinary team approach is utilized, and the team may include a speech pathologist, reading specialist, classroom teacher, psychologist, learning disabilities specialist, principal, special education director, counselor, social worker, and the parents (Robertson and Freeman, 1974).

One of the critical features of the team approach is the determination of who is going to what to whom. A clinical-educational approach, as previously discussed, requires the coordination of historical information, observations of behavior, and test results. In the case of a given child and an educational team composed of members whose professional competencies and functions frequently overlap, who is responsible for the provision of such data; who assumes the role of the primary case manager?

With regard to children with language disorders, it appears that at least three disciplines—speech pathology, reading, and learning disabilities—increasingly have vested interests. The specialists in these areas have fundamental concerns about the relationships among a child's linguistic competence, academic achievement, and personal-social adjustment. Although each may view the presenting problems in terms of his or her own specialization, the professional roles often overlap.

An educational-team approach is based on the premise that the competencies of each member will be integrated into a unified program. This premise serves to eliminate professional territorial boundaries in favor of providing the most comprehensive service by the most competent providers, whoever they may be. The premise requires matching a child's needs to the educator or educators who are most able to meet them.

Although speech pathologists and reading specialists increasingly are cognizant of the relationship between oral language development and the acquisition of basic reading skills, few reading specialists have had formal course work in oral language development; most speech pathologists have little training or background related to reading. Each discipline independently may provide the most competent service to some children. For example, children whose reading problems are not based on primary language disorders clearly fall within the prerogatives of the reading specialist; similarly, children whose communicative disorders do not interfere with reading skills may be served exclusively by speech pathologists. However, in the case of other children, the two must meet on common ground to plan and implement unified strategies based on each other's strengths.

In accord with current practices in academic training, reading specialists should anticipate that most speech pathologists will have knowledge about language acquisition and its relation to the normal development of children, the varying disorders of language, distinctions between language differences (dialectical variations) and language disorders, and strategies for evaluation and remediation. Speech pathologists, on the other hand, may expect reading specialists to have knowledge about the developmental reading process, alternative strategies to teach reading, skills related to word analysis and reading comprehension, and techniques for the diagnosis and remediation of reading problems.

Because of variations in the training, background, and experience of each professional worker, however, these general expectations may prove inadequate. In specific situations, therefore, each team member should reveal his or her own strengths and weaknesses and utilize the other as a resource for personal continuing education. Under such conditions the distinctions between professional roles become less important than the common goal of providing the best available program to the child with a language problem.

A final word relates to classroom teachers and the need to enlist their support in the remedial language programs. Regardless of which member of the support staff takes the lead in the implementation of the plan for a child, this plan should be integrated into the school program. One of the chief challenges in doing so involves convincing instructional personnel that the development of auditory-verbal skills significantly relates to a child's academic achievement in other language modes. Even speech pathologists and reading specialists, both concerned with the continuum of language functions, are not yet committed to this concept on a widespread basis. Therefore, it is not surprising that other educators frequently are unaware of the integrative aspects of linguistic skills.

Experience has demonstrated that the most effective way to interpret language problems to classroom teachers is through emphasis on description rather than on classification. To say that a child has a "syntax problem" is insufficient; it tends to legitimize the child's failures as they exist. It provides no information to teachers regarding the specific skills on which to capitalize in order to promote educational objectives within the classroom.

Frequent consultation between specialists and teachers is necessary regarding a child's changing linguistic skills and abilities and the effects of his or her limitations on achieving success in the classroom. When such discussions emphasize behavioral descriptions, a child-centered rather than a disorder-centered conference is promoted (Freeman, 1969). Further, the descriptive analyses provided by specialists are more understandable than the diagnostic vernacular which often is used. Descriptions also may corroborate some of the teachers' impressions, immediately indicating areas of mutual concern.

A behavioristic context for consultations also helps to demonstrate that the overall structure of a language program is similar to that with which most educators are familiar. In many ways the approaches used to enable a child to learn appropriate language patterns resemble teachers' daily goals with respect to other skills. The individual characteristics of a child, on the one hand, and the application of principles and theories of learning, on the other, are common concerns of specialists and classroom teachers. These points should be highlighted in facilitating integrating of remedial programs and daily classroom activities; they promote the establishment of a comfortable communicative environment in which a child's acquisition of language skills can be related to other aspects of her or his behavior and school adjustment.

SUMMARY

It is essential for speech pathologists and reading specialists to cooperate in the planning and implementing of remedial programs for children whose reading failures are related to primary language disorders. The clinical-educational scheme presented here for the evaluation of children's primary language skills promotes such cooperation. The approach is designed to assess a child's linguistic code and conceptual system in a behavioristic context. It stresses the overlapping areas of concern of speech pathologists and reading specialists, the need to account for the integrative aspects of language modes, and the creation of an environment in which professional workers may engage in those areas of assessment and remediation in which each is most competent.

REFERENCES

Bloom, L. *Language Development: Form and Function in Emerging Grammars,* Cambridge, Mass.: MIT Press, 1970.

Brown, R. *A First Language: The Early Stages,* Cambridge, Mass.: Harvard University Press, 1973.

Burgemeister, B. B., L. H. Blum, and I. Lorge *Columbia Mental Maturity Scale,* New York: Harcourt Brace Jovanovich, 1972.

Carroll, J. B. "Words, Meanings and Concepts," *Harvard Educational Review* 1 (1964): 178–202.

Carrow, E. "Assessment of Speech and Language in Children," in J. E. McLean, D. E. Yoder, and R. L. Schiefelbusch, eds., *Language Intervention with the Retarded: Developing Strategies,* Baltimore: University Park Press, 1972.

Carrow, E. *Carrow Elicited Language Inventory,* Austin, Texas: Learning Concepts, 1974.

Chappell, G. E. "A Cognitive-Linguistic Intervention Program: Basic Concept Formation Level," *Language Speech and Hearing Services in Schools,* 1976 (in press).

Dunn, L. M. *Peabody Picture Vocabulary Test,* Circle Pines, Minn.: American Guidance Service, 1965.

Freeman, G. G. "An Educational-Diagnostic Approach to Language Problems," *Speech and Hearing Services in Schools* **1,** 4 (1971): 23–30.

Freeman, G. G. "The Speech Clinician—As a Consultant," in R. J. VanHattum, ed., *Clinical Speech in the Schools,* Springfield, Ill.: Charles C. Thomas, 1969.

Frostig, M., and D. Horne *The Frostig Program for the Development of Visual Perception,* Chicago: Follett, 1964.

Gesell, A., et al. *The First Five Years of Life,* New York: Harper and Brothers, 1940.

Johnson, D. G., and H. R. Mykelbust *Learning Disabilities: Educational Principles and Practices,* New York: Grune and Stratton, 1967.

Kavanaugh, J. F., ed. *Communicating by Language: The Reading Process,* Bethesda, Md.: U. S. Dept. Health, Education, and Welfare, National Institutes of Health, 1968.

Kephart, N. C. *The Slow Learner in the Classroom,* Columbus, Ohio: Merrill, 1960.

Kirk, S. A., and J. Elkins "Characteristics of Children Enrolled in the Child Service Demonstration Centers," *Journal of Learning Disabilities* **8** (1975): 630–637.

Lee, L. L. *Developmental Sentence Analysis,* Evanston, Ill.: Northwestern University Press, 1974.

Lee, L. L. "Developmental Sentence Types: A Method for Comparing Normal and Deviant Syntactic Development," *Journal of Speech and Hearing Disorders* **31** (1966): 311–330.

Lee, L. L. *Northwestern Syntax Screening Test,* Evanston, Ill.: Northwestern University Press, 1971.

Lerea, L. "Assessing Language Development," *Journal of Speech and Hearing Research* **1** (1958): 75–85.

Montessori, M. *The Montessori Method,* Cambridge, Mass.: Robert Bentley, 1965.

Piaget, J. *The Language and Thought of the Child,* Cleveland: World, 1955.

Rees, N. S. "The Speech Pathologist and the Reading Process," *ASHA* **16** (1974): 255–258.

Richardson, S. O. "Language Training for Mentally Handicapped Children," in R. L. Schiefelbusch and R. H. Copeland, eds., *Language and Mental Retardation,* New York: Holt, Rinehart and Winston, 1967.

Robertson, M. L. and G. G. Freeman "Applying Diagnostic Information to Decisions about Placement and Treatment," *Language Speech and Hearing Services in Schools* **5** (1974): 187–193.

Stark, J. S. "Reading Failure: A Language-Based Problem," *ASHA* **17** (1975): 832–834.

Strauss, A. A., and L. E. Lehtinen *Psychopathology and Education of the Brain-Injured Child,* New York: Grune and Stratton, 1947.

Venezky, R. L. "Spelling-to-Sound Correspondences," in J. J. Kavanaugh, ed., *Communicating by Language: The Reading Process,* Bethesda, Md.: U. S. Dept. Health, Education, and Welfare, National Institutes of Health, 1968.

Wallace, G., and J. M. Kauffman *Teaching Children with Learning Problems,* Columbus, Ohio: Merrill, 1973.

Wepman, J. M. *Auditory Discrimination Test,* Chicago: n.p. 1958.

Zigmond, N. K., and R. Cicci, *Auditory Learning,* Sioux Falls, S. D.: Adapt Press, 1968.

Appendix:
Sample of Language Tests
Organized According to Table 7.1

(A) Encoding/Phonemes

Fisher-Logemann Test of Articulation Competence
Houghton Mifflin Company
Boston, Massachusetts

Goldman-Fristoe Test of Articulation
American Guidance Service, Inc.
Publisher's Building
Circle Pines, Minnesota

McDonald Deep Test of Articulation
Stanwix House, Inc.
3020 Chartiers Avenue
Pittsburgh, Pennsylvania

Photo Articulation Test
Interstate Printers
Danville, Illinois

Templin-Darley Tests of Articulation
Bureau of Educational Research and Services
State University of Iowa
Iowa City, Iowa

(B) Decoding/Phonemes

Goldman-Fristoe-Woodcock Test of Auditory Discrimination
American Guidance Service, Inc.
Publisher's Building
Circle Pines, Minnesota

Short Test of Sound Discrimination (Templin)
M. Berry and J. Eisenson
Speech Disorders (Appendix 3)
Appleton-Century-Crofts, 1956

Wepman Auditory Discrimination Test
Joseph M. Wepman, Ph.D.
950 E. 59th Street
Chicago, Illinois

(C) Encoding/Semantics

Michigan Picture Vocabulary Test (Subtest of the Michigan Picture Language Inventory)
Speech and Hearing Clinic
University of Michigan
1111 E. Catherine Street
Ann Arbor, Michigan

(D) Decoding/Semantics

Peabody Picture Vocabulary Test
American Guidance Service
720 Washington Avenue, S.E.
Minneapolis, Minnesota

Van Alstyne Picture Vocabulary Test
Harcourt, Brace, and World
Tarrytown, New York

(E) Encoding/Syntax

Carrow Elicited Language Inventory
Learning Concepts
2501 N. Lamar
Austin, Texas 78705

Northwestern Syntax Screening Test
Northwestern University
Evanston, Illinois

(F) Decoding/Syntax

Assessment of Children's Language Comprehension
Consulting Psychologists Press
599 College Avenue
Palo Alto, California 94306

Northwestern Syntax Screening Test
Northwestern University
Evanston, Illinois

Test for Auditory Comprehension of Language
Learning Concepts
2501 N. Lamar
Austin, Texas 78705

1. Encoding and Decoding

Action-Agent Test
A. Gesell *et al., The First Five Years of Life,* Harper, 1940

Kent EGY Scale
Kent, Series of Emergency Scales, The Psychological Corporation, 1946

2. Language Batteries

Communicative Evaluation Chart From Infancy to Five Years
Educators Publishing Service
75 Moulton Street
Cambridge, Massachusetts 02138

Detroit Tests of Learning Aptitude (Language Subtests)
Bobbs-Merrill Co.
4300 W. 62nd Street
Indianapolis, Indiana

Hannah Gardner Preschool Language Screening Test
Joyce Publications
18702 Bryant Street
P.O. Box 458
Northridge, California 91324

Illinois Test of Psycholinguistic Abilities
University of Illinois
Urbana, Illinois

Preschool Language Scale
Charles E. Merrill
1300 Alum Creek Drive
Columbus, Ohio 43216

Utah Test of Language Development
Communication Research Associates
P.O. Box 11012
Salt Lake City, Utah 84111

Chapter 8

AN INTERDISCIPLINARY APPROACH TO THE ASSESSMENT AND MANAGEMENT OF SEVERE LANGUAGE-LEARNING PROBLEMS

NATHANIEL A. PETERS • *Oakland Schools, Pontiac, Michigan*

The resolution of complex problems through a cooperative sharing of diagnostic and intervention responsibilities has contributed to the solution of seemingly overwhelming societal problems. For example, improved treatment strategies for the mentally impaired and severely motor-impaired child can be attributed to the combined efforts of educators, physical therapists, psychologists, rehabilitation engineers, physicians, speech and hearing specialists, computer scientists, and vocational rehabilitation specialists. Any of these specialties functioning in isolation can address themselves to only a facet of the child's total functioning—just a glimmer of the child's "hidden wholeness," to paraphrase Thomas Merton. It is the individual with complex problems who benefits from multidisciplinary intervention strategies in at least two ways: (1) through the increased expertise brought to bear on the problems, and (2) from the level of commitment of individual team members. If a person plays a role in the decision making, he or she will make a more concerted effort to see that the intervention program is carried out successfully. Conversely, if major intervention decisions are made by one individual or by a nucleus of "key professionals" and then are channeled as directives to other people interacting with the individual, the probability of full cooperation by the individual receiving the directive is diminished. In some cases, those who are on the receiving end of such directives feel professionally disenfranchised and even consciously or subconsciously subvert intervention as if to prove the "experts" incorrect.

RATIONALE FOR AN INTERDISCIPLINARY PERSPECTIVE

The complicated set of interrelationships, particularly between learning disorders and linguistic, socioeconomic, biological, and psychological variables, necessitates interdisciplinary investigation and treatment of serious difficulties in learning. A thorough understanding of the more serious problems in learning transcends the knowledge of any one individual or profession. To provide a seriously disabled learner with appropriate treatment demands comprehensive assessment. Obviously, the realities of comprehensive assessment will be related to such factors as: (1) severity of the problem; (2) associated disorders, such as emotional or behavioral problems, primary language problems, chronic health problems, or peripheral sensory defects; (3) age of the child; (4) availability of well-qualified professionals to participate on the interdisciplinary team; (5) financial resources of the school district; and (6) location of diagnostic and treatment facility, i.e., elementary/secondary school, regional education center, or community mental health center. These factors, as well as other related variables, determine the composition of an interdisciplinary team. In all teams there will be a nucleus of specialists, usually the classroom teacher, the remedial specialist (clinical educator,* reading consultant/specialist, learning disability specialist, or speech and hearing consultant), the school psychologist, and the speech and hearing specialist. Depending on the specific nature of the problem, social workers, neuropsychologists, psychiatrists, vocational rehabilitation specialists, and other specialists can be called on to contribute their expertise.

TEAM COMPOSITION

Not all teams are comprised of the same professionals. More often than not, the composition of an interdisciplinary team reflects the location of the intervention. Landreth, Jacquot, and Allen (1969) describe a university-based pupil appraisal center comprised of counseling, reading, and speech and hearing specialists. Kappelman and Ganter (1970) describe a hospital-based interdisciplinary "school health team" composed of a pediatrician, a clinical psychologist, a psychiatric social worker, a social work assistant, a speech and hearing specialist, a psychometrician, and an experimental psychologist. To complement this team, "an educational consultant from the school system's special education division provides liaison between the clinic and the school." Elaborating on an amalgam of the university-based and hospital-based interdisciplinary teams, Wolcott (1972) describes a team comprised of psychoeducational and medical specialties: a neuropsychologist, a social worker, an occupational therapist, a speech therapist, an educator, and a pediatric neurologist. At times a psychiatrist, an ophthalmologist, and an otolaryngologist are consulted on specific cases.

---

* For a discussion of this role, see Chapter 13.

Caution must be exercised to control the tendency to assume that the more members there are on a team, the better the service. Size is not the critical variable; the potential usefulness of the diagnosis is. A cast of thousands of individuals who are only peripherally involved in the actual remediation of a serious learning disability or who have never attempted to teach a child with a language-comprehension or reading problem will not generate recommendations imbued with remedial strategies that facilitate learning in a classroom or clinic setting.

Presently, most state legislation has created *de jure* interdisciplinary teams which operate in the school rather than in a university or medical setting. Michigan, for example, has mandated the creation of educational planning and placement committees which have as part of their responsibility determining a pupil's eligibility to receive special educational programs and/or services and establishing instructional goals and identifying outcomes expected as a result of the special education placement. State law requires that as a minimum, the committee shall be comprised of a representative of the administrative personnel serving the child (building principal and/or special education director), diagnostic personnel (school psychologist, reading specialist, speech and language specialist, teacher consultant, school nurse, mental or public health representatives, or other clinical practitioners, including private-sector physicians and psychologists), and instructional personnel (special education, general and vocational education teachers, teacher consultants, occupational and physical therapists, work-study coordinators, representatives from community agencies, such as vocational rehabilitation). The child's parents complete the composition of the team. Obviously, it would be neither economically practical nor programmatically valuable to have representatives from each of these disciplines present at a thorough interdisciplinary evaluation. Each child and the problems she or he presents are unique. It is incumbent on the professional who has major responsibility for the child (depending on the setting, a psychologist, remedial specialist, or physician) to determine what kind of supportive information is required to serve the child or young adult in question. For an interdisciplinary team to function properly, each individual's role must be clearly defined.

SPECIFIC ROLES OF INTERDISCIPLINARY TEAM PERSONNEL

To clarify role definition, possible interdisciplinary team appraisals will be discussed as they apply to either elementary or secondary students. This division is predicated on the assumption that the composition of the interdisciplinary team varies with the student's age. For example, it would be highly unlikely to find a vocational rehabilitation specialist functioning on a team planning for an elementary age child, or a speech and hearing specialist participating on a team planning for a secondary school student. However, with most learners experiencing academic difficulty, an interdisciplinary team is usually comprised of a nucleus of individuals: remedial specialist, psychologist, classroom teacher, social worker, and parents; other specialists should be consulted if additional information is required to provide a more accurate diagnosis.

MEMBERS OF THE ELEMENTARY SCHOOL TEAM

The age of the referred child, the setting of the diagnosis, and the possibility of dysfunctions associated with learning difficulties, such as peripheral sensory defects, neurological impairment, and chronic health difficulties, determine the composition of the interdisciplinary team.

Parents

Parents are the most important participants in interdisciplinary team planning for a child. Although child specialists have long been cognizant of the awesome role parents play in educating their children, only limited recognition has been afforded parents as allies of professionals serving children. When examining the realities of the complex interaction between home and school, one is immediately aware of how little parents are included in extending, reinforcing, and broadening the wide array of social and cognitive skills important in the classroom. Zigler (1972) has assessed the deleterious effects of failing to involve parents in both educational planning and programming for children and predicts that educational programs conducted in isolation from the home and without parental involvement will inevitably fail.

Classroom teacher

Another key person who is sometimes neglected as a source of information in interdisciplinary evaluation of learning disorders is the classroom teacher. The typical classroom teacher has invaluable information about how the referred child learns in the natural milieu where most academic learning takes place—the child's classroom. The classroom teacher can provide the team with such data as the child's level of distractibility, ability to process oral directions, relationships with peers, and the degree to which a child copes with frustrations in learning.

Information must be obtained from the teacher prior to a final staffing.

In some settings the teacher is invited only to the final meeting of the team. It is not uncommon at this meeting for the teacher to be deluged with information about the child that is both contributory and noncontributory to the treatment of the child's problem. Because of time limitations, little information is obtained from the classroom teacher. Understandably, when they are only on the receiving end of the information flow, some teachers get the impression that they are peripheral to the intervention program; ideally, however, they are one of the key agents for change. The teacher should be regarded as a source of information throughout the diagnostic process. If the teacher cannot observe some of the assessment or clinical teaching, the team conducting the evaluation should communicate via telephone, questionnaires, or checklists with the classroom teacher. No matter how sophisticated or thorough an interdisciplinary assessment might be, the intervention program will have a minimal impact without the involvement and understanding of the team's diagnostic conclusions and recommendations by the classroom teacher.

Remedial specialist

Major responsibility for assessment and clinical teaching will be assumed by the remedial specialist, who might be trained as a remedial reading specialist, speech and hearing specialist, learning disability specialist, or school psychologist. The remedial specialist will diagnose strengths and weaknesses in the child's processing of verbal and written symbols, perceptual-motor, and cognitive functioning. It is hoped that the remedial specialist will be a thoroughly trained child specialist whose training and professional expertise will correspond to that of the role of clinical educator, explained in Chapter 13. If the remedial specialist does not possess the training necessary to function as a clinical educator, he or she must exercise self-constraint so as to avoid performing diagnostic and intervention strategies for which he or she is not trained.

A major role of the remedial specialist is to integrate the findings from noneducational members of the interdisciplinary team into the educational program for the referred child. Since it is the remedial specialist who works the most closely with the classroom teacher, it is critical that he or she have had extensive experience with the problems faced by the classroom teacher, who is attempting to both individualize instruction for a severely disabled learner and assess and develop intervention programs for language-reading disabled children.

School psychologist

The level of training and professional experiences will determine the role the psychologist performs on the interdisciplinary team. Ideally, all interdisciplinary teams evaluating children with learning problems should include a school psychologist, who functions as more than a psychometrist. Although intellectual, personality, and perceptual-motor assessment can contribute valuable information for educational programming, broadly trained psychologists can provide additional services to the interdisciplinary team. Specifically, such services might include: consultation with the parents of the referred child to assist them in understanding the emotional-behavioral components of the child's learning problem; psychological counseling of children and parents who are experiencing difficulty coping with the frustrations and stresses that are frequently caused by academic failure; and consultation with the child's classroom teacher in the development and implementation of procedures and techniques designed to facilitate learning.

Child psychiatrist

Some interdisciplinary teams also include a child psychiatrist, who collaborates with the remedial specialist and school psychologist to investigate possible constitutional-emotional components of the child's learning problem. On some interdisciplinary teams the child psychiatrist provides consultation and counseling to the referred child, his or her parents, or both. If psychoactive drugs might be indicated as adjuncts to psychoeducational intervention, the child psychiatrist would be instrumental in coordinating the efforts of the parent, teacher, and remedial specialist in assessing the effectiveness of the psychopharmacological intervention. As with all specialists on an interdisciplinary team, caution must be exercised in selecting a child psychiatrist who thoroughly understands the complexities of learning disorders and who has had extensive experience with normal children in public school settings. A psychiatrist whose training has been mostly in a medically oriented treatment facility with children who manifest signs of severe psychopathology will in most cases be of limited value to the interdisciplinary team evaluating children with learning problems.

Social worker

The social worker interviews the child and parents in an effort to understand the home milieu. In some cases the social worker will assemble past social, psychological, and medical histories for evaluation by the team. If it is felt that counseling will aid the child and family in overcoming the child's learning deficit, the social worker will share responsibility with the psychologist and/or psychiatrist for appropriate psychotherapeutic intervention.

Neurologist

Some interdisciplinary teams also make use of a consulting neurologist to assist the team in determining if neurological impairment is a contributing variable to the child's learning problem. Depending on the major presenting problem, a neurologist might utilize electro-encephalographic techniques or skull X-ray films, in addition to the standard neurological evaluation to complete the assessment.

Two suggestions can be offered on the inclusion of a neurologist. First, in most cases, do not expect the neurologist to intervene beyond the diagnostic level. The neurologist is a skilled diagnostician whose expertise does not lie in the remediation of dysfunctions of the learning process. Second, an educationally oriented team should insist that a neurologist have both board certification as a pediatric neurologist and extensive experience with school-age children.

Neuropsychologist

Clinical neuropsychology is fast becoming a discipline capable of providing diagnostic and treatment information to the interdisciplinary team. Until recently, neuropsychology as a profession was closely identified with the profession of neurology in the assessment of cognitive and sensory-motor skills associated with neurological disease. However, in recent years, it has begun to shift away from diagnosis and assessment toward therapy and remediation (Costa, 1976). Neuropsychologists can, among other things, provide the team with information about brain functioning and its implication for remedial intervention with reading-disabled children or about language retraining for children experiencing language-production or comprehension problems.

Pediatrician

A pediatrician who is part of the interdisciplinary team first takes a medical history and then gives the child a physical examination to determine underlying physical problems that might contribute to the learning disorder. If physical abnormalities are detected, the pediatrician usually recommends referral to other child specialists, such as audiologists or ophthalmologists. Since most interdisciplinary teams do not have the services of a pediatrician, it is strongly recommended that evaluation teams see that all children referred to them have had a recent physical examination.

MEMBERS OF THE SECONDARY SCHOOL TEAM

It is my bias that the interdisciplinary team for secondary, or high school, students should in certain very essential characteristics vary from the interdisciplinary team for elementary school children. Most importantly, the team must include as many of the student's content teachers (English, science, social studies, mathematics) as can possibly involve themselves in the assessment and intervention process. (In Chapter 13 I formulate caveats about diagnostic and treatment facilities that are physically and, more important to the continuity of intervention, psychologically removed from the school. The potential problems created by this distance are compounded with secondary school students. By virtue of their subject-matter training, content teachers understand little about child development, language development, or the reading process. They find it difficult to fathom that a ninth or tenth grader may experience difficulty learning because of a serious reading problem. Sadly, young adults with academic problems are sometimes perceived as unmotivated, uninterested in intellectual subjects, or just plain unintelligent by their content-area teachers. Carlson (1972) suggests that the typical young adult will in most cases spend about 90 percent of the average day with content teachers rather than with specialists who understand his or her problem and are sensitive to the resulting frustrations. Content-area teachers must be helped to understand what they can do to facilitate learning in a young adult. Content specialists must come to understand that he or she is a most critical component in the intervention process; without their full cooperation, gains will be minimal.

To elicit full cooperation of content teachers, several adjustments must be made in the interdisciplinary team. Foremost, the remedial specialist should have a thorough understanding of secondary school curriculum and the cognitive-linguistic demands of the secondary disciplines. Preferably, this person should have had high school teaching experience, so as to fully understand the pressures placed on a secondary American and world history instructor who faces more than 150 students and makes two preparations daily. Secondary teachers will respond more favorably to a remedial specialist who can provide them with techniques for reducing the complexity levels of textual material, suggest workable teaching strategies, and locate supplemental material written at lower levels of complexity. The content teacher must be able to relate to the diagnostic conclusions and recommendations. To tell a high school English teacher who is doing his or her best to teach a unit on the American short story that a child has an auditory sequencing problem will understandably draw only a vacant stare. Even if the teacher understands the terminology, it is doubtful whether she or he could incorporate such specific diagnostic statements into teaching methodologies planned for a class of 30 or more students, without first being given longer-term guidance on how to work with students who are severely disabled learners. It is well worth the time of a secondary remedial specialist to meet with all content teachers individually if they cannot be assembled as a team. To plan an intervention program for a secondary student without involving content teachers is to significantly lower the probability of a positive out-come.

VOCATIONAL TEACHERS AND VOCATIONAL REHABILITATION SPECIALISTS

Before beginning this discussion, I want to emphasize that in no way do I believe that all young adults with learning problems should be channeled into vocational education programs. However, if a young adult shows inter-est in vocational or technical programs offered in high school or after high school, an interdisciplinary team should help the student explore this possi-bility. To do otherwise would be a violation of professional responsibility to a referred young adult.

A vocational education teacher would be asked to affiliate with the team if during the evaluation it was found that a referred young adult had an expressed interest in a vocational area. It has been our experience at the Oakland Schools Reading and Language Center that vocational educators are willing members of an interdisciplinary team. The vocational teacher can discuss with the young adult the specifics of a given vocational program and even invite the student to participate on a trial basis in the vocational program. If the referred client elects to participate in the vocational pro-gram, the remedial specialist or reading consultant can then assist the voca-tional teacher in selecting reading materials and adjusting the reading de-mands for the referred student.

A federally funded research project conducted by the Oakland Schools Reading and Language Center (Butz, 1972) forcefully underscores the need for a systematic evaluation of the reading demands of vocational subjects. Butz found that many textbooks used in vocational courses were written four to five grade levels beyond the mean comprehension range of students placed in the course. For example, the textbook utilized in a course on air conditioning servicing was written at a level of complexity four grades be-yond the mean comprehension scores of young adults in the course. Between 50 and 67 percent of the students enrolled in the class achieved comprehen-sion scores below the mean readability of the textbook. Assuming that these data can be generalized to other vocational-technical programs, the message is clear. Vocational teachers need to be incorporated into the interdisciplin-ary team.

Taking on a different role from the vocational teacher, the vocational rehabilitation specialist assists the interdisciplinary team in determining if the referred client is eligible for vocational rehabilitation services, especially services offered to post-high-school-age students. Usually this specialist will be an employee of the state agency responsible for vocational rehabilitation services and can be invited to participate on interdisciplinary teams.

PRESENT REALITIES OF INTERDISCIPLINARY INTERVENTION

No matter how sound in principle the concept of interdisciplinary intervention is, several realities must be reckoned with:

1. Interdisciplinary intervention is not widespread. In fact, only a small minority of children presenting problems are evaluated from a multidisciplinary perspective.

2. Some settings that provide interdisciplinary services are concerned only with diagnosis, leaving the classroom teacher to winnow and sift through a plethora of noncontributory diagnostic statements about sagittal and coronal circumference, facial asymmetry, external ocular movements, and the status of the deep tendon reflexes.

3. Interdisciplinary intervention is expensive. A school district must have the resources to compensate well-trained specialists. The expense is well justified if parents and teachers are able to obtain specific information about a child without following the usual treadmill from one specialist to another.

4. Interdisciplinary intervention demands a rare virtue in human interaction—the ability to cooperate among individuals who represent different professional orientations and training experiences.

Finally, the real test of the efficacy of the interdisciplinary team approach is the quality of information generated for teachers and parents by the team. The assessment results must be teacher- and parent-based and readily translatable into intervention appropriate for both school and home. To fail to communicate diagnostic information that is pertinent and jargon-free is to fail the purposes of an interdisciplinary team.

BIBLIOGRAPHY

Butz, Roy J. "End of Budget Period Report for *Vocational Reading Power Project*," MDE–0671, (ERIC listing pending), Pontiac, Michigan: Oakland Schools, 1972.

Carlson, Thorsten R., ed. *Administrators and Reading*, New York: Harcourt Brace Jovanovich, 1972.

Costa, Louis "Clinical Neuropsychology: Respice, Adspice, Prospice," *The INS Bulletin*, March 1976.

Kappelman, Murray M., and Robert S. Ganter "A Clinic for Children with Learning Disabilities, *Children* 17 (1970): 137–142.

Landreth, Garry L., Willard S. Jacquot, and Louis Allen "A Team Approach to Learning Disabilities," *Journal of Learning Disabilities* 2 (1969): 82–87.

Wolcott, George J. "Learning Disability a Cooperative Team Approach," *Wisconsin Medical Journal* 71 (October 1972): 223–226.

Zigler, Edward F. "Child Care in the 70's." *Inequality in Education,* Number Thirteen, Cambridge, Mass.: Harvard Center for Law and Education, December 1972.

Chapter 9

DIAGNOSIS OF READING PROBLEMS

CHARLES W. PETERS • *Oakland Schools, Pontiac, Michigan*

Diagnosis is a fundamental element in a reading program; without it, a program has no direction, accurate instructional decisions cannot be made, and appropriate pedagogical techniques or materials cannot be selected. For these reasons, we must closely examine the diagnostic process. Diagnosis is predicated on the precept that before one can accurately detect deficiencies a reader may possess, the diagnostician must have a thorough knowledge of the reading process. Most of the information that preceded this chapter dealt with either the reading process itself or its correlates (language development, sociolinguistics, and psychological difficulties). Obviously, it is very difficult, if not impossible, to diagnose or assess a phenomenon you do not understand. A comprehensive knowledge of the reading process is therefore imperative in deciding appropriate instructional methodology.

Before we delve into a detailed analysis of the diagnostic process, take a few seconds to write down as many words as possible that come into your mind when you think of the term "diagnosis." Once you have completed your list, compare it to the one that follows:

Reading tests	Judgments
Evaluation	Decisions
Assessment	Placement
Teaching	Grouping

Probably many of the terms you listed were very similar to these. Now check each word that you believe denotes diagnosis. How many did you check? If you checked any at all, you have fallen victim to a very pervasive problem that exists within the reading profession, namely, the interchanging of terms that should have *one* agreed-on usage. For example, some of the criticism levied against standardized reading tests can be related to a misuse of the term. Contrary to what some educators believe, the results obtained from reading tests are not synonymous with diagnosis. A reading test merely assesses the behaviors related to reading; diagnosis, by contrast, involves the use of many procedures (assessment, judgments, decisions, etc.), one of which may include the use of a standardized reading test.

DEFINING THE TERMS

Evaluation involves establishing tentative hypotheses, gathering information, and utilizing that information in formulating instructional decisions. Evaluation, as it relates to the reading process, is a systematic, comprehensive analysis of information. Varying types of information should be incorporated into the evaluative process. For example, such information might include scores from informal reading inventories, questionnaire results (to ascertain the effectiveness of a specific diagnostic procedure), comparison of test scores on a districtwide basis (to make certain administrative judgments and to determine the effectiveness of material). Thus evaluation can range from individual to districtwide programs. In short, evaluation is based on a series of identified activities which must be continuous and systematic.

Reading diagnosis is a microcosm of reading evaluation; both procedures are based on the scientific method of inquiry. Hypotheses must be developed, data gathered, and interpretations made. Diagnosis is a very comprehensive and complex process of attempting to determine what information is appropriate, what decisions have to be made, and what procedures are best utilized in implementing those decisions.

Reading tests assess the manifested behaviors associated with the reading process. As a result, tests represent the operational definition of that process. As Evans (1968, p. 43) cogently points out:

> When I ask you what you are teaching, don't show me your behavioral objectives; show me your post test. The post test is the ultimate operational measure of what you are trying to teach.

In other words, show me your reading tests, and I will tell you your definition of reading. Reading tests are, then, a collection of behaviors that reflect the reading process. Reading tests can be formal (standardized) or informal (without norms), group or individual, general or specific. The use of standardized reading tests is a much-debated issue in the field of reading. Some of the skepticism about standardized reading tests centers on what may be called an abuse of test results. Many times people who attempt to diagnose reading problems have selected an instrument or group of instruments that in no way will allow them to make accurate decisions about reading problems. Therefore, when the validity of the results is questioned, apparent inaccuracies are blamed on the instrument rather than on the process used in selecting a specific instrument. Such an inappropriate use of a test or tests has caused some people to confuse testing or assessment with diagnosis. Therefore, part of the problem that has developed in regard to diagnosis can be related to this misperception. A reading test is not synonymous with diagnosis.

This misperception, of course, helps illustrate one very important problem—too much testing without any type of interpretation. Tests have been used to evaluate programs, to assess a student's reading performance, and to group students. The validity of these uses of tests depends on the purposes for testing. This is a very important issue and will be discussed in greater detail later in this chapter.

Reading assessment is the systematic collection of data based on the systematic utilization of test and nontest procedures (interviews, personal teaching records, conversations with parents) which provide insights into reading behaviors. It is this systematic collection of information that allows diagnosis and evaluation to take place.

Reading measurement is the quantification of reading behavior. Presently the quantification of reading behaviors can be broken down into two very general approaches—the criterion-referenced approach and the norm-referenced approach. These approaches are discussed more fully later in this chapter.

Figure 9.1 gives two views of evaluation and diagnosis. In the diagram on the left, the various components are seen operating as isolated entities. The second view suggests that all components are related and that at the core

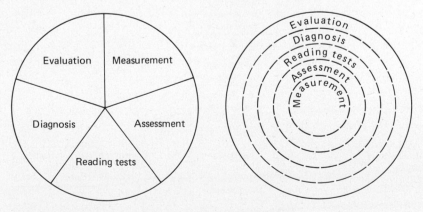

Fig. 9.1. Alternative views of evaluation and diagnosis.

of evaluation and diagnosis are assessment, measurement, and testing. It is the interrelation of those components that allows the diagnostic process to function.

DEVELOPING A DIAGNOSTIC MODEL

Diagnosis is an interrelated process through which a teacher attempts to ascertain the specific strengths and weaknesses of individual students. Diagnosis is, therefore, predicted on the systematic collection, interpretation, and utilization of information. However, a mere definition of terms does not provide the teacher or reading specialist with a conceptual framework from which sound diagnosis must flow. To make diagnosis functional, it must be broken down into several instructional components (see Fig. 9.2).

The diagnostic process must be based on a series of related steps and have as its ultimate goal a sound instructional program that seeks to build a balance between the student's strengths and weaknesses. First, the classroom teacher or reading specialist must *specify the decisions to be made*. In other words, before any instruments can be selected or information gathered, the diagnostician must have some idea as to what the information will be used for. The decision to be made might be as simple as determining which reading group a particular student will be assigned to or as complex as attempting to ascertain the possible causes of a specific reading disorder. Whatever the decision, it must be clearly delineated at the outset. Without such information, it is impossible to implement the other steps inherent in the diagnostic process.

Second, the information needed must be *described*. For instance, do you

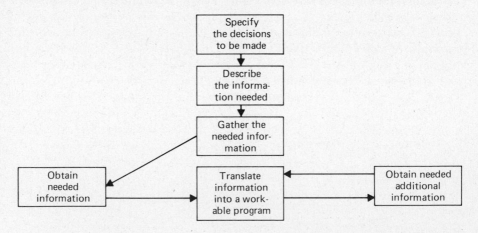

Fig. 9.2. The diagnostic process. (Adapted from Terry D. TenBrink, *Evaluation: A Practical Guide for Teachers*, New York: McGraw-Hill, 1974, pp. 12–19.)

need information about cognitive abilities or language development? Is it psychometric or personality information that is required? Regardless of the specified area, the teacher must be able to describe the needed information. One cannot obtain information unless one knows what is needed.

Third, the information must be *gathered*. This process involves several related steps. First, all existing information that is pertinent to the diagnosis must be located and its utility determined. Parents, personal teaching records, results of classroom work, and permanent records—all are resources to be consulted before any additional data are collected. However, the information utilized must be valid and reliable. This can be achieved by first eliminating any duplication of information and then deciding when and how to gather the additional information that is required. For example, would you use an informal reading inventory or informal observations or both? Would you, as a reading specialist at the secondary level, want to include the classroom teacher in the diagnosis? Would you utilize a checklist or questionnaire? All of these specific questions must be answered at this point in the diagnosis, for without answers to these questions, it is impossible to determine how the information will be gathered. The last step in the information-gathering process is to select or construct the instruments needed to gather the required information. This is a very important step in the process, because the information collected will be no better than the instrument(s) used. Related to the selection of appropriate instruments are such factors as the standards utilized in selection of the specified instrument(s), the validity and reliability of the instrument(s), and the appropriateness of criterion- or norm-referenced tests.

Fourth, the information must be *obtained*. At this point the reading specialist or classroom teacher must realize that in order to accurately diagnose possible causes of reading disability, other correlates of the reading process must be included in the diagnosis. This might involve the inclusion of other specialists (school psychologist, learning disabilities specialist, speech pathologist, psychiatrist). For a more detailed description of the interdisciplinary approach, see Chapters 8, 12, and 17.

Fifth, the information must be *analyzed* and *recorded*. In oral reading, for instance, an agreed-on marking system should be identified. In addition, one must determine whether a quantitative or qualitative analysis of errors will be utilized. This is an extremely important part of the diagnostic process, because it is here that some teachers, erroneously, terminate the process. The results must be translated into a program. This is why the teacher must at the outset identify the needed information, describe it, and then determine the process for collecting the information. If the teacher does not understand the purpose of each piece of information, it cannot be properly analyzed. For example, if I do not know the significance of the flashed untimed presentation of words on the Gates-McKillop Reading

Diagnostic Tests, I cannot translate those results into an effective program. A raw score is not tantamount to diagnosis.

Sixth, once the information has been analyzed, the teacher will have to determine whether it is sufficient or whether additional information is required. The need for additional information must be predicated on the results derived from existing information. The ultimate measure of the utility of any information is the degree to which it can be translated into a program that works.

The goal of this entire process is to identify the needed information, decide how the information should be collected, and then translate that information into a workable program. What follows is a more detailed explanation of each step in this process.

Specify the decisions to be made

At the outset the reading specialist or classroom teacher must clearly delineate the type of diagnostic decisions to be made. Contrary to popular belief, the first step is not to select the test or desired procedures needed to assess reading performance. How many people performing a diagnosis have been approached by a peer and asked, "What reading test should I use in my classroom?" Such a question implies that the test will provide all the necessary information. However uninsightful that question may seem, many individuals do not think beyond the test. All they are interested in acquiring is a score that either confirms or raises questions about individual performance. In other words, some teachers are more interested in *quantifying* than in *interpreting* reading performance. Such questionable practices in the name of diagnosis must be avoided. To a considerable extent, the success of the diagnosis ultimately depends on how accurately the teacher has identified the diagnostic decisions to be made. It is here that the diagnosis must begin, not with the selection of a test.

Specify the type of decision to be made   Teachers and administrators are confronted with many different types of decisions about reading performance —instructional, administrative, and evaluative. Table 9.1 presents a checklist of potential decisions and a means for categorizing each of those decisions. First, the teacher or administrator must identify the decision(s) to be made. For example, is the main concern placement in reading materials, skill groupings, or comparison of performance? Once the type of decision has been identified, it can be categorized as instructional (individual or group), administrative, or evaluative. Differentiating among the three categories should help simplify the description of the information needed, the method to use in gathering the information, and the procedure to employ in obtaining the information. Since these categories can be overlapping, it may be possible in some instances for an instructional decision to be categorized as

Table 9.1. Guide to decision making

	Instructional (group and individual)	Administrative	Evaluative
Determine placement in materials			
Evaluate the effectiveness of a program			
Determine instructional reading level to adopt material			
Determine strengths and weaknesses in specific skill areas			
Determine readiness skills			
Make decisions about grouping			
Assess effects of experimental and innovative programs			
Monitor progress of individual students			
Determine effectiveness of instructional procedure			
Determine individual placement			
Compare performance within levels			

either evaluative or administrative. The attempt is not to create arbitrary divisions, but rather to categorize the types of decisions to be made so that the appropriate diagnostic techniques can be utilized. Table 9.1 presents such a method for classifying decisions. However, it is obvious that not all decisions are diagnostic. Nevertheless, the strategies must vary with the decision, because part of the problem related to inadequate diagnosis can be attributed to pedagogically unsound diagnostic procedures. Unfortunately, in the past many diagnostic decisions were predicated more on the availability of an instrument than on its appropriateness. The first step in this model seeks to eradicate such inconsistencies.

Identify the level of diagnosis In attempting to categorize decisions, it is helpful to specify the type of detailed information desired. To facilitate this process, levels of diagnosis have been delineated. According to Otto, McMenemy, and Smith (1973), there are three levels of diagnosis—survey, specific, and intensive. This trichotomy is particularly useful in the interdisciplinary approach to diagnosis, because it is based on the assumption that the more complex the problem, the more intermeshed it will be with other complicating problems. This, of course, means the involvement of other professionals in the diagnostic process.

The primary concern at the survey level is to obtain a general overview of reading performance, perhaps by administering to all students such instruments as the Gates-MacGinitie Reading Tests, the Iowa Silent Reading Tests, or the Sequential Tests of Educational Progress. The results would be used to identify those students who need further diagnosis. The specific level of diagnosis is designed to collect such information. The primary concern at this level is to identify through individual assessment specific instructional strengths and weaknesses. Instruments used at this level might include the Gates-McKillop Reading Diagnostic Tests, the Stanford Diagnostic Reading Tests, or the Gilmore Oral Reading Test. Both the classroom teacher and reading specialist would be involved in the diagnosis.

If, as a result of previous attempts by the classroom teacher or reading specialist to determine the nature of the problem, there still is some doubt about the cause or causes of the disability, a more intensive diagnosis will be needed. At the intensive level, as the term implies, very specific information is obtained. For the more severely disabled child, the diagnostic process might begin here. Since the problem seems to be more complex at this level, other members of the interdisciplinary team should be involved. The important point is that the level of diagnosis must match the diagnostic information required. In considering the type of information needed, one must also identify the level at which the information will be sought.

Describe the information needed

The second step in the diagnostic process is to describe the information needed. At this point it becomes obvious just how important one's knowledge of the reading process is to conducting a successful diagnosis. Each teacher or reading specialist must have an understanding of how reading is operationally defined; for without such an understanding, it will be impossible to accurately describe the diagnostic information needed. This inability to adequately describe the information desired continues to contribute to a breakdown in the diagnostic process. Most people are perceptive enough to know when a reading problem exists, but they lack sufficient knowledge to identify those behaviors associated with the problem.

The inability of teachers to accurately describe the behaviors associated with the reading problems is readily apparent in the referral process. For example, many reading specialists frequently receive referrals from teachers who merely state that the child has some sort of problem with word recognition, without attempting to explain what specifically they mean by word-recognition problems. For this reason it is essential that the behaviors associated with word recognition be described. For instance, does the student need to know words in isolation or in context? Is knowledge of phonological and morphological processes important? Is the application of word-recognition skills in a variety of situations an essential requisite? Most likely an inadequate knowledge of word-recognition skills will be only part of the problem. In addition, the teacher should be concerned with such other related factors as auditory and visual perception, auditory and visual memory, sequencing, recognition of letters, as well as with language development and cognitive development.

The information sought by the reading specialist or classroom teacher also varies from level to level. For instance, at the secondary level, teachers are more concerned with critical reading skills, which means that the reading specialist is confronted with an additional problem—not knowing which specific comprehension skills are needed by a student to successfully survive in a specific content area. For example, if a social studies teacher refers a student to a reading specialist, the reading specialist must, in addition to possessing a well-defined concept of reading, be cognizant of how the social studies teacher has operationally defined reading in the context of his or her classroom. Therefore, the reading specialist must work closely with content teachers who refer students. A device such as the one mentioned in Chapter 13 will assist in getting content teachers to describe the specific information they seek. Without such information it is impossible for the reading specialist to adequately diagnose content-related reading problems. As these examples imply, diagnosis is only as detailed or sufficient as the information described.

In addition to instructural information, behaviors associated with other aspects of the reading process should be considered. For example, in some cases the classroom teacher or reading specialist might wish to have an intelligence test administered. If the problem is one of limited potential, the student may be working up to capacity and require adaptive instruction rather than remedial instruction. Likewise, it might be important to ascertain whether emotional disorders are inhibiting reading performance. If they are, they must be dealt with first, before any effective instructional program can be implemented. For this reason, input from all members of the interdisciplinary team is important. Once these decisions are made and the behaviors described, the next step in the process is to determine how to gather the information.

Gather the needed information

Determining how to gather information is a very crucial step in the diagnostic process, because many times teachers and reading specialists have merely duplicated existing information. In addition, teachers have tended to utilize external sources (commercially prepared materials) for collecting information rather than internal sources (informal observations, anecdotal records, informal tests, checklists, or informal reading inventories).

Existing internal sources should always be checked first. Many times classroom exercises may prove to be an invaluable source for diagnostic information, since classroom materials reflect the structural makeup of the reading program. For example, if comprehension is an area of concern, the classroom teacher could check the types of reading assignments utilized, the types of questions asked, and the type of materials read. In checking additional internal sources, the diagnostician should ask: Were there any standardized tests reported in the permanent record? How has progress in reading up to this point been determined? Does the student have a psychological profile? What outside agencies have been utilized? Have the parents been consulted? All of these factors might be useful sources of information.

External sources also provide important diagnostic information. There are several different types of external sources that should be considered by the classroom teacher or reading specialist. First, attitude inventories can be particularly useful. Research has shown that one's attitudes and interests have a significant effect on the comprehension process. Since many different types of inventories exist (Dulin and Chester, 1974; Estes, 1972; and Kennedy and Halenski, 1975), the teacher should select the one most suitable for her or his needs. Second, since individual personality traits are also significantly related to reading achievement, they too might serve as a potential source of information. For example, such personality traits as motivation, attention span, and maturity frequently affect reading performance. Third, although emotional characteristics have long been an enigma, such factors as antisocial behavior and aggressiveness may influence reading performance. Therefore, instruments that seek to identify emotional problems that might disrupt the instructional process might be utilized (see Chapter 6). Fourth, checklists designed to aid and structure informal observations can assist in the collection of information. Such lists can be used to gain insights into a student's self-concept, peer relationships, or interaction with teachers. The Durrell Analysis of Reading Difficulty contains a good example of a checklist designed for oral reading.

There are many varieties and many types of resources to consider when attempting to gather information. Therefore, the information itself should reflect the type of diagnosis the teacher desires. For example, most secondary-level educators have relied on a general measure of reading performance (e.g., Gates-MacGinitie Reading Tests, Nelson-Denny Reading Test, the Iowa Silent Reading Tests) to predict reading ability. However, Peters and Peters (1976) examined the interaction among general reading performance, specific reading performance (teacher-constructed content reading test), student self-evaluation (both cognitive and affective), teacher assessment of reading ability, and grades to ascertain which variables were the best predictors of reading performance. The results of their study seemed to indicate that each of the five variables was measuring significantly different ($<.001$) elements of the reading process. However, not all the variables seemed to be uniquely different. For example, grades and student attitudes (affective component) did not appear to provide information that was not already contributed by other measures. The single variable that seemed to be most predictive of reading performance when considered in conjunction with general and specific reading performance was the cognitive component of the Student Attitude Inventory.

The relationship among these variables seems to suggest that a diagnostic process that seeks to incorporate the student's assessment of his or her abilities provides valuable information. The results of their study seem to confirm the need to incorporate a number of variables into the diagnostic process. Further, the results suggest that those who are responsible for making instructional decisions based on reading performance need to be more concerned with the interaction among variables and the significance each variable has to the diagnostic process. An important implication drawn from this study is that there exists a need to systematize the utilization of such information, since not all variables are equally significant in contributing useful information. The message to teachers seems clear: utilize a number of sources, but be cognizant of the fact that each contributes different information and of varying utility.

Concurrent with the need to collect information that will contribute to the overall understanding of specific reading disorders, guidelines for selecting such information should be developed. TenBrink (1974, p. 134) has established four rules of thumb to help guide teachers in the selection process.

1. If the judgments and decisions are important and if it is relatively easy to obtain more accurate information, obtain the new information.

2. If any information you will obtain is likely to be no more accurate than what is available, use what is available.

3. If it is relatively easy to obtain new information, do so.

4. If more accurate information is needed but there is neither time nor money available for obtaining it, use what is available. But use it with caution, supplementing it with other information where possible. Continually seek confirmation (or lack of it) that the information you had was essentially correct.

Underlying these four guidelines is the assumption that all information must be both reliable and valid. Without reliable and valid information, the diagnosis becomes an exercise in futility. Methods for determining the reliability and validity of information will be discussed in a later section of this chapter.

Selecting or constructing information-gathering instruments   Much has been written in recent years on the differences between criterion- and norm-referenced tests. Before going on, however, see if you can distinguish between a criterion-referenced and a norm-referenced test item.

1. How does the farmer's impression of government control of railroads compare with the lawyer's view of government control of railroads?
   a) Both the farmer and the lawyer favor government control of the railroads.
   b) Both the farmer and the lawyer favor private ownership of the railroads.
   c) The farmer favors private ownership, whereas the lawyer favors government control.
   d) The farmer favors government control, whereas the lawyer favors private ownership.
   e) Neither takes a position in the article.

2. In the following sentence, "The planes went out to drop food and bullets to the *marooned* men," marooned means:
   a) Stranded
   b) Lonesome
   c) Worried
   d) Deserted
   e) Scared

If you had difficulty determining which item was taken from the criterion-referenced test and which item was taken from the norm-referenced test, do not become overly depressed or feel that you should repeat an introductory course in reading. Even the erudite would have difficulty with this task. Actually, on the basis of the information provided, it is impossible to distinguish between the two. To do so requires a much more detailed examination of theories on which each is predicated.

Standardized and norm-referenced tests. A standardized test can best be defined as an instrument that attempts to compare students or groups of students to a common standard. In attempting to make comparisons, the standardized test uses such devices as grade equivalencies, percentiles, and stanines. This use of internal standards differs markedly from that of a criterion-referenced test, which is based on instructional objectives. Instructional objectives are generated by the teacher or specific reading program. According to Glaser and Nitko (1971, p. 653), a criterion-referenced test

> is deliberately constructed so as to yield measurements that are directly interpretable in terms of specified performance standards. . . . The performance of standards are usually specified by defining some domain tasks that the students should perform. Representative samples of tasks from its domain were organized into a test. Measurements are taken and are used to make a statement about the performance of each individual relative to that domain.

Rather than comparing a student to an internal standard, as in a norm-referenced test, the criterion-referenced test utilizes the concept of mastery. A student either does or does not demonstrate a functional knowledge of whatever skill is being measured. In other words, a very specific criterion has been established and a mastery level determined. The results derived from the test are interpreted only in light of individual performance.

Since individual performance is predicated on the concept of "mastery," this term has been the source of much contention. Although mastery may vary from subtest to subtest and even from test to test, most experts set the level of mastery at 75 or 80 percent accuracy. However, it is still unclear how this range was determined. For a more detailed description of establishing levels of mastery, see Millman (1973) and Block (1972).

A second major distinction between norm- and criterion-referenced tests is the acceptable range of difficulty for each test item. In ascertaining the acceptable range of an item to be used on a norm-referenced test, most experts would approve of an item with a p-value (percentage of test takers answering the item correctly) of between .40–.60. Since a norm-referenced test attempts to discriminate between individuals, comparisons can be made. However, criterion-referenced test items have a much wider range of acceptability (.00–1.0), because theoretically a criterion-referenced test has a point at which a person is said to master specific items. Therefore, the item difficulty can be as high as 1.0 and still be considered a good item.

There are advantages and limitations to both criterion- and norm-referenced tests. The main advantage of a norm-referenced test is that it can be utilized for making comparisons, an important asset when you are attempting to evaluate programs or make comparative-type decisions. A second advantage of the norm-referenced test is that it has translated raw scores into standard forms of measurement—grade equivalencies, percentiles, and stanines. The main advantage of the criterion-referenced test is the one-to-one relationship between the objectives of the reading program and the test itself. Second, since there is a high correlation between the test and the instructional program, criterion-referenced tests assist teachers in instructional planning. Third, since criterion-referenced tests are designed to measure individual performance, a student's strengths and weaknesses are easily discernible.

Each type of test also has several limitations. First, many psycholinguists with an interest in reading question the ability of any instrument to measure many of the skills or subskills attributed to the reading process. They contend that the reading process cannot be fragmented and that, therefore, any attempt to measure each minute segment could provide the teacher with a distorted view of the student's ability to read. Second, the format of some criterion- and norm-referenced tests lends itself to a choice between right and wrong answers, thus limiting the tests to certain types of questions. As a result, the evaluative or affective dimensions of the comprehension process are totally negated. Third, many times the items themselves are weak, with structural clues imbedded in the question, and as a result the correct answer is often conveyed to the readers. In the case of criterion-referenced tests, the objectives themselves may be inadequate, thereby making the results inadequate. Fourth, many times the item does not measure the skill it purports to measure. Fifth, the method used to report test results in both norm- and criterion-referenced tests may be deceiving. For example, many times an individual can score at a certain level on a norm-referenced test merely because the norms do not go below the third or fourth grade level. Therefore, by placing his or her name on the answer sheet, a student appears to possess certain specific skills. On the other hand, a criterion-referenced test has an inherent problem of mastery. What is mastery, and does a student truly demonstrate it by correctly answering four or five questions related to a specific skill?

Womar (1974) stated it very ably when he said that differences do exist between criterion-referenced and norm-referenced tests, but that these differences do not place them in separate categories. He goes on to say (p. 43):

> Just as ability and achievement measurements differ at some point, they overlap at others. The best norm referenced test will contain items that are closely tied to desired outcomes, objectives, or other criteria. The best criterion referenced test will furnish item statistics that help to provide normative information.

In other words, differences do exist between the two types of tests, but both contribute useful diagnostic information. Each should be viewed as supplying information not obtainable through other sources. Therefore, the use of a norm- or criterion-referenced test depends on the type of information needed.

Criteria for selecting tests. Despite the differences that exist between criterion- and norm-referenced tests, the reading specialist and classroom teachers are confronted with another very important problem—establishing appropriate standards by which to judge reading tests. Too many educators presently use instruments that are inappropriate for their needs. For this reason criteria for test selection must be developed and adhered to. There are certain standards that must be used when selecting the appropriate test: reliability, validity, test length, normative data, the method used to measure the skills assessed, and professional opinions of the test.

1. *Validity.* One of the most important factors to consider when selecting a test is its validity. Validity can be defined as a measure of the instrument's appropriateness to meet the identified instructional needs of the teacher. In other words, does the test measure what it purports to measure? There are four types of validity: content validity, concurrent validity, construct validity, and predictive validity.

Content, or face, validity is probably one of the more important components of validity. The teacher must determine whether the items on the test are similar to the materials used to teach reading. If there is not a close relationship between such factors as the concept level of the material and the types of questions asked, the content of the test is probably inappropriate. For example, if narrative material was used to teach students how to read, it would not be a valid measure of their knowledge of the reading process to use expository material to test that knowledge. Likewise, a social studies teacher would not use material taken from an English class to determine knowledge of social studies concepts. In both cases there is a lack of content validity.

If a test possesses concurrent validity, the results should be consistent with those of other instruments that purport to measure the same skill or skills. For example, the test used to measure a student's word-recognition skills should provide the same results as classroom exercises, activities, or other instruments that measure this skill. If a high correlation does not exist, the instrument lacks concurrent validity.

A test possesses construct validity to the extent that the ideas or theories on which it is predicated exist. In other words, is the construct a test seeks to measure identifiable? Has its existence been verified by research or other instruments outside the field of reading? Since there is much disagreement as to whether reading comprehension can be subdivided into subskills, the constructs of a test that claims to measure such skills as cause-and-effect relationships, predicting outcomes, or comparing and contrasting information must be verified. A test has construct validity if the existence of such skills can be confirmed.

Predictive validity refers to the ability of an instrument to predict future reading performance. When teachers are concerned with predicting certain types of reading behaviors, the ability of a test to establish predictive validity is essential. If an instrument indicates that a student is deficient in certain auditory perceptual skills, for example, the student should have difficulty with tasks that require the use of that skill. If the teacher desires a test that predicts certain types of reading behavior, the test must present evidence that it possesses those capabilities.

One important aspect of validity still remains; at what point is the test considered to be valid? Validity is generally established through a statistical process that yields a coefficient that can range from .00 to 1.00. Experts argue that in order for a test to be considered valid, the coefficient should be at least .80 or above. Any coefficient below this level should be considered questionable. At the .80 level, 64 percent of the variation in one's measurements is caused by real differences between the individuals being measured, and only 36 percent is due to random error in the measurement process. Such information is generally located in the test manual. If none exists, it is impossible to determine whether the instrument is valid. Part of the problem that exists today in our profession stems from the fact that we are willing to accept and use instruments without appropriate standards. If the instrument does not provide such information, do not use it. Utilizing such instruments perpetuates the assumption that standards are of no importance.

2. *Reliability.* Reliability refers to the ability of a test to measure accurately a phenomenon consistently. A test should be constructed so that the score a student receives today will be similar to the one he or she would receive if the test were administered again tomorrow.

There are several types of reliability—internal consistency, equivalent or alternative form, and interjudgment. The most common form of reliability is the internal consistency. Internal consistency attempts to measure relationships between various items on the test. The two most widely used procedures in computing internal consistency are the Kuder-Richardson formulas (KR-20 and KR-21) and the split-half method. The Kuder-Richardson formulas merely analyze the relationship between items across the test or within the various subtests; the split-half method refers to dividing the test in half and correlating the scores. Formulas such as Spearman Brown may be used for this procedure.

A second type of reliability is the equivalent, or alternative, form. When two equivalent forms of a test are available, both instruments are administered to the same group and the scores correlated. A high correlation between the two (.80 or higher) produces a coefficient of equivalency.

Interjudge reliability is established when two or more observers consistently report the same results after observing the same phenomenon. This form of reliability is used primarily when observational techniques are employed.

3. *Standard error of measurement.* Unlike reliability, which estimates the overall accuracy of a measure, the standard error of measurement refers to the accuracy of each individual score. The standard error of measurement can be best defined as the difference between the true score and the obtained score. Since one expects scores to vary to some degree when a test is repeated, the true range of a score must be established. This is done by calculating the standard error of measurement. For example, if a standard error of 2 exists between the true score and the obtained score of 45, the true score ranges from 43 to 47. In some cases the range in a score can be extremely important, because a standard error of 2 may change an individual's percentile rank, grade-equivalency score, or level of performance on a criterion-reference test. For this reason, be sure that the test provides the user with a standard error of measurement; without it, the true range of an individual's performance cannot be determined.

4. *Normative data.* Norms are generally used in order to make comparisons between students. Normative comparisons can be made in at least three ways: grade equivalencies, stanines, or percentiles. Grade equivalency merely refers to the translation of a raw score into a grade-level score. For example, rather than expressing a score in terms of 55 correct out of a possible 100, one reports the score in terms of year and month of academic performance. If a student is performing at the level of fourth grade–third month, the score would be reported as 4.3. (It should be kept in mind that in reporting scores in terms of grade equivalencies, the school year has been divided into ten months.)

There are two basic limitations associated with the use of grade-equivalency scores. First, since reading growth does not take place in equal intervals, a range from 1.0 to 12.0 does not imply equal intervals of growth. Reading involves the acquisition of many more skills in grades 1–3 than it does in grades 7–9. Therefore, an increase in performance of one year in a lower grade might be much more significant than a two-year growth in reading performance at an upper grade. Second, the results are sometimes thought to be transferable to actual reading or classroom materials. Teachers often attempt to place students who scored at the 4.4 level into materials that are designed for that level. It should be kept in mind that 4.4 merely refers to the point at which a particular individual scored in comparison to the rest of the members of the group taking the same test. Therefore, such test results should not be used to place students in materials that are concomitant with their level of performance. More appropriate instruments are available for such tasks.

A stanine refers to dividing the range of scores into nine equal parts. By using stanines, the teacher can determine how far below or above the average (the fifth stanine) a student falls. If a student's score falls in the second stanine, the student is below average. Conversely, a score in the seventh stanine would be considered above average. The major limitation in utilizing stanines is that it is much easier for a person to move from the fourth to fifth stanine than from the first to the second; as is the case with a normal population curve, the range in scores is much more extreme at the two ends of the distribution. For example, in order for a student to move from the fourth to the fifth stanine, an increase of only four points in score might be required, whereas an increase of seven points might be needed to move from the second to third stanine. Therefore, comparisons in growth can sometimes be deceiving.

A percentile is a means of reporting scores in terms of percentage of students who receive lower scores. For example, a score at the 60th percentile means that 60 percent of the students taking the test had lower scores. As is the case with stanines, the major limitation in reporting scores in percentile rankings is that unequal intervals of growth are reported. For example, those individuals who scored at the 23rd percentile might have to increase their scores by five points in order to move to the 24th percentile, whereas students who scored at the 54th percentile might have to increase their score by only two points to move to the 55th percentile. Again, comparisons based on percentile rankings can be deceiving.

If normative information is employed, the test should report the procedures used to norm the instrument. The normative information should include a description of the group in terms of age, sex, educational level, socioeconomic status, race, geographical setting, and size. Without this information, it would be impossible to ascertain whether the results of the test are applicable to the population tested. For instance, it would be extremely difficult to apply the results obtained from an instrument normed on a rural population comprised largely of individuals from the lower socioeconomic strata to a group of students from an upper-middle-class metropolitan area. Obviously, the results would have to be questioned, based on the inconsistent makeup of the two groups. Even if the groups are comparable, the normative data must be current; values, roles, curricular materials, and methodologies change over time. Therefore, a group of middle-class students of the 1950s might differ from urban middle-class students of the 1970s. For this reason, unless both the test and normative data are continually updated, validity becomes questionable.

Many of these recommendations are not new. However, even though some of the more popular tests today have no norms, they still report their results in terms of stanines, percentiles, or grade equivalencies. Even without this information and despite repeated warnings, teachers and administrators still religiously use the results. One begins to believe that the educational profession is composed of slow learners. If the normative data do not exist, two options are available to the user: first, do not use the instrument; second, if you use the instrument, disregard the normative scores.

5. *Skills assessment.* How does the instrument operationally define the skills it seeks to measure? Steps 1 and 2 in the diagnostic process are essential requisites to the successful completion of this step, in that the skills and behaviors you seek to diagnose must be identified prior to testing. Only after these have been identified should a teacher ascertain how the various diagnostic instruments operationally defined those skills.

Unfortunately, this step is often deleted from the diagnostic process. Too frequently the only criterion utilized to determine whether a test or subtest is appropriate is its title. However, with some tests a one-to-one correlation does not always exist between the descriptive title of a subtest and the skill or skills it seeks to assess. In addition, the numerous formats for assessing the same skill also contribute to the variance between title and operational definition. Some of the following examples should help illustrate why this often neglected aspect of test selection must be considered more carefully.

Vocabulary. In a classic study Kelly and Krey (1934) analyzed the methods utilized by reading tests to assess *vocabulary* development and found at least 26 variations. Listed below are the various techniques used by tests to assess vocabulary development.

1. Unaided recall
    a) Checking for familiarity
    b) Using words in a sentence
    c) Explaining the meaning
    d) Giving a synonym
    e) Giving an opposite

2. Aided recall
    a) Recall aided by recognition
        (1) Matching tests
        (2) Classification tests
        (3) Multiple-choice tests
            (a) Choosing the opposite
            (b) Choosing the best synonym
            (c) Choosing the best definition
            (d) Choosing the best use in sentences

      (4) Same-opposite tests
      (5) Same-opposite-neither tests
      (6) Same-different tests

  b) Recall aided by association
      (1) Completion tests
      (2) Analogy tests

  c) Recall aided by recognition and association
      (1) Multiple-choice completion tests
      (2) Multiple-choice substitution tests (p. 109)

After analyzing the results of Kelly and Krey's study, it becomes very obvious as to why a teacher must closely examine the method a particular instrument employs to assess vocabulary development. If, for example, a teacher wishes to test vocabulary in terms of context, a test that seeks to present one-word synonyms in isolation would not be appropriate. Therefore, it is essential that the teacher closely scrutinize subtests before making a selection.

Ending sounds. The example below comes from the "Ending Sounds" subtest of the Doren Diagnostic Reading Test. In this particular subtest the student is asked to draw a circle around the word that *makes sense.*

1. The boy (walked, walking) fast.
2. Sally was (runs, running) home.

Obviously, more than merely ending sounds is being assessed in this example. Although the endings of the words differ, it is the student's knowledge of syntactic structure that is paramount. In addition, the student has a 50 percent chance of selecting the correct answer based on format alone. A teacher who is truly interested in assessing knowledge of ending sounds should select a more appropriate test.

Whole-word recognition. In the following example the student is asked to find two words that are alike and to draw a circle around them. The words are: "yellow," "little," "kitten," "pretty," and "little." If the teacher wished to ascertain more than just visual discrimination, this test would not be an appropriate task. Further examination of the list reveals that the child does not even have to discriminate among words. Since none of the alternatives begin with the letter "l," all the child must do is see that the first letter in the two words is the same.

Comprehension. A number of very important factors must be considered when selecting an appropriate measure of comprehension. First, if the reading specialist or classroom teacher is interested in assessing more than literal or inferential comprehension, a noncommercial test will probably have to be used. Most of the commercial tests on the market ask only convergent, or closed-ended, questions, which have agreed-on answers. If commercially prepared materials are utilized, the comprehension component should be augmented.

Second, in addition to using different types of questions to assess comprehension, tests also employ different formats. For example, rather than asking comprehension questions, the Stanford Diagnostic Reading Tests and the Gates-MacGinitie Reading Tests utilize a modified cloze procedure. If you are interested in assessing specific types of comprehension skills, such as literal recall of information, sequence, main ideas, and cause-and-effect relationships, these instruments would not be suitable.

Third, the reading specialist or classroom teacher should determine whether a student would be able to answer the questions without reading the selection. For example, in the question "Does a spider have big or little feet?" few students would have difficulty answering the question.

Fourth, questions should require more than a yes or no response. Such a format gives the student a 50 percent chance of answering the item correctly without prior knowledge of any information contained in the selection. If teachers wish to avoid such a problem, they should eliminate questions that can be answered as yes or no or true or false.

Fifth, sometimes the questions themselves provide answers to other questions that follow. Questions of this type should also be eliminated. For this reason, instruments that use unaided recall prior to aided recall are superior.

Oral reading. Oral-reading tasks can differ greatly, depending on the test selected. For example, the Gates-McKillop Reading Diagnostic Tests has seven short paragraphs, but requires oral reading without any check of comprehension. If comprehension is a critical factor to be considered, the Gates-McKillop Reading Diagnostic Tests would not be appropriate.

Recording errors made while reading may also be an important consideration.

Spache (1976) has made a comparison of word-recognition errors from five diagnostic instruments (the Durrell Analysis of Reading Difficulty, the Gates-McKillop Reading Diagnostic Tests, the Gilmore Oral Reading Paragraphs, the Gray Oral, and the Spache Diagnostic Reading Scales). As this analysis reveals, the differences that exist among the five instruments appear to be the result of the variations in scoring procedures. For example, the range in the number of errors in oral reading is from a high of 95 percent on the Durrell Analysis of Reading Difficulty to a low of 50 percent on the Gates-McKillop Reading Diagnostic Tests. Since the number of errors differs from instrument to instrument, the teacher or reading specialist should determine an acceptable level and use only those instruments that adhere to that level.

In addition, the teacher concerned with both a qualitative and quantitative interpretation of oral-reading errors would have to find an instrument containing such a scoring procedure. Again, if the teacher feels that appropriate background information must be given prior to oral reading, he or she should select a test that provides this type of information. Similarly, the teacher who is concerned with whether the material reflects language patterns that are consistent with those of his or her students should give close consideration to the type of language and sentence structure contained in the reading material.

6. *Length.* A sixth criterion to consider when selecting a test is the length of the instrument. Two factors must be contemplated when determining the appropriate length of a test. First, each subtest should provide its user with an in-depth coverage of each skill area. For example, if the diagnostician desires an in-depth analysis of a student's knowledge of morphology, the brief subtests contained in the Durrell Analysis of Reading Difficulty, the Gates-McKillop Reading Diagnostic Tests, or the Spache Diagnostic Reading Scales may not be adequate.

The length of a subtest can also be deceiving, however. Length alone does not necessarily imply quality. A good rule of thumb about test length is that each subtest should contain a sufficient amount of information to make the required diagnostic decisions. Second, the length of the total test battery should not be so cumbersome that it is impossible to administer.

7. *Time.* Obviously, in many standardized tests, norms are based on a timed performance. But time can have a negative impact on the diagnosis. For instance, time can affect reading comprehension in a very important way. Timing a comprehension selection may result in a measure not of comprehension, but rather of speed of comprehension. If the teacher does not place a high priority on timed reading, it should not have a high priority in diagnosis. However, there are very legitimate reasons for using a timed presentation, e.g., recognition of sight words.

8. *Reviewers' opinions.* The most extensive review of reading tests is Oscar Buros's *Seventh Mental Measurement Yearbook,* Vol. VII, Highland Park, New Jersey: Gryphon, 1972. In this and his six previous editions (1938, 1940, 1949, 1953, 1959, 1965), Buros has reviewed most of the tests in print. A second source is the professional reading journals, which have for years published articles on various reading tests. For example, the October 1974 issue of the *Journal of Reading* contained an excellent review of secondary- and college-level reading tests—*"Concise Guide to Standardized Secondary and College Reading Tests,"* by Mavrogenes *et al.* Reviews of tests also appear in a variety of preservice and inservice publications (William Blanton, Roger Farr, and Joap Tuinman, *Reading Tests for Secondary Grades: A Review and Evaluation,* Newark, Del.: IRA, 1972; Roger Farr, *Reading: What Can*

Be Measured? Newark, Del.: IRA, 1969; and George D. Spache, *Diagnosing and Correcting Reading Disabilities,* Boston: Allyn & Bacon, 1976).

Testing has been a very popular topic in the past ten years, and there is a plethora of information available. Therefore, before using a test, it would be wise to consider the views of other professionals.

9. *Special requirements.* Does the test require any type of professional training to administer or interpret the test results? For example, it would be impossible for reading specialists to administer the Weschler Intelligence Scale for Children unless they had received appropriate psychological training. The Reading Miscue Inventory (Goodman and Burke, 1972) is another example; unless the person using the test is familiar with both the psycholinguistic concepts on which the test is predicated and the elaborate marking system, the test might prove difficult to score and interpret. Before utilizing any test or subtest, a teacher should be sure that she or he is qualified to administer the instrument and interpret the test results.

10. *Organization of the manual and cost.* The test manual should be clearly organized and readable. The instructions to the teacher and the statistical data (on reliability, validity, item analysis, and normative information) should be in a form that facilitates interpretation; otherwise, the teacher may find it very difficult and tedious to administer and interpret the results. The final criterion to consider is the cost of the test, which is an extremely important variable. If the cost is prohibitive, the teacher may decide to devise an instrument.

Teacher-constructed instruments. If standardized tests do not meet your diagnostic needs, another alternative exists—utilization of teacher-made instruments, which might include informal reading inventories, teacher-constructed content reading tests, or classroom exercises or activities.

An informal reading inventory (IRI) is an excellent method for assessing individual reading performance. An IRI can be as general or as specific as the needs dictate. However, the format remains relatively the same. Generally, the IRI is based on a series of graduated paragraphs taken from the teacher's own reading material. In addition, the IRI might also contain a word list adapted from the reading material used in class and subtests designed to assess the student's phonological and morphological skills. Obviously, the use of the teacher's own materials will result in a high correlation between the testing and teaching situations. In constructing such an instrument, the teacher must be continually cognizant of the need to incorporate into the IRI those skills that have been identified as essential in the diagnostic process.

The teacher should adhere to certain standards in constructing the IRI.

First, a standard for the interpretation of oral-reading errors must be established. The most widely used approach (Betts, 1941) consists of three performance levels: (1) *independent level*—one error in oral reading per 100 words and 90 percent or better on comprehension; (2) *instructional level*—five errors in oral reading per 100 words and 75 percent or better on comprehension; and (3) *frustration level*—more than ten errors per 100 words and 50 percent or below on comprehension. This approach generally reveals such word-recognition errors as substitutions, repetitions, omissions, additions, and refusals.

Another method used to interpret oral-reading errors is the miscue approach, developed by Goodman and Burke (1972). Their elaborate system is based on the theory that miscues are primarily grammatical substitutions predicted by semantic and syntactic redundancies in the language. Rather than merely quantifying errors, as in Betts's approach, Burke and Goodman look at the quality of the miscue in terms of the following questions. (1) Was the miscue graphically similar (e.g., there for three)? (2) Was there similarity in sound (e.g., bought for bat)? (3) Was the miscue syntactically acceptable (e.g., substituted a noun for a noun)? (4) Was the miscue semantically acceptable (e.g., home for house)? (5) Did any of the miscues result in a change in sentence meaning? (6) Do corrections make the sentence semantically correct?

The second standard to consider when constructing an IRI is the establishment of a balanced questioning strategy; thus representative questions from all dimensions of the comprehension process should be used. For example, if Barrett's taxonomy (Smith and Barrett, 1974) is used, literal, inferential, evaluative, and appreciative questions would be asked. Since the questions themselves occasionally provide clues to some answers, unaided recall should be utilized before the teacher initiates any questions. Students are told at the outset that after completing the selection, they will be asked to retell everything they can remember from the selection. Once the student has concluded this task, aided recall should begin. Figure 9.3 is an example of a coding sheet that can be used with both unaided and aided recall.

Teachers can also construct their own reading tests. At the middle school and high school levels, teacher-constructed content reading tests can provide insights into reading performance that cannot be derived from standardized reading tests. Research seems to indicate that a difference in *general* reading performance (reading performance assessed by such instruments as the Gates-MacGinitie Reading Tests or the Sequential Tests of Educational Progress: Reading) and *specific* reading performance (reading performance assessed by the teacher-constructed content reading tests) does exist (Artley, 1944; Peters, 1975; Peters, Peters, and Kaufman, 1975; and Swenson, 1942). In other words, teacher-constructed reading tests tend to be more predictive of reading performance than do general measures. At this level, reading skills are juxta-

Student's name _____

Grade _____

Reading level	% Correct	Quality of recall			Type of error (UNAIDED RECALL)			Type of error (AIDED RECALL)	
		Poor	Ave.	Good	Sequence	Main idea	General recall	Inference	Literal recall
2–A									
2–B									
3–A									
3–B									
4–A									
4–B									
5–A									
5–B									
6–A									
6–B									
7–A									
7–B									
8–A									
8–B									
9–A									
9–B									

Fig. 9.3. Coding sheet for use in unaided and aided recall.

posed with content and should be assessed as part of the content process. Therefore, in order to obtain an accurate assessment of reading ability, one must assess reading skills within the context of the various disciplines that comprise the curriculum.

One of the major difficulties in utilizing standardized reading tests to assess reading difficulties at this level is that many of them are composed primarily of narrative-type material. The use of such material violates a very basic tenet of diagnosis, i.e., materials used in diagnosis should be closely related to those utilized for classroom instruction. Therefore, secondary teachers and reading specialists should be encouraged to develop content-related reading tests that more accurately reflect their own priorities.

The following guidelines can be used in constructing a content-related reading test.

1. In order to construct a reading test that reflects your own reading-skill priorities, try to identify those skills. This may be difficult to do, since content teachers are not accustomed to thinking in terms of content-related reading skills. In the appendix at the end of this chapter is an example of a skills checklist that has proved most useful. The checklist has two major functions: (1) to identify those content-related reading skills that should be taught at the secondary level, and (2) to establish the importance of each skill. Once the checklist has been completed, the teacher uses the results as the basis for constructing the test. By using a checklist, the teacher identifies his or her own priorities, thus avoiding the problem of having them imposed by someone else. If the test is to be utilized at the departmental level, the checklist can also serve as a means for resolving differences that may exist among departmental members. Since each teacher has indicated the relative importance of each skill, those with a low priority can be deleted.

2. After establishing skill priorities, the teacher must operationally define each skill by using his or her own classroom material. For example, a math teacher who wants to know how well students could comprehend word problems should select a representative sample of word problems.

3. The same standards used in selecting standardized reading tests should also be applied to the construction of teacher-made instruments, e.g., length, type of comprehension question, and time.

4. Next, teachers should give careful consideration to the writing of test questions. The following guidelines should be used to develop multiple-choice questions.

    a) Guidelines for stem construction:

        (1) Use clear, succinct language
        (2) Avoid the use of negatives or double negatives

(3) Use only one question per stem

(4) Use incomplete statements if possible

(5) Utilize an interrogative at the beginning of the stem

(6) Attempt to establish a balance between inferential and literal-level comprehension questions

(7) Control the difficulty level of the stem

b) Guidelines for constructing answers:

(1) Utilize only one correct answer

(2) The correct answer should be the same length as the alternatives

(3) The correct answer should have the same syntactic structure as the alternatives

(4) Ensure complete agreement by all judges on "best" answer selections

(5) Avoid placing key words from the stem in the answers

(6) Control difficulty level of the answer

c) Guidelines for constructing alternatives or distractions:

(1) Use plausible alternatives

(2) Order numerical responses from smallest to largest

(3) Alphabetize single-word responses

(4) Develop independent alternatives

(5) Utilize clear, concise language

(6) Control difficulty level of alternatives

The use of these guidelines should result in better questions.

Obtain diagnostic information

Diagnostic information should be obtained from a variety of sources—student records, questionnaires, other professionals, informal and formal instruments. After identifying these sources, the teacher can ascertain when and how to collect the information. This is why the development of the interdisciplinary team approach becomes so important; each member is particularly qualified to gather a certain type of information (see Chapters 5 and 8).

Collecting the data   It is extremely important to decide *how* the data will be gathered. Since testing is an ominous experience for many children, the teacher should attempt to mitigate any tension or emotional strain by seeking to place the student at ease, perhaps by finding out about the student's personal interests. Another technique is to inform the student that his or her responses will be recorded. This should allay any fears by the student that only incorrect responses will be recorded.

A second point to bear in mind is that some students find it difficult to concentrate on one task for long periods of time. If the student appears fatigued or if she or he does not attend to the task, stop the testing. A test need not be administered in a single sitting. Information collected under such conditions will be of questionable validity.

Third, a balanced information-gathering technique should exist. It is a good idea to alternate questionnaires and inventories with tasks that do not require sustained concentration. For instance, oral reading might be followed by a gamelike activity that is nevertheless diagnostic in nature. Remember that many poor readers spend only a relatively small percentage of their time in instructional interaction with the regular classroom teacher. Therefore, when they spend 30 to 40 minutes in a one-to-one testing situation, it can be a very demanding and tiring task.

Fourth, the reading specialist should observe the child in the classroom environment. Many times the reading specialist encounters the student only in a special class. Valuable insights can be obtained from observing the student's interaction with peers and the classroom teacher. Observations should be structured so that they occur when the student is engaged in activities that contribute useful diagnostic information. There is nothing more distressing for a diagnostician than to walk into a classroom and find the student watching a film or engaged in some other activity not suitable for observational purposes. Similarly, it can be quite revealing for the classroom teacher to observe the reading specialist at work with a student. Many times teachers who send students to the reading specialist think that they can then abdicate all responsibilities for reading. These teachers believe that someone else will solve the student's reading problem. However, classroom teachers must work closely with the other members of the interdisciplinary team in order to maximize the student's progress.

Fifth, the purposes and results of the test should be shared with mature students. Too many times, students are left without any feedback. By sharing the test results with students, the teacher can gain insights into the reasons for the student's responses. The explanation might provide additional insights into the student's problems. Finally, the teacher cannot gather accurate data without having the appropriate material, understanding all of the directions, and knowing how to administer each subtest.

Recording and analyzing results To be interpreted correctly, the data must be accurately recorded. In order to accomplish this goal, several important factors must be considered. First, determine the system that will be utilized in recording diagnostic information. For whatever recording system will be used, the ultimate criterion is the system's usefulness in contributing meaningful diagnostic information.

Unlike the controversy over what methods to use when interpreting word-recognition errors in oral reading, most of the other procedures for recording information derived from questionnaires, informal observations, classroom activities, or attitude inventories are relatively straightforward. A cumbersome checklist that requires more time to record data than was spent in observing the student will be of questionable validity. Likewise, a system that requires an inordinate amount of paperwork will result in more time being spent marking rather than analyzing the data. However, not possessing enough information can be just as frustrating. To eliminate this problem, be precise and succinct in your analysis. If the information is recorded hastily or if vague terminology is used, the analysis will be superficial and imprecise.

The analysis of information is a very crucial step in the diagnostic process. In the past many teachers tended to believe that the diagnostic process was completed once the data had been collected and the results recorded. As a noted educational guru once stated, "Results are not expected to just sit there; they must be interpreted."

To some, the obvious is not always apparent. A number of things can be done to facilitate the interpretation of diagnostic data. First, analyze the information as soon after it has been collected as possible. The longer the lapse between collection and interpretation, the more likely it is that valuable insights will be forgotten. Second, save samples of students' work so comparisons can be made. This will help you relate the results obtained from the diagnosis to classroom activities. Third, look for patterns that may emerge. For example, in attempting to sound out unknown words, does the student focus only on the initial, medial, or ending elements? Does the student confuse past and present tenses? Does the child have problems sequencing information? In attempting to discern diagnostic patterns, it is sometimes helpful to chart information. Fourth, do not jump to conclusions. Once you have made the tentative diagnosis, test your hypotheses by comparing them to other available information. Fifth, share your insights with other members of the interdisciplinary team. Sixth, analyze *all* information. If a student could not successfully complete a task, analyze what skills were either explicit or implicit in the activity. As much as possible, isolate the skills involved in the activity and determine which ones the student has and has not mastered. For example, if a task requires both visual and auditory perceptual skills and a student could not successfully complete it, your next step would be to determine if either the visual or perceptual component is the source of the problem. Such follow-up is extremely important, because how you label a student will to a large extent determine your teaching strategy. Seventh, the analysis of the data must be continual and ongoing. The ultimate test of any diagnosis is how effectively those results can be transformed into a workable program. If the information is incorrect, the program will be incorrect.

Translate the results into a workable program

The actual strategies for translating the results into a workable program are discussed in great detail in Chapters 12, 13, and 14. Here, several guidelines will be presented to assist the classroom teacher and reading specialist implement the remedial program.

1. *Establish an instructional sequence.* The teacher should establish an instructional sequence based on the information derived from the diagnosis. This instructional sequence should be consistent with the teacher's concept of reading.

2. *Combine strengths and weaknesses.* Since most poor readers will have a number of related problems, the program should seek to combine the student's strengths and weaknesses. It is difficult for students to view themselves as successful if all they encounter is a series of tasks that continually emphasize their weaknesses.

3. *Utilize various instructional strategies.* Sometimes the nature of the disability might require the use of a variety of teaching strategies. Some students may function better in a behavior-modification program. Others may find the language-experience method more appealing, whereas still others would prefer a more structured approach, e.g., Charles Fries's linguistic approach. Teachers working with remedial students must be willing to use a variety of approaches, because the instructional technique should vary according to the student's needs.

4. *Focus reading instruction.* Since poor readers have so many problems, the teacher can begin almost anywhere. However, the instruction must be clearly focused in terms of individual needs based on the priorities established by the diagnosis.

5. *Vary the reading materials.* The teacher should not be hesitant to use a wide variety of materials—books, magazines, newspapers, catalogs, records, tapes, menus, and comic books. In other words, the program should not be limited to instructional materials, but should also include recreational and functional material. Unless the student sees use or enjoyment in reading, the program will fail.

6. *Build in skill transfer.* Skills cannot be taught in isolation. Teachers should realize that for students to be successful readers, they must be able to transfer the skills learned in reading classes to all types of materials. Read-

ing is not a subject, but a process. In addition, if materials specifically designed to teach a certain skill are used, make sure that other, more realistic, materials are also included in the instructional program.

7. *Use reinforcement activities.* Contrary to popular belief, there is nothing sinister about drill. Students learn through reinforcement, but activities that seek to reinforce previously taught skills do not have to be boring, uninteresting, or tedious. Games are an excellent method of reinforcement. However, like any other type of instructional material, games must serve an instructional purpose. They should never be used to *teach* a skill; rather, they should be used to *reinforce* it.

8. *Stimulate interest in reading.* Poor readers should not be deprived of exciting and interesting material. Too many poor readers believe that reading is a workbook filled with activities. If you had to answer questions or do a worksheet every time you read the newspaper, you would soon lose interest in reading. The same is true with the poor reader.

9. *Build a positive self-concept.* Too many poor readers view themselves as failures. The program should seek to enhance the reader's self-image. Although the development of self-concept is related to many factors besides reading, research has shown that if a child possesses a poor self-concept, his or her success in reading could be jeopardized.

SUMMARY

Diagnosis is an interrelated process involving many steps—specifying the decisions to be made, describing the information needed, gathering the needed information, obtaining the needed information, and translating the information into a workable program. Through these steps the classroom teacher attempts to ascertain the specific strengths and weaknesses of individual students. Therefore, diagnosis must be predicated on the systematic collection, interpretation, and utilization of information. The end result should be an effective program that seeks to remediate those problems identified through diagnosis.

REFERENCES

Artley, S. A. "A Study of Certain Relationships Existing Between General Reading Comprehension in a Specific Subject-Matter Area," *Journal of Educational Research* **37** (1944): 464–473.

Blanton, William E., Roger Farr, and J. Jaap Tuinman, eds. *Measuring Reading Performance,* Newark, Del.: IRA, 1974.

Blanton, William, Roger Farr, and J. Jaap Tuinman, eds. *Reading Tests for Secondary Grades: A Review and Evaluation,* Newark, Del.: IRA, 1972.

Block, J. H. "Student Evaluation: Toward the Setting of Mastery Performance

Standards." Paper presented at the annual meeting of the American Educational Research Association, Chicago, 1972.

Buros, Oscar K., ed. *The Seventh Mental Measurements Yearbook,* Vol. VII, Highland Park, N. J.: Gryphon, 1972.

Dulin, Kenneth L., and Robert D. Chester "A Validated Study of the Estes Scale Attitude Scales," *Journal of Reading* 15 (1974): 56–59.

Estes, Thomas H. "A Scale to Measure Attitude Toward Reading," *Journal of Reading* 15 (1971): 135–138.

Evans, J. "Behavioral Objectives Are No Damn Good," in *Technology and Innovation Education,* New York: Praeger, 1968.

Farr, Roger *Reading: What Can Be Measured?* Newark, Del.: IRA, 1969.

Glaser, R., and A. J. Nitko "Measurement in Learning and Instruction," in R. L. Thorndike, ed., *Educational Measurement,* Washington: American Council of Education, 1971.

Goodman, Yetta M., and Carolyn L. Burke *Manual for Reading Miscue Inventory: Procedure for Diagnosing and Evaluation,* London: Macmillan, 1972.

Kelly, T. L., and A. C. Krey *Tests and Measurements in the Social Sciences,* New York: Scribner, 1934.

Kennedy, Larry D., and Ronald S. Halinski "Measuring Attitudes: An Extra Dimension," *Journal of Reading* 18 (1975): 518–522.

Mavrogenes, Nancy A., Carol K. Winkley, Earl Hanson, and Richard T. Vacca "Concise Guide to Standardized Secondary and College Reading Tests," *Journal of Reading* 18 (1974): 12–22.

Millman, J. "Passing Scores and Test Lengths for Domain-Referenced Measure," *Review of Educational Research* 43 (1973): 205–216.

Otto, Wayne R., Richard A. McMenemy, and Richard J. Smith *Corrective and Remedial Teaching,* 2d ed., Boston: Houghton Mifflin, 1973.

Peters, Charles W. "Predicting Reading Performance in Social Studies Classrooms." Paper presented at the annual meeting of the National Council for the Social Studies, Atlanta, 1975.

Peters, Charles W., and Nathaniel A. Peters "A Systematic Approach to Predicting Reading Performance at the Secondary Level," in the *Twenty-fifth Yearbook of the National Reading Conference,* 1976.

Peters, Charles W., Nathaniel A. Peters, and B. Darwin Kaufman "A Comparative Analysis of Reading Comprehension in Four Content Areas," in George H. McNinch and Wallace D. Miller, eds., *Reading: Convention and Inquiry,* Urbana, Ill.: NRC, 1975.

Smith, Richard J., and Thomas C. Barrett *Teaching Reading in the Middle Grades,* Reading, Mass.: Addison-Wesley, 1974.

Spache, George D. *Diagnosing and Correcting Reading Disabilities,* Boston: Allyn & Bacon, 1976.

Spache, George D. *Investigating the Issues of Reading Disabilities,* Boston: Allyn & Bacon, 1976.

Swenson, E. A. "A Study of the Relationship among Various Types of Reading Scores on General and Science Materials," *Journal of Educational Research* 36 (1942): 81–90.

TenBrink, Terry D. *Evaluation: A practical Guide to Teachers,* New York: McGraw-Hill, 1974.

Womer, Frank B. "What is Criterion-Referenced Measurement?" in William E. Blanton, Roger Farr, and J. Jaap Tuinman, eds., *Measuring Reading Performance, op. cit.*

TESTS

Durrell, Donald D. *Durrell Analysis of Reading Difficulty,* New York: Harcourt Brace Jovanovich, 1955.

Farr, Roger, ed. *Iowa Silent Reading Tests,* New York: Harcourt Brace Jovanovich, 1972.

Gates, Arthur I., and Walter H. MacGinitie *Gates-MacGinitie Reading Tests,* New York: Teachers College Press, 1970.

Gates, Arthur I., and Anne S. McKillop *Gates-McKillop Reading Diagnostic Tests,* New York: Teachers College Press, 1962.

Gilmore, John V., and Eunice C. Gilmore *Gilmore Oral Reading Test,* New York: Harcourt Brace Jovanovich, 1968.

Goodman, Yetta M., and Carolyn L. Burke *Reading Miscue Inventory,* London: Macmillan, 1972.

Gray, William S., and Helen M. Robinson, *Gray Oral Reading Tests,* Indianapolis: Bobbs-Merrill, 1967.

Karlsen, Bjorn, Richard Madden, and Eric F. Gardner *Stanford Diagnostic Reading Tests,* New York: Harcourt Brace Jovanovich, 1966.

Sequential Tests of Educational Progress, Series II: Reading, New York: Educational Testing Service.

Spache, George D. *Spache Diagnostic Reading Scales,* Del Monte Research Park: California Test Bureau, 1963.

Appendix:
Essential Skills
to Function in Your Classroom

DIRECTIONS

This questionnaire is designed to identify the reading skills essential to understanding material utilized in your content area. It has been divided into two parts: (1) the level at which the skill is taught, and (2) the importance of the particular skill within your content area. Please make sure that all skills are checked. If a skill is not applicable to your content area, check the column labeled "Skills not identified with my content area."

Please rate each response according to the following scale. Circle the appropriate number.

1 = very important
2 = moderately important
3 = moderately unimportant
4 = unimportant

Skills taught before entering high school	Skills taught after entering high school	Developmental skills taught at both levels	Skills not identified with my content area	
				1. *Contextual analysis* (use of context to determine the meaning of unknown words). 1 2 3 4
				2. *Structural analysis* (use of prefixes, suffixes, and roots to determine meaning of unknown words). 1 2 3 4
				3. *Phonetic analysis* (use of sound to determine meaning of unknown words). 1 2 3 4
				4. *Dictionary* (use of dictionary to determine meaning of unknown words). 1 2 3 4

				5. *Vocabulary development* (use of denotation, connotation, synonyms, homonyms, and antonyms to expand vocabulary). 1 2 3 4
				6. *Set purpose for reading* (establish important ideas, concepts, details, relationships, etc., to look for while reading). 1 2 3 4
				7. *Scan* (develop the ability to rapidly locate material on the printed page without reading every word). 1 2 3 4
				8. *Skim* (develop the ability to locate specific material without reading every word on the printed page). 1 2 3 4
				9. Adjust reading speed to the type and difficulty level of the material. 1 2 3 4
				10. *Main ideas and details* (can distinguish between central ideas and related minor points of a chapter). 1 2 3 4
				11. Distinguish fact from opinion. 1 2 3 4
				12. *Critically analyze material* (critically evaluate or judge ideas, material, etc.). 1 2 3 4
				13. Draw inferences from material read. 1 2 3 4
				14. Summarize and draw conclusions from materials read. 1 2 3 4
				15. Apply concepts gained from reading to real or hypothetical situations. 1 2 3 4

Skills taught before entering high school	Skills taught after entering high school	Developmental skills taught at both levels	Skills not identified with my content area	
				16. Discern cause-and-effect relationships. 1 2 3 4
				17. Paraphrase material read. 1 2 3 4
				18. Organize material into understandable units. 1 2 3 4
				19. Knows how to use the table of contents. 1 2 3 4
				20. Knows how to use an index. 1 2 3 4
				21. Knows how to use an appendix and cross-references. 1 2 3 4
				22. Knows how to use maps. 1 2 3 4
				23. Knows how to use charts. 1 2 3 4
				24. Knows how to use graphs. 1 2 3 4
				25. Knows how to use diagrams. 1 2 3 4
				26. Knows how to use tables. 1 2 3 4
				27. Knows how to interpret symbols. 1 2 3 4
				28. Knows how to interpret illustrations. 1 2 3 4

				29. Knows how to utilize pictures. 1　　　2　　　3　　　4
				30. Knows how to utilize atlases. 1　　　2　　　3　　　4
				31. Knows how to utilize globes. 1　　　2　　　3　　　4
				32. Knows how to interpret abbreviations. 1　　　2　　　3　　　4
				33. Can recognize propaganda. 1　　　2　　　3　　　4
				34. Can recognize inconsistencies. 1　　　2　　　3　　　4
				35. Can recognize bias. 1　　　2　　　3　　　4
				36. Can recognize author's purpose. 1　　　2　　　3　　　4
				37. Can recognize author's point of view. 1　　　2　　　3　　　4
				38. See relationships between ideas. 1　　　2　　　3　　　4
				39. Recognize time-order relationships. 1　　　2　　　3　　　4
				40. Compare and contrast ideas. 1　　　2　　　3　　　4
				41. Recognize the plot (major/minor) of stories. 1　　　2　　　3　　　4
				42. *Characterization* (ability to describe the qualities, traits, etc., that make up the various characters in stories). 1　　　2　　　3　　　4
				43. Recognize the author's mood. 1　　　2　　　3　　　4

Skills taught before entering high school	_Skills taught after entering high school_	_Developmental skills taught at both levels_	_Skills not identified with my content area_	
				44. Recognize the author's tone. 1 2 3 4
				45. Recognize symbolism in stories. 1 2 3 4
				46. Can take notes in an organized manner. 1 2 3 4
				47. Can outline material in an organized manner. 1 2 3 4
				48. Recognize figurative language. 1 2 3 4
				49. Recognize visualizations and dramatic action (imagery and sensory impression). 1 2 3 4
				50. Sequentially place events in their proper order. 1 2 3 4
				51. Recognize rhythm and meter. 1 2 3 4
				52. Recognize the theme of the story. 1 2 3 4
				53. Please add any additional skills you feel have been omitted. 1 2 3 4

Chapter 10

ORIENTATION TO REMEDIAL TEACHING

WAYNE OTTO · *University of Wisconsin–Madison*

In the preceding chapters, we talked about the reading process and reading problems. First, we examined the overall process and factors that influence its development. Then we introduced ways of viewing and means for diagnosing problems that arise when individuals tackle the complex process of learning to read. In the chapters that follow, we focus on how to deal with reading problems. The role and function of reading specialists and other resource people are examined, and guidelines for their optimum functioning are laid out. Specific approaches to dealing with reading problems at the elementary, secondary, and adult levels are offered. Consideration is given to matters of method, organization, and training as means for dealing with reading problems in the schools. Earlier, we examined the problem; in the chapters that follow, we suggest solutions.

This chapter takes a close look at what the whole book is about—remedial teaching. Insofar as organization of the book is concerned, this chapter is transitional, the bridge between problems and solutions. Insofar as the reality of dealing with people who have reading problems is concerned, remedial teaching offers an effective bridge from failure to success in reading. In fact, success or failure of any specific remedial technique or any general remedial program depends largely on the quality of remedial teaching that is offered. Excellent remedial teaching is empathetic, well focused, realistically paced instruction that *facilitates* learning. It proceeds from a thorough understanding of the reading process and the problems that interfere with its development. Yet it transcends the methods, materials, techniques, and organizational schemes that are the raw materials for efficient remediation. It involves observable acts, but it defies definitive description because it always amounts to the acts of individual teachers responding to the attributes and needs of individual learners.

The purpose of this chapter, then, is to present an orientation to remedial teaching. Everyone who works with people who have reading problems—whether a classroom teacher or a supporting specialist—ought to give some thought to what *remedial teaching* is all about. The discussion in this chapter deals more with how-to-*pursue*-it than with the how-to-do-it of remedial teaching. The how-to-do-it suggestions are given in chapters that follow. Here, the emphasis is on personal perceptions, developing a personal style, and formulating a point of view.

The discussion begins with a consideration of how—or whether— remedial teaching differs from developmental teaching and how remedial teaching relates to the overall developmental teaching of reading. Next, a framework for getting organized to deal efficiently with reading problems is discussed. Finally, a point of view for remedial teaching is offered.

REMEDIAL TEACHING IN THE OVERALL
READING PROGRAM

The most basic overall goal for any reading program is to permit each individual to cope with the reading tasks encountered in one's life. An assumption implicit in a goal so stated is, of course, that the strengths, limits, and needs of the individual define the specific outcomes to be pursued. The basic goal for a remedial program is exactly the same. Reality suggests, however, that specific goal(s) for any individual must be stated in terms that reflect such factors as personal capacities, background, and previous achievement, as well as the reading demands imposed by the school and society. The effective teaching of reading, whether in a developmental or a remedial setting, demands that close attention be paid to individuals, even though the overall goal remains the same.

Given an identical overall goal and recognition of the need to attend to individual differences, does it make any sense at all to differentiate between *developmental* (overall) and *remedial* reading? The *theoretical* answer is an unequivocal *no*. With a common goal and common stipulations, any reasons given for any other answer could be considered purely academic, because the teaching considerations would always be the same. Nevertheless, the pragmatic answer is an unequivocal *yes*. The fact is that school practices differentiate between developmental and remedial programs in very tangible ways, such as allocation of resources and class size, and personal perceptions differentiate in such intangible ways as expectations, pressures, and rewards. In practice, more often than not, remedial programs are set apart as being *special,* and readers with problems are set apart as being *different.* So long as the present practices and perceptions persist, it will make sense to differentiate between *developmental* and *remedial* programs.

Let us consider, then, some of the ways in which developmental and remedial teaching differ and the place of the remedial program in a school's overall developmental program.

Developmental/remedial teaching

With the kind of insight that comes from experience and *perceptive* observation, Heilman (1969) got right to the heart of the matter of differences between developmental and remedial teaching when he said that "in remedial reading we conscientiously adhere to the principles that we often only verbalize in the regular classroom instruction" (p. 457). And so it is. The goal of reading instruction remains the same, but the pursuit of the goal changes. Most observers would agree that in good remedial teaching, diagnosis is more intensive, instruction more finely focused and more carefully paced, reinforcement more systematic, and assessment of mastery more rigorous.

A cynic might say that if this is so, *all* teaching of reading ought to be considered remedial from the start. And who could quarrel if simply changing the term would ensure conscientious adherence to sound teaching principles? But of course Heilman was making a point more profound than a cursory look might reveal.

Why *does* remedial teaching tend to be more rigorous than developmental teaching? There seem to be two equally sensible reasons. First, learners with reading problems *need* more careful teaching than do learners who experience little or no difficulty with the reading process. So to say that remedial teaching conscientiously adheres to sound principles is not to say that developmental teaching is sloppy and insensitive. Unlike learners who succeed, learners who fail in reading are characterized by their general inability—or at least great difficulty—to put things together for themselves. One remedial reading teacher put it this way: "It's as if they [poor readers] just don't know how to play the game. Good readers will have a dozen different ways to figure out words and what they mean. They play the game without even thinking about the rules. But I have to teach the poor readers what to do, and then I have to help them do it." To say that poor readers *get* more help because they *need* it may be to oversimplify to the point of glibness. Certainly there is no wisdom in that statement. Nevertheless, the adage that the squeaky wheel gets greased is a wise one—and both perceptive and sensible to boot. Greasing greasy wheels just isn't very smart.

The second reason can be stated as follows.

> Adherence to sound principles is made workable in part by modifications in the conditions under which teachers function, e.g. lower teacher: pupil ratios, availability of varied supplementary materials, more time allotted for skill development. Even more important, much stress is placed upon the fine focusing of instruction through careful diagnosis and consideration of the needs of individuals rather than upon the demands of curriculum guides. (Otto, McMenemy, and Smith, 1973, p. 32)

In other words, the teaching conditions are modified in such a way as to make them more conducive to the application of principles.

Remedial teaching, then, tends to be more rigorous than developmental teaching because there is a *need* for rigor and because there has been, at least in some instances, an inclination to provide the *means* for seeing to it. Of course, the teacher ultimately determines whether remedial teaching is in fact different from developmental teaching.

If the goal of developmental and of remedial teaching is the same, the background and attributes of the teachers involved ought to be similar. In fact, more often than not, the same classroom teacher handles whatever remedial teaching is done as well as the developmental teaching in a given classroom. Yet as the notion of differentiated roles for teachers becomes more widely accepted and implemented, discussion of differences between developmental and remedial teachers can be more than academic.

> Because disabled readers must overcome greater obstacles of previous failure and frustration than the adequate learner, his need for instruction that is thoughtfully conceived and sensitively executed is greater. Therefore, the teacher who accepts responsibility for . . . remedial teaching ought to have certain training and personal attributes that will permit him to deal effectively with special problems. (Otto, McMenemy, and Smith, 1973, p. 400)

Note the choice of words in the preceding quotation: ". . . the teacher who accepts responsibility for . . . remedial teaching. . ." That might be a classroom teacher who wants to deal with special problems in a special way *in the classroom*. Or it might be a teacher in any of a variety of specialties that can be brought to bear in dealing with reading problems in a variety of settings. The point here is that because remedial teachers deal with more complex problems, at least with regard to developing reading ability, they need to be more skilled in diagnosis, more aware of their students' attributes and needs, and more able to focus instruction for individuals. Whatever the setting, the demands of remedial teaching are equally rigorous. Some of the demands can be met through training, experience, and cooperation.

These things are discussed throughout this book. But ultimately the success of an individual remedial teacher will be determined by that teacher's _____.* That is what this chapter is supposed to be about.

Remedial teaching/overall program

Perhaps by now the point that remedial teaching is at the same time similar to and different from developmental teaching is overmade. Yet the considerations involved are sufficiently important to merit careful examination when it comes to implementing programs designed to deal realistically with reading problems. Now, to put remedial teaching into the perspective of an overall reading program, we need to consider the full scope of instructional needs. One conception of the instructional aspects of an overall reading program is summarized in Fig. 10.1.† Note that the overall program comprises a number of instructional aspects, all of which are interrelated and contributing, but nonetheless subsidiary, parts. Note, too, that each instructional aspect is directed toward the goal of the overall developmental program: *reading achievement that approaches the limit of each pupil's capacity.*

The instructional aspects of an overall program that are identified in Fig. 10.1 are intended to provide means for thinking about and dealing with the diverse instructional needs that exist in virtually any reading program. Each of the instructional thrusts deals with genuine and legitimate concerns of a program that is designed to meet the real-life reading needs of individuals in an orderly, systematic manner. Remember, though, that the program can function effectively only when all of the aspects are integral working parts of the overall program. Classification schemes like the one given can be useful in designing a coherent program, but successful implementation requires the understanding and support of every person involved.

---

* Fill in the blank with something like *point of view, style, technique,* or even *charisma.* The specific term should not stand in the way of the notion that successful remedial teaching is more than a bag of tricks or the content of a course or training program.

† Figure 10.1 and the related discussion are adapted from several sources in which I have discussed the instructional aspects of the overall reading program: *Corrective and Remedial Teaching,* 2d ed. (Otto, McMenemy, and Smith, 1973), in which the focus is on the corrective and remedial aspects of the instructional program in the several basic-skills areas; *Administering the School Reading Program* (Otto and Smith, 1970), in which the overall developmental reading program is discussed in detail; and *The Wisconsin Design for Reading Skill Development: Rationale and Guidelines,* 3rd ed. (Otto and Askov, 1974), in which an objective-based approach to reading instruction is presented.

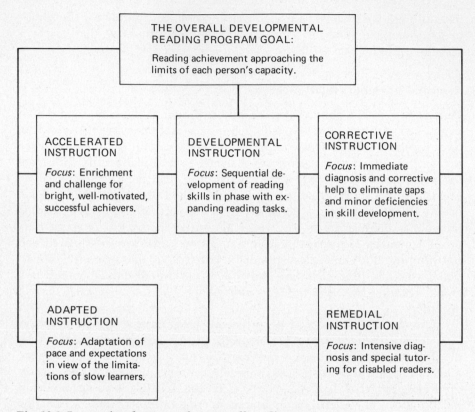

Fig. 10.1. Instructional aspects of an overall reading program.

Developmental instruction   Schiffman (1966, p. 241) has characterized developmental instruction as follows:

> The developmental program of instruction involves systematic instruction at all school levels and in all content areas for those who are developing language abilities commensurate with their general capacity levels. This developmental program is the responsibility of every teacher, affects all the pupils, is provided for in the regular curriculum, and is a continuous, ongoing process. A balanced program includes instruction in the basal, curricular, and recreational reading areas.

Thus developmental instruction is pitched to and adequate for the normal child who moves through the skill-development sequence without complications. Corrective, accelerated, adapted, and remedial instruction—which should be forthcoming in response to special problems and/or needs—must, of course, be carefully coordinated with the ongoing developmental instruction.

Corrective instruction   Corrective instruction is differentiated from developmental instruction mainly to underscore the need for (1) continual assessment of individual performance in order to discover minor problems and confusions early, and (2) prompt provision of additional help as needed. Designed to find and eliminate gaps and minor problems early, corrective instruction is best offered by the classroom teacher as a part of the day-to-day developmental instruction.

Accelerated instruction   Like corrective instruction, accelerated instruction is based on continual assessment. Students who are experiencing no difficulty should—if they have the ability and adequate motivation—be able to respond positively to a more rapid pace or a broader scope of work, or both. To permit—or worse yet, to force—such students to loaf along with work that is not challenging is wasteful and unpardonable. Continual assessment can help us find problems while they are still minor. But equally important, though far less prominent in much planning, continual assessment can also clear the way for accelerated instruction.

Adapted instruction   *Adapted instruction,* with its *emphasis on modification of pace and expectations in view of the limitations of slow learners,* is possibly the most neglected area of the overall reading program of the typical school. Unfortunately, in age-graded schools children who belong in adapted instruction are often pushed into remedial classes, where they remain because they are never able to get "up to grade level." A sensible approach to this area of instruction begins with the acceptance of the limited ability of these children and goes on to provide adapted instruction, whereby the pace and long-term expectations are appropriately modified. This in no way labels certain children as inferior. Rather, it amounts to recognizing and responding to each child in appropriate ways. As with other areas of the total reading program, success depends on instructional adaptations which permit realistic pacing according to the strengths and weaknesses of the individual.

Remedial instruction   Remedial instruction differs from corrective instruction mainly in degree and from adapted instruction in expectations. Remedial instruction is offered to pupils with severe deficits in skill development, with the expectation that the deficit will be eliminated or substantially reduced as a result of the teaching. Pupils with limited intellectual ability need adapted instruction; pupils who are not achieving at capacity need remedial instruction. The instructional setup is modified to insure that adequate time, sufficient materials, and an optimum setting are available to permit the intensive diagnosis and tutoring required.

Perspective   A scheme like the one developed above can help to identify concerns and to focus discussion. But it can also cause problems if the categories are treated as if they were inflexible. In the classroom, there would be a very fine line between, say, developmental and corrective instruction. To label a given student or a given instructional act either "developmental" or "corrective" would usually be both unproductive and plain foolish. We talk about corrective teaching mainly as a way to underscore the need to handle little problems before they become big ones. Likewise, we talk about remedial teaching mainly to underscore the need for special resources when it comes to handling more demanding problems.

The point here is that everything must fit together, because there is a single goal. Continual assessment is what makes the fitting possible. If we continue to look at and deal with the strengths and limits of individuals, labels and schemas will serve, not dictate, our purposes.

GETTING ORGANIZED FOR REMEDIAL READING

All good teaching is assessment-based. Some teachers seem to be able to use informal assessment techniques, such as observations and work samples, very effectively; others tend to rely on more formal testing and record keeping in their assessment. Whichever personal style a teacher finally develops, the fact is that teaching that is efficient and effective is *assessment-based.* In other words, teaching that is focused, properly paced, and individualized is based on thorough and specific information about the learner. But if good teaching is *based on* assessment, it is *guided by* perceptive consideration of such things as *resources available, viable teaching alternatives,* and *realistic outcomes.* Good remedial teaching simply underscores all the positive aspects of good teaching.

A teacher's style is a very personal thing that reflects many factors that are beyond influencing in the space of a single chapter. Yet certain aspects of an effective style can be identified. Together they amount to what we call an *assessment/alternatives approach* to teaching. The characteristics of such an approach are discussed in the subsection that follows. In effect, the discussion has to do with getting organized on a personal basis. Organization is also required if communication and movement are to proceed smoothly among teachers and across aspects of the overall reading program. Some suggestions are offered in the subsequent subsection.

To some people, any talk about getting organized will be seen as heavy-handed and confining. Organization can turn out that way. But it can also provide structure and means for dealing efficiently with recurring tasks and/ or problems. Positively perceived, organization can set you free!

An assessment/alternatives approach

One model for teaching in general, but for remedial teaching in particular, has been the Diagnosis → Prescription model borrowed from the medical profession. Application calls for prescribing treatment on the basis of all relevant information. The model tends to break down in the classroom, however, because the teacher must deal with about 30 individuals at once, not with the single individual for which the model was devised in the first place. In a modified *remedial* teaching situation, the limitation is less severe, but even then individual tutoring is more often the exception than the rule. The *Assessment/Alternatives* model suggested here is a modification of the classic medical model insofar as it builds in consideration for numbers and for the total situation. The model is presented schematically in Fig. 10.2. Each of the main aspects is considered in the discussion that follows. Note now that the model provides, as indicated by the lower set of arrows, for not only regeneration after action is completed, but also possible modifications— through further evaluation and/or generation of additional alternatives—as action proceeds.

Acquire information   Good teaching is, as we have pointed out, assessment-based. But assessment must be broadly conceived. Unfortunately, too many teachers have come to view assessment as little more than paper-and-pencil testing, so they have experienced the disillusionment that comes from trying to make sensible instructional decisions on the basis of test scores only. Test scores are sterile until they can be viewed in a larger context.

More broadly conceived, assessment amounts to information gathering *directed by a sense of what can and should be done.* Direction is important because unrestricted information gathering can dissipate energy and resources in a most unproductive manner. How much information is enough? Any answer to such a question is likely to be either too pat or too general to be very useful, but it deserves careful consideration because it has important implications for allocating resources.

Otto, McMenemy, and Smith (1973, Chapters 3 and 4) offer at least a partial answer in their discussion of *levels of diagnosis*. Acknowledging that

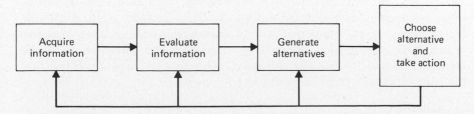

Fig. 10.2. The assessment/alternatives model.

all reading problems do not demand equally comprehensive treatment, they suggest three levels of diagnosis: *survey, specific,* and *intensive.* At the *survey,* or screening, level, the purpose is to locate learners who are having difficulty and appear to need corrective or remedial help. The information required would be quite limited, and it could readily be obtained by consulting cumulative records, examining achievement test scores, consulting teachers, giving a screening test, or some combination of these. Since the purpose is simply to locate problems, there is no need for background information on individuals or for any information regarding the specific nature of the problems.

At the *specific* level, the purpose is to identify the deficiencies and gaps in reading-skill development that are the immediate causes for an individual's poor performance in reading. Because the focus is on skill development, information gathering would focus on the assessment of performance related to specific reading skills. The direction of information gathering is set by an assumption that is made at the specific levels of diagnosis: that the most straightforward way to tackle a reading problem is first to identify and eliminate specific deficiencies in skill development. The information sought is, therefore, limited to the diagnosis of strengths and weaknesses in skill development.

The *intensive* level is reserved for cases that are unusually severe and that have not responded to skill-centered teaching. At this level, any and all information that relates to causes for the problem and ways to tackle it becomes relevant, so a comprehensive case study may be in order. Such a case study would include information about (1) the individual's academic performance, particularly in the area of difficulty; (2) the individual's background—home, school, health, personality, social adjustment; (3) the success or failure of previous remedial teaching, if any; (4) promising directions, if any, for further treatment. The information would come from a variety of sources and, equally important, the assumption would be that intensive treatment could and would be made available.

Again, how much information is enough depends on the purpose that is set and the outcome that is expected. A hierarchy of levels of diagnosis, such as the one suggested by Otto, McMenemy, and Smith, tackles successively more complex problems, sets progressively broader constraints with regard to next steps, and demands more information at each level. Whether or not such a progression in levels of complexity and information can be identified, questions like the following ought always to be asked *before* information is gathered:

1. What kind of information is needed to accomplish the purpose?
2. What are the best sources of needed information?
3. How can and will the information be used?

If information is purposefully gathered in the first place, there will be less need for sorting through the relevant and the irrelevant at the next step—evaluation.

Evaluate information   Purposeful information gathering can be at least partially sidetracked for remedial teachers by the fact that they often work with information that comes to them from a variety of other sources, e.g., classroom teachers' verbal or written reports, cumulative folders and test-score summaries, psychologists' reports, and medical evaluations. Although such information is potentially useful to a remedial teacher, it is often gathered for purposes only tangentially related to the remedial teacher's. But regardless of its source, information once gathered should always be evaluated in terms of the specific and immediate context in which it will be used. Good remedial teachers evaluate information by giving consideration to its *validity, appropriateness, credibility,* and *relevance.* Lest we appear to suggest that the evaluation process be heavy-handed and formalistic, we shall simply characterize the considerations as they might be encountered by a remedial teacher.

Validity. Test validity finally boils down to whether a test really measures what it claims to measure. Unfortunately, test titles can be very misleading. Many so-called tests of intelligence (or capacity or potential or whatever) really measure reading ability. "Comprehension" tests may in fact bog down in word-attack problems. "Phonics" tests may never get beyond auditory discrimination. Although there are very formalistic ways to assess test validity, common sense is the most readily available guide. *If you want to judge what a test truly measures, don't look at the title; look at the test.*

All information, not only tests, ought to be examined for *validity.* A valid test can yield a *score* that has no validity for an individual if, for example, it is given under inappropriate conditions. A teacher's report *can* convey more feelings than facts. A psychologist's or medical doctor's report *can* be so biased or so dated as to be quite invalid. In short, information must be examined with regard for its *source* and the *context* in which it is given. Only information that presents the facts as they *really are* is valid.

Appropriateness. Information must be appropriate to the purpose for which it will be used. A quick survey test, e.g., the *Wide Range Achievement Test* (Jastak, Jastak, and Bijou, 1965), might yield scores that would be quite appropriate at the survey level of diagnosis, but the scores from such a test would be of no value at the intensive level. Conversely, detailed case-study information could be completely relevant at the intensive level of diagnosis, but be much too detailed to be useful at the survey or specific levels.

There is no need to belabor the matter of *appropriateness* of information. The point is important but very straightforward; information must be on target in view of the immediate purpose. Any information that is not on target does not meet the critical test of appropriateness. Once a judgment is made, such information should be put aside so that it will not clutter up the assessment process.

Credibility. In addition to being appropriate to a given purpose, information must be credible in view of the clientele. Stress consideration for the individual. Such is the case with many ostensible tests of achievement; be *valid* in a strict measurement sense, *appropriate* in terms of level of diagnosis, but not *credible* in view of a cultural bias to the disfavor of a given individual. Such is the case with many ostensible tests of achievement; certain items are out of step with reality as it is experienced by certain individuals. Equally common are instances in which children who must participate in group testing strictly on the basis of their grade placement are forced to respond to tests that are too hard or too easy. The credibility of scores for such individuals is questionable, because the scores reflect only random responding if the test was too hard or, on the other hand, a ceiling effect if the test was too easy. Again, the point is simple but extremely important; consider the *individual* involved in judging the credibility of information.

Relevance. In terms of reality, the judgment of relevance of information to a given *situation* may be most important of all. Remember, we said that the *Diagnosis* → *Prescription* model tends to break down when teachers must deal with groups rather than single individuals. The main problem is that diagnostic and teaching routines that would be appropriate and feasible in one-to-one situations are not practicable when there are, as is most often the case, one teacher and more than one—possibly many more—individual. Adaptations must be made in order to accommodate group, as contrasted to strictly individual, needs and to reflect the reality prescribed by such things as group size, time and resources available, and group characteristics. The strategy—which we discuss in the next sections—is to develop and select alternative means for dealing with group realities. The relevance of information in view of given situational constraints must be considered in the evaluation of information.

In summary, the evaluation of information ought to include careful consideration of (1) its *validity,* the most basic factor; (2) its appropriateness in light of a specific *purpose;* (3) its credibility with regard for a given *clientele;* and (4) its relevance in view of *situational* constraints.

Generate alternatives   Assessment amounts to purposefully gathering and carefully evaluating information, and it should provide a basis for generating teaching alternatives insofar as the needs and characteristics of learners are concerned. At the stage of generating teaching alternatives, the sky is the limit. Creative thinking, or brainstorming, is in order because the goal is to *generate,* not to implement, alternatives. The single trait that probably most definitively sets excellent remedial teachers apart from the crowd is their ability to generate creative, innovative, worthwhile alternatives to dealing with assessment information. New grouping patterns; the use of small group, large group, and individual tutoring options; the effective use of material and personnel resources; realistic motivational techniques; the development of new materials—all of these are considered in generating alternatives for dealing effectively with individual needs.

Many factors influence the generation of alternatives: time available, resources, point of view about reading and the reading process, number of students, characteristics of the students, and others. A teacher of economically and/or culturally deprived students would come up with alternatives different from those devised by a teacher of middle-class students with enriched backgrounds of experience. The same teacher would probably come up with many more alternatives for dealing with a heterogeneous group of 30 than for a smaller, more homogeneous group. The teacher operating from a language-development base for teaching reading might come up with quite different alternatives from the teacher with a systematic skill-development orientation. But whatever the alternatives, the generative step is important because it transforms the information base into plans for action.

Choose alternatives/take action   At this stage the teacher chooses the plan of action that seems most appropriate in view of the information available, the teaching situation as it exists, and personal expertise and preference. Too often, the element of personal expertise and preference is ignored, when in fact it is likely to be at least as influential in making a final decision as any other set of factors. Certainly the personal resource is important and deserves consideration. The single point for comment here is that there is a danger of choosing an alternative simply because it fits into a comfortable routine. The ultimate choice must reflect personal and situational limitations, but it ought to be the one that comes closest to meeting all of the instructional needs, not merely the one that comes most easily.

Good teachers have always worked with an implicit *Assessment/Alternatives* model. Those who *aspire* to be good remedial teachers will benefit from applying the model as they develop or sharpen a personal style.

Objective-based teaching

In addition to the need for some scheme for getting personally organized for remedial teaching, there is a need for organization in the reading program.

Rather than attempt to survey the alternatives that have been devised, we shall describe the elements of a framework for organizing instruction by objectives. The discussion is excerpted and adapted from *Objective-Based Reading* (Otto and Chester, 1975). Objectives provide not only the structure that is required by an overall reading program like the one discussed earlier in this chapter, but also the basis for assessment of reading problems and progress. There are five main elements of an objective-based framework for teaching reading.

1. *Identify essential skills.* First, we must decide *what* we want children to learn if we hope to deal effectively with their individual differences as we teach them to read. This means that the first step toward organizing instruction in reading must be to identify the skills that are essential to success in reading. Until this is done, there is no basis for *focusing* instruction.

Unfortunately, at the present time there is no empirically derived list of essential skills in reading. That is, the massive task analysis and research job required to determine precisely which skills must be mastered, and in what order, has not been done. One of the problems is that people in reading education and research are still having trouble agreeing how to define reading. In any event, an empirically derived and validated list of skills is not likely to be available in the near future.

This does not mean that nothing can be done now. The fact is that reading is being taught successfully, and there is reasonable agreement among teachers as to what the essential skills are. Once you have decided which skills you consider essential to success in reading, you have a basis for proceeding with the differentiation of instruction. Your main task is to help each child to master the skills as rapidly and efficiently as possible. Continual progress—that is, moving each child along at a rate that is right for him or her, not at a rate that is tied to a curriculum guide or a basal reader —is possible because you know what you want each child to learn.

2. *State objectives.* Once the essential skills have been identified, it is useful to pin them down with objectives that describe either mastery levels of behavior or situations for developing the skills. *Behavioral objectives* serve two purposes. First, since they make explicit the behaviors that are essential for mastering a given skill, they give you a basis for discussing a skill with other people and for setting a goal for teaching the skill. Second, they establish observable criteria that permit you to decide when a child has mastered a given skill. *Expressive objectives* are useful when mastery levels cannot, or should not, be prescribed. See Otto, Chester, McNeil, and Meyers (1974) for a detailed discussion of objectives and lists of essential objectives.

3. *Examine individual skill development.* If we can decide which skills we consider essential, and if we can describe our expectations regarding mastery of those skills, we are in a position to examine the skill-development status

of individuals. We can observe the behavior of individuals to determine their strengths and weaknesses. Such knowledge about each individual is the practical basis for assessment information at the specific level of diagnosis.

4. *Identify appropriate teaching/learning activities and materials.* Appropriate instruction involves more than focusing on strengths and weaknesses in skill development. It also involves providing differentiated instruction for students with different learning styles. That is, given a common objective, some pupils will respond well to one instructional approach, others will respond best to an alternative approach, and still others will do best with still other approaches.

What this means is that teachers must not be lulled into a false sense of well-being by an objective-based approach to teaching reading. They must remain eclectic in their approach to teaching. In other words, they must select and use the best from all approaches. Most important, they can adapt their approach with a given individual because they are aware of and comfortable with a variety of approaches.

So by all means, be an eclectic. But in order to avoid being overwhelmed by the vast quantities of materials and the varied procedures that are available for teaching reading, remember that your goals are described by objectives and prescribed by your list of essential skills. In other words, once you decide what is important, you have an efficient way to bring instruction into focus. You can organize your teaching and your instructional materials around your objectives. With an individual pupil, you may follow any one of several paths, but you always know exactly where you are going.

5. *Evaluate the results.* Two levels of evaluation are essential when specific skills are the focus of instruction. First, there must be assurance that the skill-related objectives are being reached. Second, there must be assurance that the attainment of specific objectives is accompanied by functional reading ability, an ability to cope with the reading tasks encountered both in and out of school. The ultimate payoff from objective-based instruction comes at the second level.

We focus on essential skills and specific objectives in order to systematize teaching and encourage efficient learning. But the mastery of specific objectives is nothing unless it is accompanied by an ability to get them all together and to read connected text. Many opportunities to apply the skills must be provided, and assurance that functional reading ability is increasing must be sought. Any evidence of a breakdown at either level is a signal to go back and reevaluate the entire process.

A breakdown in specific skill development may indicate too rapid pacing, inappropriate teaching, overwhelming personal difficulties, or other problems that can be identified through careful reexamination. A breakdown in functional reading ability may indicate inadequate skill mastery, inability to apply known skills, or inappropriate choice of reading materials at a given stage of skill development. Such problems, too, can be identified through reexamination. A major advantage of a skill-centered approach to reading instruction is that it establishes a basis for tracing back to see what went wrong if the desired end results are not forthcoming. We can do a better job of teaching if we first decide exactly what we want children to learn and then facilitate that learning.

Objectives provide the building blocks of a comprehensive, overall reading program and a vehicle for communication among teachers. For individual remedial teachers, objectives provide a basis for gathering information about students' specific strengths and weaknesses in reading and a means for organizing instruction. Viewed with perspective and used with common sense, objectives provide direction without prescribing teachers' actions.

SOME POINTS OF VIEW FOR REMEDIAL TEACHERS

A point of view is a very personal thing, so it would be presumptuous to suggest here a point of view to be adopted by remedial teachers. Instead, we offer some personal viewpoints that were developed in a variety of contexts, in the hope that they will be useful to teachers who are shaping their own points of view about remedial teaching.

The individual/person paradox

The point of view expressed here is from *Objective-Based Reading* (Otto and Chester, 1975).

The individual The complex process of reading is translated to real-world behaviors only when human beings tackle the tasks of mastering the composite skills and of making sense out of printed symbols. The process is abstract and lifeless until a reader is involved. Yet the reader, while making the process come alive, also adds to its complexity by bringing to it the full range of personal idiosyncrasies.

The concept of individual differences is easier to accept than the consequences. Many teachers who readily accept, say, the normal, or bell-shaped, distribution of IQ scores do little or nothing in their classrooms to adapt the instruction accordingly. But to single out just one dimension of individual differences, such as intelligence, is to greatly oversimplify the problem. Perhaps this tendency to oversimplify, by fixing on but one dimension at a time, is at least partly responsible for our typically poor attempts to cope with individual differences. If we would take a look at the larger, more complex picture, there would be no way to avoid the conclusion that instruction must indeed be individualized. Then we could get on with the task of figuring out how to get the job done.

A number of points are well supported by the existing work in individual psychology. Taken together, they demonstrate the wide range of concerns we must have in order to work effectively with each individual.

1. *Children achieve at different rates.* This point is obvious to anyone who has ever worked with children. Some children learn almost spontaneously, whereas others learn only after much repetition and belabored effort. The only effective way to deal with different achievement rates is to pace the rate of instruction so that it is suitable to each individual's pace of learning. Proper pacing is based on a thorough knowledge of each individual's achievement rate and an explicit knowledge of exactly what it is that we want each child to learn. A major purpose of the remaining chapters of this book is to establish the knowledge base required to deal effectively with individual learning rates.

2. *Differences in achievement increase as children advance through school.* Two additional facts are relevant here. First, the *better* the teaching, the *greater* the differences. Certain critics of education seem to be suggesting that the goal ought to be a preestablished level of performance for all. What a waste of human potential that would be! Well-focused, effective teaching will maximize the realization of each child's full potential and ensure a range in achievement that is as great as the range in individual differences. Second, given *equal* amounts of practice, good and poor achievers will, all other things remaining equal, *increase* their differences in performance. Again, the outcome is an increase in the range of differences in achievement.

The more general issue of *teaching for mastery* is also relevant here. Reduced to essentials, mastery teaching amounts to setting specific objectives and then seeing to it that every child masters the objectives. Handled in a mechanistic, heavy-handed manner, mastery teaching *could* put a lid on achievement, thereby decreasing the range in differences. This would, of course, amount to a dreadful misuse of a sound idea. Mastery teaching of the basic reading skills is essential, but the *pace* of such teaching must vary greatly from individual to individual, and there is more to *mature* reading than essential skills. In other words, *how fast* and *how far* will remain highly individual matters.

3. *Achievement is often marked by spurts and plateaus.* Achievement rate in any given area is a highly personal matter, but whether it is fast or slow it is likely to be marked by periods of relatively little progress and periods of rapid growth. This phenomenon is particularly apparent in remedial-reading situations, in which the periods of no measurable progress may tend

to be prolonged. Apparently, from time to time children have a need for an opportunity to assimilate new information, to fit it into existing cognitive frameworks, and to organize it all into a manageable whole.

4. *Native endowment (biological factors) plays a large role in a child's development.* Up to this point we have been focusing mainly on psychological and experiential factors, both of which are powerful forces in shaping human differences. The fact remains, however, that each human being is bounded by his or her biological attributes. Consider a homely analogy: The *size* of a box establishes limits on what can go into it. The size does not dictate *what* can go in or determine whether the box will be partially or completely filled. Similarly, biological attributes establish limits on potential, but do not dictate whether that potential will be realized.

5. *Environmental factors play a large role in a child's development.* The old notion that intelligence is fixed by hereditary factors and is unchangeable has now been quite thoroughly discredited. Certainly, as suggested in the preceding point, hereditary biological endowment establishes a base, but there is considerable evidence that such things as nutrition, experiences, and training can and do have a profound influence on human intelligence *as it is currently measured.* Environmental factors, then, *can s*erve as equalizers by offsetting many kinds of individual strengths. Poor teaching can be a great equalizer by encouraging mediocrity. Poor nutrition can prevent the realization of potential, as can an impoverished experiential background. Conversely, enriched environments can make the most of individual strengths and qualities.

6. *Membership in a particular group may lead to erroneous attribution of a certain characteristic to an individual.* This point has strong social-psychological overtones, but it focuses clearly on the individual. The important thing to remember is that we must always consider each individual human being, not the group with which we happen to identify the person. Consider the following: "Your brothers and sisters were all good students, so you must be. . . ." "So you're in remedial reading. You must be. . . ." "Are you saying, Johnny, that you'd really rather take home ec than go out for baseball? You must be. . . ." "This medical report says that you were a premature baby. That means that you must be. . . ." The message, we think, is clear.

7. *Intraindividual differences may be as great or greater than interindividual differences.* Everything we have said about individual differences pertains to the differences *among* individuals. The fact is that there are also differences *within* individuals that must not be overlooked. Each individual is a collection of both strengths and weaknesses. To cite an obvious example, good readers are not necessarily good spellers. Individual uniqueness is indeed an individual matter.

The person Concern for individual differences and for carefully focused instruction can cause problems as well as help to solve them. These problems are implicit in two paradoxes—the individual-person paradox and the teaching-learning paradox.

The individual-person paradox. The individual-person paradox was described by Otto and Smith (1970, pp. 5–6) as follows:

> In our zealous attempts to understand and to provide for the individual we tend often to forget about the person.
>
> MacDonald (1965) has discussed the individual-person paradox. "The *person* . . . in contrast with the individual, is not prized for his uniqueness. . . . The person is valued because of what he shares in common with all other persons: The human condition. . . . To treat persons as individuals (in the psychological sense) is in essence to treat them as objects for our study and control."
>
> Individuals are indeed unique, and they do indeed seem to respond to instruction that is sensitive to their idiosyncratic strengths and weaknesses. Ultimately, though, the acceptance of these factors can—and often does—cause students to be treated as if they were little more than "objects for our study and control," as MacDonald put it. In this case what began as a sound and desirable attempt to personalize instruction becomes an extremely impersonal complex of procedures and categories.

Each child presents us with a paradox. On the one hand, the child is a unique individual in the world. That uniqueness must be treated in unique ways. We must cater to the child's strengths and minister to weaknesses. Yet, on the other hand, the child has a common human status with all other human beings. The child is valued not for idiosyncrasies, but for his or her common human status.

If the paradox is complex, however, its resolution is straightforward. We must not lose sight of the person as we focus on the individual. The individual can be assessed in terms of unique strengths and weaknesses and taught accordingly, but the person must remain unclassified, free to strive and free to learn. But as teachers, we are confronted by still another paradox when we attempt to strike a balance in dealing with the individual-person.

The teaching-learning paradox. Educators have traditionally addressed themselves to the methodology—the how-to-do-it—of teaching. That is, or so it would appear, as it ought to be, for if we are to focus instruction, we must first have a clear notion of what the task is and how to tackle it. Unfortunately, such an emphasis usually tends to stress the *manipulation* of pupils rather than the *participation* of each pupil in the learning process. Thus if we truly believe that active participation is an important aspect of efficient learning, we can see a teaching-learning paradox. On the one hand, once we decide what we want children to know, we want to get on with teaching them. On the other hand, we want to ensure that they take major initiative for their own learning. In effect, we want to be free to manipulate and yet be assured that everyone will participate.

This paradox, too, can be resolved if we will make the main function of teaching the *facilitation of learning*. Here again, concurrent concern for the individual and the person is critical. We can facilitate learning by helping the learners to focus on what they need to know. This must involve not only a thorough understanding of the idiosyncrasies of each individual, but also an abiding concern for the integrity of each person.

Counseling point of view

Here the point of view is adapted from the final chapter of *Corrective and Remedial Teaching*, 2d ed. (Otto, McMenemy, and Smith, 1973).*

Counseling and remedial teaching   Not all disabled learners are emotionally maladjusted, nor are all emotionally maladjusted pupils disabled learners. Yet success in the basic skills—especially reading—is an essential step in normal development, for failure precludes the sequential acquisition of the higher-level academic skills and learnings. Failure in the basic school subjects, then, is likely to interfere with adequate adjustment. To attempt to decide whether an individual pupil's learning problems were caused by emotional problems or vice versa is less important than to recognize the probability that many learning disabilities will be accompanied by varying degrees of emotional maladjustment.

Many children with severe emotional maladjustments need intensive psychotherapy before they can respond to remedial teaching; every attempt should be made to secure competent professional help in such cases. But in the majority of cases it is up to the remedial teacher to deal with emotional problems along with learning problems. Mastery of diagnostic and remedial techniques provides the teacher with a means for outlining a plan of instruction, but success in remedial teaching is often as dependent on meeting emotional needs as on meeting instructional needs. This does not mean that remedial teachers must be highly trained counselors, but it does mean that teachers who can establish relationships that communicate acceptance and understanding with their pupils are more likely to be successful than those

---

* Robert C. Fredricks, Counselor at the Portland (Oregon) Community College, is responsible for much of the discussion of the counseling point of view.

who depend entirely on the manipulation of diagnostic and remedial techniques.

Counseling relationships   One of the characteristics of the counseling relationship, *uniqueness,* is paradoxical. Although certain general statements can be made about the relationship, each relationship is unique because individuals are unique. Thus a counselor must have self-knowledge and understanding, have a generally positive feeling toward human beings, and be flexible enough to adapt basic counseling techniques to the particular needs of each client. The paradox is not a new one for teachers who know from experience that what works with one child does not necessarily work with another.

The counseling relationship also contains the paradox of *objective thoughts* and *emotional feelings.* A counselor must maintain an intricate balance between these two diverse positions. In order to apply the scientific principles of human behavior to what the client is presenting, the counselor must remain, to a degree, removed or detached from the remarks, avoiding personal reaction. However, the counselor must, at the same time, be emotionally involved with the client, communicating sensitivity to and awareness of the feelings the client is expressing. This also enables the client to remain emotionally involved. A counselor who becomes too detached takes on the characteristics of a computer; one who becomes too emotionally involved loses objectivity and starts reacting personally. Thus the counselor must strive to be both emotionally involved in and objectively detached from the counseling situation. This simultaneous dual role makes counseling both an art and a science.

The counseling relationship must also be *real;* it must be genuine, sincere, and honest. People carrying on conversations in everyday life mask their true feelings with small talk; but if such a façade is maintained in the counseling relationship, conversation instead of counseling takes place. But a counselor cannot merely say, "I am interested in you"; he or she must show it through behavior.

Another important characteristic of the counseling relationship is *acceptance* of the individual by the counselor. To accept is to value an individual for his or her characteristics of infinite worth and dignity, to place extreme value on a human being for having an inner self, for being unique, for producing original thoughts and ideas. The client who is accepted by the counselor feels valued for his or her unique self and in possession of the qualities necessary for positive development; thus the client enhances self-acceptance.

Sympathy is not a part of acceptance. A counselor who expresses sympathy is saying, "I agree with your suffering—you must feel awful—let me help you." Sympathy teaches the client to be dependent, to rely on the counselor instead of learning to operate independently. A counselor must feel *with* a client, which is empathy, not *for* a client, which is sympathy. Remedial teachers who do not guard against dependent relationships may find that children who have learned to function effectively during remedial sessions cannot do so when they return to the classroom.

Application   A counseling point of view can be extremely beneficial to a remedial teacher's efforts in working with children. A warm, positive, accepting relationship created by the teacher can enable a pupil to be more receptive to remedial teaching. As a student who has met defeat and failure in one or more school subjects experiences the teacher's positive attitudes of acceptance and understanding, the foundation for improvement is laid. Then, when remedial work is geared to the unique needs of the individual, the stage is set for the student to experience success, perhaps for the first time in his or her school experience. Motivation is created as the remedial teacher is able to give honest, genuine compliments, praise, and encouragement. This in turn produces a greater degree of self-confidence, additional educational goals, and forward movement. Just as failure tends to beget failure, so too can success beget success.

By projecting a counseling point of view, remedial teachers can contribute to more positive learning situations by creating rewarding interpersonal relationships. Rogers (1961, p. 287) was speaking of such relationships when he wrote:

> As I think back over a number of teachers who have facilitated my own learning, it seems to me each one has this quality of being a real person. I wonder if your memory is the same. If so, perhaps it is less important that a teacher cover the allotted amount of curriculum, or use the most approved audiovisual devices, than that he be congruent, real, in his relations to his students.

The case for eclectic teaching

The best remedial teachers are *eclectics*—that is, they select and use what in their judgment is best in a given situation rather than follow a prescribed course of action. The case for eclectic teaching presented here is from a paper prepared for an International Reading Association publication dealing with the improvement of reading instruction (Otto, 1971). The paper has to do generally with the *training* of reading teachers, but its rationale for an eclectic approach is relevant here. All teachers are probably well advised to be eclectics; given the diversity of learning problems, the eclectic view is imperative for remedial teachers.

The need for eclectic teaching   Frieder (1970) gets it all together when he says: "Many alternatives are currently available to the prescriber in the area of media and strategies; but despite the advances in diagnosis and instruction, research has provided little concrete information about the prescriber's task—putting diagnosis and instruction together to reach objectives." A cynic might say that if we don't really know what we're doing, the only thing we *can* do is take an eclectic approach. But I prefer to "accentuate the positive," even though it may be impossible to "eliminate the negative." In another context (Otto, McMenemy, and Smith, 1973, p. 405) it was put this way:

> We doubt that research-based knowledge is forthcoming in the foresee-able future . . . teachers will need to continue to make judgments regarding the instruction of individual pupils. Such judgments will best be made by sensitive teachers with clear perceptions of pupils' needs, explicit objectives, and knowledge of a wide range of methods and materials.

We may not be able to do much to make anyone sensitive, but we can help teachers-in-training to recognize diversity, to accept limitations, to establish objectives, to become familiar with a wide range of methods and materials, to question pat answers, and ultimately to take an eclectic, problem-solving approach to remedial teaching. *Eclectic* means not following any one system, but selecting and using what are considered the best elements of all systems. *That* is the desired approach after the training program is completed, for we have no evidence whatever to support any single system to the exclusion of all others. But if we want teachers to be in a position to take a creative, problem-solving approach to each case they encounter, we must devise training programs that encourage such behavior as well as supply the basic knowledge required.

Rationale for eclectic teaching   The only rationale needed for an eclectic approach is inherent in the following quotations. James (1915, pp. 8–9) put it this way more than half a century ago:

> The art of teaching grew up in the classroom, out of inventiveness and sympathetic concrete observation. Even where . . . the advancer of the art was also a psychologist, the pedagogics and the psychology ran side by side, and the former was not derived in any sense from the latter. The two were congruent, but neither was subordinate. And so everywhere the teaching must *agree* with the psychology, but need not necessarily be the only kind of teaching that would so agree; for many diverse methods of teaching may equally well agree with psychological laws.

That seems to be a clear invitation to eclecticism—not hit-or-miss eclecticism, but eclecticism based on diverse knowledge.

In her excellent article on individual differences, Tyler (1969, p. 639) makes this observation:

> It is psychological individuality which is of the greatest importance to education. Each student in a classroom, no matter how carefully selected as a member of a "homogeneous" group, will of necessity react in his own unique way to the situation. There are differences in talents and aptitudes, in interests and motives, in habits and response styles, in emotional needs and vulnerabilities. In education as in medicine, there is really no "norm." When a teacher makes an assignment to a class of 30, it is actually 30 different assignments that are carried out.

Most teachers would heartily agree with this opinion, even those who have never made a differentiated assignment in their lives. The message is very clear. No single approach or focus is likely to be adequate to deal with the vast range of individual differences in any school situation.

The latter point was also made quite vigorously by Bracht (1970, p. 627):

> Bloom . . . Cronbach . . . Gagné . . . Glaser . . . Jensen . . . and other educational psychologists have suggested that no single instructional process provides optimal learning for all students. Given a common set of objectives, some students will be more successful with one instructional program and other students will be more successful with an alternative instructional program. Consequently, a greater proportion of students will attain the instructional objectives when instruction is differentiated for different types of students.

Bracht (1970) also makes this statement on experimental factors related to aptitude-treatment interactions: "The goal of research on ATI (aptitude-treatment interactions) is to find significant disordinal interactions between alternative treatments and personalogical variables, i.e., to develop alternative instructional programs so that optimal educational payoff is obtained when students are assigned differently to alternative programs." Such research would hopefully and ultimately serve to provide guidelines for the systematic matching of pupils and treatments. Presently, however, the surface has barely been scratched. Until the scratch has been deepened considerably—and to get on with the task of identifying viable alternatives to be researched—we are well advised to maintain a repertoire of treatment options to be employed as they appear appropriate. And the name of the game is eclecticism—not hit-or-miss, trial-and-error fumbling, but careful selection of the treatment that appears to be most appropriate for a given pupil at a given point in time.

The selection of treatments for pupils is what Harris (1970) is talking about in the introduction to his *Casebook on Reading Disability*:

> A combination of teaching methods was used with most of these children, teaching visual recognition of common words while also teaching phonics, and devoting part of the lesson to oral and silent reading. The Gillingham method of phonics instruction was followed in Cases 4, 14, and 16, and was sometimes combined with kinesthetic procedures (Case 10). The Fernald kinesthetic or VAKT method was employed in several of the cases, usually with some modification. For example, in Case 2 the child's lack of fine motor control made writing difficult, so typing was substituted. A language experience approach utilizing the child's own dictation was employed at the beginning in several cases, at times combined with reading of easy printed material.*

He goes on, but the point is adequately made that case studies are likely to be the bases for the variety of approaches. Again, eclecticism is the name of the game. The rationale for an eclectic approach to both teaching and teacher training is implicit in what people who have considered the diversity in pupils and in teaching have had to say.

Espousing eclecticism and actually practicing eclecticism in any sensible way can, of course, turn out to be two quite different matters. Here we have dealt with *why* to do it. One learns *how* to do it by keeping open to ideas and by acquiring a broad background of knowledge and experience. Studying this entire book ought to be a step in the right direction. But the pursuit of eclecticism is a way of life, not just another book or another course.

A FINAL WORD

Richard Pirsig's book, *Zen and the Art of Motorcycle Maintenance* (Pirsig, 1974), carries a subtitle in small print: *An Inquiry into Values.* The subtitle is more descriptive of the content than the full title, and the book is worth reading by anybody who teaches or aspires to teach. Among many quotable passages, one in particular is worth contemplating in the present context:

> I see a deer move about two hundred yards
> ahead and above us through the pines. I try

> to point it out to Chris, but by the time
> he looks it's gone. (p. 231)

Remedial teachers get plenty of invitations to look. The good ones do so before what is there is gone.

REFERENCES

Bracht, G. H. "Experimental Factors Related to Aptitude Treatment Interactions," *Review of Educational Research* **40** (1970): 627–645.

Frieder, B. "Motivator: Least Developed of Teacher Roles," *Educational Technology* **10** (1970): 28–36.

Harris, A. J. *Casebook on Reading Disability,* New York: McKay, 1970.

Heilman, A. W. *Principles and Practices of Teaching Reading,* 2d ed., Columbus, Ohio: Merrill, 1969.

James, W. *Talks to Teachers,* New York: Henry Holt, 1915.

Jastak, J. F., S. R. Jastak, and S. W. Bijou *Wide Range Achievement Test,* rev. ed., Wilmington: Guidance Associates of Delaware, 1965.

MacDonald, J. B. "The Person in the Curriculum." Speech delivered at the 1965 Teachers College Curriculum Conference, Columbia University, November 1965.

Otto, W. "An Eclectic Approach to Training," in Joseph S. Nemeth, ed., *Reading Rx: Better Teachers, Better Supervisors, Better Programs,* Newark, Del.: International Reading Association, 1975, pp. 117–122.

Otto, W., and E. Askov *The Wisconsin Design for Reading Skill Development: Rationale and Guidelines,* 3rd ed., Minneapolis: National Computer Systems, 1974.

Otto, W., and R. D. Chester *Objective-Based Reading,* Reading, Mass.: Addison-Wesley, 1975.

Otto, W., R. D. Chester, J. McNeil, and S. Meyers *Focused Reading Instruction,* Reading, Mass.: Addison-Wesley, 1974.

Otto, W., R. A. McMenemy, and R. J. Smith *Corrective and Remedial Teaching,* 2d ed., Boston: Houghton Mifflin, 1973.

Otto, W., and R. J. Smith *Administering the School Reading Program,* Boston: Houghton Mifflin, 1970.

Pirsig, Robert M. *Zen and the Art of Motorcycle Maintenance: An Inquiry into Values,* New York: Morrow, 1974.

Rogers, C. R. *On Becoming a Person,* Columbus, Ohio: Merrill, 1961.

Schiffman, G. "Program Administration within a School System," in J. Money, ed., *The Disabled Reader,* Baltimore: Johns Hopkins Press, 1966.

Tyler, L. E. "Individual Differences," in R. L. Ebel, V. H. Noll, and R. M. Bauer, eds., *Encyclopedia of Educational Research,* 4th ed., New York: Macmillan, 1969.

Chapter 11

THE READING SPECIALIST

DANIEL A. BRIGGS · *Russell Sage College*

FLORENCE C. COULTER · *Oakland Schools, Pontiac, Michigan*

EVOLUTION OF THE ROLE OF THE READING SPECIALIST

Although reading instruction in one form or another has been part of the American school scene since the earliest colonial period, little if any material is available which would enable current generations of Americans to understand how this reading instruction took place. Almost nothing was done to provide teachers in the early colonial period with a structure and a set of methodologies which they could then translate into classroom experiences. In other than a few isolated instances, Smith (1965) notes that teachers and school people were on their own in presenting structured reading programs. It was not until the middle 1800s that textbooks designed to be sources of information for teachers and prospective teachers became available. One of the earliest, John Gill's *The Introductory Textbook for School Education Methods and School Management,* appeared in 1867. Published in London, it was designed to give teacher-education candidates a general overview of how school should be "kept." The material covers school education, school management, and methodology, with a heavy emphasis on reading. Gill discusses methods and use, principles and rules, work and standards, exposition, and derivation. In addition to these specific reading fields, spelling, writing, penmanship, and grammar are also treated. It is interesting to note that the material on reading occupies more space than the other three language arts combined.

Of interest also is the fact that long before the phonics look/say controversy raged in the 1950s, Gill carefully pointed out the variety of ways in which words and reading could be taught. He specifically named the alphabetic method, the phonic method, the look/say method, and the phonic-analysis method. One notes few differences between the things Gill said well over one hundred years ago and those things which currently are being said by proponents of particular approaches to word analysis or decoding. Although Gill devoted most of the material in his book on reading to word analysis, he did not ignore comprehension. Without specifically designating comprehension as such, he described a series of techniques which teachers could use to develop what we label "comprehension skills" today. Again without naming it as such, Gill carefully covered ground that current writers define as content-area instruction. He asked teachers to be concerned with those materials in texts that could prove a hindrance to youngsters' understanding and went on to develop the point that when teaching from a textbook, the teacher must develop special vocabulary as well as sentence and paragraph comprehension of the concepts presented.

In the period following Gill's publication and continuing through into the early twentieth century, other professional writings on the subject of reading instruction appeared in England and America. These included Huey's scientific contribution to the field, *The Psychology and Pedagogy of Reading,* published in New York in 1908. It is safe to say, however, that little attention was paid in the literature or in practice to supervising reading instruction. Historically, what supervision took place was accomplished by the elementary school principal. Among the first books to be devoted to the subject were *The Teaching and Supervision of Reading* by Gist and King, published in 1927, and *Supervision and Teaching Reading* by Harris, Donovan, and Alexander, also published in 1927. Gist and King directed their efforts primarily toward the responsibilities of principals. Harris and her associates addressed their publication to supervisors and teachers. As these and other American educators began thinking of reading supervision, attention was also being directed toward the conceptualization of teaching strategies which eventually became known as remedial reading. The development of such techniques grew out of a complicated set of interconnecting circumstances, including the perfection of some of our earliest tests of reading vocabularly and comprehension. The trend of the period was toward keeping pupils in school rather than encouraging them to drop out. Educational philosophers such as Dewey and Kilpatrick were influencing thought. There was increasing public acceptance of a changing relationship in education. Schools were responsible to students, not students to schools. Each of these factors played a part, too.

The reading specialist who finally emerged in the early 1930s was a supervisor responsible for the improvement of the teaching of reading. The trend toward general elementary supervision had been accelerating so rapidly that the move to specialists for basic subjects was a natural outgrowth. Unfortunately, the idea of a reading supervisor as such did not "catch fire" at that time. The literature supplies no solid explanation as to why this occurred. One can only speculate that not one reason, but rather a multiplicity of factors, was responsible. Whatever the cause, two decades later, at the beginning of the 1950s, there were few reading supervisors or coordinators on the educational scene. A relatively limited number of state, county, and district school systems had joined the small minority of big cities whose administrative staffs included someone responsible for the total reading program.

In the aftermath of World War II, a move to afford a more professional status to teachers coincided with a period of national concern about academic achievement, which grew out of medical and technological advancement and the cold war. Critics of education were legion. It was an unusual year when a prominent American from education itself, from government, or from the business community did not make some pronouncement about reading instruction and problems associated with it. In order to cope with the critics, schools began to employ the so-called remedial-reading teachers. At the same time, a proliferation of professional books and remedial materials occurred. These all but guaranteed newly hired remedial-reading teachers and school systems employing them the solutions to problems encountered by children learning to read. The scope of the job assigned to the new reading specialist, who was largely untrained, was that of providing instruction to individual or small groups of children "reading below grade level." With the position of reading supervisor still not fully developed, countless school districts in the United States had reading programs staffed by such remedial teachers but were without leadership in reading. Like Topsy, these remedial-reading services just "growed," aided and abetted by government at all levels and by private foundations quick to provide grants or funding for such programs. In a sense, schools had begun the process by hiring workers without realizing the need for supervisors to direct the projects.

Professional groups organized to promote knowledge and research in reading had appeared early in this period. Later, a few farsighted reading educators, recognizing the need for a strong, comprehensive organization, were instrumental in bringing together two competing groups. When the International Council for the Improvement of Reading Instruction and the National Association of Remedial Teaching were merged in 1956, the resulting organization was to become known as the International Reading Association. The newly formed group moved quickly to establish a Professional Standards and Ethics Committee to define the role of the reading specialist and to suggest educational training requirements. Probably because there was so little commonality among reading programs at that time, no hierarchy of functions was delineated. Instead, the reading specialist was broadly defined as a person who could work directly or indirectly with those pupils who had failed to benefit from regular classroom instruction in reading and/or who could work with teachers and administrators to improve and coordinate the total reading program of the school.

The minimum standards for professional training developed by the Board of Directors of the International Reading Association in 1961 represented an important milestone. For the first time, guidelines were available to aid those wishing to use them: colleges setting up educational training programs, school administrators judging the competency of candidates for reading positions, and members of state agencies establishing certification requirements for reading specialists.

Unfortunately, the need to establish direction for the development of the specialist role had not yet been recognized. In a 1965 revision and extension of those guidelines, the committee suggested limiting application of stated minimum standards to those specialists spending the majority of time in developmental or remedial reading activities. It further acknowledged that the responsibilities of a reading clinician, consultant, or supervisor necessitate greater training and experience. However, it was not until 1968, in a second revision, that responsibilities and qualifications were enumerated for these more sophisticated positions. Four major roles were discussed in the new guidelines: special teacher of reading, reading clinician, reading consultant, and reading supervisor (coordinator or director).

ROLE, RESPONSIBILITIES, AND QUALIFICATIONS*

Special teacher of reading

A special teacher of reading would have major responsibilities for remedial and corrective and/or developmental reading instruction. In this role the reading specialist would:

1. Identify students needing diagnosis and/or remediation;
2. Plan a program of remediation from data gathered through diagnosis;
3. Implement such a program of remediation;
4. Evaluate student progress in remediation;
5. Interpret student needs and progress in remediation to the classroom teacher and the parents;
6. Plan and implement a developmental or advanced program as necessary.

To qualify as a special teacher of reading, candidates should have completed the following.

---

* For a more detailed discussion, see the brochure *Roles, Responsibilities and Qualifications—Reading Specialist* (1968), available from the International Reading Association, Newark, Delaware.

1. A minimum of three years of successful classroom teaching in which the teaching of reading was an important responsibility of the position;

2. A planned program for the master's degree from an accredited institution, including:

    a) A minimum of 12 semester hours in graduate-level reading courses, with at least one course in each of the following:

        (1) *Foundations or survey of reading,* a basic, first course whose content is related exclusively to reading instruction or the psychology of reading;

        (2) *Diagnosis and correction of reading disabilities,* one or more courses whose content includes the causes of reading disabilities, observation and interview procedures, diagnostic instruments, standard and informal tests, report writing, and materials and methods of instruction;

        (3) *Clinical or laboratory practicum in reading,* a clinical or laboratory experience that might be an integral part of a course or courses in the diagnosis and correction of reading disabilities (students diagnose and treat reading-disability cases under supervision);

    b) Undergraduate or graduate work in each of the following areas:

        (1) Measurement and/or evaluation;
        (2) Child and/or adolescent psychology;
        (3) Psychology, including such aspects as personality, cognition, and learning behaviors;
        (4) Literature for children and/or adolescents;

    c) Fulfillment of remaining portions of the program from related areas of study.

Reading clinician

A reading clinician would provide diagnosis, remediation, or the planning of remediation for the more complex and severe reading-disability cases. In this role, the reading specialist would:

1. Diagnose and treat more complex and severe reading-disability cases;

2. Provide internship training for prospective clinicians and/or special teachers of reading.

To qualify as a reading clinician, candidates should have completed:

1. Requirements stipulated for the special teacher of reading;

2. A sixth year of graduate work, including:

   a) An advanced course in the remediation and diagnosis of reading and learning problems;
   b) A course or courses in individual testing;
   c) An advanced clinical or laboratory practicum in the diagnosis and remediation of reading difficulties;
   d) Field experiences under the direction of a qualified reading clinician.

Reading consultant

A reading consultant would work directly with teachers, administrators, and other professionals within a school to develop and implement the reading program under the direction of a supervisor with special training in reading. In this role, the reading specialist would:

1. Survey and evaluate the ongoing program and make suggestions for needed changes;
2. Translate, with the help of the principal of each school, the district philosophy of reading into a working program consistent with the needs of the students, the teachers, and the community;
3. Work with classroom teachers and others in improving the developmental and corrective aspects of the reading program.

To qualify as a reading consultant, candidates should have completed:

1. Requirements stipulated for the special teacher of reading;
2. A sixth year of graduate work, including:

   a) An advanced course in the remediation and diagnosis of reading and learning problems;
   b) An advanced course in the developmental aspects of a reading program;
   c) One or more courses in curriculum development and supervision;
   d) A course and/or experience in public relations;
   e) Field experiences under a qualified reading consultant or supervisor in a school setting.

Reading supervisor

The reading supervisor (coordinator or director) would provide leadership to every phase of the reading program in a school system. In this role, the reading specialist would:

1. Develop a systemwide reading philosophy and curriculum and interpret this to the school administration, staff, and public;

2. Exercise leadership with all personnel in carrying out good reading practices;

3. Evaluate reading personnel and personnel needs in all phases of a schoolwide reading program;

4. Make recommendations to the administration regarding the reading budget.

To qualify as a reading supervisor, candidates should have completed:

1. Requirements stipulated for the special teacher of reading;

2. A sixth year of graduate work, including:
   a) Courses listed as (a), (b), (c), and (d) in the requirements for a reading consultant;
   b) One or more courses in administrative procedures;
   c) Field experiences under a qualified reading supervisor.

Beyond the qualifications described for each of the four roles, some general competencies would be needed. All reading specialists should demonstrate:

1. Proficiency in evaluating and implementing research;

2. Willingness to make a meaningful contribution to professional organizations related to reading;

3. Willingness to assume leadership in improving the reading program.

Despite the efforts of the International Reading Association, certification bureaus in many states, and teacher education institutions throughout the country, there remains a confusing array of reading specialists operating in a multitude of fragmented reading programs. Nationwide data would undoubtedly show the preponderance of individuals providing specialized reading service to be employed in the capacity of a special teacher of reading. Reading clinicians, consultants, and supervisors remain comparatively few in number.

PROBLEMS RELATED TO CURRENT FUNCTIONING OF READING SPECIALISTS

Although hundreds of millions of dollars have been invested in special reading instruction over the past 25 years, the incidence of reading failure continues to be depressing. According to statistics reported by the United States Office of Education (1971), more than eight million children still are not learning to read adequately. Sixteen percent of the children enrolled in grades 1 through 12 require special reading instruction. In most large city school systems, at least half the students are unable to read well enough to handle their assignments. Each year some 700,000 youngsters drop out of public schools. Studies show that the average dropout is at least two years behind his or her age group in reading and other basic skills. There are more than three million illiterates in our adult population. Finally, about 18.5 million Americans lack the practical reading skills necessary to complete simplified application forms for such common needs as a driver's license, a personal bank loan, or a job application.

Why do we face such a dilemma when we have been funding reading-support services at a higher level than at any previous time in the history of American education? The answer is not a simple one. Hindsight strongly suggests that many programs to combat reading failure have been undertaken too hastily and with too superficial an awareness of the true dimensions of the problem. Given the sweeping technological and social changes of recent decades, however, even more carefully conceived and executed actions might have proved powerless to do more than hold the line while achieving moderate successes here and there. Yet clearly the reading specialist has not been a catalyst for improvement to the degree anticipated. Some probable reasons merit further exploration.

Attention to developmental reading

First, the fact cannot be disputed that the majority of our efforts toward improvement have been and continue to be concentrated in remedial rather than developmental instruction. This practice continues despite the advocacy of reading educators and implications of research that the classroom teacher is the most important variable in the process of learning to read. The Bond and Dykstra report, *Interpreting the First Grade Reading Studies* (1967), supported that opinion. Wide differences in achievement among classes using a single approach, which persisted even when pupil variations were held constant by statistical means, led the researchers to conclude that the differences may have been due to differences in teachers. Chall and Feldman (1966), participating in one of those same first-grade studies, found other evidence that what teachers know and do can make a difference in reading success. Overall teaching competence, a thinking approach to learning, a sound-symbol emphasis rather than the reading method per se, and appropriateness of reading lesson difficulty levels—all showed significant positive relationships to success in reading.

Focusing on the aspect of teacher competence is not to indicate that the classroom teacher is the primary cause of reading failure. Rather, the intent is to point out the continuing failure to recognize the inadequacies of preservice teacher education for reading and the absence of appropriate staff-development programs to compensate for such inadequacies. In reporting on a national survey of undergraduate methods-course requirements, Roeder

(1975) found that ten percent of the institutions surveyed did not require prospective teachers to complete even one course in reading methods. Approximately 30 percent of the others included the teaching of reading with instructional procedures for other basic disciplines or incorporated it in the language arts. The majority of these, however, did not allocate the amount of time and credit the combined subject matter merited. Nonacademic methods for classroom teachers fared much better. For music, art, physical education, and religion, more than three semester hours of work was usually required. Though frivolous, Roeder's comment that given the sad state of undergraduate reading programs, religious training might be justified on the grounds that it would prepare the teacher to pray for divine pedagogic guidance, is understandable.

Research has not been able to describe conclusively the exact process by which children learn to read. There is no study that has not generated as many questions about the complexities involved as it has answered. It is an unusual journal report that does not conclude with a statement by the author concerning implications for future research. Yet the classroom teacher is expected to plan and implement reading instruction without benefit of adequate training or constructive direction. Professional books and journals are virtually nonexistent in public schools. Instructional guidance for the teacher is generally limited to teachers' manuals for the basal or other district-adopted materials. Despite such deficiencies, it is assumed that the classroom teacher can be expected to perform at the high level of proficiency necessary to determine and meet the reading needs of children representing a wide range of abilities.

It is inevitable that statistics of failure continue to plague us. The omissions cited in the area of teacher training undoubtedly have fostered many questionable developmental reading practices that can be observed in classrooms. Teachers know little of materials other than district-adopted texts. Instructional planning is being viewed in terms of materials to be covered —books to be completed during the school year, stories to be read this week, workbook pages to be finished before starting the next story—rather than a sequence of skills to be developed. Teaching is being accomplished through directed activities that are conceived of as ends in themselves, not as means to the overall goal of developing capable readers. Assumptions are being made about what children know, particularly as that information relates to reading level. Children move from book to book in developmental materials on the basis of completion of activities rather than competencies demonstrated. Even when publishers' tests show performance falling below standards supposedly indicative of adequate mastery, it is the unusual situation in which a child does not "go on" to the next book or level. Continuity between grade levels is lacking. Children may repeat or skip materials on the basis of imprecise teacher judgments or grade-level equivalence scores achieved on standardized reading tests. The latter practice has been labeled as one of the greater misuses of such tests by Farr and Anastasiow (1969). Direct teaching of reading all but disappears beyond the primary grades.

The consequence of all these facts is that many children are using developmental materials beyond their instructional levels and are experiencing daily frustration. This is especially true in secondary content-area classes; textbooks often are too difficult for a relatively high percentage of students expected to read them. Unfortunately, the rule in such situations usually becomes: "If you can read this book, I can teach you. If you can't read it, I cannot." Furthermore, many other children regularly use reading materials below their instructional levels and participate in activities designed to teach skills they already have.

Quality of remedial programs

A second factor to be considered is the quality of remedial services being provided by special teachers of reading. To be effective, prescriptive instruction must be given individually or in very small groups and distributed according to a time schedule that will permit mastery. Yet the number of students being identified for special help programs invariably exceeds the teaching time available to serve them adequately. In such situations, the options are to deny service to disabled students or to overextend the reading specialist. Either solution ultimately frustrates the goal of remedial instruction—the overall improvement of reading performance.

Articulation between remedial and developmental teachers

A lack of articulation between remedial and regular classroom programs is a further aspect of the problem. For the most part, special reading services operate in a vacuum, largely independent of the classroom and with no impact on the pattern of developmental instruction. Nothing makes less sense than for a child to be sent regularly to the "reading room" for special help while receiving daily reading instruction in the classroom from materials in which she or he has been inappropriately placed by a well-intentioned but misguided teacher. Without doubt, neither teacher is cognizant of what the other is doing. The child is like a ping-pong ball, propelled from one teacher to the other, making it over the net in remedial sessions, but programmed to crash headlong into it when faced with classroom reading demands. A further irony may be a requirement that the disabled reader be responsible for completing classroom work missed while attending remedial reading classes. Such situations occur because specialists and/or classroom teachers fail to understand the need to support each other if disabilities are to be overcome. Instead, classroom teachers see responsibility for corrective instruction belonging to the specialist and want them to accept the burden. More often than not, specialists are happy to do so and devote the school day exclusively to work with disabled readers, leaving classroom teachers free to maintain their individual spheres of influence, including whatever reading instruction they deem appropriate. This pattern has become firmly established over the past two decades.

Resistance to change

The universal phenomenon of resistance to change is yet another factor frustrating reading-improvement efforts. Once a practice has been initiated and the initiators have stamped it successful, it is almost a certainty that the practice will continue unaltered unless a major event forces a change. There is relative security in doing things the way they have always been done, even when the way has been shown to be of questionable value. To some degree, agreement of remedial and classroom teachers to operate independently of each other may reflect conditions under which these reading specialists appeared on the educational scene. Largely untrained and selected to operate in vaguely defined programs, remedial teachers themselves shaped the role. Their general consensus to avoid the appearance of dictating to co-workers with equivalent credentials was not surprising at the time. Now, however, neither group seems to be anxious to change the status quo. In the unusual situation in which teachers and administrators seem to be in agreement on the need to modify a reading support system, there are still likely to be differences in the ways the respective parties view their mutual goals.

Wylie (1969) found such differences when he surveyed elementary classroom teachers and reading consultants to determine their respective perceptions of the consultant's role. Three of his four conclusions described divergent opinions. First, classroom teachers saw the consultant as a supplier of materials, demonstrator of techniques, or director of diagnostic and corrective procedures. By contrast, consultants placed emphasis on administrative needs—organization, time allotments, grouping, and the school curriculum. Second, teachers wanted consultant aid to be accomplished through personalized, informal, small-group activity. Consultants favored involvement with greater numbers through grade-level meetings, orientation programs, or bulletins for teachers. Finally, classroom teachers believed that depth of background in reading and related areas, ability to criticize constructively, and willingness to consult were necessary attributes of an effective reading consultant. Consultants, on the other hand, felt that being able to establish rapport, to offer constructive criticism, and to be impartial were of importance in the order named. Information, materials, and procedures for helping new teachers produced the only area of agreement between the two groups. If Wylie's sample is representative of the two groups nationally, changes leading to greater consultant influence on developmental reading procedures still remain uncertain.

A further commentary also seems to be warranted here. It would be difficult to defend a major objection to the prioritization by classroom teachers that sets in-depth knowledge of the reading process as the most important qualification of the reading consultant. One wonders, therefore, that consultants in the study did not also consider it so. At the very least, subject expertise would seem to outrank criticizing constructively and treating all teachers alike. Without the first, the second certainly would appear to be of questionable quality.

Inadequate certification requirements

A final dimension remaining to be explored is the adequate training and certification of reading specialists. Research demonstrates clearly that we have never really addressed ourselves to that consideration. Kinder (1969), after reviewing the national scene concerning state certification for reading personnel, reported only eight reading credentials of a supervisory nature which appeared to meet the minimum standards suggested by the International Reading Association. A total of 38 other credentials requiring special reading training were found among 23 states. According to Kinder, further study of those 38 credentials showed most of them failing to meet criteria set forth in the IRA minimum standards noted above. The picture was no better in 1974, according to data reported by Stinnett in *A Manual on Standards Affecting School Personnel in the United States,* published by the National Education Association that year.

A picture of a situation that results from such inadequate standards can be constructed from information obtained from the New York State Education Department Office of Basic Educational Data Systems. During the 1974–75 school year, 9254 individuals who functioned as reading specialists were employed by the public schools of that state. Of that number, 855 were listed as administrators. Titles included coordinator, assistant director, supervisor, consultant, department head or chairman, and a category entitled "other" to indicate that the responsibility was outside the classroom. There were 8399 reading teachers classified as developmental reading, corrective reading, or remedial reading specialists. The state of New York is currently preparing certification recommendations which will establish credentials for special reading teachers and reading consultants/supervisors. Until then, no specific reading certification is available at any level. The only credentials that can be required of those presently employed are of a general teaching or supervisory nature. Without certification requirements there is no way to insure that persons functioning in reading positions in the state have adequate qualifications or indeed any which classroom teachers do not possess.

In light of the research cited previously, the New York picture undoubtedly is representative of most other states.

Responsibility for inadequately trained and certified reading support personnel does not rest with state education departments alone. Certainly graduate education institutions granting advanced degrees in reading must share a substantial part of the blame. Colleges and universities do not always have the depth of faculty necessary to fulfill program requirements. Practicum offerings designed to develop practical competencies often lack the simplest quality control—a reasonable professor-student ratio. Unusual latitude in elective or independent study courses may encourage candidates to invest a minimum of time and effort to meet mandated degree requirements.

In a related context, the International Reading Association has also contributed to the problem. This organization seems to be satisfied to describe a hierarchy of roles, responsibilities, and qualifications for reading specialists without becoming involved in enforcement of standards. It has settled instead for an innocuous statement about ethical responsibilities of professionals: "that it is the obligation of all members of the IRA to observe the code of ethics of the organization and to act accordingly so as to advance the status and prestige of the Association and of the profession as a whole" (1968). In the matter of services, reading specialists are admonished that they "must possess suitable qualifications for engaging in consulting, clinical, or remedial work. Unqualified persons should not engage in such activities except under the direct supervision of one who is properly qualified" (1968).

Beyond that, the IRA Committee on Professional Standards and Ethics, acting on charges set forth by the Board of Directors (1975–76), continues to examine the roles, responsibilities, and qualifications of reading specialists; to move to refine, clarify, and extend the description of competencies needed by reading personnel; to recommend criteria and methods for the assessment of those competencies; to study the need for IRA involvement in the evaluation and approval of teacher education programs leading to various categories of certification in the field of reading; and to make recommendations to the board concerning the advisability and feasibility of mounting such a review procedure. The charges to the committee notwithstanding, no evidence of its activity under similar charges has been reported in the last two *IRA Annual Reports* (1973–74, 1974–75). Both of those publications, however, detail operations and recommendations of other committees that are less closely related to the national reading instructional scene.

As states move toward more adequate certification of reading specialists, the issue of individuals already holding such titles will arise. There has been an unwritten law within state education department certification divisions that those individuals currently serving in designated positions are "grandfathered" into the new certification when the requirements are eventually approved. The purpose of the action is to provide the stabilizing effect of not routing personnel from positions in a wholesale manner. But at the same time, it has the debilitating effect of permitting individuals who may not be competent to continue in those positions until they decide to change jobs or retire.

Agreement among reading educators with the preceding analysis of problems of current reading-improvement efforts will hardly be unanimous. Nevertheless, it would be difficult to imagine many arguing seriously against an immediate need for some carefully considered change in direction. Ironically, present circumstances surrounding public education may be militating against rather than fostering such a change. Remedial programs funded by special titles of laws administered by the United States Office of Education and various state education departments have traditionally been considered to be "soft money" projects which would eventually be phased out. However, recent financial pressures in many places have resulted in such programs becoming the only reading services included in local school budgets. Consultant and supervisory positions supported by district revenues appear to be disappearing at an ever-increasing rate. Since funding for special programs under state and federal laws is designed primarily to provide direct service to children, there is little real opportunity for the development of adequate supervision or consultant-type positions. Unless and until the categorical nature of special funds for reading instruction is changed, the inefficient remedial reading services so commonly noted in school systems today could continue by default. Such a commentary becomes especially sad when considered in light of the following statement from an editorial in *The Reading Teacher* by Stauffer (1967, p. 474):

> As the reports in this issue show, a change is slowly being effected. Reading specialists are being sought—not to serve as remedial reading teachers and work in the bottomless pit, but as reading consultants. The role of the consultant is to prevent reading failure by working with teachers, school psychologists, guidance and counseling specialists, administrators, and parents. At last we are on the "ounce of prevention" phase.

A PLAN FOR MORE EFFICIENT UTILIZATION OF THE READING SPECIALIST

Stauffer's euphoria was premature. Today, a decade later, there is little evidence in the literature of any widespread reliance on the reading specialist to prevent failure. Yet as we continue to search for remedies to the problems we face, the reading consultant described by Stauffer again emerges as a practical and reasonable solution. Freed from classroom teaching assignments and/or instruction of special reading groups, such a specialist would work with teachers, administrators, and other school personnel to develop and coordinate a total school reading program. Major responsibilities would include:

1. Planning and directing evaluation of the ongoing program and making recommendations for change;
2. Assisting the building principal and other administrators in the planning and implementation of the school reading program;
3. Working with school administrators and support staff to coordinate the reading program with the total curriculum;
4. Keeping the community informed as to the purposes and progress of the reading program;
5. Consulting regularly with classroom teachers on matters relating to reading instruction;
6. Helping teachers to diagnose reading strengths and weaknesses and to match those skills with appropriate techniques and materials;
7. Recommending materials to aid instruction;
8. Orienting beginning teachers and school aides to the philosophy, procedures, and materials for the school reading program;
9. Providing continuous and systematic procedures and opportunities for professional growth for classroom teachers, e.g., demonstrations, in-service courses, workshops, seminars, conference reports, etc.;
10. Working as a resource person for special cases whose difficulty or complexity requires a high degree of professional skill and knowledge;
11. Keeping school staff informed about new developments in reading;
12. Encouraging and facilitating implementation of promising ideas;
13. Encouraging and facilitating development of research projects with appropriate experimental designs.

Within the framework of responsibilities outlined above are nine areas in which the reading specialist should be able to demonstrate competency: program assessment, goals development, materials and methodology, instructional management, evaluation of pupil progress, staff development, multi-disciplinary team operations, parent and community relations, and professional standards. Although no single plan of operation would be universally feasible, a basic design to guide specialists moving toward reorganization of reading instruction is offered in the rest of this chapter. The model, which incorporates all responsibilities listed previously, should be adapted to coincide with the philosophies and needs of individual school systems.

Program assessment

A first step in implementing the model would be a comprehensive survey of the existing total reading program. Data collection to establish necessary baseline information should focus on the following specific aspects.

Pupil achievement   All evidence of pupil achievement of a standardized, informal, or diagnostic nature should be considered. Input need not be confined to test results alone, but should include subjective records as well. If pupil data available are insufficient, appropriate testing would become the major priority.

Scope and quality of instruction   The extent of the overall reading instructional program is important and should be viewed in relation to district curriculum and philosophy statements. Of greater importance, however, would be some determinations about how well basic fundamentals of reading instruction are being met in individual classrooms, including those of a special and remedial nature. Interest should focus on observable provisions for developmental, functional, and recreational reading. As the specialist examines the developmental phase of classroom instruction, a sequentially organized word-attack program, activities to develop sight vocabulary, and opportunities for oral and silent reading practice would be indicative of attention to the decoding aspects of reading. In addition, structured comprehension experiences, both literal and nonliteral, should be apparent. In the matter of functional reading, the consultant should look for instruction to promote effective use of study skills and reading in content-area materials. Finally, it should be readily discernible that all children are participating in recreational reading. It is equally important that such independent-reading programs enable youngsters to develop and refine literary tastes and judgments as grade levels increase.

Of underlying significance in establishing a total picture of teaching quality should be the question of whether instruction is being provided at appropriate levels of difficulty. It is imperative that students not be placed in materials above or below instructional level as that concept is most commonly defined. Teacher awareness of individual student weakness in specific skill areas should be a related concern.

Materials for instruction   Without making specific judgments about quality, attention should be directed to the depth, breadth, and variety of reading materials available, whether or not in current use. Also, some analysis should be made as to accessibility of those materials not in classroom environs.

Staff development   Assessment of this aspect of the reading program would require determination of staff development and support programs which have been available in the immediate past, are in current operation, or have been planned for the future. Consideration should not be limited to reading, but should include a broad range of in-service opportunities which could help teachers integrate reading with other classroom experiences.

Goals development

Analysis of data collected should permit the specialist to hypothesize about possible directions for action, leading to the second step in the process—setting long- and short-term objectives. Goals, however, should not be established by the specialist alone. Attainment would be most unlikely in the absence of input from all individuals concerned. Rather, it should be the role of the specialist to guide teaching and administrative staff members in the formulation process so that objectives reflect district philosophy. In addition, they must be clearly stated, attainable, and agreed to by all.

Since many circumstances cannot be foreseen when goals are established, there may be occasions when modifications will be necessary. The specialist, therefore, would have continuing responsibility for periodically reviewing progress and suggesting that objectives be restructured whenever that course seems advisable.

Materials and methodology

Goals selected directly influence the instructional program. Therefore, the reading specialist would next qualitatively analyze materials in relation to stated objectives, detailing developmental approach as well as strengths and weaknesses of design. If additional or more appropriate materials are required, the specialist would recommend possible choices and guide staff in the selection process. Toward that end, the specialist must be able to communicate conclusions of pertinent research to all concerned.

Efficient utilization of reading instructional materials seems to demand location of a wide variety of such materials in a central resource area. Supplementary developmental series, trade books, high-interest/low-vocabulary offerings, periodicals, workbooks, teacher-made worksheets, games, and audio-visual equipment should be included. Quantities should be sufficient to permit teachers to draw supplies from time to time to solve immediate problems with individual or groups of children. Organizing and keeping resource-center materials current would be handled by the specialist, too.

Instructional management

In this phase of implementation, the specialist should provide leadership in helping teachers to organize for instruction. Individual assessment if recommended, appropriate grouping and instruction, short- and long-term planning, lesson-plan development, scheduling procedures, and classroom and schoolwide record keeping should be considered. Flexibility would also be important, for no approach will be appropriate for every situation.

Beyond the classroom aspect of instructional management, time should be devoted to working with paraprofessionals or volunteers engaged in reading activities. Assisting building aministrators in selecting and arranging for the use of facilities for classroom and remedial instruction would be a less dramatic but nonetheless important role of the reading specialist, too. This would include working with school personnel who direct such special-use facilities as the media center, library, or learning resource center.

Evaluation of pupil progress

A function of the reading specialist in this area would be to advise teachers about the selection and interpretation of appropriate classroom assessment instruments. Beyond that would be the task of helping teachers to become more proficient in the use of self-selected techniques for determining the effectiveness of specific instructional practices. When evaluation of the total school program is deemed necessary, the specialist would analyze and interpret the results for school and district administrators.

Staff development

At this point, specialist efforts should be focused on promotion of satisfactory learning experiences for children. Strengths and weaknesses noted during the initial assessment phase should suggest the direction for work with teachers. Whatever the instructional approach, the charge would be the same: to insure attention to all elements of a comprehensive reading program consistent with district philosophy. This means that every teacher must know not only the spectrum of reading skills, but also their sequence and interrelation in the development of a mature reader. In this context it would be important to remember that functional reading skills must be practiced in content-area classes. Teachers of those classes must know how to use simplified materials and substitutes for print as sources of information for severely disabled readers.

Staff development traditionally has been accomplished in a variety of ways. Informal lunchtime discussions, meetings during free periods or after school, classroom demonstrations, and college extension course offerings have been popular. Although such methods have, admittedly, fostered improvement, the continuing incidence of reading failure suggests the wisdom of taking a different approach. Utilization of released and paid vacation time opportunities for in-service should be considered as a more viable approach.

In the final analysis, however, the school administrator will have to determine the direction such activities should take, after studying recommendations of the reading specialist in light of district policy and contract provisions.

Multidisciplinary team operations

In his statement cited previously, Stauffer (1967) noted the need for reading consultants to work with school psychologists and guidance counseling personnel to prevent reading failure. Although that premise is obviously sound, a multidisciplinary effort is also the most effective approach to remediation. Except for evident physical or mental handicaps, failure to learn can seldom be attributed to a single cause. Neurological, psychological, emotional, and instructional concerns are possible contributing factors. The reading specialist's responsibility for instructional planning in cases of potential or actual reading disability would require interaction with the social worker, learning disabilities consultant, and language development professional in addition to those already identified by Stauffer.

Parent and community relations

The reading specialist should also serve as an important bridge between school and parent or community groups. Willingness to attend PTA and other local organization meetings to explain the school reading program would ensure the most favorable presentation of the facts and could reap important dividends in community support. The opportunities for feedback from such groups should not be overlooked either. If there is a public relations problem, the sooner the problem can be faced, the better.

Professional standards

The final phase concerns the need for a commitment by the specialist to maintain a high level of professional expertise. Such a commitment would demand that the specialist keep abreast of developments in the field through the literature, professional conferences, and continued study.

CONCLUSION

The model that has been presented does not preclude the need for the reading specialist to function in roles recognized by the International Reading Association other than that of consultant. There will always be children who require greater individual attention than is possible in a developmental situation. In those cases prescriptive instruction might still be provided by the special teacher of reading but would be carefully coordinated with regular classroom activities. Specialized reading personnel could still coordinate districtwide programs from central-office positions. However, we must begin to invest the majority of our time, talent, and financial resources in the prevention of reading failure rather than waiting for problems to arise before taking action. The specialist operating in the role described in this chapter would have the greatest impact on such an effort. Yet realization of that potential will be possible only if demonstrated competency becomes a condition for employment for the position.

State departments of education will have to take the lead by establishing strict certification requirements to ensure availability of competent reading specialists in various categories. Some states, Wisconsin for one, have already established new regulations for reading teachers and for more highly trained specialists as well. Other states are moving in the direction of strong certification controls, too. New York is one of them. The State University (1974) has asserted that the basis for certification must be demonstrated competence in general knowledge, subject-matter knowledge, and teaching skill rather than completion of college course work. Proposed certification for classroom teachers, reading teachers, and reading consultants will require completion of competence-based programs of preparation which provide acceptable evidence that through the collaborative efforts of representatives of colleges and universities, school districts, and professional staffs of school districts, there exists:

1. An analysis and statement of the roles, responsibilities, and functions of the professional positions for which persons are being prepared;

2. A readily available statement of the skills, knowledge, and attitudes expected of program graduates, stated as explicitly and objectively as possible;

3. A statement of what constitutes acceptable evidence of the attainment of the expected skills, knowledge, and attitudes, as well as the standards and conditions by which the evidence is gathered;

4. An instructional program that is congruent with the expected outcomes;

5. A means by which the program is monitored, evaluated, and modified in light of the evaluation.

A competence-based system permits the widest variety of program design, since it does not prescribe any set of courses or learning activities (1974, p. 2).

Assuredly, the most important part of the program will be the procedures and conditions under which assessment is to be accomplished. The greater the degree to which students are assessed doing those things that are actually demanded on the job, the more reliable the judgment will be. Evaluation based on term papers and written reports cannot compare with evaluation procedures based on the reality of a working situation. Unquestionably, many assessment procedures widely used at the present time measure only the ability of students to bring together on paper ideas they have gained from reading and research. Such an evaluation may not even mean that the student actually understands what has been written. It may reflect only the fact that the student has been capable of organizing the thoughts of others and presenting them in a most attractive package.

Finally, the International Reading Association cannot justify continuing to "study the need for IRA involvement in the evaluation and approval of teacher education programs leading to various categories of certification in the field of reading and make recommendations to the board concerning the advisability and feasibility of mounting such a review procedure" (1976, p. 70). The organization must become involved.

REFERENCES

Bond, G. L., and R. Dykstra "Interpreting the First Grade Reading Studies," in R. G. Stauffer, ed., *The First Grade Reading Studies: Findings of Individual Investigations,* Newark, Del.: IRA, 1967, pp. 1–9.

Chall, J., and S. Feldmann "First Grade Reading: An Analysis of the Interactions of Professed Methods, Teacher Implementation and Child Background," in Stauffer, *op. cit.,* pp. 20–26.

Farr, R. G., and N. Anastasiow *Tests of Reading Readiness and Achievement: A Review and Evaluation,* Newark, Del.: IRA, 1967, p. 9.

Gill, J. *Introductory Textbook for School Education Methods and School Management,* 11th ed., London: Longmans, Green, Reader, and Dyer, 1867.

Gist, A. S., and W. A. King *The Teaching and Supervision of Reading,* New York: Scribners, 1927.

Harris, J. M., H. L. Donovan, and T. Alexander *Supervision and Teaching Reading,* Chicago: Johnson, 1927.

Huey, E. B. *The Psychology and Pedagogy of Reading,* New York: Macmillan, 1908.

International Reading Association, Professional Standards and Ethics Committee *Minimum Standards for Professional Training of Reading Specialists,* Newark, Del.: IRA, 1961.

International Reading Association, Professional Standards and Ethics Committee *Minimum Standards for Professional Training of Reading Specialists,* Newark, Del.: IRA, 1965.

International Reading Association, Professional Standards and Ethics Committee *Professional Preparation in Reading for Classroom Teachers Minimum Standards,* Newark, Del.: IRA, 1965.

International Reading Association, Professional Standards and Ethics Committee *Reading Specialists: Roles, Responsibilities, and Qualifications,* Newark, Del.: IRA, 1968.

International Reading Association *Annual Report 1973–1974,* Newark, Del.: IRA, 1974.

International Reading Association *Annual Report 1974–1975,* Newark, Del.: IRA, 1975.

International Reading Association *1975–1976 IRA Directory,* Newark, Del.: IRA, 1976.

Kinder, R. F. "State Certification of Reading Teachers and Specialists," in J. A. Figurel, ed., *Reading and Realism* 13 (1968): 381–386.

Roeder, H. H. "A National Survey of Methods Courses," in J. S. Nemeth, ed., *Reading Rx: Better Teachers, Better Supervisors, Better Programs,* Newark, Del.: IRA, 1975, pp. 19–24.

Smith, N. B. *American Reading Instruction,* Newark, Del.: IRA, 1965.

Stauffer, R. G. "Change, But ——," *The Reading Teacher* 20 (1967): 6, 474, 499.

Stinnett, T. A. *A Manual on Standards Affecting School Reading Personnel in the United States,* Washington, D.C.: NEA, 1974.

United States Office of Education *Reading Seminars,* Washington, D.C.: USOE, 1971.

University of the State of New York, State Education Department, Division of Teacher Education and Certification *Basic Competencies in Reading, and Certificates for Reading Personnel,* Albany, N.Y.: 1973.

University of the State of New York, State Education Department, Division of Teacher Education and Certification *Teacher Education Program Proposals,* Albany, N.Y.: 1974.

Wylie, R. E. "Diversified Concepts of the Role of the Reading Consultant," *The Reading Teacher* 22 (1969): 519–522.

Chapter 12

THE COMPREHENSION PROCESS

CHARLES W. PETERS • *Oakland Schools, Pontiac, Michigan*

As Samuels mentioned in Chapter 2, reading is a complex process comprising many interrelated factors: language, visual discrimination, auditory discrimination, memory, and cognitive development. An essential element inherent in this process is comprehension, for without it the process is incomplete. But what do we mean by comprehension? This vexing question has confronted researchers as well as practitioners for more than a century. Much has been written and published on the topic, but no conclusive determinations have been reached. Nonetheless, it is a very fundamental question, regardless of the lack of professional consensus, because without some operational definition, one cannot ameloriate inadequate comprehension. How can someone develop an instructional program that has as one of its essential elements an undefinable process? Before we can teach comprehension, we must attempt to ascertain what it is.

TOWARD UNDERSTANDING THE NATURE OF THE COMPREHENSION PROCESS

Because good readers can process most of the information on the printed page with relative ease, they often forget what it is like to experience some difficulty with material. As you read the following selection, mentally note those factors which seem to inhibit or impede your understanding of the passage.

> It is impossible to be certain of the identity of the earliest forebrain nuclei and tracts. A few neuroblasts appear around the optic stalk of 6-mm embryos, sending thin axons ventral to it in a caudal direction toward the mammillary recess. They are joined by a few others from above

and just behind the stalk, as shown diagrammatically in Fig. 10. A few fibers of this thin peripheral tract course caudally as far as the interstitial nucleus. They comprise a diffuse system containing the first components of the medical forebrain tract and, more rostrally, a preopticohypothalamic tract.*

The selection illustrates a number of important factors related to the comprehension process. First, although you know many of the words in the passage, the density of important key concepts probably made it difficult for you to ascertain the definition of words such as *neuroblasts, interstitial nucleus,* and *preopticohypothalamic.* Second, the heavy reliance on pronouns makes it difficult to reliably associate all of them with their appropriate referents. Third, undoubtedly this was not the most interesting passage you have ever encountered, and for many people interest alone may be enough to affect their abilities to adequately comprehend a reading selection. Fourth, cognitive strategies that allow you to impose meaning through manipulation of ideas are impeded by both concept load and language structure. For example, having read the selection, you know that its topic deals with the physiology of the brain. But you would probably find it more difficult to answer other specific questions, such as "The preopticohypothalamic tract is part of what section of the brain?" because of the relationship between your own cognitive strategies and such factors as the language structure and conceptual level of the material. Fifth, if specific information or comprehension-related tasks were identified as a major goal of this passage, they may assume a skill sophistication you as a reader may not possess. For example, a comprehension-related task might be to identify the various segments of the brain. This activity would require specific clusters of comprehension skills; as a result, a portion of your success would be based on your ability to complete adequately the designated comprehension task. If you do not possess these skills or lack the appropriate cognitive strategies, you must be instructed in the applications of these skills. Therefore, based on the analysis of the selection, there appear to be at least five factors related to the comprehension process: conceptual attainment, language, cognitive strategies, interest, and comprehension skills related to specific instructional outcomes.

Product versus process

Many factors contribute to the difficulties students encounter when they attempt to comprehend print. However, research findings do not agree on

---

* Ethel Toback, Lester R. Aronson, and Evelyn Shaw, eds., *Biopsychology of Development,* New York: Academic Press, 1971, p. 151. Reprinted by permission.

whether all five of the factors identified comprise the mental operations which we define as comprehension. Since the comprehension process cannot be observed directly, any investigation of the process is circumscribed by this imposed barrier. Nevertheless, the product generated by this covert mental operation can be closely scrutinized, and on the basis of those manifested behaviors, characteristics of the process can be inferred.

Since the comprehension process has to be inferred, it has resulted in the development of opposing views about what factors comprise the comprehension process. Two of the more prominent views are the skills approach and the psycholinguistic approach.

The skills approach   Some reading researchers have attempted to describe the comprehension process by delineating skills thought to be necessary requisites to understanding the message conveyed through print by the author. Considerable research has been influenced directly or indirectly by this belief, and much of the research investigating this area has been designed to measure or verify the existence of such comprehension skills. It is further believed that these skills can be broken down into teachable components. One of the leading advocates for this position is Fredrick B. Davis.

Over the past 30 years a number of studies seem to indicate that five skills can be experimentally distinguishable: recalling word meanings, finding answers to questions answered explicitly or in paraphrase, drawing inferences from the content, recognizing a writer's purpose, attitude, tone, and mood, and following the structure of a passage. The research conducted by Spearritt (1972) seems to confirm Davis's findings in all skill areas except one—finding answers to questions answered explicitly or in paraphrase. The research findings of Peters and Peters (1976) also seem to verify the existence of separately distinguishable skills. In their study teachers identified seven comprehension skills they believed essential for success in their classrooms. A comprehension test was developed to assess the skills. All seven reading skills were found to measure significantly different segments of the comprehension process. Although not all researchers have reached similar conclusions, it does appear that specific comprehension skills are identifiable.

Many skills-management systems—e.g., Communication Skills Program (Southwest Regional Laboratory, 1971); Reading Instructional Management (Oakland Schools, 1972); and the Wisconsin Design for Reading Skill Development (Wisconsin, 1971)—also subscribe to the skills approach. In the Wisconsin Design, comprehension skills have been clustered to provide an overall sequential arrangement without attempting to impose an arbitrary sequence. The basis for such an approach is partially predicated on research such as Davis and Spearritt's logical examination of both elementary and secondary curriculum and input from classroom teachers. The Wisconsin Design has identified six comprehension skills: (1) main idea, (2) sequence,

(3) reading for detail, (4) affixes, (5) use of context, and (6) reasoning (Otto, Chester, McNeil, and Myers, 1974). Taken together, skill-centered approaches appear to be predicated on several assumptions: (1) reading comprehension can be subdivided into a number of subskills; (2) subskills define discrete, or at least teachable, behaviors; and (3) although instructional sequences can be identified, they do not imply hierarchial structure.

Psycholinguistic views of the comprehension process   At the other end of the continuum are those who advocate a holistic approach to the teaching of comprehension. Kenneth Goodman is one of the leading spokesmen for this group. To psycholinguists, reading comprehension involves the use of both language and cognition. They believe in a holistic approach, because in their view, to subdivide the comprehension process into discrete skill categories fractionates the process. They also strongly react to the notion that there is a specifically identifiable sequence associated with the teaching of comprehension skills or that such a sequence can be arranged in a hierarchical taxonomy.

Much of the support for the psycholinguistic approach comes from the research conducted by Chomsky. This approach emphasizes the importance of transformational generative grammar to the comprehension process. Those who advocate the importance of transformational grammar believe that the structure inherent within language—the syntactic and semantic elements— makes it possible for comprehension to occur. According to this theory, the structure inherent within language consists of two elements—the surface structure and the deep structure. Surface structure consists of the relationship between words in sentences; deep structure involves the manipulation of the syntactic elements contained within the surface structure to derive meaning. This is an important distinction, because a single surface structure may have several different deep-structure meanings. For example, in the sentence, "Flying planes can be dangerous," the deep structure conveys two different interpretations. First, all planes flying in the air are dangerous; second, flying in a plane can be dangerous. Such obfuscation can be eliminated only at the deep-structure level. Therefore, comprehension occurs when surface structure can be transformed into deep structure. The more complex the surface structure, the more difficult the transformation.

Language structure and the process of deriving meaning from language are essential elements of the psycholinguists' approach to comprehension. The child must use language that he or she is familiar with and be encouraged to rely on the clues inherent in that language. As Simons (1971, p. 356) points out, in order to comprehend a sentence such as "What was taken?" the reader must be able to retrieve the following information:

1. that something was taken;
2. that something was taken by someone (unspecified);

3. that the person producing the sentence seeks information, i.e., is asking a question;

4. that the sentence refers to a past action;

5. that the person asking the question is more interested in what was taken than in who took it.

A combined approach to comprehension   Both positions contain pedagogically sound views. No one would argue with the position that reading comprehension involves the use of language and cognition. Likewise, a program that advocates a systematic skill-development approach to the teaching of comprehension does not have to be mechanical. Both approaches have pupils' interests as their primary concern. As a result, comprehension becomes inextricably linked to the language and thinking processes. Therefore, for instructional purposes we must identify those factors that allow the student to function in different educational and occupational environments. The remainder of this chapter will deal with how one can seek to combine the two approaches by adopting the most pedagogically and pragmatically sound strategies for teaching comprehension without losing sight of our concerns for individual differences and needs.

Breaking down the comprehension process into teachable components. For instructional purposes it is important to distinguish between the desired instructional outcomes or uses of comprehension skills and the enabling skills or pedagogical techniques used to teach comprehension. Simons (1971) cogently points out that although many lists of "essential" skills for comprehension exist, most of them have arbitrarily grouped skills together without differentiating between uses and techniques employed to teach the skill. For example, it is not uncommon to find the following skills included in materials designated to teach comprehension:

1. predicting outcomes;

2. distinguishing fact from opinion;

3. recognizing literary devices;

4. reading to follow directions;

5. offering a new title for a paragraph;

6. underlying key words in a paragraph;

7. finding the topic sentence;

8. summarizing a paragraph in one's own words;

9. reading in thought units;

10. finding the main ideas of a paragraph;

11. making generalizations;

12. grasping and assimilating relevant details.

The problem with such a list, however, is that it confuses uses with techniques and conversely, techniques with uses. For example, a teacher's desired instructional outcome may be to have the student be able to recognize key transitional words in paragraphs. A pedagogical technique utilized to teach such a skill might involve having the student underline key transitional words in a series of paragraphs. Although the pedagogical activities may vary, the desired instructional outcome remains the same.

This is an important distinction and one that should be kept in mind when determining instructional priorities. Instructional priorities should be consistent with both the desired instructional outcomes and the pedagogical techniques utilized to teach the skill. Analyzing instructional priorities is not a simple task. At the elementary level the process is a little more straightforward. Generally, at this level reading exists as an identified curricular subject. It is taught by utilizing material designated for that specific purpose. Instructional priorities can be ascertained by examining the material and activities utilized to teach reading. For example, if critical reading is the desired instructional outcome, enabling activities that stress only literal recognition would not produce the desired result, thus creating a conflict between what is desired and what is produced.

At the secondary level reading is not usually taught independently of content, as it is at the elementary level. Since content teachers utilize the reading process to disseminate printed information, students with comprehension problems find most of the reading material too difficult. To develop a pedagogically sound program to ameliorate inadequate comprehension problems, the reading specialist must work closely with content teachers to ascertain instructional priorities related to the uses of comprehension.

One method for identifying instructional priorities is the "Reading Skills Priorities Checklist" (see Fig. 12.1). Both the reading specialist and the classroom teachers can utilize it to determine the instructional outcomes they will require of their students. For example, at the middle-school level a reading specialist must continually deal with referrals from all content areas. Therefore, in order to establish an instructionally sound program, the reading specialist must be able to identify not only comprehension deficiencies related to reading in general, but also specific comprehension deficiencies related to functional reading demands made by content teachers.

The checklist can also assist the content teacher and reading specialist to identify essential comprehension skills. The reading specialist should ask the content teacher who referred the student or who has students assigned to the reading specialist to use the checklist in analyzing instructional demands. By placing a check in each appropriate box, one can obtain an overview of the

ASSIGNMENT	CRITICAL READING								TEXTBOOK-RELATED SKILLS						LISTENING AND STUDY SKILLS					
	Understand main idea	Provide supporting detail	See relationship between ideas	Summarize	Analyze	Synthesize	Apply	Evaluate	Locate information	Utilize formulas	Understand symbols	Use table, charts, etc.	Understand concepts	Read pattern	Follow directions	Take notes	Outline	Organize idea in proper relationship	Interpret graphic aids	Research reading
Textbook reading																				
Research work in library																				
Listening to presentation in class (film strip, lecture, discussion, etc.)																				
Practical application of skill (taking carburator apart)																				
Lab exercise																				
Handout readings (prepared classroom handouts)																				
Additional assignment																				

Fig. 12.1. Reading skills priorities checklist.

reading demands made on the student by the content teacher. The checks appearing in each column identify skill demands; those in each row identify the type of assignment in which the skill or skills appear. Tabulating the results vertically and horizontally produces an instructional reading profile.

These instructional priorities can be compared to the diagnostic information obtained by the reading specialist, and on the basis of this information a program that reflects both the educational and functional needs of the student can be developed. Such a process has actively involved both the content teacher and the reading specialist in the identification of instructional priorities. This process replaces the more traditional approach taken by many content teachers—that of abdicating all responsibilities for reading improvement to the reading specialist. In this manner reading is viewed as a process rather than a subject; and as a result, reading improvement becomes a shared responsibility.

Once various instructional outcomes have been identified, the appropriate pedagogical techniques or enabling skills can be developed. For example, one identified priority might be the recognition of the central thought of a paragraph. In order to teach this task, the teacher may have the students engage in some of the following activities: (1) read a paragraph and select the appropriate title, (2) underline the topic sentence in a paragraph, and (3) identify the main idea of several related paragraphs. The appropriate enabling skills should be identified for each such instructional outcome. This process is shown in Table 12.1. The classroom teacher or reading specialist can correctly match the appropriate activity with the desired behavior by dividing each priority into instructional outcomes and enabling skills. Once this process has been completed, the teacher can identify potential problem areas and pedagogical techniques designed to alleviate those problems.

Table 12.1. Classifying enabling skills

Desired instructional outcome	Enabling skill or pedagogical technique
1. Recognizing the central thought of a passage	1a. Select the appropriate title for a reading selection 1b. Underline the topic sentence in a paragraph 1c. Identify the main idea in several related paragraphs
2. Recognizing the sequence embedded within various types of reading material	2a. Place pictures in their proper order 2b. Identify the sequence in a short mystery 2c. Place historical events in their proper sequence
3. Recognizing imposed organizational patterns	3a. Know how to construct an outline 3b. Identify problem-causes-solution pattern 3c. Identify the narrative pattern

PROBLEMS RELATED TO COMPREHENSION DIFFICULTIES

There are at least four types of problems related to comprehension difficulties: (1) inadequate knowledge of key concepts, (2) insufficient language skills, (3) inadequate reading-skill competencies, and (4) insufficient cognitive strategies. The rest of this chapter will discuss these four major areas and offer practical suggestions for attempting to eradicate each problem.

Inadequate knowledge of key concepts

As the paragraph about the brain demonstrated, without knowledge of key concepts—or, for that matter, general vocabulary—a reader's comprehension will be limited. However, it is not the aim of this section to deal with the various techniques related to contextual, structural, or phonic analysis, but rather to present a technique designed to facilitate comprehension of key concepts.

Research (Peters, 1975) related to inadequate comprehension of concepts seems to suggest that the present approach utilized by many textual materials is insufficient. Two basic problems confront students attempting to adequately comprehend concepts presented in textual materials: (1) insufficient explanation of concepts, and (2) insufficient organizational patterns of written material, i.e., the style in which the material is written makes it difficult for poor readers to discern main ideas, cause-effect relationships, time-space relationships, or any other information the writer seeks to convey through print to the reader.

Both of these factors have made it difficult for good and poor readers to adequately comprehend concepts. Because of these inadequacies, the reader is not provided with sufficient semantic clues. In the case of conceptual attainment, these additional semantic clues consist of such factors as non-examples of the concept and relevant and irrelevant attributes of the concept. Without the inclusion of such additional semantic clues, the reader is unable to chunk information into meaningful units. As Pearson (1975) points out, "semantic chunks" are hypothetical storage units ("tall man," "short girl," or "the tall man hit the short girl") which facilitate the synthesizing process of cementing ideas together. Without the additional structure to facilitate the chunking of information, alternative approaches must seek to incorporate those elements which, when included in the material, will provide the reader with more structure in the form of semantic clues. The Frayer model of concept analysis incorporates those elements into its approach.

The Frayer approach to concept analysis Frayer, Frederick, and Klausmeier (1969) have outlined a procedure that appears to facilitate the comprehension process for both good and poor readers. Their model of concept classification can be utilized to both analyze and test concept attainment. As Peters (1975) states: "The method proposed by Frayer *et al.* classifies concepts according to several dimensions: relevant attributes, irrelevant attributes, examples, non-examples, and relationships established between other concepts." He goes on to say (pp. 91–92):

> The first means utilized to clarify a concept involves the identification of its relevant attributes. Relevant attributes are the intrinsic qualities which are common to all examples of the concept. For instance, relevant attributes of a globe would be the facts that it is (1) spherical and (2) a representation of the earth.
>
> A second means of clarifying a concept is by noting its irrelevant attributes, which can be defined as the qualities of a specific concept that are not endemic to all concept examples. For instance, an irrelevant attribute of globe would be size. As Tabachnick, Weible, and Frayer (1970, pp. 15–16) state:
>
>> One approach used to determine the relevant and irrelevant attributes of a concept was to think of as many different examples of the concept as possible. Those characteristics common to all of these examples were usually relevant attributes of the concept. Characteristics which occurred only in particular examples were irrelevant attributes of the concept. As an example of this type of approach, think of the concept *delta*. A delta is always a type of river mouth where land was formed when soil was deposited from that river. The relevant attributes would be that a delta is part of a river mouth, is an island formed by the river, and grows larger as more soil carried by the river is deposited. Every delta in the world would share these characteristics. However, not every delta in the world is at the end of the Mississippi River, not every delta has good land for growing cotton, not every delta is exactly fan shaped; therefore, these characteristics of location, kind of soil and shape are irrelevant attributes of the concept delta.
>
> On the basis of relevant and irrelevant attributes, a definition of the concept is generated.
>
> A third means of clarifying a concept is to utilize non-examples. A non-example lacks one or more relevant characteristics. For instance, in the concept *globe*, a wall map could be employed as a non-example, because it would lack the relevant characteristic of spherical shape. The function of a non-example is to help determine whether the student has accurately comprehended the concept by offering him a plausible alternative which requires the student to discriminate the concept upon the basis of its relevant or irrelevant attributes.

A fourth means of clarifying a concept is to determine the relationship it has to other concepts. For example, Jacksonian Democracy and democracy are related in that they deal with the concept *government*. A democracy is a specific form of government which means that the concept government is in a superordinate relationship with both concepts. However, Jacksonian Democracy is different from democracy in that it pertains to a specific period in history and is associated with specific changes which obtained more rights for the people. Democracy is then a superordinate, the more general concept, while Jacksonian Democracy, the subordinate concept, is the more specific. By establishing a relationship between concepts, it is possible to determine a hierarchical structure and, therefore, provide a more systematic means for ordering concepts and establishing relationships between concepts.

The Frayer model is a very systematic approach to concept analysis. Concepts are defined according to their critical attributes. Based upon a concept's critical attributes examples and non-examples are generated. In addition to providing the reader with both examples and non-examples the concept is placed within a superordinate-coordinate-subordinate relationship.

The Frayer model for presenting concepts differs greatly from the present methods employed by many textual materials. Most textual materials provide a general definition of the concept and give only one example. This type of conceptual presentation makes it difficult for poor readers to comprehend the material. Through the utilization of a systematic approach similar to the one outlined by Frayer *et al.,* which identifies the intrinsic qualities of a concept and then presents them within the framework of a hierarchical structure, it is possible to assist the reader in imposing order on the material. Not only does the material provide more external structure in the form of additional semantic clues, i.e., those elements (the listing of relevant attributes, the inclusion of examples and nonexamples, etc.) of the Frayer model that require the writer to adopt a more structured organizational pattern within material, but it also provides a more systematic procedure for presenting concepts. Klausmeier (1971) found this latter element to be an essential requisite for improving concept attainment. Therefore, it is the elements contained within this systematic procedure that provide the reader with additional semantic clues. These semantic clues are designed to improve the reader's organization of information, thus facilitating the comprehension of concepts.

Application of the Frayer model. The Frayer model can be utilized in a number of ways in classrooms at both the elementary and secondary levels. First, as concepts are introduced as a part of prereading activities, each concept can be discussed in terms of its relevant and irrelevant attributes. Klaus-meier (1971) has stated that one of the first operations in acquiring a concept is for the student to discriminate and label attributes of the specific concept. To facilitate that process several activities could be employed.

1. Given the name of an attribute, can the student select an example of the attribute? For instance, if the teacher is attempting to introduce the concept *desert,* one of the relevant attributes might be that it is an area where temperature varies greatly from day to night. The student could be asked the appropriate question to elicit the desired response.

2. Another, similar procedure would be that once the relevant and irrelevant attributes of a concept were identified, the student could be given a list and asked to classify the attributes.

Second, once students have completed these activities, they should be able to classify examples and nonexamples of the concept. A variety of strategies can be employed:

1. Given an example of the concept, a student should be able to select another example of the concept.

2. Given the concept, a student should be able to select a nonexample of the concept.

3. Given the example of the concept, a student should be able to select the name of the concept.

As Markle and Tiemann (1969) revealed in their research, part of the problem students have experienced in mislabeling concepts can be attributed to overgeneralization. For example, if students were asked to define the concept *globe,* they might include a wall map as an example of globe. If this occurs, students have incorrectly included a nonexample within their definition of globe. This occurs when students formulate too broad a definition of the concept. The problem of overgeneralization can be significantly reduced by using examples and nonexamples. Therefore, if overgeneralization is to be avoided, it is important to include strategies similar to the ones outlined above.

Third, the Frayer model can be utilized by teachers who write their own materials or develop their own handouts. Research conducted by Peters (1975) seems to indicate that when material is rewritten according to the guidelines established by the Frayer model, comprehension is significantly improved for both good and poor readers. The results of this study also seem consistent with research conducted by Bransford and Franks (1971), who found that comprehension was facilitated when more semantic clues in the form of additional external structures were provided.

Language skills

A basic knowledge of the English language is an essential requisite for reading comprehension. Teachers often forget just how important language is to the comprehension process. The following paragraph is designed to help us see to what extent we do rely on language.

THE MARLUP

A marlup was poving his kump. Parmily a narg horped some whev in his kump. "Why did vump horp whev in my frinkle kump?" the marlup jufd the narg. "Er'm muvvily trungy," the narg grupped. "Er heshed vump norpled whev in your kump. Do vump pove your kump frinkle?" (Goodman, 1973)

Although you may have had some difficulty at first, most individuals could answer some basic questions about the story, even though many of the words are synthetic or have no lexical meaning by themselves. Meaning is associated with these words once they are placed in the context or structure of the story. For example, some of you probably think that the marlup is a person and that the narg is another person or possibly an animal. It is not important whether we all concur as to what the marlup is, but rather that we attribute some meaning to the word, and that meaning must be predicated on its relationship with other words in the sentence. Our knowledge of the language system also provides us with other additional information about the story.

1. A marlup was poving his kump.

   (a) Whatever the marlup was doing happened in the past.
   (b) The marlup's poving indicates some form of action.
   (c) The marlup apparently owned or possessed kump.

2. "Er'm muvvily trungy," the narg grupped.

   (a) Muvvily describes trungy.
   (b) The narg was speaking.

This paragraph helps illustrate two fundamental language skills a reader must possess in order to comprehend written language. First, he or she must possess a concept for each word. Generally, this information is provided through background experiences. Second, the reader must possess a knowledge of the grammatical relationships inherent in the structure of language. In other words, the reader must understand the morphologic (word formation), syntactic (surface structure), and semantic (deep structure) elements in the language system before comprehension can take place.

Strategies for dealing with limited language skills   Many activities can be utilized by the reading specialist or classroom teacher in eradicating language deficiencies. Four such techniques are: (1) structural words, (2) the cloze procedure, (3) multiple-meaning words, and (4) additional symbol systems.

Structural words. Sometimes the meaning of a paragraph or selection might be altered or misconstrued if the reader incorrectly comprehends key structural words. Key structural words assist the reader in following the author's transitions from idea to idea or from paragraph to paragraph. For example, the following words make it possible for the writer to present *contrasting ideas* (opposed to, conversely), *additional ideas* (and, plus, furthermore), and *final or concluding ideas* (consequently, thus, finally).

Shepherd (1973) has developed a highly organized list of key structural words. However, a word of warning before approaching the teaching of these words. They should not be taught or memorized in isolation; rather, they should be infused in the lesson when the need arises. Second, the overall structural relationship in which the words are presented also provides a good organizational schema and one that should further assist students in the learning of these important words. For example, many students have difficulty recognizing that many of these words are related or have similar meanings. However, when these words are presented in relationship to one another (space relationships, time relationship, etc.), it assists the reader in incorporating them into his or her vocabulary in a structured manner. As Gerhard (1975) points out, such organizational schemas help facilitate the comprehension process. Shepherd's list of commonly used structural words follows.*

    I. Structure words indicating additional ideas

       A. Words pointing to coordinate ideas, adding to the total thought

and	furthermore	besides	likewise
also	plus	too	similarly
another	otherwise	after that	again
in addition	moreover	as well as	since

---

* David Shepherd, *Comprehensive High School Reading Methods,* Columbus, Ohio: Merrill, 1973, pp. 92–93. Reprinted by permission.

since then   not only,
               but also

B. Words pointing to final or concluding ideas

consequently	in conclusion	then
thus	in summation	to sum up
hence	at last	in brief
therefore	finally	in the end

II. Structure words indicating a change in ideas by reversing, qualifying, or modifying ideas already presented

in contrast	on the other hand	for all that
to the contrary	but	nevertheless
opposed to	in spite of	yet
conversely	although	still
however	either-or	even if
even though		

III. Structure words indicating concrete application of a thought

because	specifically	provided
for example	for instance	like

IV. Structure words pointing to relationships among and between ideas

A. Time relationships

in the first place	last	previously
at the same time	now	hereafter
thereafter	later	at last
in retrospect	after	at length
meanwhile	before	following
finally	immediately	

B. Space relationships

here	close	by	farther on	to the east
there	far	away	above	westward
yonder	near	under	across	beneath
everywhere				

C. Related in degree

many	little	some	best	fewer	greater
more	less	all	worst	fewest	greatest
most	least				above all

D. Pointing to show emphasis

this	that	one	some	few
these	those	several		

Another teaching technique to employ with structural words is to present them in the same sentence and have students indicate whether the substitution has altered the meaning.

Football is my favorite sport, *but* my parents will not let me play it.
Football is my favorite sport, *although* my parents will not let me play it.
Football is my favorite sport; *consequently* my parents will not let me play it.
Football is my favorite sport; *moreover* my parents will not let me play it.
Football is my favorite sport, *and* my parents will not let me play it.
Football is my favorite sport; *however* my parents will not let me play it.

For students at the secondary level, examples can be drawn from their own textbooks. Before reading key passages, have students underline important structural words. The following selection could be used to demonstrate key structural words that indicate time relations. (The key structural words are in italics.)

DESERTERS

Every war has its deserters. Desertion figures during the Civil War were high—278,000 out of 1.5 million soldiers in the North, 103,000 out of 1 million in the South.

Why were desertion figures high? *First,* many deserters were boys between the ages of fourteen and eighteen. They found war a rude shock, and they ran away.

Second, bounty jumpers helped run up the desertion figures. These were men who enlisted for a bounty, or cash bonus, served a few days, deserted, *and then* volunteered in a different county a few days later, collecting a new bounty.

Third, many men deserted because of wretched conditions. Southern soldiers, especially, were often without basic necessities. For example, General James Longstreet of the Confederacy reported in November 1862 that over six thousand men in his corps were without shoes. Sanitation and medical facilities were poor. Twice as many Civil War soldiers died of disease—typhoid, dysentery, pneumonia—as died in action.

Finally, many men on both sides felt little loyalty to the cause and had little understanding of military discipline. A homesick boy often saw nothing wrong with going home to see his parents. A man from a farm might slip off to put in a crop, fully intending to return, but somehow just never getting around to it.*

Words such as *it, they, this,* and *their* often contribute to the difficulty level of materials. For example, some publishers have attempted to "write down" material so that it can be used at lower levels. To reduce the difficulty level of the material, multisyllable words are often replaced by single-syllable pronouns. Although this might reduce the difficulty score, it might also inhibit the reader's understanding of the passage. Several activities can be used to both increase student awareness of such words and illustrate their significance to the comprehension process.

One method would be to see if students can match the italicized pronoun to its appropriate referent.

The police figure that most of the time when a car is stolen, somebody knows something about *it.*

_____ 1. the police

_____ 2. the car

_____ 3. the theft

When I think back to that time, *it* almost makes me sick because of what happened to my dog.

_____ 1. the time the event took place

_____ 2. the person speaking

_____ 3. what happened to the dog

Cloze procedure. The cloze procedure—deleting every fifth, eighth, or tenth word—was initially developed by John Bormuth as another means for assessing the difficulty level of printed material. However, it can also be used to measure a student's knowledge of linguistic principles. The cloze procedure is predicated on the Gestalt principle of closure, which states that one can accurately replace the missing word by utilizing one's knowledge of the language system. Since the reader must study the surrounding context and

* From *Promise of America: Breaking and Building* by Larry Cuban and Philip Roden. Copyright © 1971 by Scott, Foresman and Company. Reprinted by permission of the publisher.

make a judgment based on his or her understanding of the author's message, the teacher can use this procedure as a diagnostic tool to assess the student's language skills.

The grammar of the sentence provides clues to the missing word. Thus an understanding of both the syntactic and semantic elements of the language process enables the reader to supply the appropriate word. By using such an activity, the teacher can analyze the results to determine such things as whether indeed the student is substituting nouns for nouns and verbs for verbs, or whether he or she has followed the semantic flow of the passage. For additional insight, it might be useful to have the student explain any incorrect choices. The results from the cloze procedure should assist the teacher in ascertaining the nature and type of activities needed to facilitate the student's use and understanding of language.

Multiple-meaning words. Students encounter many words whose meanings are determined solely by the context in which they are presented. For example, the student who identifies a *radical* in a math text as an "extremist" rather than "the root of a quantity" will be in deep trouble. Some of the following activities will help the learner expand his or her knowledge of multiple word meanings.

Some words have more than one meaning. Two of the sentences in each group below have the same meaning. Place an "X" by the sentence that has the different meaning.

_____ 1. He said that he would only be a *minute*.

_____ 2. May I see you for a *minute?*

_____ 3. She is no bigger than a *minute*.

_____ 1. The *wind* blew the branch off the table.

_____ 2. The runner could not get his second *wind*.

_____ 3. The curtains on the window were blowing in the *wind*.

Listed below are two games that emphasize words with multiple meanings.

1. Materials: On an 18″ × 12″ piece of paper, place a series of multiple-meaning words ("pick," "light," "crop," "root," "draw," etc.).

   Procedure: Each student illustrates the word selected by drawing or cutting pictures from a magazine. The student is to draw or illustrate as many different meanings for the word as possible.

2. Materials: A wheel divided into colored segments, a spinner on the wheel, and cards with multiple-meaning words written on them. The word cards should match the colored segments.

Procedure: The children take turns spinning the arrow. When it comes to a stop, the child picks a card that corresponds to the appropriate color, gives two different definitions for the word, and then use the words in a sentence. No child may use repeated definitions or sentences.

Additional symbol systems. In mathematics or science material, students encounter a double symbol system—the traditional, written symbol system and the number, sign, and symbol system of mathematics and science. The reader must master both symbol systems in order to comprehend such material. Activities, such as the one provided below, should be engaged in by both the classroom teacher and reading specialist to assist students who experience difficulties in these areas.

Read the statements under A. Look at each number sentence under B. Some statements in A are the same as the number sentences in B. Some are not. Write the letter of the number sentences next to the statements they go with.

A

_____ 1. Three triangles times three are equal to nine triangles.

_____ 2. Milton divided six candy bars equally between two friends. Then Mr. Cohn gave each boy three times as many bars as Milton had given them. That meant each boy had nine candy bars.

_____ 3. Bert was trying to push his cart up a hill. Each time he pushed it, it went 10 feet. But then it would roll back three feet before Bert could get to it. He did this four times before he reached the top of the hill. This meant the hill was 28 feet long.

_____ 4. Ten minus three plus four is equal to 28.

_____ 5. Five times two minus three plus one divided by two is equal to what number?

_____ 6. One set of triangles divided by one set of three triangles is equal to one.

B

(a) $(10 - 3) \times 4 = 28$

(b) $(6 \div 2) \times 3 = 9$

(c) $\{\triangle, \triangle, \triangle\} \div \{\triangle, \triangle, \triangle\} = 1$

(d) $5 \times 2 \div 3 + 1 - 2 = \boxed{?}$

(e) $(6 \div 2) + 3 \neq 9$

(f) $10 \div (3 \times 4) \neq 28$

Now look at each number sentence under B. This time, underline each number sentence that is correct. It may not match a statement under A.*

Reading-skill competencies

As was mentioned earlier, comprehension skills have been the source of much controversy in the field of reading. However, despite the "great debate," students are required to read and to react to information being disseminated via the printed page. Many times the ultimate success or failure of reading-related activities depends to a great extent on whether a student has mastered the skills that are either implicit or explicit in the assignment. Some of the most frequently used reading skills are: (1) determining the main idea of a passage, (2) determining supportive details, (3) recognizing the sequence of a passage, (4) determining cause-and-effect relationships, (5) being able to compare and contrast ideas, and (6) making appropriate judgments. Each of these six skills will be discussed and enabling activities or pedagogical techniques suggested. The enabling activities are designed to guide the student toward independent use of the skill.

Main idea   One of the basic skills required of a reader is determining the main idea of a passage. To identify the main idea of a passage, a reader must be able to synthesize and interpret information. In addition, the student might have to utilize other related skills, such as recognizing supporting details, sequence, or cause-and-effect relationships in order to formulate the main idea. The following exercises illustrate the various pedagogical techniques a teacher may employ to develop a student's ability to ascertain the main idea of a passage.

Editorial cartoons. Editorial cartoons provide an excellent method for getting students to formulate a concept of main idea. Two possible activities are: (1) have the student label what she or he believes is the main idea of the cartoon and then give a rationale for choosing that title; (2) as a follow-up activity, have the student read a selection and draw an illustration of what he or she believes is the main idea of the passage.

---

* Harold Herber and Mary Lee Johansen, *Go: Reading in the Content Area,* New York: Scholastic Book Services, 1973, p. 92. Reprinted by permission.

Outlining. The use of an outline helps students discern the structural relationship between major and minor points, an essential requisite to understanding the difference between main ideas and details. In the activity that follows, the student must read the paragraph and insert the main idea into the blank that follows.

> The American Civil War was fought by the North and the South between 1861 and 1865. Most historians agree that there were many causes for this conflict: economic differences (agrarian versus industrial) political differences (strong central government versus state's right form of government), and social differences (slaves versus nonslaves). However, some historians have argued that there is only one cause of the Civil War, the Abolitionist Movement. Despite the differences in interpretation over causes of the Civil War, it is important to keep in mind that rarely can an event as complex as the Civil War be caused by a single factor.

I. _____

_____

   a. The Civil War took place between 1861 and 1865.
   b. The Civil War was a conflict between the North and the South.
   c. There were many differences between the North and the South.
   d. The Abolitionist movement was a contributing factor to the Civil War.

In a follow-up to this activity, the teacher could give students a list of words or phrases, such as the ones below, and ask each student to identify the word or phrase that best depicts the main idea.

1. Causes of the depression
2. Crash and panic
3. Bank failures
4. Black Friday
5. The stock market and disaster
6. Buying on margin
7. Bank lost money

Specially prepared material. There presently exists a variety of commercially prepared materials developed specifically to teach students how to recognize main ideas. Such materials do serve as a good model for teaching reading skills. However, some caution should be shown; because of the contrived format of these materials, students may have difficulty transferring the skill to materials they encounter in other classrooms. For instance, in a math class the student is sometimes confronted with the task of solving word problems. Many times success or failure depends on the student's ability to identify what is considered to be the "main idea" of the problem. In mathematics terminology, this is generally referred to as "what is to be found." If only contrived materials have been employed, some students may experience difficulty in recognizing the "main idea" of the math problem. The following is an example of an activity that can be utilized to insure that transfer of the skill is made to varying types of printed materials.

Have the student circle each statement he or she feels presents what is to be found. The student should be able to justify the response based on the information presented in the word problem. Be sure to emphasize that it is merely a reading task and does not involve any mathematical computation.

A gallon of water weighs 8.3 pounds. The water in a tank weighs 1494 pounds. How many gallons of water are in the tank?

What is to be found in the problem?

a. The size of the tank

b. The time it takes to drain the tank

c. The number of gallons the tank will hold when full

d. The number of gallons in the tank

e. The weight of a gallon of water.

Noting important details   The importance of details in the overall reading task often depends on the established purpose for reading. For instance, when students are conducting lab experiments or are following written or oral directions, they must pay careful attention to all details. Exercises that require students to pay close attention to details should be developed and utilized. However, in employing activities that require students to note important details, the following points should be kept in mind: (1) ask for information that is important to the completion of the overall reading task, and (2) identify the purpose of the reading task so that students can clearly focus on the required detailed information.

Following written directions. Listed below are several activities designed to focus the student's attention on important details. In the first activity, students should be given the following list of directions and asked to complete them in their proper sequence.

1. Read all directions.

2. Take out a piece of paper.

3. Write your first name then your last in the upper right-hand corner.
4. Fold the paper in half.
5. Write today's date in the upper left-hand corner.
6. Determine how many days are left in the month.
7. Stop here if today is your birthday.
8. Write the present time.
9. Determine how many minutes are left in class.
10. Do no homework tonight if there is less than 10 minutes in the class.
11. Do not follow any of the above directions and take out any book and read for the next 10 minutes.

As a follow-up to the preceding activity, have each student in the class write directions for an activity that can be performed in the classroom. One student should read the directions while another follows them. The task can be as simple or as complex as the need dictates. Another activity that can be performed in the classroom is to have the students attempt to simplify directions that are difficult to follow. Ask the students to explain what made the directions difficult and how their revisions have simplified the original directions.

Answering specific questions from a passage. This is a very straightforward task. The student is provided with a short passage to read, and the teacher identifies appropriate questions that elicit details.

THE MYSTERIOUS CAT

The girl's name was Laura. She was known in the village as the girl with the mysterious cat. Her cat's name was Snappy Tom. Some people believed he was possessed. But no one really knew for sure.

QUESTIONS

1. What was the cat's name?
2. What strange features did he seem to have?
3. Who owned the cat?

Directing attention toward specific details. Give a student specific information to locate in the want ad section of a newspaper. For example, you might say to the student, "You are to purchase a 1968 Pontiac Lemans with air conditioning and power brakes for less than $500." Or, use a catalog from a large department store to purchase certain articles at a specific price. For a change of pace, have a student decide what additonal information is needed to solve a specific problem, as in the following example.

Chet and his two friends want to go to a spy movie. You can probably give Chet and his friends lots of ideas how to get into the movie, but if you read this number story carefully, you will find there is not enough information to know whether the boys really have enough money to buy tickets. What else do you need to know?

How much money do Chet's friends have if they have $2.50 between them? Check any statement you agree with. Also list the additional information that is needed to solve the problem.

_____ 1. They each have $2.50.

_____ 2. One friend could have $1.00 and the other $1.50.

_____ 3. They could each have $1.25.

_____ 4. They could have any combination of coins that add up to a total value of $2.50.*

Sequence   Sequence involves the ability to place events, ideas, or actions in their proper order. This very fundamental skill causes many poor readers great difficulty, because in most materials sequence is implicit rather than explicit and requires the reader to impose some organizational structure on the material. Since many poor readers lack this ability, activities such as the following may help them improve their ability to discern sequence.

First, since most students enjoy reading mysteries, such stories are an ideal instrument for teaching sequence. The minimystery, a short selection that is easy to read, can be utilized as such an instructional device. As is the case with most mysteries, the student is given the events in an inverted order. To solve the mystery, the student must arrange the clues in their proper sequence. After solving the mystery, the student should be able to list the events in their proper sequence.

Second, break down a paragraph into several sentences and see if the student can reassemble the paragraph in its correct sequence. One word of caution: be sure you can determine its proper order before giving it to a student. An example follows.

The group of sentences below makes a single paragraph. Read each of the sentences and decide in what order they would have to be arranged to make a single well-written paragraph. Write the order of sentences to the right of the sentences.

---

* Harold Herber and Mary Lee Johansen, *Go: Reading in the Content Area,* New York: Scholastic Book Services, 1973, p. 92. Reprinted by permission.

ELI WHITNEY

A. With this machine a laborer could clean fifty pounds of   _____ 1.
   cotton in a single day.

B. In 1792, he visited Georgia where he saw workers picking   _____ 2.
   the tiny seeds from the raw cotton.

C. By 1800, the cotton production reached thirty-five million   _____ 3.
   pounds a year.

D. In 1793, Whitney invented a machine to do the picking,   _____ 4.
   the "cotton gin."

E. Eli Whitney, a New England inventor, made cotton "king"   _____ 5.
   of the south.

F. Just to prepare one pound of cotton to be made into cloth   _____ 6.
   took the worker one full day.

G. During the year before Whitney invented the "cotton gin,"   _____ 7.
   the United States produced a few hundred thousand
   pounds of cotton.

H. Then the cotton production boomed.*   _____ 8.

Third, a similar activity can be performed with a series of pictures. Cartoons usually are an excellent resource for such an activity. Cut the cartoons into segments and then have the student arrange the pictures in their proper sequence. It is a good idea to have the student describe what is in each picture before attempting the activity; this should help obviate any misperceptions that might develop.

Fourth, many times writers indicate sequence through structural words. An example of such an arrangement was provided earlier in this chapter. Students should be encouraged to identify words that indicate sequence. Some examples of such words are: "in the first place," "last," "now," "then," and "before."

Fifth, have students read a short story and identify the correct sequence of events. An example of the procedure is provided below.

NEW RESPONSIBILITIES

Before the winter season set in, Jeff had to check his trapping equipment, because once the first snow fell he would not have the time, and any delay could mean that local trappers would beat him to the most

---

* *Organizational Skills,* Newton, Mass.: Curriculum Associates, 1973, p. 24. Reprinted by permission.

productive hunting areas. It was important to make sure his snow shoes were in excellent condition, since his life might depend upon them. Once he had checked all his equipment, he glanced over the map to locate what he thought would be good trapping areas. His father had broken his collar bone in an accident and could not make the annual trip. Since Jeff was the oldest, his family had depended upon him for this extra income. Two weeks later the snow fell, and Jeff's family waved to him as he and his dog Keshka headed for the woods.

Number the statements in the order in which they were presented in the story.

_____ Jeff checked over his map.

_____ Jeff needed all the time he could get.

_____ Jeff would do the trapping by himself.

_____ Jeff was the oldest in the family.

Cause and effect   Understanding a cause-and-effect relationship is an essential requisite for ascertaining the relationship between ideas, actions, or events. It is one thing to know that an event took place, but another to know that there is a relationship between the events and that this relationship is one of cause and effect. Many times such a relationship is implicit in the organizational structure of material and needs to be understood if the material is to be adequately comprehended. The activities that follow are designed to assist readers in identifying cause-and-effect relationships.

Draw one line under the cause and two lines under the effect.

The "Maine" is sunk. Less than a week later, Americans were shocked by a great tragedy. Because of the disorders in Cuba, the United States battleship "Maine" had been sent to Havana to protect American lives and property. On the night of February 15, 1898, a terrific explosion sank the "Maine" with the loss of two officers and 258 of the crew. An American naval court of inquiry at once conducted an investigation.*

A follow-up to the preceding assignment would be to have the students read a designated selection and then see if they can identify those events which are causes and those events which are effects. An example follows:

Place the letter "C" in front of the statements that are *causes* of the de-

---

* Richard C. Wade, Louise C. Wade, and Howard B. Wilder, *A History of the United States,* Vol. 2, Boston: Houghton Mifflin, 1970, p. 259. Reprinted by permission.

pression. Place the letter "E" in front of the statements that are *effects* to the depression.

_____   1. The stock market crash.

_____   2. The high rate of unemployment.

_____   3. Bank failures.

_____   4. Overproduction of goods.

_____   5. Decline in the price of stocks.

_____   6. Workers' lack of money to buy surplus goods.

_____   7. Little demand for U.S. goods.

_____   8. No control over regulations governing the stock market.

_____   9. The Bonus Army's demands.

_____ 10. The AAA.

_____ 11. The WPA.

_____ 12. The NRA.

_____ 13. The FDIC.

_____ 14. Labor unrest.

_____ 15. Formation of the UAW.

_____ 16. The Dust Bowl.

_____ 17. People losing their homes.

_____ 18. Artists working for the government.

_____ 19. Construction of dams to control floods.

_____ 20. Migration of people to California.

_____ 21. Hoover's response to the unemployment problem.

_____ 22. Huey Long and "Share the Wealth."

_____ 23. Plowing under crops.

Comparing and contrasting   In order to compare and contrast, a student must be able to identify similarities and differences. Several activities are suggested as a means for improving this skill.

Before reading a selection, have the student divide a piece of paper in half; one side will be used for listing similarities and the other for differences. Each time the student locates what he or she believes is a similarity or difference between the objects or events being compared (two characters in a story), it should be added to the appropriate list.

Pictures are also a good device to utilize when atempting to establish the concept of difference and similarity. For example, the student could be asked to compare two pictures of the same person taken by different people.

If your town has two newspapers, many times they will cover the same event. Compare and contrast their pictorial coverage.

A follow-up to this activity might involve comparing and contrasting the national coverage of a major news story in one of the national weekly periodicals (*Newsweek, New Republic, U.S. News and World Report,* or *Time*). Students could note the similarities and differences in the news stories.

Judgment   In order to judge or evaluate materials, a student must develop a standard that can be readily applied to a variety of materials. In the development of such standards, the student must consider such criteria as the accuracy of the information, the validity of the information, the source of the information, and whether the information is fact or opinion. The activities that follow are designed to assist students in formulating judgments and in making evaluations of printed materials.

Have students evaluate the accuracy of a local school event that has been seen by members of the class and reported in the local school or metropolitan paper. As a follow-up activity, have students write a review of a television program they all have viewed. Have a few students read their reviews and then determine who has the "most" accurate one. This should help illustrate both the variety of standards and the variation in judgments utilized by the students in making an evaluation.

In the following activity, have the students attempt to ascertain which statement is fact and which statement is opinion.

Which of the following statements are fact, and which ones are opinion? Keep in mind that a fact must be proved true through the use of an objective standard.

_____ 1. Andrew Johnson was impeached.

_____ 2. Skiing is fun.

_____ 3. July is always a summer month.

_____ 4. A pound of feathers weighs the same as a pound of gold.

_____ 5. Ford was a good President.

Finally, students could view or listen to several commercials to determine what information is fact and what is opinion.

Insufficient cognitive strategies

Many activities discussed thus far in this chapter can be viewed as cognitive strategies which allow the reader to more efficiently assess printed information. Without such guidance, disabled readers would have difficulty comprehending much of the material they encounter. However, a very important cognitive strategy that many disabled readers do not possess is the ability to impose organizational structure on material. Ausubel, Rothkopf, and Gagné have conducted considerable research in this area, and their results seem to support the theory that when poor readers are provided with some advanced organizational restructuring of material prior to engaging in the act of reading, comprehension is facilitated. Therefore, it seems that poor readers would benefit from instruction that provides additional organizational assistance.

The classroom teacher can use many techniques to alleviate organizational inadequacies: the SQ3R approach, the Instructional Framework (Herber, 1970), the Directed Reading Activity (DRA), the Frayer model of concept attainment, and the advanced organizer. All of these approaches seek to facilitate comprehension by providing the poor reader with a cognitive strategy for imposing organizational structure on the material read. The basic premise underlying each of these approaches is that by providing external structure, the reader can more clearly focus on the designated reading task. For instance, the SQ3R approach is designed to direct the reader's attention toward the external structure many textbooks build into each chapter, i.e., introductions, summaries, graphs, charts, titles, subtitles, key words, etc. These aids provide the reader with a sense of organization and can be utilized as a means for organizing information prior to reading. Too many teachers and students have viewed such structural aids as "filler material" provided by authors to help break up the flow of printed information. In other words, these structural aids have a minimum of instructional value for the reader. However, many times such aids assist the reader overcome insufficient cognitive strategies.

A second strategy for helping the disabled reader overcome insufficient cognitive strategies is the advanced organizer, a pedagogical technique designed to assist the reader to organize information prior to reading. Instead of merely providing the reader with a general overview or summary of the material, as in the SQ3R approach, the advanced organizer presents the information at a higher level of organization. As Ausubel (1963, p. 82) states, this organizational format assists the learner, because it:

(a) gives him a general overview of the more detailed material in advance of his actual confrontation with it, and (b) also provides organizing elements that are inclusive of and take into account most relevantly and efficiently both the particular content contained in the material and relevant concepts in cognitive structure. It thereby makes use of established knowledge to increase the familiarity and learnability of new material.

Many instructional techniques can be utilized with the advanced organizer. However, all activities should be designed to enhance the reader's ability to impose organizational structure on material. For instance, many teachers introduce important concepts before reading. Rather then merely listing the words, as in List I, arrange them in some hierarchical manner so that the student can see that there is a relationship between the concepts (see List II).

LIST I

concurrent powers	implied powers
constitutional division of powers	inherent powers
delegated powers	interstate compacts
division of powers	interstate relations
exclusive powers	privileges and immunities
expressed powers	republican form of government
extradition	reserved powers
federal state cooperation	revenue sharing
full faith and credit	supremacy clause
grants-in-aid	

LIST II—CONSTITUTIONAL DIVISION OF POWER

A. Division of powers
   1) Delegate powers
      a) Expressed powers
      b) Implied powers
      c) Inherent powers
   2) Reserve powers
   3) Exclusive powers
   4) Concurrent powers

B. Federal-state cooperation
   1) Federal grants-in-aid
   2) Revenue sharing

C. Interstate relations
   1) Interstate compacts
   2) Full faith and credit
   3) Extradition
   4) Privileges and immunities

A third cognitive strategy the reader must possess is the ability to perceive the organizational structure imposed by a writer on the material. This structure allows the reader to recognize such things as the relationships between ideas or the sequence in which information is presented (Pauk, 1975). Writers utilize several discernible patterns: (1) a chronological pattern, which is based on events and experiences occurring in a time sequence, (2) a spatial pattern, which develops mental pictures of objects authors describe, (3) a pattern of increasing complexity, which gives an example that proceeds from simple to complex, and (4) an enumeration pattern, which breaks ideas into major and minor components by mnemonic devices of numbering, lettering, etc. Through such organizational arrangements, the writer seeks to convey meaning to the reader. The reader must be able to impose some type of structural order on the material in order to derive meaning. Since most writers present their ideas in some order, the reader must be able to perceive this structure. By attempting to make the reader more cognizant of such patterns, it is possible to facilitate comprehension. Activities such as those designed by Pauk (1975) assist the reader in the devlopment of those abilities. Two examples of such activities follow.

If you still think me mad, you will think so no longer when I describe the wise precautions I took for the concealment of the body. The night waned, and I worked hastily, but in silence. First of all I dismembreed the corpse. I cut off the head and the arms and the legs.

The organizational structure of this passage is designed

_____ a. to provide the reader with lurid details.

_____ b. to establish that the speaker is, indeed, sane.

_____ c. to establish that the speaker is insane, but careful.

_____ d. to show the ironical twist of an insane mind.

At first I hated school, but by and by I got so I could stand it. Whenever I got uncommon tired I played hooky, and the hiding I got next day done me good and cheered me up. So the longer I went to school the easier it got to be. I was getting sort of used to the widow's ways, too, and they warn't so raspy on me. Living in a house and sleeping in a bed pulled on me pretty tight mostly, but before the cold weather I used to slide out and sleep in the woods sometimes, and so that was a rest to me. I liked the old ways best, but I was coming along slow but sure, and doing very satisfactory. She said she warn't ashamed of me.

The ideas in this passage are organized by explaining

_____ a. why the widow wasn't ashamed.

_____ b. the consequences of playing hooky.

_____ c. two sides of the story.

_____ d. what it means to be civilized.*

---

* Walter Pauk, *A Skill at a Time: Perceiving Structure,* Providence, R.I.: Jamestown Publishers, 1975, pp. 18, 20. Reprinted by permission.

Through the use of techniques such as those outlined above, the disabled reader is provided with cognitive strategies that will allow him or her to impose organizational structure on the material to be read.

SUMMARY

As this chapter has attempted to point out, comprehension is a very complex process to define. Much controversy exists within the profession as to what factors comprise the process and what pedagogical strategies should be employed to teach this process. It was the premise of this chapter that although philosophical differences exist between those who advocate the psycholinguistic approach and those who advocate the skills approach, both approaches contain elements that are pedagogically and pragmatically sound. Reading comprehension, as it was defined here, seeks to combine both approaches into a systematic process inextricably linked to the language and thinking processes. In breaking down comprehension into teachable components, several factors emerge: (1) conceptual knowledge, (2) language skills, (3) reading-skill competencies, and (4) cognitive strategies. Various techniques can be used to eradicate the weaknesses related to each of these areas.

REFERENCES

Ausubel, D. P. "The Role of Discriminability in Meaningful Parallel Learning," *Journal of Educational Psychology* 54 (1963): 331–336.

Bransford, John, and Jeffery Franks "The Abstraction of Linguistic Ideas," *Cognitive Psychology* 2 (October 1971): 331–350.

Communication Skills Program Inglewood: Southwestern Regional Laboratory, 1971.

Cuban, Larry, and Philip Roden *Promise of America: Breaking and Building,* Atlanta: Scott, Foresman, 1971.

Frayer, Dorothy A., Wayne C. Fredrick, and Herbert J. Klausmeier "A Schema for Testing the Level of Concept Mastery." Working paper from the Wisconsin Research and Development Center for Cognitive Learning, The University of Wisconsin, April 1969, No. 16.

Gerhard, Christian *Making Sense: Reading Comprehension Improved through Categorizing,* Newark, Del.: International Reading Association, 1975.

Goodman, Kenneth "The Marlup," Wayne State University, 1973 (monograph).

Herber, Harold L. *Teaching Reading in the Content Areas,* Englewood Cliffs, N.J.: Prentice-Hall, 1970.

Klausmeier, Herbert J. "Cognitive Operations in Concept Learning." Paper presented at the meeting of the American Psychological Association, Washington, D.C., September 1971.

Markle, Susan M., and Paul W. Tiemann *Really Understanding Concepts: Or Infruminous Pursuit of the Jebberwock,* Cambridge, Ill.: Stipes, 1969.

Otto, Wayne, Robert Chester, John McNeil, and Shirley Myers *Focused Reading Instruction,* Reading, Mass.: Addison-Wesley, 1974.

Pauk, Walter. *A Skill at a Time,* Providence, R.I.: Jamestown Publishers, 1975.

Pearson, David P. "The Effects of Grammatical Complexity of Children's Comprehension, Recall, and Conception of Certain Semantic Relations," *Reading Research Quarterly* **10** (1975): 155–192.

Peters, Charles W. "The Effect of Systematic Restructuring of Material upon the Comprehension Process," *Reading Research Quarterly* **11**, 1 (1975–1976): 87–111.

Peters, Charles W., and Nathaniel A. Peters "A Systematic Approach to Predicting Reading Performance at the Secondary Level," in the *Twenty-fifth Yearbook of the National Reading Conference,* 1976.

Reading Instructional Management Pontiac, Michigan Oakland Schools, 1972.

Shepherd, David L. *Comprehensive High School Reading Methods,* Columbus, Ohio: Merrill, 1973.

Simons, Herbert D. "Reading Comprehension: The Need for a New Perspective," *Reading Research Quarterly* **6** (Spring 1971): 338–363.

Spearritt, Donald "Identification of Subskills of Reading Comprehension by Maximum Likelihood Factor Analysis," *Reading Research Quarterly* **8** (Fall 1972): 92–111.

Tabachnick, B. Robert, Evelyn Weible, and Dorothy A. Frayer "Selection and Analysis of Social Studies Concepts for Inclusion in Tests of Concept Attainment." Working Paper from the Wisconsin Research and Development Center for Cognitive Learning, The University of Wisconsin, November 1970, No. 53.

Toback, Ethel, Lester R. Aronson, and Evelyn Shaw, eds. *Biopsychology of Development,* New York: Academic Press, 1971.

Wisconsin Design for Reading Skill Development Madison: University of Wisconsin, Research and Development Center for Cognitive Learning, 1971.

Chapter 13

APPROACHES TO REMEDIAL TEACHING

NATHANIEL A. PETERS • *Oakland Schools, Pontiac, Michigan*

HISTORICAL PERSPECTIVE

For better or worse, the notions of disabled learners and concomitant re-medial-teaching methodologies have persisted as long as teachers and learners have interacted. Among the first remedial learners were probably our Cro-Magnon progenitors who did not possess the necessary eye-hand coordination to successfully clobber a succulent woolly mammoth or the necessary visual perceptual skills to differentiate a tryannosaurus from a brontosaurus. Perhaps the cave student's teacher attempted to individualize, or at least differentiate, instruction by pairing a remedial learner with a more advanced peer, who would model adequate spear-tossing strategies (peer tutoring), or by finding a younger child whom a problem learner could instruct and thereby develop and reinforce his or her own competence (cross-age tutoring).

Remedial teaching has been with us for a long time, but only in relatively recent times has remedial teaching become a structured body of knowledge. Even though it is a body of knowledge or process, some laymen and professionals have tended to reduce remedial teaching to one approach or philosophy—a "bag of tricks" that the teacher produces on command when confronted with a problem learner. The idea that disorders of learning are highly complex problems worthy of sophisticated diagnostic and treatment methodologies has become more accepted. One finds fewer examples of undimensional treatment strategies—e.g., the EDL Controlled Reader, "Visual Perceptual Training," or the Readers Digest Skill Builders—for all children with learning problems; the supposition that all problems warrant the same intervention is no longer an accepted approach. Mostly gone are the days when children would be systematically cycled and recycled through the same materials year after year. Young adults in their late teens and early twenties sometimes can offer candid and realistic accounts of this pedagogical malaise. Once when I was talking with a young adult who had referred himself to our center for help with his reading problem, I asked him to recall what had been the most beneficial approach in assisting him with his problems when he was in school. "I don't know," he said, "every year I did the same thing, nothing but read and reread the booklets from the SRA Reading Laboratory. In fact," he continued, "I've read *Brown and Red* three times!" Simple solution to a complex problem.

THE HISTORICAL-CULTURAL MILIEU THAT NURTURED REMEDIAL TEACHING

Concern for the child who found learning difficult did not unfold in a vacuum. In Europe and North America the development of an interest in teaching children whose learning abilities diverged from the normal because of intellectual differences, experiential differences, or socioeconomic differences emerged from a political and cultural milieu fertile with the conditions necessary to ignite the desire of professionals and laymen to develop the potentialities of all children. Throughout the Western world there was a passionate commitment to reform that would abolish age-old practices that smother the human spirit.

First, paralleling the growth of remedial education were the elimination of European colonies in South America and the Caribbean, the worldwide movements for the abolition of slavery, and the concern for the abolition of child labor and for the rights of workers. Second, the rise of industrialization created excess wealth that philanthropists used to further humanitarian efforts. Last, but certainly not the least important consideration, was the belief that all individuals are entitled to an education that would make them more effective citizens and members of the human family.

Early models of intervention with children with special needs

Among the first to conceptualize a complex model of educational intervention for children with distinct special needs were Edouard Sequin and his mentor, Jean-Marc-Gaspard Itard. Ironically, neither Itard or Sequin was trained as an educator, and their techniques were not conceptualized and refined in educational settings. Both were trained as physicians, and their remedial curriculum reflects a rigorous adherence to the observation and treatment of the individual; techniques exist for the development of social skills in group settings, but major remediation takes place in the interaction between a single teacher and child. Itard's *The Wild Boy of Aveyron* gives a detailed yet sensitive and poignantly moving account of Itard, then the school physician for Abbe Sicard at the National Institute for the Deaf and Dumb in Paris, and his experiences with Victor, a feral child found wandering near Paris in 1799. Through pedagogical techniques based on the ideas of the French educator Abbe de Condillac, Itard nurtured the development of Victor from a child functioning without language and apparently incapable of socialization to a young man with expressive language and the ability to read.

Sequin, Itard's student, had a more significant impact on educational practices than did his mentor. Drawing primarily on the philosophical and educational theories of such diverse predecessors as Henri Saint-Simon, Auguste Comte, John Locke, and Jean-Jacques Rousseau, Sequin derived the theory on which his philosophy of remedial education was based. It was Itard, however, who gave Sequin his teaching techniques and the pedagogical diagnoses and prescriptions which Sequin believed to be essential to educational as well as medical treatment (Talbot, 1964, p. 40).

To the layman, the best-known educator of the twentieth century whose ideas are associated with remedial teaching is Maria Montessori. Although now Montessori's methodologies seem to be ensconced primarily in suburbia and a Montessori program is a cachet of middle-class education for parents, Maria Montessori gave shape to her educational theories as a young physician assigned to institutions for the emotionally disturbed in Rome. She believed that the mentally impaired who were callously placed with the disturbed could profit from a unique educational milieu. Finding a dearth of pedagogical ideas to help these unfortunate children, she delved into the ideas of Itard and Sequin, translated their major works into Italian, and even traveled to Paris and London to study the work of those early pioneers.

WHAT IS REMEDIAL TEACHING?

After a cursory examination of the historical antecedents of remedial teaching, it behooves the practitioner to examine the most important question of what constitutes remedial teaching and who should be the recipient of such teaching. The position taken in this chapter is that remedial teaching should be reserved for the learner of average or higher ability who has not responded to a sound developmental or corrective educational curriculum devised by a competent, well-trained classroom teacher. This is not to say that remedial teaching is reserved only for settings outside the classroom; in fact, it is hoped that every classroom teacher would attempt to use the assessment and teaching models discussed in this chapter with all children. However, in some settings, reality and legislation may dictate that children with very serious reading problems be placed in specialized environments within the school in order to obtain the help they need. Fortunately, a trend is growing in the schools that is highly critical of remedial specialists who are working in isolation from the classroom teacher, collecting diagnostic information and generating hypotheses about the child's learning strengths and weaknesses without communicating with the classroom teacher or the child's parents. It is not unusual to find high school students who are reading at second- or third-grade level and who are receiving "remedial help" from the specialist "down the hall," but who are nevertheless required to read science, English, and social studies texts at the high school level.

Remedial teaching involves not only the gathering of diagnostic information, but also, and more importantly, the use of this information in planning an educational program for a disabled learner. Unless diagnostic insights find their way out of the reading center or clinic, the impact of remedial teaching is diminished. Remedial teaching also requires that the training of a person taking on the responsibility of teaching learners who may have a history of academic frustration and failure will be of a different nature from that of the teacher responsible for developmental or corrective reading. In many areas training experiences would overlap, but it would be hoped that the committed remedial teacher would be a specialist who needs a background not only in reading and disorders of reading, but also in language development, language disorders, psychological assessment, and techniques of parent consultation and training. More specific recommendations for training are discussed later in this chapter.

WHO SHOULD RECEIVE REMEDIAL TEACHING?

Remedial teaching should be made available to all children who are not actualizing their learning potential, regardless of associated secondary conditions. The definition developed by state departments of education, professional organizations, and individuals representing various professional orientations excludes psychogenic-emotional problems (Myklebust, 1963; National Advisory Committee on Handicapped Children, 1968; National Council on Exceptional Children, 1968) or sociocultural differences (Clements, 1966; Kirk, 1962; National Advisory Committee on Handicapped Children, 1968) as factors in learning disability. However, it is my position that children with these compounding difficulties too would benefit from remedial teaching. I do not want to convey the impression that all educators and psychologists embrace the concept of remedial teaching with equal degrees of enthusiasm. Some believe, as does Hans Furth, a psychologist and Piagetian scholar, that remediation is of questionable value.

> Remediation, rehabilitation, redoing—these remedies are in store for a few of them from a benevolent society which is perhaps not as unkind as some would judge, but which is quite irrational in not providing appropriate opportunities for mediation, for habilation, for doing the appropriate thing when the time is ripe, when chances of success are high and financial expenditure would be relatively small. (1970, p. 1)

To disagree with Furth is to be hopelessly myopic. As Satz points out in Chapter 3, most authorities in the field of learning disorders concur that a valid early-detection system is necessary if intervention is to take place when the "time is ripe." However, early intervention should be aggressively pursued only when based on an accurate early-detection procedure.

A SPECIFIC REMEDIAL TEACHING MODEL

Johnson and Myklebust (1967) and Severson (1970) offer a most cogent and pragmatic explanation of remedial teaching. In their model the role of the remedial specialist has been redefined and broadened to that of a clinical or diagnostic teacher. Clinical or diagnostic teaching emphasizes the importance of direct observation of the learner based on objective, diagnostic information gathered from testing, classroom observation, and interviews with the learner's teachers and parents. In order to successfully implement this model, the teacher must be fully aware of the learner's disabilities, strengths and weaknesses in processing oral and written language, and understanding of mathematical operations. The teacher also needs to obtain nonacademic information about the child. Some of the following questions need to be asked to obtain such information: What are the sources of ego strength outside of the purely academic world of the classroom? Is the child successful in athletics, music, drama, 4H activities, Girl Scouts/Boy Scouts? Does the child make friends easily? Do peers select the child for leadership in class activities? Are the parents aware of their child's problems without viewing him or her as a remedial learner first and as a child with many assets second?

To Johnson and Myklebust, remedial teaching (or "clinical teaching," according to their terminology) must involve a skilled teacher who determines the integrities and deficits of a child in light of the level of involvement, the type of involvement, the child's readiness levels, and the nature of the task. "Integrities" and "deficits" refer to the degree of intactness of the learning processes (information-processing strategies) the child brings to a learning situation. Determination of strengths and weaknesses requires a person sophisticated in the various modes of information gathering: formal assessment (norm- and criterion-referenced instruments), informal assessment (informal reading inventories, teacher-made instruments, or activities that give the teacher insights into the child's learning processes), and observation systems for classroom and playground (Good and Brophy, 1970; LeBlanc and Etzel, 1967).

Essentially, Myklebust and Johnson believe that the process of learning can be viewed as a hierarchy of experiences. At the lowest level is *sensation,* which involves only an automatic, neurophysiological response to incoming stimuli. Dysfunction at this level involves developmental handicaps such as deafness or blindness. Beginning with the next level, *perception,* there is a behavioral component of central nervous system functioning that can be directly observed. At this level, dysfunction in the perceptual processes takes the form of difficulties in perceiving and differentiating visual and auditory stimuli. It is too simplistic to state that an inability to visually differentiate a "p" from a "b" or a tendency to auditorally confuse *tin* and *ten* indicates a disturbance in perception. The referral of large numbers of children for "perceptual training" or perceptual-development classes when experiencing a normal amount of confusion with our complex sound and writing systems indicates a poor understanding of normal obstacles in learning to read. The existence of dysfunctions of perception in the visual or auditory channels cannot be denied—to do so would also be simplistic—but the diagnosis and treatment of disorders at this level require cautious and knowledgeable interdisciplinary evaluation and treatment.

Johnson and Myklebust believe the next level in the hierarchy, *imagery*, has been neglected in American psychology and education. To them, imagery encompasses what most educators would regard as memory in its broadest sense. Both auditory and visual memory could be subsumed under the concept of imagery, because an individual engaging in imagery retrieves from memory some aspect of past experience without remembering the actual words surrounding the experience. A child with a deficit in auditory imagery might experience difficulty recalling environmental sounds such as those made by a jet airplane, waves crashing into rocks at the beach, or a cow. At a higher level, this same child might encounter difficulty remembering his or her address or the sounds associated with letters in our English writing system. Children with deficits in visual imagery may experience difficulty in recalling what the oak tree in their back yard looked like when it changed colors in the fall or the appearance of the face of the child in the next seat in school.

Common sense tells us that imagery is an important ability that underlies much learning, but more recently the investigations of experimental psychologists (Anderson and Kulhavy, 1972; Paivio, 1969; Paivio and Yuille, 1967) have added experimental evidence that image-evoking is the most important determiner of the learnability of words. A child will learn more from reading a prose passage and retain more sound/symbol association in a paired-associate learning task if she or he can form images of the things and events described in the passage.

Symbolization, the fourth level in the hierarchy, has been historically and principally viewed in terms of verbal symbolic behavior. Myklebust and Johnson (1967, p. 35) state that "symbolic behavior is highly inclusive, encompassing both verbal and nonverbal types of learning and recall, and refers to the ability to represent experiences." This ability to represent experience enables the human organism to conceptually structure his or her complex environment. Symbolization allows humans to develop a stock of concepts through which they come to understand internal and external reality.

Werner and Kaplan (1963) regard symbolization as the basic "tool for knowing." Without adequate symbolization abilities, a child encounters difficulty not only in the more commonly understood manifestation of language —inner, receptive, and expressive—but also in what Rees (1963) designates as the "noncommunicative function of language in children," or language not directed to a listener or not communicating meaning or feeling. Although most of us view language as an essential tool for communication, recent contributions from psycholinguists and psychologists indicate that the less transparent functions of language—its role in concept formation, the control and direction of behavior, and the establishment of self-image or self-consciousness—are of critical importance in understanding both child growth and development and disorders of learning.

The last level in the Myklebust and Johnson hierarchy is *conceptualization*. Conceptualization represents a group of experiences with a common denominator, usually obscure and abstract, but having some association one with another. The ability to conceptualize differentiates humans from other species of life. A child may have intact perception, imagery, and symbolization, but yet encounter great difficulty with the critical ability of conceptualization. It is incumbent on the teacher to maintain a continual awareness of a child's level of concept attainment. As mentioned earlier in this chapter, and by Charles Peters in Chapter 12, those of us who interact with children, either in a classroom or clinical setting, frequently are guilty of assumptive teaching—the practice of assuming, often mistakenly, that the learner understands a concept. Assumptive teaching can occur at all levels of learning, from preschool to graduate school, and is more likely to occur when the teacher neglects to probe a student's understanding of the conceptualization process. Confusing understanding with the mechanical, rote, regurgitation of a concept, teachers run the risk of subjecting learners to conceptual overload. How many preschoolers can parrot complex relational concepts, such as *in between, next to the last,* and *in the middle,* without being able to apply the concept in a variety of contexts, as "the house in the middle of the block" or "in the middle of the room," or "in the middle of the afternoon"? How often does the junior high school student of European history memorize the definition of "feudalism" or "dictatorship" without being able to transfer this knowledge in learning situations? A plausible explanation of the failure to transfer conceptual understanding is that at the conceptualization level, the learner has a vague grasp of *middle of, feudal,* or *dictatorship* and is unable to generalize these concepts outside of the context in which they were learned.

Johnson and Myklebust outline a conceptual framework that a well-trained teacher could utilize to obtain insights into a learner's perceptual, imagery, symbolic, or conceptual abilities. The teacher should be aware that the processes both overlap and are interwoven and that any cognitive process will fall somewhere within the framework, with the more complex cognitive skills, such as reading, involving all four processes. A disturbance in any one of the processes disrupts all processing above it. As an example, Myklebust and Johnson indicate that a deficit among the processes of perception, imagery, and symbolization would impede concept formation. At a more basic level, a child with impaired auditory perceptual processes—an inability to correctly differentiate two similar sounds—could possibly encounter great obstacles when given a task that demands language-comprehension abilities, a task falling at a higher level in the framework (see Table 13.1).

When using a hierarchical schema, such as Myklebust and Johnson's, the teacher or clinician must be careful to avoid postulating that causation of all problems of learning emanates from the lowest levels in the hierarchy. As an example, often a reading specialist diagnoses the "cause" of the academic problems of a ninth grader reading at a sixth-grade level as a problem in "auditory discrimination," when in fact more in-depth diagnosis reveals comprehension difficulties with the recall of specific facts or the understanding of dialogue in narrative writing. This child's ability to "recode" the written symbols into oral language equivalents or to "sound out" words is intact; the greatest difficulty lies in the child's inability to comprehend specific types of written messages. To emphasize the development of "auditory discrimination" abilities would do this learner a great disservice. Because of a penchant for the obscure, or possibly poor training, that emphasizes a limited or reductionist intervention model—Delacato's neurophysiological retraining (1963) being an example—some learning specialists focus on variables that research has found to be noncontributory or peripheral to the teaching-learning process. In addition to offering little to the understanding and remediation of problems of learning, an emphasis on inappropriate variables causes some specialists to unwittingly build barriers separating them from classroom teachers who are reluctant to involve children in language-learning activities—both oral and written—because the child has an "auditory or visual discrimination problem" that is being "treated" by a professional in the schools or in the community.

Although the teacher is told that this professional is dealing with the underlying causes of the learning problem, the teacher is kept ignorant of the specific ways of individualizing instruction so as to facilitate learning in the classroom. Sometimes the underlying message conveyed to the teacher is that the complexities of the problem are so arcane as to be beyond the ken of the classroom teacher. After much contact with professionals on both the giving and receiving ends of such information, I firmly believe that those who fail to relate their diagnostic and remedial insights to the classroom teacher do not fully understand the nature of the problem and are reluctant

Table 13.1. Levels of behavior, in descending order

5. Conceptualization

Definition: The ability to determine the common relationship among experiences that have some association, either obvious or obscure.

Characteristics of a deficit at this level: An inability to see the common denominator among experiences. For example, an inability to see that cats and dogs are mammals; or that the common domestic cat and the siamese are members of the feline family; or that squares, circles, and triangles are curves in mathematics.

4. Symbolization

Definition: The ability to mediate or represent experience in a symbolic form, either verbal or visual.

Characteristic of a deficit at this level: Although nonverbal symbolization should not be neglected, deficits coming to the attention of the teacher or learning specialist normally are of a verbal nature encompassing inner, receptive, or expressive language.

3. Imagery

Definition: A reproduction of a sensory experience when that experience has already been received and perceived.

Characteristics of a deficit at this level: Any disturbance in retrieving sensory input, especially visual or auditory input.

2. Perception

Definition: The ability to organize sensory input into understandable patterns of experience.

Characteristics of a deficit at this level: Any disorder that reflects difficulty organizing sensory input can occur with input from any sense organ (olfactory, skin, auditory, visual), but pedagogically the perception of visual and auditory input is of more significance.

1. Sensation

Definition: The immediate awareness when a peripheral sensory organ is stimulated.

Characteristics of a deficit at this level: Sensory disturbances such as deafness or blindness.

---

to let the teacher know it. Such failures to communicate can be attributed to: a lack of experience with a variety of intervention modalities, an inability to transduce clinical insights into classroom programs, or a hyperprofessionalism that views the classroom teacher as unable to comprehend complex

insights into the learning process. Such divisive attitudes only further exacerbate the distance between the specialist and the classroom teacher and can
best be overcome by a concerted effort to create an environment in which
consultant and teacher feel secure enough to jointly plan a coordinated
intervention program in the milieu where the action takes place—the classroom.

GUIDELINES FOR CLASSROOM ASSESSMENT

As with any schema or model that purports to explain the manner in which
a child processes information, its value is related to the degree to which it
aids a remedial specialist in educational programing for a child in the classroom. The intent of this section is to adapt the Myklebust and Johnson
assessment model for classroom use. The discussion will begin with a consideration of the limitations of norm-referenced instruments for educational
assessment. Next, the utility of criterion-referenced instruments and other
instruments will be analyzed to ascertain whether the information obtained
from such instruments can be translated into recommendations for classroom
activities. Third, general guidelines for assessment will be presented. Finally,
specific instruments that measure the behaviors comprising the Myklebust
and Johnson model will be discussed.

Limitations of norm-referenced testing

The use of norm-referenced testing has provided the foundation for educational assessment in American schools. Although there is no question that
norm-referenced testing supplies the specialist and teacher with valuable
information, it rarely accounts for the *reasons* the child performs in a particular way. Because norm-referenced tests do not closely parallel classroom
instruction, they offer the specialist or teacher only limited information for
remediation.

    An alternative to norm-referenced assessment is the criterion-referenced
test, which is based on the objectives of the specific child's instructional program. Such an alternative is criterion-referenced assessment, which tells the
teacher how an individual child performs on learning tasks. No attempt is
made to compare the child to other learners. (A more thorough discussion
of criterion-referenced testing is presented in Chapter 9.) Boehm (1973) suc-
cinctly outlines the essential characteristics of norm-referenced and criterion-
referenced tests in Table 13.2.

    In recommending instruments that test the behaviors in the Johnson and
Myklebust model, I have attempted to rely on criterion-referenced instruments because of the specificity of the instructional information yielded. In
no way should you interpret the discussion that follows as an endorsement

Table 13.2. Characteristics of norm-referenced and criterion-referenced tests

	Norm-referenced	Criterion-referenced
1. General purpose	To make comparisons among individuals	To determine how an individual functions relative to a criterion
	To make decisions about placement in programs in which only limited numbers of individuals can be accepted	To program specifically for the individual
	To determine for whom a program "works"	To determine whether an instructional program "works" in developing criterion behaviors
2. Item types	Items must discriminate among individuals	Items must correspond to criterion levels
	Items all subjects pass or fail eliminated	Items must provide explicit information about what an individual can or cannot do
3. Content	Content may or may not match particular classroom goals	Content *must match* classroom objectives which have been behaviorally defined beforehand
	Sampling is made from the larger task domain	Criterion levels can be set at each content level of a program and must specify minimal levels of competence
4. Scores	Variability among scores is essential	Variability is irrelevant
	Scores can mask what an individual can do but provide indication of his or her relative standing	Scores must reflect (not mask) what an individual can or cannot do
5. Type of ranking	Use of age and grade norms; percentiles; standard scores	Percentage passing a criterion level
		Pass/fail information on each item

of a specific assessment battery. Assessment batteries, as the name implies, are frequently just barrages of tests thrown at beleaguered children by clinicians who may be themselves at a loss as to how the diagnostic information can be used by the person teaching the child. More often than not, batteries of tests appear to be administered by professionals removed from the schools who convey information to school personnel through a written report. Usually this intermediary "interprets" the conclusions of the team to the teacher without demonstrating remedial techniques or reviewing materials found to be effective with the referred child. Any learning specialist working apart from the schools, e.g., in a medical or mental health setting, must continually scrutinize his or her evaluation process to see that relevant, contributory information is conveyed to the teacher. Reliance on a battery usually results in a plethora of diagnostic data that the teacher is left to unravel without guidance. Figure 13.1 is a verbatim example of diagnostic data gathered from a battery of tests conducted at a large metropolitan hospital and put into a format that more than likely will not be understood by the person implementing the recommendations.

Fig. 13.1. Educational evaluation.

Jane _____
Birthdate: 10/6/65   Grade: 1
Age: 7   Date of Testing: 11/7/72

BEHAVIOR OBSERVATION RELATED TO LEARNING TASKS

Jane appears to be an interesting, happy, blond girl of just 7 years who exhibits a fine sense of humor. Rapport was easily established and attention skills were good despite fatigue. Jane's attitude was continually negative concerning her ability; however, with encouragement and praise, her skills improved and she became more positive. She appeared more proficient with auditorally directed tasks than those visually presented; however, these skills fluctuated.

Difficulties were noticed in the area of language, both expressive and communicative, visual motor, visual memory, sequencing, and visual discrimination, and integration.

PROFICIENCY AND LEVEL OF ACADEMIC SKILLS

  I. *Language-arts skills*

    A. *Reading*
      1. Sight-vocabulary level—none
      2. Listening and comprehension level—3.3
      3. Word-analysis skills—none visually
      4. Sentence memory—4.0 years

    B. *Vocabulary development*
      1. Oral vocabulary—good vocabulary knowledge and usage; however, she has a language disability.

    C. *Spelling*
    Auditorially responsive to beginning and final consonant sounds.

    D. *Developmental test of visual perception*
      1. Eye-motor—4.0
      2. Figure-ground—6.6
      3. Form constancy—6.0

Fig. 13.1 (cont.)

    4. Position in space—6.3
    5. Spatial relations—6.6

II. *Mathematics*

  A. *Computation*
    1. Recognition—109
       Production of numbers—120 with auditory assistance
    2. Number facts (automatic memorization level)
      a) Addition facts—age inappropriate
      b) Subtraction facts—age inappropriate
    3. Numerosity and sequence—named days of the week,
       counted by 10s and 5s.
    4. Mathematical operations—beginning 1st Stanford Achievement Test I
      a) Addition (concrete)—age inappropriate
      b) Subtraction (concrete)—age inappropriate

  B. *Concepts*
    Beginning 1st—age inappropriate

  C. Applications—(ability to apply numerical principles to practical situations)
    Age inappropriate; however, was able to figure these concretely.

III. *Handwriting* (visual motor)

  Right—difficulty noted—unable to reproduce the alphabet.

DIAGNOSTIC IMPRESSION

Jane appears to be functioning at a readiness level in the language arts area. She is unable to read; however, proficiency is noted in ability to match words. She is able to discriminate beginning and final consonants. Difficulty with visual motor, memory, sequencing, and visual perception seem to interfere with Jane's ability to produce the alphabet independently; however, with visual cues she is able to complete this task. During the Frostig Test of Visual Perception, she held the booklet three inches from her face, and with much body shifting and attempts at paper turning, had difficulty completing this test. Jane appeared to be more proficient with auditorally directed tasks in Wepman Test, following directions and listening and comprehension. Grammatical and syntactical errors are noted in her language plus inability to explain words verbally, which resulted in gestures and diagrams in the air.

Mathematically, Jane is able to perform at a first-grade level. She was able to produce numbers to 120, add and subtract at a basic, concrete level, and could analyze story problems correctly.

Jane did not appear bothered by auditory stimuli. She does need many visual cues to achieve successfully. She watched the examiner's lips closely at all times. Jane seemed conditioned to failure; however, with praise and encouragement she became more diligent in her efforts to succeed.

Recommendations

1. Proper classroom placement pending staff conference, preferably small.
2. A strong tutorial program to assist Jane in building skills needed for successful achievement.

Teaching techniques and suggested materials

1. Provide visual cues whenever possible until Jane is able to work independently.
2. SeeQuees for v-m sequencing.
3. Classifying similarities.
4. Learn finger plays.
5. Permit Jane to trace—use templates.
6. Sterns structural reading and math series.

Where to begin

The instruments that will be discussed all yield information with direct implications for classroom or clinical use. With the exception of the instruments used to measure *sensation,* which are administered by a school nurse, audiologist, or physician, classroom teachers with a supervised practicum in assessment and test interpretation can use the instruments in their classrooms. Again, the caveat that these tests neither constitute a battery nor are administered to all children having learning problems must be made. It is important that teachers view a child's problems with learning as unique to that child; to do otherwise is to deny the complexity of learning problems. If one approaches assessment with the caution it merits, the child will benefit. If assessment is approached casually, the child will be harmed, even though the effects of poor assessment may not be apparent until months or years later.

Obviously, all classroom assessment must have a beginning point. To Otto (1973), this beginning point is *screening-level* assessment, since concentration is on *identification* of children demonstrating difficulty learning. It is hoped that after identification, more intensive assessment and intervention will follow. Until school districts make use of well-designed and thoroughly validated early-detection programs for large numbers of children, major responsibility for detecting children who need assistance will fall on classroom teachers and other educational and psychological specialists. Since a plethora of instruments exist, it is necessary that caution be exercised both in the selection and the administration of assessment screening instruments. Potential problems can be at least more manageable if classroom teachers and specialists become more judicious in evaluating instruments from the standpoint of test construction, validity, and reliability. Guidelines for test evaluation (Anastasi, 1968; Cronbach, 1970; Joint Committee on Revision of Standards, 1974) should be consulted when selecting a screening instrument.

The Joint Committee on Revision of Standards, comprised of representatives from the American Psychological Association Committee on Psychological Tests, the American Educational Research Association, and the National Council on Measurement in Education, has published a document, *Standards for Development and Use of Educational and Psychological Tests,* which explicitly makes available to the test user standards to apply in selecting, administering, or interpreting a test. Although the intent of the *Standards* is to provide guidelines about the obligations of test constructors, all of the guidelines can be applied to the test user in selecting, administering, scoring, or interpreting a test. The standards apply to any assessment procedure, assessment device, or assessment aide, i.e., to any instrument or procedure for making inferences about characteristics about children.

> An essential principle underlying these standards is that the test user, in selecting, administering, scoring, or interpreting a test, should know what he is doing and the possible consequences of his activity. He should, most of all, have a clear idea of why he is testing. It is not enough to have benign purposes; the user must know what procedures are necessary to maximize the effectiveness of the testing program and to minimize unfairness in the use of test results. (p. 3)

Because such test manuals can never give all of the information and test users can never follow all of the desirable procedures in testing, the standards are grouped in three levels: essential, very desirable, and desirable. Teachers and specialists should make every effort to see that the tests they use in decision making meet many of the standards characterized as essential by the Joint Committee.

Characteristics of tests essential to good testing   Classroom teachers and learning specialists can utilize the Joint Committee's guidelines in test selection, administration, scoring, or interpretation. The extensiveness of the guidelines and their intent as guidelines for test producers can be distilled into major guidelines for use by classroom teachers and learning specialists. The guidelines are in checklist format to assist you in organizing your impressions of a given test. These guidelines were followed in selecting instruments that test the processes in the Myklebust-Johnson model.

By following these guidelines, the teacher's chances of selecting an inadequate instrument are reduced; by eliminating inadequate instruments, assessment—and more importantly, teaching—is not cluttered with noncontributory, functionally barren test results. Ideally, a teacher or learning

NAME OF TEST _____

Yes   No

1. The selection of this test or assessment procedure has been based on clearly formulated goals and hypotheses.

2. Using the test manual, I have evaluated the history of development of the test and its original and developing rationale.

3. Using the test manual, I understand the psychological, educational, or other reasoning underlying the test and the nature of the process or skill it is intended to measure.

4. Do I meet the special qualifications required to administer the test and interpret it properly?

5. Evidence of the test's validity and reliability is clearly presented.

6. If the test is criterion-referenced, are the measures of criteria completely and accurately described?

7. Directions for administration of the test are clearly presented in the test manual.

8. Language of the test's instructions is understandable to the children I will be testing.

9. Procedures for scoring the test are clearly presented in the test manual.

10. Norms presented in the test refer to defined and clearly described populations.

11. Characteristics of the children I will be testing are comparable to the norming population.

12. Does the test manual report whether scores vary for groups differing in age, sex, race, or locale?

specialist should answer "yes" to a majority of the statements if she or he is to have confidence in the test results.

After survey-level assessment detects those children experiencing difficulty with learning, the teacher or specialist can begin more in-depth testing and clinical teaching. Table 13.3 is a diagrammatic representation of tests that can be used to assess the Myklebust-Johnson model.

Table 13.3. Tests that can be used to measure the processes in the Johnson-Myklebust model

5. *Conceptualization*

a. Boehm Test of Basic Concepts (Boehm, 1969)
b. Basic Concept Inventory (Engelmann, 1967)

   4. Symbolization

   a. Test for Auditory Comprehension of Language (Carrow, 1973)
   b. Peabody Picture Vocabulary Test (Dunn, 1965)

   3. Imagery

   a. Detroit Tests of Learning Aptitude: Subtest 9 (Visual Attention Span for Objects); Subtest 16 (Visual Attention Span for Letters) (Baker and Leland, 1958)
   b. Illinois Test of Psycholinguistic Ability: Subtest of Visual-Sequential Memory
   c. Slingerland Screening Tests for Identifying Children with Specific Language Disability (Slingerland, 1970)

2. *Perception*

a. Skills Tests from Pre-Reading Skills Program (Board of Regents of the University of Wisconsin System, 1974)
b. Slingerland Screening Tests for Identifying Children with Specific Language Disability (Slingerland, 1970)
c. Auditory Discrimination Test (Wepman, 1958)

1. *Sensation*

a. Can be evaluated by school or public health nurse, audiologist, or physician.
b. A reading or learning disability specialist with specific training in the use of visual screening instruments, e.g., the Bausch and Lomb Orthorater or the Keystone Telebinocular, and/or puretone, air conduction screening audiometers, can also conduct basic evaluations of sight and hearing.

Toward a responsible use of test results   Selection of an appropriate instrument is only one step in the assessment process. The correct utilization of an instrument in diagnostic teaching is a more complex and challenging task for the teacher or specialist. The objective of this section is to assist the teacher or specialist in making proper use of test results. The following topics will be discussed:

1. the responsibility of validating diagnostic insights through remedial teaching;

2. the confusion of diagnosis with remedial teaching;

3. the importance of well-ordered observations;

4. the importance of conveying diagnostic information to the classroom teacher.

The responsibility of validating diagnostic insights through remedial teaching. Although diagnostic instruments are of utmost importance in assessment, their results are not infallible. Some professionals report diagnostic information gathered from tests *ex cathedra,* as if the test or tests in question increase their hammerlock on truth. The fact of the matter is that variables within individuals, such as an anxiety, fatigue, and low tolerance to frustration, and those outside the individual, or environmental variables, such as the noise or light density of the room where testing takes place or the degree of rapport the examiner has with the child, all influence the child's performance on a diagnostic test. For this reason, it is incumbent on the teacher or learning specialist to validate testing results through teaching. As an example, one should not necessarily accept the reading-competency levels yielded by an informal reading inventory without determining if they correspond to the curriculum materials the child must read in the classroom. If an informal reading inventory indicates that a child's independent reading level is approximately fifth grade, we would want to validate this by seeing how well he or she can read curricular materials designed for use in fifth-grade classrooms. Failure to validate test results can result in a child's being over- or underplaced in reading materials, either of which does harm to the child. If the results of tests that purport to measure visual perception were validated by classroom teaching, fewer children in middle- or upper-elementary grades or above would be subjected to unnecessary materials that supposedly improve visual perception. In some instances children who demonstrate perceptual confusion (e.g., rotations, inversions of letters or geometric shapes) on diagnostic tests do not demonstrate such confusions when they avail themselves of syntactic or semantic clues present when reading connected prose.

The confusion of diagnosis with remedial teaching. Although the practice is declining, the confusion of diagnosis with remedial teaching still plagues teaching. The collection of diagnostic data without translation into sound intervention programs is both a dubious use of time and of questionable professional ethics. However, a teacher or specialist who lacks the necessary expertise to begin teaching usually resorts to excessive testing, as if the testing itself will solve his or her dilemma. The reader who is currently functioning as a teacher-consultant or who aspires to be one should watch for the teacher who relies on excessive testing without making use of the results.

Frequently, this is the teacher who asks the consultant for names of the most current tests without specifying what information she or he expects to obtain or what will be done with the test results. The teacher with this difficulty frequently cannot explain what he or she plans to do after extensive testing; it is as if testing is an end in itself. With this type of problem, the message for the consultant is clear: instead of supplying the teacher with an endless array of tests, focus on improving the teacher's ability to interpret diagnostic tests and to use test results for educational planning.

The importance of well-ordered observations. Care should be taken to avoid a reliance on test results as the only source of insights for remedial teaching. Without question, the use of tests by a skilled consultant or teacher provides a framework for sampling complex cognitive-linguistic behaviors important to school learning. But observation and intuition are also important to the learning process. The importance of well-ordered observations by experienced teachers and consultants is not to be underestimated. Obviously the key factor is the experience of the teacher or consultant. The insights of a person who is a product of a training program with a well-supervised clinical practicum will develop insights and sensitivities about children with learning problems that are impossible to learn when a student is one of 25 or 30 competing for supervision from one or possibly two practicum supervisors. Sadly, it is more common to find the poorly supervised practicum than the well-supervised one. Ironically, in some training settings practica are supervised by junior members of the department or are left to graduate students. The underlying message of this slipshod form of training is that the pragmatic elements of a training program are not important enough to warrant the attention of the senior members of a department. This training perspective seems unique to teacher education departments and is not as prominent in the training of other service-oriented professionals, e.g., social workers, dentists, psychologists, or physicians.

The importance of conveying diagnostic information to the classroom teacher. Whether by omission or commission, classroom teachers frequently do not receive diagnostic information or teaching suggestions from a specialist who is concurrently seeing a child from his or her classroom. As discussed earlier, the greater the psychological or physical distance that separates the consultant from the classroom, the higher the probability that communication will be impaired and insights and recommendations will not be shared.

The Oakland Schools Reading and Language Center has developed a procedure that facilitates communication between a specialized setting and the classroom. Since a sizable distance separates us from the classrooms of many of our clients, we realized that communication would have to be open and direct, or the child would suffer. As in most facilities providing clinical services to educational institutions, the majority of our referrals came from classroom teachers seeking help for a severely disabled learner. For this reason, we felt that the referring teacher would both welcome and benefit from an opportunity to interact directly with the clinician assisting the child in our Center. From the beginning of the diagnostic teaching sessions, the clinician communicates the findings and makes recommendations about teaching strategies to the classroom teacher through the utilization of a form developed for communication purposes. The teacher then returns the form to the Center, responding to the classroom recommendations. In this way we find out if our recommendations are useful to the child's classroom teacher.

After sufficient diagnostic teaching, we invite the classroom teacher and other specialists assisting the child to our Center for a half-day conference to discuss our findings. Since the child is the focal point of the discussion, we spend part of the conference modeling effective teaching strategies that can be implemented in the classroom. Attention is also given to the selection of appropriate reading materials for the child. If the client is a junior or senior high school student, we spend considerable time working with the consultant and content teachers selecting appropriate subject-matter textbooks. When consulting with content teachers, we provide them with an annotated bibliography of subject-matter reading materials appropriate for the high school student with a serious reading problem (Peters and Peters, 1973a and b).

In most cases the Reading and Language Center clinicians also meet with subject-matter teachers at the client's school to do more in-depth educational planning. We have found in most cases that teachers appreciate being included in the remedial process and respond with a high level of commitment. Including the classroom teacher also helps to eliminate the possibility of the teacher's abdicating major responsibility for the child to the specialist. In some cases teachers reduce the amount of help they are giving a child if they feel that the specialist has primary responsibility for the child. This is especially true if the specialist projects an air of hyperprofessionalism, making the teacher feel peripheral to the treatment of the problem.

DETERMINING THE OPTIMAL CONDITIONS UNDER WHICH A CHILD LEARNS NEW MATERIAL

Severson (1970) has generated a model of assessment and teaching that is both highly individualized and flexible. His model can be used with learners from preschool through high school. Like Myklebust and Johnson, Severson does not tie his model to any diagnostic testing battery; in fact, Severson excoriates the widely used practice of extensive diagnostic testing with a so-called test battery prior to teaching. Instead, he advocates a continual system of diagnosis and treatment existing as an ongoing, interwoven process. Severson believes that a remedial teacher should not abandon all standardized tests, but should retain and utilize components of the instrument that give important insight into both the deficiencies a child demonstrates and the unique way in which he or she learns new information. Severson also is concerned with assessment that is too far removed from the actual teaching-learning process. For this reason, he regards the obsessive concern to determine if a child is "dyslexic," "minimally brain damaged," or "perceptually handicapped" to be of dubious value. As he states:

> Rather than seeking to make differential diagnosis between various underlying processes presumably related to learning abilities, we approach the learning disabled child as a person who has brought, and now brings, certain personal patterns of skill, ways of behaving, and learned emotional reactions to each learning situation. A multitude of historical ingredients have affected him in various ways, and as a result of the composite interaction over time, the child has evolved into a current pattern of considerable complexity. It is our task to understand this complex pattern as best we can, not primarily with a sense of history, nor by trying to get at inferred brain-behavior relationships, but with increasingly more precise ways of measuring the current functional relationships which determine the reactions of the child. (p. 8)

Severson considers his model to be quite close to a *system analysis* point of view with an exploration of input-throughput-output of language/cognitive information. Concern is not for the discrepancy between I.Q. and performance or grade-level placement and performance; rather, the emphasis is on an analysis of the conditions for contributing to adequate learning. It is the responsibility of the remedial teacher to determine the optimal learning environment in which the child learns. Essentially, the success or failure of an intervention program rests on the ability of the remedial teacher to determine how much the child knows, how he or she learns new material, and how varying certain aspects of the teaching-learning process influences the effectiveness of learning.

Determining how much the child knows

Severson advocates sound assessment as the first step in the remedial process. Flexibility is the merit of the Severson model as it pertains to assessment, since it values both standardized test-based and informally derived data. Severson retains many of the desirable qualities of standardized testing while recognizing that observation of the child *in a learning situation* is a much more useful activity. Using an assess down–teach up approach, the teacher will assess down to the point where the learner experiences deficiencies in learning and begin teaching at that level. For the preschooler the deficiencies could occur at what Myklebust and Johnson would call the symbolic or conceptual level, perhaps with a confused awareness of important relational concepts, e.g., *first* or *second;* for a high school student, an inability to scan for salient points when reading.

The teacher or specialist can determine a child's strengths and deficits by relying on the Myklebust and Johnson hierarchical approach for classifying diagnostic data, any of the objective-based formats for reading instruction (Fountain Valley Reading Program, 1971; Wisconsin Design for Reading Skill Development, 1971), informal measures drawn from classroom observation or teacher-constructed instruments for preschool children, or Freeman's (1971) educational-diagnostic approach to assessing language skills. All of these approaches provide a framework for obtaining diagnostic information. The most important consideration at this point is to begin to identify the child's learning deficiencies and strengths. Until this is done, there is no beginning point for remediation.

As Otto indicated in an earlier chapter, there is no empirically derived list of essential skills in reading, and the same can be said of the readiness skills that are viewed as prerequisite to the acquisition of reading—visual processing skills, language skills, and the array of abilities that can be subsumed by the term "attention." Although a precise catalog of these specific skills is lacking, the teacher should not become immobilized by anxiety and stress.

It should be noted in passing that in a few isolated instances the absence of an empirically derived sequence of skills has precipitated a general pedagogical malaise. This lack of consensus has resulted in viewing language and reading as complex skills that escape analysis and assessment to the point that such terms as "assessment" or "skills" are taboo, and any attempt to assess or focus instruction places one firmly in the nonhumanist camp.

At the present time, applied and basic researchers are attempting to determine which skills are requisites for success in language acquisition and reading. In fact, the psycholinguistic research of Venezky, Calfee, and Chapman (1968) has attempted to isolate the prereading skills that are predictive of subsequent success in reading; other researchers (Carrow, 1973; Ruddell, 1970; and Samuels, 1970) are currently investigating the specific abilities that contribute to the language and reading process. Also, professionals who work with children in the classroom or clinic are intuitively aware that certain psycholinguistic skills precede others and that the concept of "multiple readiness levels" formulated by Johnson and Myklebust (1967) should be utmost in a teacher's mind when planning for children who find learning difficult.

Because of these complex linguistic-cognitive demands, many teachers are aware that it is more beneficial for a child's learning to view "readiness" not as a global, unitary factor, but as a factor that is a prerequisite to all learning. When a complex process such as reading is in the context of such a framework, an insightful teacher is aware that "readiness" viewed as a general construct is overly imprecise and that certain specific skills precede others in a quasi-hierarchical style. For example, many teachers intuitively know that a child must be able to auditorially blend sound units into words *before* he or she can be expected to use a "phonics" approach to word recognition. When given the sounds /k/ + /a/ + /t/ orally, a child who cannot recognize the word as "cat" may have problems that would lead to difficulty learning to read through an approach that involves "sound out" words. Most teachers also know that a child who has language-comprehension problems will in most cases have difficulty with reading comprehension. A Peanuts cartoon demonstrates this very well.

© 1974 United Feature Syndicate, Inc.

A linear-hierarchy of skills is not needed to recognize that certain skills are prerequisite to others. Through experience, training, and professional reading, a committed remedial teacher attempts to better understand the learning process and its analysis in order to be better prepared to begin educational remediation.

Determining how a child learns new material

After determining a point at which to begin intervention, the next step in the Severson model is to systematically ascertain the best reinforcement contingencies under which a child learns new materials. Let us take the teaching of survival vocabulary at the junior high school level as an example. The teacher selects 15 unknown survival words (such as *danger, caution, slow, poison*) to teach the young adult. The 15 unknown words are presented to the student in three groups of five. A record of correct responses is kept, and feedback is limited to telling the child if his or her response was correct or incorrect ("Yes, it's _____." or "No, it's _____."). This is the only kind of reaction given the child. A record of the number of trials the child requires to get all five words correct is made (see Fig. 13.2). The trials are discontinued

DIAGNOSTIC TEACHING

Date _____ Child _____

Teacher _____ Session number _____

Feedback (FB)	Trials

```
 5 | 5  5  5  5  5  5  5  5  5  5     Items:        3._____
 4 | 4  4  4  4  4  4  4  4  4  4     1._____  4._____
 3 | 3  3  3  3  3  3  3  3  3  3     2._____  5._____
 2 | 2  2  2  2  2  2  2  2  2  2     Observations and comments:_____
 1 | 1  1  1  1  1  1  1  1  1  1     _____
 0 | 0  0  0  0  0  0  0  0  0  0     _____
     1  2  3  4  5  6  7  8  9  10    _____
```
(# Correct)

Social praise (SP)	Trials

```
 5 | 5  5  5  5  5  5  5  5  5  5     Items:        3._____
 4 | 4  4  4  4  4  4  4  4  4  4     1._____  4._____
 3 | 3  3  3  3  3  3  3  3  3  3     2._____  5._____
 2 | 2  2  2  2  2  2  2  2  2  2     Observations and comments:_____
 1 | 1  1  1  1  1  1  1  1  1  1     _____
 0 | 0  0  0  0  0  0  0  0  0  0     _____
     1  2  3  4  5  6  7  8  9  10    _____
```
(# Correct)

Tangible (T)	Trials

```
 5 | 5  5  5  5  5  5  5  5  5  5     Items:        3._____
 4 | 4  4  4  4  4  4  4  4  4  4     1._____  4._____
 3 | 3  3  3  3  3  3  3  3  3  3     2._____  5._____
 2 | 2  2  2  2  2  2  2  2  2  2     Observations and comments:_____
 1 | 1  1  1  1  1  1  1  1  1  1     _____
 0 | 0  0  0  0  0  0  0  0  0  0     _____
     1  2  3  4  5  6  7  8  9  10    _____
```
(# Correct)

Fig. 13.2. Form for charting student's responses in diagnostic teaching.

whenever the child does not make an improvement within four to eight trials or when the child's behavior reflects lack of attention or discomfort.

The next step involves presenting the child with another five words of similar difficulty as the first five. This time, the teacher responds with enthusiastic praise (e.g., "Excellent," "Good work") for correct responses and simply corrects the incorrect responses. Again, a record is kept of correct responses per trial. The final step involves presenting another five unknown words, but following each correct response with a tangible reinforcer (a token that can be exchanged for candy or a Coke, a star, or a smiling face on a piece of paper). Severson suggests combining the tangible reinforcer with social praise, since it is important to know if the tangible reinforcer will improve the learning rate over social reinforcement.

The form devised by Severson for charting a student's responses is given in Fig. 3.3. The important thing to remember is that the teacher or specialist is attempting to determine under what conditions a child maximizes his or her learning rate. Since different children respond to different types of reinforcers, this information has instant, pragmatic utility for all learning occurring in the classroom. Some children respond more favorably to praise, whereas others find tangible rewards more motivating in a learning situation. Not all curricula fit into this format as easily as building sight vocabulary, but a creative teacher will find other processes that can be subjected to this type of analysis.

A PROPOSED MODEL FOR TRAINING SPECIALISTS WORKING WITH DISABLED READERS

Most training programs preparing specialists to teach the severely disabled reader do not significantly differ from training programs constructed for the reading consultant responsible for a district- or schoolwide reading program or the classroom teacher desirous of improving his or her skill as a teacher of developmental reading. Although this practice has some redeeming virtues, it just is not defensible to have a unitary training model for all reading specialists. To the extent that a core of courses and experiences should be made available to reading specialists, there will be a certain degree of overlap. All reading specialists must have a knowledge of tests and measurements, child development, language development, developmental reading in the elementary school, developmental reading in the secondary school, and remedial reading. Graduate students preparing to become elementary or secondary reading consultants, more knowledgeable classroom teachers, or specialists servicing the severely disabled reader would, in addition to sharing required courses, pursue a curriculum emphasizing one of these three specialties. A student earning a master's degree in reading education would not automatically be prepared to serve as a reading disability specialist, elementary consultant, or secondary consultant, as is now the case in many training programs.

An alternative model for training teachers of disabled readers: The clinical educator

Bryant (1966) first formulated the role of clinical educator, emphasizing the function this specialist would serve in community mental health clinics or psychoeducational clinics either within the school or apart from it. The clinical educator would normally function as part of a team comprised of a clinical psychologist or psychiatrist, social worker, and assorted medical specialists, such as neurologists and pediatricians. After diagnosing a child, staff members would convey to the teacher information about the team's diagnostic findings.

Bryant's model never had much of an impact either in community mental health clinics or the schools. Part of this nonacceptance can be attributed to the psychological distance separating many community mental health clinics or psychoeducational clinics from the school personnel who have daily contact with the child. The teacher was peripheral to the diagnostic process, receiving information either at a short staff meeting or through a written report. This might suffice for a teacher with a great deal of experience with disabled readers, but a relatively untrained person might not possess the necessary skills to translate the diagnostic team's recommendations into a classroom-based intervention program.

Another limitation of this model is the availability of such services in the community. Most reading-learning-disabled children do not live in a community where there is a mental health center that offers comprehensive services to reading-learning-disabled children or a psychoeducational clinic sponsored by the school district or a university. Since for the vast majority of children, services are provided by the school district, attention should be given to upgrading these services. Thus the school is the most natural place for intervention. Hobbs (1975) in his visionary book, *The Futures of Children,* summarizes the recommendations of 93 experts contributing to a government-sponsored Project on Classification of Exceptional Children. One of the major outgrowths of the project was the recommendation that the institution in our society that can serve almost all children without creating nonfunctional categories and isolating conditions is the public school. Specifically, the project demands that "the public schools should be the institution with primary advocacy responsible for providing or obtaining educational and related services for all children in need of special assistance whose condition or life circumstances does not require their institutionalization" (p. 250).

Ironically, schools frequently appear to be the most resistant to the Project's recommendations. The most complex, challenging problems are often referred to other public agencies or private practitioners in the community. Sometimes the *raison d'être* of school evaluation committees appears to be to refer learning-disabled children to agencies and individuals who are not affiliated with the schools.

If diagnostic and intervention services are to be provided in the schools, school-affiliated professionals must improve the delivery of services to children in need. A beginning is the differentiation of training for those providing essentially different services for children with severe reading problems. The person functioning as a "clinical educator" would be a product of a multivariate training program. Such a program might be housed in a department of reading education, educational psychology, or communicative disorders. The important factor is not the professional identity of such clinical educators, but their professional competence. Course work would be interdisciplinary, encompassing developmental and remedial reading, language development and language disorders, an introduction to childhood psychopathology, and group dynamics.

An understanding of language disorders is especially important for those clinical educators working with children of elementary school age, since language problems sometimes are associated with reading problems. Because of the high incidence of emotional and behavioral disturbances coupled with severe reading problems (Eisenberg 1966; Gates, 1968; Kline, 1972; Saunders and Barker, 1972), the clinical educator must have a basic understanding of such disturbances and their treatment. This is not to imply that a clinical educator will serve as a counselor or therapist, but rather that she or he will be prepared to support mental health professionals assisting the child with the emotional/behavioral components of academic failure. An undestanding of group dynamics will strengthen the clinical educator's abilities as a consultant to classroom teachers or other specialists. With additional training in individual, group, or family counseling, clinical educators could also assume more responsibility for dealing with the emotional/behavioral components of academic problems. The clinical educator would serve as the coordinator of any intervention involving professionals from agencies outside the schools and would also share major responsibility with the classroom teacher for communicating with parents about their child's learning problem.

The clinical practica or supervised teaching experiences for the clinical educator would differ from those for consultants or classroom teachers wishing to become more knowledgeable teachers of reading. Practica experiences for the clinical educator would entail exposure to the most disabled readers, eliminating the customary practice of placing practica students with less complex cases of reading disability. Practica would also give the prospective clinical educator experience working in an interdisciplinary mode with speech and hearing specialists, school psychologists, and social workers. Such training would prepare the student for the realities of working with other specialists, an experience for which few reading specialists are prepared.

In addition to diagnostic teaching responsibilities with referrals, the clinical educator would serve as a consultant to the teachers of referred children. This form of consultation varies from the consulting services performed by the reading consultant. The reading consultant typically assists classroom teachers with what should be called problems of a curricular nature geared to improving reading instruction for the "average student." Such problems could include the following: implementation of a systematic skill-development program, grouping of children into appropriate reading groups, or selecting a basal reader or supplemental reading materials for a school or classroom. The clinical educator, in addition to providing direct diagnostic teaching services to children, consulting services to parents, and coordinating school services with professional services offered outside the schools, would also consult with classroom teachers about the management of specific children in the teacher's classroom. The clinical educator would not replace the reading consultant, but instead would have a commitment to and responsibility for specific children rather than for broader problems involving the improvement of the reading curriculum.

In summary, the clinical educator would be a unique professional, possessing both clinical and consulting expertise. Well trained in the diagnosis and treatment of serious reading problems, oral-language development and disorders, and childhood development and disorders in general, the clinical educator would be an asset to any teaching staff.

CONCLUSIONS

Obviously, if the recommendations for assessment made in this chapter are given serious consideration, there will have to be greater—I cringe at the cliché—individualization in classrooms with severely disabled learners. Individualization has been bandied about by educators for decades; each year brings with it more innovations—paraprofessionals, volunteer aides, computer-assisted instruction—which if used correctly provide a greater degree of individualization for the disabled learner. Even with these innovations, forces beyond the control of teacher and specialist militate against individualization: parsimonious budgets, unwieldy numbers of children in school classrooms, and even the attitudes of teacher educators who, while justly criticizing the room-at-the-end-of-the-hall concept of assisting disabled learners, continue to prepare teachers who do not have the skills to help disabled learners. It is to be hoped that society, taxpayers, school districts, and schools of education will someday recognize that a significant move in overcoming the effects of learning problems can be accomplished only through educational intervention committed to as much individualization as feasible. Costs will be higher, but as Satz so cogently argues in his chapter, the costs are

Lilliputian in proportion to the human, social, and economic costs of juvenile delinquency, emotional disorders, and unemployment associated with reading problems.

REFERENCES

Anderson, R. C., and R. W. Kulhavy "Imagery and Prose Learning," *Journal of Educational Psychology* 3 (1972): 242–243.

Anastasi, Anne *Psychological Testing,* 3rd ed., New York: Macmillan, 1968.

Baker, H. J., and B. Leland *Detroit Tests of Learning Aptitude,* Indianapolis: Bobbs-Merrill, 1958.

Board of Regents of the University of Wisconsin System *Pre-reading Skills Program,* Chicago: Encyclopaedia Britannica Education Corporation, 1974.

Boehm, A. E. *Boehm Test of Basic Concepts,* New York: Psychological Corporation, 1969.

Boehm, A. E. "Criterion-Referenced Assessment for the Teacher," *Teachers College Record* 75, 1 (1973): 117–126.

Bryant, N. D. "Clinical Inadequacies with Learning Disorders—the Missing Clinic Educator," in *Learning Disorders,* Vol. II, Seattle: Special Child Publication, 1966, pp. 265–279.

Carrow, E. *Test for Auditory-Comprehension of Language,* Austin: Learning Concepts, 1973.

Clements, S. D. *Task Force I: Minimal Brain Dysfunction in Children,* U.S. Department of Health, Education and Welfare, National Institute of Neurological Disease and Blindness, Monograph N. 3, 1966, pp. 9–10.

Cronbach, L. J. *Essentials of Psychological Testing,* 3rd ed., New York: Harper & Row, 1970.

Delacato, C. H. *The Diagnosis and Treatment of Speech and Reading Problems,* Springfield, Ill.: Thomas, 1963.

Dunn, L. M. *Peabody Picture Vocabulary Test,* Minneapolis: American Guidance Service, 1965.

Eisenberg, L. "The Epidemiology of Reading Retardation and a Program for Preventive Intervention," in J. Money, ed., *The Disabled Reader: Education of the Dyslexic Child,* Baltimore: Johns Hopkins University Press, 1966, pp. 3–20.

Engelmann, S. F. *The Basic Concept Inventory,* Chicago: Follett Educational Corporation, 1967.

Fountain Valley Teacher Support System in Reading Huntington Beach, Calif.: Richard L. Zweig Associates, 1971.

Freeman, G. "An Educational-Diagnostic Approach to Language Problems, *Speech and Hearing Services in Schools* 4, 1971, pp. 23–30.

Furth, H. G. "Reading as Thinking: A Developmental Perspective" (unpublished monograph).

Gates, A. I. "The Role of Personality Maladjustment in Reading Disability," in G. Natchez, ed., *Children with Reading Problems,"* New York: Basic Books, 1968, pp. 80–86.

Good, T., and J. E. Brophy "Teacher-Child Dyadic Interaction: A New Method of Classroom Observation," *Journal of School Psychology* 8 (1970): 131–137.

Harriman, P. L. *Handbook of Psychological Terms,* Totowa, N.J.: Littlefield, Adams, 1965.

Johnson, D. J., and H. B. Myklebust *Learning Disabilities: Educational Principles and Practices,* New York: Grune and Stratton, 1967.

Kirk, S. A. *Educating Exceptional Children,* Boston: Houghton Mifflin, 1962.

Kirk, S. A., J. J. McCarthy, and W. D. Kirk *Illinois Test of Psycholinguistic Ability,* Urbana: University of Illinois Press, 1968.

Kline, C. S. "The Adolescents with Learning Problems: How Long Must They Wait?" *Journal of Learning Disabilities* 5 (1972): 262–271.

LeBlanc, J. M., and B. C. Etzel (in collaboration with the University of Kansas Head Start Evaluation and Research Center Staff), "Social Interaction Observation Procedure Training Manual," U.S. Head Start Evaluation and Research Center, Sept. 1967, mimeo.

Myklebust, H. R. "Psychoneurological Learning Disorders in Children," in S. A. Kirk and W. Becker, eds., *Conference for Children with Minimal Brain Impairment,* Urbana: University of Illinois, 1963, p. 27.

National Advisory Committee on Handicapped Children "Special Education for Handicapped Children, Toward Fulfillment of the Nation's Commitment," January 31, 1968.

Otto, W., R. A. McMenemy, and R. J. Smith *Corrective and Remedial Teaching,* 2d ed., Boston: Houghton Mifflin, 1973.

Paivio, A. "Mental Imagery in Associative Learning and Memory," *Psychological Review* 76 (1969): 241–263.

Paivio, A., and J. C. Yuille "Mediation, Instruction and Word Attribute in Paired-Associate Learning," *Psychonomic Science* 8 (1967): 65–66.

Peters, N. A., and J. I. Peters "Better Reading Materials for the Content Areas," *The Volta Review* 6 (1973): 375–387, 445–448.

Peters, N. A., and J. I. Peters "Better Reading Materials for the Content Areas," *The Volta Review* 8 (1974): 500–507.

Rees, N. S. "Noncommunicative Functions of Language in Children," *Journal of American Speech and Hearing Disorder* 38, 1 (1973): 98–110.

Ruddell, R. B. "Language Acquisition and the Reading Process," in Harry Singer and Robert B. Ruddell, eds., *Theoretical Models and Processes of Reading,* Newark, Del.: International Reading Association, 1970.

Saunders, W. A., and M. G. Barker "Dyslexia as a Cause of Psychiatric Disorder in Adults," *British Medical Journal* 4 (1972): 759–761.

Severson, R. "Behavior Therapy with Severe Learning Disabilities," 1970, p. 8 (unpublished monograph).

Slingerland, B. H. *Slingerland Screening Tests for Identifying Children with Specific Language Disability,* Cambridge, Mass.: Educators Publishing Service, 1970.

Talbot, M. E. "Édouard Sequin: A Study of the Treatment of Mentally Defective Children," New York: Columbia University, Bureau of Publications, Teachers College, 1964.

Venezsky, R. L., R. C. Calfee, and R. S. Chapman "Skills Required for Learning to Read: A Preliminary Analysis," Working Paper No. 10, University of Wisconsin at Madison: Wisconsin Research and Development Center for Cognitive Learning, September 1968.

Wepman, J. M. *Auditory Discrimination Test,* Los Angeles: Western Psychological Services, 1958.

Werner, H., and B. Kaplan *Symbol Formation,* New York: Wiley, 1963.

Wisconsin Design for Reading Skill Development Madison: University of Wisconsin, Research and Development Center for Cognitive Learning, 1971.

Chapter 14

PROBLEMS, PRESCRIPTIONS, AND POSSIBILITIES IN HIGH SCHOOL READING INSTRUCTION

HARRY SINGER · *University of California, Riverside*

ALAN RHODES · *Upland High School, Upland, California*

INTRODUCTION

High school reading instruction is not a recent phenomenon in American education. As early as post–World War I, high schools organized reading programs in the aftermath of the country's discovery of the large number of draftees who had been rejected from Army service because they were deficient in reading ability. But the concept of developmental reading (instruction in reading that starts in elementary and continues through high school) was not prominent among educators until the 1950s (Hill, 1971; Smith, 1965). Ruth Strang's research and writing (Strang, 1938, 1942; Strang, McCullough, and Traxler, 1946) was credited with making the difference in establishing postelementary instruction in reading (Russell, 1961; Singer, 1970).

A concomitant trend was the increase in the number of students remaining in school. Instead of dropping out for jobs in industry or agriculture, more students began to remain in school until graduation. For example, from 1930 to 1960, enrollment of 14–17-year-olds in secondary school increased from 51.3 to 83.2 percent (Tyack, 1967). Recently, Jencks (1975) reported that 85 percent of students who had been in school in ninth grade were still in school in the twelfth grade. Aiding this increase in the schools' holding power was the initiation of the 100 percent social-promotion policy in elementary school; for example, after marshalling convincing evidence against the nonpromotion policy, Caswell and Foshay (1950, p. 380) advocated 100 percent promotion along with an appropriate curriculum: "a program should be developed in which the curriculum is so well adjusted to the individual needs of pupils that all can progress regularly. In such a situation, 100 per cent promotion results from the development of an adequate program."

Also, during the 1960s civil rights groups urged integration of minority groups into the schools (Singer and Hendrick, 1967) and admonished minority students to remain in school and to make schools adapt instruction to their needs, interests, and abilities. In 1950, anticipating this trend toward a 12-year common school, Caswell and Foshay (1950, p. 385) wrote:

> For a long period of our national life, for all practical purposes, it [elementary school] was the common school. Now, however, conditions have changed. Compulsory attendance age limits have been raised in most states to include a portion or all of the secondary school years. Under normal conditions, employment of youth has been delayed longer and longer. At the same time more and more complex social problems have increased the need for education.
>
> The secondary school has accepted the challenge of becoming in fact a common school, and its leaders are moving forward to develop a program adapted to the needs of all youth of secondary school, regardless of ability. In brief, we are now seeking to create in America a twelve-year common school program which truly meets the needs of all children and youth, affording them an equalized educational opportunity for the entire period.

Consequently, high schools today do not have the more selective group of students they had some 50 years ago. Instead, high schools now have a more heterogeneous group of pupils with a wider range of achievement in reading.

Range in reading achievement

Range of achievement in reading increases with progression through school (Cook, 1951). In a heterogeneous group whose members' IQ's vary from a low of 67 to a high of 132, the range of achievement is two-thirds of the median age group (Bond and Tinker, 1957). Thus a representative group of tenth graders whose median age is 15 years would be expected to have a ten-year range in achievement. This range would vary in reading equivalency from fifth grade to sophomore college level. At the twelfth grade, when the median chronological age is 18 years, the range of achievement in this representative group increases to 12 years.

The basic assumption in the formula for computing this range of reading achievement is that all students have reading achievements that equal their mental age levels. If achievement in reading were not up to mental age levels, the range would be even greater; in fact, since not all students do read up

Table 14.1. Attitude inventory toward teaching reading in the content area

Directions: Read the statement on the left. Then decide whether you strongly agree, agree, are undecided, disagree, or strongly disagree with the statement. Indicate your response by circling the number on the right under the appropriate column. (If you do not want to write in your book, number 1 to 14 on a separate piece of paper. Then copy down the number you would have circled. Thus if you strongly disagree with the first statement, you would copy down "5" after the first statement, because that is the number you would have circled. The numbers change. So look and copy down the correct number.)

	Strongly agree	Agree	Undecided	Disagree	Strongly disagree
1. In the secondary school the teaching of reading should be the responsibility of reading teachers only.	1	2	3	4	5
2. Secondary school teachers can teach reading effectively without special university courses in methods of teaching reading.	5	4	3	2	1
3. The teaching of reading skills can be incorporated into content-area courses without interfering with the major objectives of these courses.	5	4	3	2	1
4. Any secondary school teacher who assigns reading should teach his or her students how to read what is assigned.	5	4	3	2	1
5. With rare exceptions, students should know what there is to know about reading before they are permitted to leave the elementary school.	1	2	3	4	5
6. Only remedial reading should be necessary in the secondary school, and that should be done by remedial-reading teachers in special classes.	1	2	3	4	5
7. Teaching reading is a technical process that secondary school teachers generally know nothing about.	1	2	3	4	5

8. Secondary school teachers cannot teach reading without special materials designed for that purpose.   1   2   3   4   5

9. Teaching reading is a necessary and legitimate part of teaching any content course in the secondary school.   5   4   3   2   1

10. Teaching reading takes all the fun out of teaching at the secondary school level.   1   2   3   4   5

11. Every secondary school teacher should be a teacher of reading.   5   4   3   2   1

12. At the secondary school level, students want to learn content, not how to read.   1   2   3   4   5

13. Integrating the teaching of reading with the teaching of specific content can be as exciting for the content teacher as teaching content only.   5   4   3   2   1

14. Content-area teachers in the secondary school are probably more competent to teach the reading skills needed for their subjects than are special reading teachers.   5   4   3   2   1

to their mental age levels, the range *is* greater. Moreover, when students' low achievement keeps them from being promoted, the range is even greater (Cook, 1951).

Attitudes toward teaching reading in the content areas

A second problem confronting high schools is the attitude of teachers toward teaching reading in the content areas. Otto and Smith (1969) examined this problem by administering an attitude scale (see Table 14.1). Using the scale on a sample of high school teachers, Otto and Smith found that the teachers wanted to teach reading in their content areas! The results surprised the researchers, who like other experts believed that high school teachers were opposed to teaching reading in their content areas. However, the high school teachers also stated that they would need further training to do so. To gain further insight into your own attitudes toward teaching reading in the content areas, simply follow the directions given at the top of the scale in Table 14.1.

Scoring and interpreting the attitude inventory

To find the score on the attitude inventory, simply add the numbers circled. The score can be interpreted by comparing it with scores derived from a sample of junior and senior high school teachers. Table 14.2 shows the attitude-inventory results for each of these school levels. A lower than average score indicates agreement with the attitude of teaching reading in content areas. A higher than average score signifies disagreement with the attitude that reading should be taught in content areas.

SCHOOL STRATEGIES

The problem of how to organize and instruct high school students with a 10- to 12-year range of general reading achievement and how to train a faculty to teach reading in each content area can be understood by con-

Table 14.2. Results of teachers on the attitude scale for teaching reading in the content areas

| | School levels | |
	Junior high	High school
Size of sample	38	48
Range of scores	22–65	19–54
Average score	42	45

trasting two approaches to a solution of the problem. For the first approach, we describe the strategy used by a composite, representative school, "Midville High School." The picture reveals the many difficulties that beset high schools as they try to establish reading programs, often with limited financial resources and little guidance.

Midville High School

Midville High School's administration, alarmed by the school's results on state-mandated achievement tests and under pressure from the community, decided that a reading program had to be established. Uncertain of what to do, the principal contacted the English department chairman, Mr. Morley, and assigned him the task of creating a reading program within the English department. Having no experience in the field of reading, Mr. Morley telephoned several other school districts that had reading programs. After locating three districts nearby, Mr. Morley was granted two days of leave time to visit and observe these schools. The Midville program was structured after these schools, which were all quite similar in their approach.

The Midville plan called for the creation of a remedial class called Reading Laboratory, which would be stocked with paperback books. There would be ten sections of the class, each with a maximum of 15 students, to insure individual attention. Since there would not be enough paperback books to supply more than one room, the lab would be occupied each period by two classes and two teachers.

No one in the English department had any experience teaching reading, and the school board was not prepared to hire additional personnel. Instead, the board believed that English teachers were already qualified for reading instruction. The administration decided that each of five English teachers would be given two reading classes, in addition to their three sections of English. Since no one on the faculty expressed any desire to teach reading, two new, young teachers were the first to be drafted. A veteran member of the department agreed to take two sections, on the condition that she be given advanced senior classes the rest of the day. Two other teachers, sympathetic to the problems of low-level readers, finally volunteered, but admitted that they were unsure of themselves and that they were accepting the assignment on a tentative, one-year basis. (Since its inception, Midville's reading lab has had a high teacher turnover rate each year, with new teachers usually filling the empty spaces.)

Incoming freshmen at Midville are channeled into reading classes on the basis of standardized test scores and/or recommendations from junior high school counselors. Students low in reading achievement who have been missed through this process are placed through teacher referrals. The system is loose; many students find themselves in reading lab, only to be moved out again because they "are too good for the class." Other students, who should be getting special help, are never discovered.

Upon entering the lab, students are given an oral-reading test. The test was selected because another reading lab in a nearby school was also using it and recommended it. One teacher complained that the oral test wasn't an accurate measure of how the students actually read, but she didn't know exactly why. A silent comprehension test was added later, but most teachers continued to rely on the oral test as the main diagnostic tool. In fact, oral reading quickly became the primary teaching method in the lab. While students silently read self-selected paperbacks at their desks, the teacher called them, one by one, to his or her desk, where each student read orally for about ten minutes. This meant that the student saw the teacher only once every four days. Most teachers made and kept packets of flashcards for students. With the exception of occasional dittoed phonics worksheets, little more was done in the way of instruction.

Students were pulled out of regular English classes and put into the lab. In theory, they were to be returned to regular classes when they overcame their reading difficulties. Some students showed gains while in the lab, but were soon floundering again when returned to the regular classroom. Other students, who enjoyed the nonthreatening atmosphere of the lab, did everything possible to stay. Students with low IQ's presented another problem. Many were never able to show any appreciable gains, because they were already up to potential (though that potential was usually several grade levels below them). Many of these pupils were to spend four years in the lab, with no noticeable improvement.

Other problems beset the reading lab. Students are quick to spot any tracking or grouping in a school; consequently, the lab soon became stigmatized as the "dummy class." Unfortunately, the lab also became a convenient depository for children with behavior problems, pupils with learning disabilities of all kinds, and bilingual students who ranged from low to high in intelligence. Most disturbing of all, the lab acquired a high ratio of black students. Midville is a predominantly white, middle-class school and has a small percentage of low-income blacks. Blacks often resented placement in the lab, regarding it as a form of discrimination.

Later, a class in developmental reading was added to the Midville curriculum. This class was created for students who were above the lab level or who had benefited as much as possible from the lab, but were still below the reading standards of regular English classes. Four sections of this class were opened, each consisting of 25 students and one teacher. All four sections were taught by a teacher who had taken two courses in adolescent literature through university extension classes. The class in developmental reading was actually a literature class; high-interest–low-level adolescent fiction was taught, but few reading skills were.

Although Midville's reading teachers worked hard and achieved some success with a limited number of students, most of the teachers felt frustrated, and they suggested that the best thing to do would be to revise the entire program. Although dissatisfaction was widespread, no one involved knew exactly what should be done. Today, Midville's reading program remains unchanged.

Evaluation of Midville's strategy   Midville's strategy is typical of one of three solutions used by many high schools to solve the problem of the wide range of individual differences in reading achievement and the need to install a program in the high school. The board or the administration of the high school (1) imports or buys a commercial reading program, (2) sends teachers to observe an outstanding reading program at another school, bring back the ideas, and install the same program in their own school—without going through the process of development originally used by the outstanding school, or (3) hires a consultant to draw up a prescription for a reading program and has teachers in the school, usually English teachers, apply the prescription without any additional staff training. None of these solutions works very well; none fits the needs of the school or trains the faculty to use the program or takes the faculty through a process of analyzing the problem and developing appropriate strategies for solving the problem.

Midville's approach, while typical, is frought with problems. We therefore recommend a second strategy, used by the idealized "Omnibus High School."

Omnibus High School

Omnibus High School is not a typical school, because it decided to use another strategy. The principal formed a steering committee of heads of departments, reading specialists, and the vice-principal to interview faculty and students to determine needs and to obtain recommended solutions for the school's reading problem.*

After analyzing reading achievement test results, the committee discovered that students could be grouped into three categories: (1) those who needed instruction in learning to read, (2) those who were beyond the elementary level of reading, but who had comprehension levels one to three years below grade level and below the readability levels of their texts, and (3) those (almost all students) who needed instruction in learning from texts in specific content areas.

To obtain solutions to this omnibus problem, the committee reviewed the research literature on high school reading instruction. In general, they

---

* For steering and interview schedules, see Burmeister (1974, pp. 281–283).

found that most high schools had a remedial reading program that was either
(1) a reading laboratory with a self-instructional program, or (2) a class that
emphasized word recognition. Although these classes were helpful, they did
not solve the school's total problem, nor did they improve the overall reading
achievement of the school. Indeed, the committee realized that although
students in remedial reading classes might benefit from the classes, they still
might not be able to handle their textbooks. Some high schools also had:
(1) corrective reading classes for students who know how to read but who are
still below grade level, (2) developmental classes for students at grade level
who want to improve their general reading ability, and (3) speed-reading
classes for students reading above grade level who want to become more
rapid readers and prepare for college courses. But none of these classes emphasized reading in the content areas. The committee concluded that the
school needed a combination of high school reading specialists and in-service
training for the faculty on teaching students to read and learn from texts in
their content areas.

In-service training programs   The committee found three models of in-
service training reported in the literature. Herber (1970a) constructed an
"open-ended" model that provides knowledge and skills for teaching reading
in content areas as needed. Five teachers from each of seven schools representing four content areas had some release time for in-service training, with
emphasis on teaching vocabulary and providing guidance to students reading
content materials. These content reading specialists prepared materials in a
supervised summer session practicum on how to integrate content with reading instruction, tried out materials with summer session students, and consulted with summer session teachers in the afternoon. In the fall, they
adopted the role of content reading specialists for their department colleagues and continued with in-service seminars.

A ten-lesson, course-model approach to in-service training, developed by
Schleich (1971), begins with a diagnostic reading test administered schoolwide. Subsequently, students scoring in the lowest decile were given the Wide
Range Achievement Test to test their basic word-recognition ability. Department heads received lessons on general reading development, readability,
informal reading inventories, directed reading activities, SQ3R, interpretation of test results, and reading skills in content areas. All students, including
those in remedial classes, received instruction on reading in the content areas.
The course instructors then did follow-up work on lesson plans with individual teachers during free periods.

The combination model consisted of an in-service training and consultation program (Singer, 1973). The in-service training program emphasized:
(1) strategies for teaching for a wide range of individual differences in reading achievement (Singer, 1973; Singer and Donlan, 1976); (2) patterns and

processes in the content areas (Robinson, 1975; Smith, 1964*a* and *b*; (3) models of reading and learning from text (Singer and Ruddell, 1976); (4) single- and multilevel text strategies; and (5) instructional framework for learning from text (Singer and Donlan, 1976). The consultation helped the reading specialists with individual strategies and the content-area specialists with classroom strategies. Finally, the committee and the consultant designed a course for incoming freshmen to teach them how to read and learn from texts in each content area. Each of these strategies (individual, classroom, and incoming freshmen) will be presented in the next three sections.

INDIVIDUAL STRATEGIES: PROBLEMS AND PRESCRIPTIONS FOR HIGH SCHOOL READERS

To say that a student is a good or poor reader is not enough. The act of reading can be divided into two major components: speed and power of reading. (Power of reading is the ability of students to comprehend passages of increasing difficulty when given unlimited time to do so. Comprehension tests can properly be called "power" tests only when their paragraphs are arrayed from easy to difficult and students have unlimited time to work on the comprehension passages.) Each of these components is composed of numerous subskills and underlying capacities. A student can be strong or weak in speed and/or power, with the cause attributable to a multiplicity of reasons (Holmes and Singer, 1966). The job of the reading specialist is to determine where a student's strengths or weaknesses lie, their causes, and how to improve the strengths and reduce the weaknesses. The first step in the adequate diagnosis of a school is to use one of the survey type of tests shown in Table 14.3 for classifying all the students.

Assessing and diagnosing high school reading achievement

A typical survey type of reading test battery contains three kinds of tests: comprehension, speed of reading, and vocabulary. These tests can be used for determining range of reading achievement and for classifying students into four categories according to their relative status in speed and power of reading. After students have been classified into these categories, further tests may be administered to arrive at educational diagnoses.

To classify students, first administer a survey test. Then divide the students at each grade level into four categories according to the test results on speed and comprehension of reading. The dividing line for each of these components is the 50th percentile level for each grade. Thus on speed of reading, a particular grade of students is separated into two groups: those in percentiles 0 to 49 and those in percentiles 50 to 99. These two groups are further subdivided into those above or below the 50th percentile on com-

Table 14.3. Some widely used survey tests of reading achievement for junior and senior high school*

Gates-MacGinitie Reading Tests, Surveys E, Grades 7–9, and F, Grades 10–12. Published by Teachers College Press, Columbia University, 1970. The test has three subscales: speed and accuracy, vocabulary, and comprehension. Test time: 46 minutes. A reliable and well-constructed test. Uses a multiple-choice type of technique for assessing comprehension.

Metropolitan Reading Achievement Test, Advanced Form, Grades 7–9. Published by Harcourt Brace Jovanovich, 1970. Measures vocabulary and comprehension. Test time: 46 minutes. A well-constructed test.

Nelson-Denny Reading Test, Grades 9–16. Published by Houghton Mifflin, 1973. Tests rate vocabulary and comprehension. Test time: 40 minutes. Mostly suitable for college prep students.

Nelson Reading Test, Grades 3–9. Published by Houghton Mifflin, 1962. Measures vocabulary and comprehension. Test time: 30 minutes. Inadequate data on reliability and test construction.

Sequential Tests of Education Progress (STEP), *Series II: Reading, Grades 4–14.* Published by Educational Testing Service, 1969. Measures only comprehension. Content includes a wide range of material: directions, announcements, newspaper and magazine articles, letters, stories, poetry, and plays.

Stanford Achievement Tests, Grades 7–12. Published by Harcourt Brace Jovanovich, 1966. Measures mostly literal and factual comprehension. A reliable and well-constructed test.

---

* For a comprehensive review of tests, see O. K. Buros, *The Seventh Mental Measurements Yearbook,* Vol. II, Highland Park, N. J.: Gryphon Press, 1972; for a summary of tests, see N. A. Mavrogenes, C. K. Winkley, E. Hanson, and R. T. Vacca, "Concise Guide to Standardized Secondary and College Reading Tests," *Journal of Reading* **18**, 1, October 1974, pp. 12–22.

prehension or power of reading. The result of this fourfold classification scheme is shown in Table 14.4.

Table 14.4 shows that students are classified into four quadrants as follows: (A) *fast, powerful* readers—above the 50th percentile in both speed and power of reading; (B) *fast, nonpowerful* readers—above the 50th percentile in speed, but below the 50th percentile in power of reading; (C) *slow, powerful* readers—above the 50th percentile in power of reading, but below the 50th percentile in speed of reading; and (D) *slow, nonpowerful* readers—below the 50th percentile in both speed and power of reading. All

Table 14.4. Classification of high school readers into four major categories

| | *Power of reading* | |
Speed of reading	More than 50th percentile	Less than 50th percentile
More than 50th percentile	A. Fast, powerful	B. Fast, nonpowerful
Less than 50th percentile	C. Slow, powerful	D. Slow, nonpowerful 1. Linguistically different readers a) Bilingual b) Dialectal 2. Low IQ reader 3. Content area–deficient reader 4. Reluctant reader a) Attitude b) Ability 5. Affectively alienated reader 6. Physiologically handicapped reader 7. Educationally under-developed reader 8. Instructionally mis-matched reader

of the students in each quadrant may be given additional tests to arrive at educational diagnoses. The resulting information can then be used to construct a reading-improvement plan for them.

Generalizations about the kinds of students found in the four quadrants are given below:

A. *The fast, powerful reader*

Although these students read rapidly and with relatively high comprehension, they can nevertheless improve and enrich their reading, particularly in specific content areas.

B. *The fast, nonpowerful reader*

These students often enjoy reading, but lack the ability to adjust their reading rates to appropriate speeds for difficult materials or lack the capability for comprehending material at the more rapid speed.

C. *The slow, powerful reader*

These students fully comprehend what they read, if given adequate time. However, they tend to process all their reading in the same time-consuming fashion. They lack flexibility in adopting a higher speed for easier materials.

D. *The slow, nonpowerful reader*

These students are all slow and nonpowerful in their reading, but for a variety of reasons. Categories of common types of slow, nonpowerful readers are:

1. *Linguistically different readers*
   a) Bilingual readers
      Upon entering school, bilingual readers are usually unable to benefit from instruction in reading in their second language. Subsequently, bilingual students may become proficient in the second language, but unless they receive special instruction when they are able to benefit (perhaps in intermediate or junior high school), they are likely to be at the bottom of their high school class in reading achievement.
   b) Dialectally different readers
      On the basis of oral reading, these students are sometimes judged deficient; in fact, however, their speech patterns are merely different. Care must be taken to determine whether their pronunciations of words are true reading errors or only dialectally different oral responses.

2. *Readers with low IQ*

Low scores in general reading ability may be a function of mental age. Even so, some yearly improvement is possible for low-IQ students; their reading ages are below their mental ages, and mental age tends to increase each year.

3. *Content area–deficient readers*

Since these students have difficulty in reading the material in a certain subject area, they need to be shown techniques appropriate for specific areas.

4. *Reluctant readers*
   a) Attitude
      Although able to read, these students refuse to do so.

   b) Ability
      These students refuse to read because they may want to hide a lack of ability.

5. *Affectively alienated readers*

These students not only refuse to read, but are openly hostile. They must be reached on a human level, have their curiosity rekindled and aroused, and their interest in reading stimulated.

6. *Physiologically handicapped readers*

Readers in this category are hindered by visual or auditory problems, speech deficiencies, glandular disturbances, or motor damage. Teachers who spot students with these problems should refer them to the appropriate specialist.

7. *Educationally underdeveloped readers*

These students have failed to learn one or more important components of the reading process (use of affixes, context, inference, etc.). Diagnosis and instruction can remediate these problems.

8. *Instructionally mismatched readers*

These students are not learning, because the wrong methods are being used. Progress can be made when the students and methods are better matched.

Working with high school readers: Selections from a reading specialist's casebook

In the following section, a high school reading specialist describes actual students he worked with. An example has been selected to illustrate categories A, B, and C from Table 14.4. Next, students who fit each of the eight subcategories in the slow, nonpowerful reader classification are discussed. To list every step taken in the treatment of every pupil would be time-consuming and redundant, so only those techniques most appropriate to each case are mentioned. Altogether, these techniques constitute a wide range of successful ways of diagnosing and solving problems in high school reading instruction.

A. A fast, powerful reader
Steve, age 15

Steve's name was first mentioned to me by his social studies teacher, Mr. Warren, while we were having lunch. "Steve's the brightest kid in class," he said. "He's a tenth grader, but his reading ability is at the college freshman level. The only thing I can do for him is keep him motivated."

"Sometimes even your brightest kids can still use some kind of reading instruction," I said. "Let's look at his test when we get back to your room."

Steve's subscores on the California Reading Test (Tiegs and Clark, 1963) were all high, but his scores in two areas were not at the same level as his scores on the others. One was reference skills. The other was the subject in which Steve's teacher had just been praising him—social studies. I suggested to Mr. Warren that he urge Steve to do his term paper in some field of social studies that would be challenging and that Steve be given the necessary work in reference skills that might enable him to make use of the nearby community college library.

One afternoon Mr. Warren and I informally interviewed Steve about his past and present schooling, as well as his interests. We discovered that Steve hadn't received any formal training in reference skills in the small junior high he had attended; moreover, the social studies teacher there had stimulated his interest the least of all his teachers. Consequently, he didn't do much reading in social studies.

While discussing one of his pastimes, science fiction, Steve mentioned a story he had read that involved an overcrowded world of the future. Later I gave Steve a copy of *The Population Bomb,* which discusses potential dangers from overpopulation. Subsequently, Steve selected population problems as the topic of his research paper.

Steve's abilities in many of the skills needed in reading social studies (use of graphs, reading statistics, etc.) improved considerably as he did his paper, largely as a result of increased exposure to this type of writing, and guidance from Mr. Warren. Steve also received regular instruction in reference skills in class, because Mr. Warren does not just assign a term paper, but also teaches his students the necessary library skills for preparing their papers. As Steve's knowledge of reference tools increased, we arranged for him to use some of the more specialized indexes and reference works at the local community college.

At the beginning of the following year, when Steve's reading was again tested, his social studies and reference skills more closely paralleled his other subscores. Thus diagnosis, guidance, and instruction in reference reading and specialized reading skills in the content area of social studies helped Steve eliminate his specific content-area deficits.

B. A fast, nonpowerful reader
Shirley, age 15

I timed Shirley as she read a passage from a relatively easy novel for young adults, then tested her comprehension. Her speed and power of reading were high. Then Shirley read a selection from a physiology text. Her speed was almost identical to her reading of the novel, but her comprehension of the material in the physiology text was close to zero.

"I know what all the words mean," Shirley protested, "and I read all the time. I just don't see how anybody can remember all that hard stuff."

Shirley's mother confirmed that her daughter read almost every night for pleasure, but all of her reading consisted of youthful fashion magazines and teenage romance novels. Shirley apparently had developed automaticity in reading this type of material, but had not learned to adjust her pace when reading material that was difficult or unfamiliar to her.

For several days Shirley came by to see me, instead of going to her last-period study hall. We discussed her class assignments and devised ways for reading in each content area. In studying history, for example, it was most helpful for Shirley to outline main events and their causes. This way she understood what had happened and why. Two techniques proved beneficial in studying biology—analysis of new vocabulary before beginning the chapter and drawing diagrams while reading. In English class Shirley was using a paperback anthology of short stories that the students had to purchase. I encouraged her to make marginal notes concerning important elements of plot, theme, characterization, and setting.

At first, Shirley complained about all of the extra time she was spending on her assignments. To demonstrate to her the effectiveness of the time spent, I had her bring in all of her grades in her classes to date and put them on graphs for each class. We observed that each graph line fluctuated in the "C" and "D" areas.

"Promise me that you'll practice all these things we've talked about," I asked Shirley. "Do it for one month, and let's see what happens."

By the end of the month, the lines on the graphs were jumping into the "B" and even the "A" range. Shirley had clear proof that her comprehension techniques were paying off.

Shirley is the type of reader who often puzzles teachers—a bright student who does read, but performs poorly in class. Showing students that there are specific ways to read each subject can often bring about dramatic changes in their abilities (see Fay and Jared, 1975, for an annotated bibliography of sources on teaching content-area skills).

C. A slow, powerful reader
Roger, age 16

Students in Mr. Victor's advanced English class were writing a paper tracing one theme through five major American novels. Mr. Victor held Roger back after class and said, "You've been a little weak lately in class discussions, Roger, so I trust you'll make up for it on your paper."

Roger lowered his eyes. "To—to be perfectly honest, sir, I've only read two of the five books."

Roger had an IQ of 125, came from a success-oriented family, and was highly motivated. As a result, he had been channeled into advanced classes and was having a difficult time. His understanding of what he read was excellent, but he couldn't keep up with his assignments. When I tested and interviewed Roger, I learned that his main interest was mathematics. In fact, the subject was almost an obsession and had occupied his full attention throughout school. Though he often neglected other subjects in favor of math, Roger had nonetheless been able to grasp other areas. However, he read everything with the slow, methodical procedure he applied to difficult math books.

Roger brought in his textbooks during the next few days. Together, we worked on ways of developing a more flexible reading rate. We took one of the novels he was reading in English and analyzed a chapter, discussing how purely descriptive passages could be skimmed, how sections dealing mainly with plot could be read rapidly, but how his rate would have to be slowed if the writing became highly symbolic or philosophical. In history, Roger was shown how to locate events and causes as he read. (This was also done for Shirley—in the preceding case—to slow her down; in Roger's case, it was done to speed his reading up.)

Graphs for each of Roger's classes were constructed. The line on each graph showed upward or downward movement of Roger's grades. The graphs were attached to one another, so progress in all areas could be seen simultaneously. Records were kept of Roger's reading speed in each subject, and comparisons were made. At first, all graph lines were at the same level for all subjects. Gradually, though, lines began to climb. Roger kept track of these comparisons over the entire semester. The mathematics line moved very little (Roger had found the proper rate for math), but those in all other subjects rose as his speed increased. Although Roger's comprehension declined somewhat at first as a result of trying new methods, it soon returned to its previous level.

Roger has graduated and is currently a college freshman. He is able to handle a course load that would have been impossible for him had he not learned to be flexible in his reading speed.

D. A slow, nonpowerful reader
    (1) A linguistically different reader
        a) Bilingual
Julian, age 16

"Why did you take this course?" I asked Julian.

The quiet Mexican-American boy thought for a moment, then said, "Well, I needed five credits, and this was the only thing I could fit in my schedule. I don't really like to read."

Julian had enrolled in my seven-week summer reading-improvement course, but had shown little initiative. The Gates-MacGinitie Reading Tests (1972) revealed that he was a slow reader and was three years below grade level in reading comprehension. His weaknesses were fairly evenly distributed over the various subskills and content areas.

In order to probe his reading development from his earliest years in school, Julian was given an in-depth interview* schedule:

1. Go over test results to find out why the student made many of the responses.

2. Look through the texts and ask how the student goes about reading and studying in each content area.

3. Ask the student to recall as much as possible about learning to read.

4. What books and magazines does the student read? What books, magazines, and newspapers are found in the home?

5. Ask the student what would be the most valuable thing to learn about reading or learning from texts.

6. Have a discussion about the student's interests and aspirations—present and future.

---

* For thorough and revealing interview techniques, see Strang, McCullough, and Traxler (1967, pp. 171, 458–472).

Note: Personal give and take should go on throughout the interview. Additional questions should arise, and the interviewer should always depart from the schedule to pursue promising areas that come up.

Upon entering school, Julian—and many of his Mexican-American friends—quickly found themselves in the low-level reading group. They were all far more proficient in Spanish than in English. Julian had normal intelligence, but reading in a second language was a task he had not yet mastered. His parents attempted to help him at home, but they were even more limited in English than their son. Julian eventually grasped most of what was taught in a lesson, but stayed well behind. He avoided reading; consequently, he never developed the automaticity (instant identification of words) necessary for fast and efficient reading.

A widely touted panacea is to give minority students materials about their own ethnic group. Although this is sometimes valid (see the case study that follows), it did not prove to be the case with Julian. An interest inventory (see Burmeister, 1974, pp. 61, 63) was used to determine areas in which Julian might be motivated. This inventory included books read, types of favorite reading, favorite TV programs, hobbies, and use of leisure time. Although Julian stated in his interview that he never read anything he didn't have to, his interest inventory indicated that he had recently read both *The Exorcist* and *Jaws*.

"Didn't those books have hard words?" I asked.

"Yeah, I skipped a lot of them."

"Why did you read these books if you don't like to read?"

"I saw both the movies, and they were really exciting. Then I saw everybody around school reading the books, so I tried them. They were good. I like stuff with lots of action."

Further analysis of Julian's process of reading *Jaws* and similar books revealed that he could eventually identify words, but could not recognize them quickly. If he tried to identify each word, he spent so much time at it that he forgot what the story was about. So he skipped words and tried to maintain the story's action. I decided that he needed to develop not only accuracy in recognizing words but go beyond accuracy to automaticity—identifying words with a minimum of attention so that he could maximize the meaning of the story. To develop this accuracy and automaticity, I selected relatively easy but interesting books for him.

Using an annotated bibliography (Reid, 1972), we selected numerous adventure books that were easy enough to develop automaticity, but not so simple as to be insulting or dull. A chart was prepared for Julian to graph his daily time spent in reading. The graph was cumulative, showing words read per session, *not* words read per minute. Thus the results were always positive, and the upward rate of the graph was under his control. Each day's number of words was added to the total number of words accumulated from the past. (For a detailed treatment showing progress in reading to students, see Singer and Beasley, 1970.)

Julian's low reading scores were no more difficult to explain than is a poor swimming performance by someone who had had a bad start learning to swim and therefore rarely swam. Julian's general reading ability could be improved by getting him to practice what he had been avoiding because of an early problem with the English language. Through reading action-filled books, doing work in reading skills he was weak in, and using a positive method of tracking his progress, Julian achieved an upturn in his reading ability in the final weeks of the summer session.

(2) A linguistically different reader
    b) Dialectally different
Mary, age 17

Mary's history teacher didn't know what to do. Mary couldn't read the textbook. She was failing the class from the start, refusing to do the work. When asked to stay after class one day and read aloud to the teacher, she mispronounced half the words in a paragraph from the text and changed many of the words and phrases.

An informal and wide-ranging interview revealed that Mary had considerable insecurity about being a member of a small black minority in a predominately white school. Until recently, she had lived in the rural South and was accustomed to a school that was almost all black.

Mary was asked to read aloud a passage from black author Sharon Bell Mathis's novel *Teacup Full of Roses*. I stopped her occasionally to ask about mispronounced words. It quickly became apparent that many of her "mispronunciations" were nothing more than regional dialect. She knew the words, but was pronouncing them in a dialect that was different from what I was accustomed to hearing. Most of the changes she made in the text were a matter of converting standard English into the patterns of the black English she had been speaking all her life.

We discussed the novel for awhile, kindling Mary's interest, and then she was asked to read silently from the book. An informal comprehension test showed that although she was a slow, uncertain reader, her reading difficulties were not as severe as her teacher had suspected.

A dual-purpose program was established for Mary. The first facet involved getting Mary interested in reading. The school she had attended in the South had few materials, and Mary had been given little exposure to books. I loaned her the copy of *Teacup Full of Roses* she had been using in our informal testing. When asked what other kinds of books she might like to see, she said that she wanted to read about black people. She was shown several books, encouraged to borrow a few, and encouraged to return any time to borrow others.

The second phase of Mary's program concerned academic reading. Mary's history teacher was urged to keep her in the class and to guide her in selecting famous black figures in American history for her papers and projects. Conferences were held with Mary's other teachers, with similar methods devised for each content area. Teachers were cautioned, above all, not to confuse Mary's dialect with a deficiency and to use comprehension of the entire passage, not just pronunciation of words in oral reading, as a criterion of her reading ability.

(3) A low-IQ reader
Sally, age 14

"I've been looking over Sally's test scores," the counselor said. "She's a freshman with a low IQ and fifth-grade reading ability. Her parents think that the elementary school didn't do a good job, and we ought to bring her up to grade level now that she's in high school."

I put down Sally's cumulative folder and told the counselor that if her IQ score of 82 was accurate, it was unlikely that Sally would ever read at grade level. "What we need to do," I said, "is take Sally's mental age of 11 and her chronological age of 14 and work out a reasonable expectation—and make sure that her parents understand the situation."

Thorough diagnosis is very important with a low-IQ student. After giving Sally the Wechsler-Bellevue individually administered IQ test and applying an expectancy formula* to the mental-age score derived from the IQ test, it was determined that the seventh-grade level was her present potential level of reading ability. Sally then took the individually administered Gates-McKillop Reading Diagnostic Tests (1962), which consist of 17 subtests. Her weakest scores were in blending word parts, auditory blending, and syllabication. Her strength lay in her sight vocabulary, but she relied too heavily on it, to the exclusion of decoding skills. Sally used initial (and sometimes final) letters when she encountered a new word, then supplied the medial letters or sounds through guesswork.

Prior to beginning work on overcoming some of her reading problems, Sally was given a learning-rate test to determine if she was able to learn under optimum conditions. Twenty-five words she had missed on the Gates-McKillop test were selected, and a chart was constructed to keep a record

---

* A commonly used, easy computational formula for establishing reading expectancy is: Reading grade level expectancy = mental age − 5. This formula can be found in Albert J. Harris (1970, p. 212).

of how many sessions it would take Sally to master all of the words. Sally moved from 23% of the words correct on session two to 100% correct on session six, with 100% correct on each subsequent session. (See Singer and Beasley, 1970, for description and rationale for a learning rate test.)

Having determined that Sally could improve, tutoring was begun to help her break her overreliance on initial sounds in words and to teach her to blend parts of words into meaningful units. Techniques designed for elementary instruction were adapted for Sally's age level. (See Hafner and Jolly (1972, pp. 55–88) for useful word-recognition techniques.) Work on word-blending skills was never done in isolation. Whenever a principle of word recognition was taught, it was applied to whatever text or novel Sally was reading. For example, after a lesson on the different ways that the letter combination "ea" could be pronounced, Sally read from a paperback novel, putting a light pencil mark under "ea" combinations as she read. After Sally had read orally for a few minutes, she went back and discussed the "ea" words that had presented difficulties, trying different pronunciations.

During her tutoring, Sally was not removed from her other classes. Instead, Sally's teachers were encouraged to provide her with easy materials and were regularly informed of her progress. She was able to use her content texts for her tutoring sessions. Since all of Sally's reading growth was charted, she had tangible evidence of her progress. As she improved in decoding abilities, I increasingly emphasized comprehension skills. Encouraged by her steady progress, Sally showed every indication of being able to achieve her expectancy level.

(4) A content area–deficient reader
Bill, age 14

Bill was talking again while the rest of the class was reading silently. This was a continual problem in his third-period class, but Bill's science teacher had been told by other teachers that it wasn't a problem in their classes. Moreover, Bill's grades were low in science, but were average and above in other subjects. Standardized test scores, however, showed that Bill was below grade level in speed and comprehension.

"If his test scores show he's below average," his science teacher asked me, "why do the low grades and poor behavior show up only in my class?"

Knowing that the science teacher was both competent and popular, I called Bill in to see what he had to say about his trouble in science. While browsing through some science texts that he had used in past grades, Bill described his reading-study techniques as merely reading the chapter and looking over the study questions prior to being tested.

"What's the hardest thing about science?" I asked.

"Learning all the big words," Bill answered.

"What do you do when you come to a word you don't know?"

"Ask the guy next to me."

That explained why Bill talked to his neighbor when he was supposed to be reading silently, but what about his low reading level? Examination of Bill's standardized test score indicated that although his overall score was low, his subscores were all at or slightly above average, except in science and following directions. These two were pulling down his total score, thus giving a false impression. Similarly, over 40% of the short paragraphs on the speed test read were science-oriented. We went over the test, determining that on other material, Bill read quickly and efficiently.

Bill said that his favorite school and pleasure reading was narrative writing. He had never learned the skills necessary for reading scientific material, and he expressed a strong aversion to the drudgery of studying new vocabulary terms.

With the help of the science teacher, Bill was taught to master difficult vocabulary *before* attempting to read scientific material. To make the learning of vocabulary painless, games, magic squares, and puzzles specifically designed for scientific vocabulary were used. (For vocabulary techniques, see Herber, 1970*b*, pp. 176–186.)

Bill's other problem—difficulty in following directions—seemed to be a matter of his lack of any systematic approach to scientific material. Spache's (1963) PQRST technique (an adaptation of SQ3R for science) was used to help Bill apply a structure to his learning. The steps in this self-study program are: Preview, Question, Read, Summarize, Test. This overview approach was combined with training in understanding the highly detailed patterns of many sentences and paragraphs in scientific writing, as well as the need to understand complex classification systems. In addition, Bill was shown that footnotes, illustrations, colored print, study questions, and glossaries are valuable *pre*reading aids.

Improvement of Bill's vocabulary and comprehension techniques brought his speed and power in science sections of standardized tests closer to the level of his other scores, thus altering his overall scores to a much more realistic appraisal of his ability. Many students are unfairly judged when only a single comprehension test score is seen. These students may suffer from a deficiency in a specific subject—a problem that can be corrected by techniques especially adapted for that content area.

(5) A reluctant reader
    a) Attitude
Mike, age 14

"He can read," the woman sighed, "but he won't. I don't think he should be in a special class. He's just lazy."

I promised the woman that I would talk with her son Mike, who had just entered high school as a freshman. Since his reading-test scores were so low, his counselor had suggested that Mike be placed in a class for low-ability students.

As I looked through Mike's cumulative folder the next day, it seemed that his mother was probably right in her feeling that he had potential. His scores on various IQ, achievement, and reading tests over the past eight years varied and appeared more likely to reflect momentary mood than ability.

When Mike came in for a conference, I opened up his latest reading test and talked with him about some of the items he had missed. Discussing test answers with the student can be one of the most enlightening techniques of diagnosis. Although Mike was a slow reader with a weak vocabulary, he understood what he read. He was able to read and answer every item he had missed on the comprehension section of the test. His errors had been caused by carelessness and lack of interest.

An important question in interviewing problem readers is: "Can you remember learning to read?" Good readers usually don't remember, because the experience was so effortless; poor readers, on the other hand, painfully recall the unpleasant situation. All of Mike's memories were negative.

Mike was kept in the regular classroom, and his English teacher gave him considerable help in finding "high interest–easy reading" books. The English teacher was given an annotated bibliography (Emery and Houshower, 1965) to use in Mike's guidance.

Rather than suggest to Mike that he avoid extracurricular activities and instead concentrate on his studies, he was encouraged to become involved in school activities. It was hoped that this would help him identify with school and, consequently, desire to do well in his academic work. As an incoming freshman, Mike was unaware that hiking and skiing clubs existed, even though these were two of his interests, as revealed in an interest inventory (see Burmeister, 1974). He was introduced to the faculty sponsors of the two clubs, who explained their activities and (as prearranged) gave Mike pamphlets and magazines on hiking and skiing.

Since the reluctant reader has often spent years developing an aversion to reading, changes in attitude are usually gradual. A patient, low-key approach, in which unpleasant connotations are removed from reading, can be an effective technique. Mike's progress was extremely slow, but improvement occurred as the year progressed.

(5) A reluctant reader
     b) Ability
Sandy, age 15

Sometimes a student will refuse to read in order to hide a problem. This was the case with Sandy, who complained of not liking to read. "It's boring," she objected, "and you can get just as much out of TV or a movie."

Formal and informal testing, as well as an interview, revealed that although Sandy could read most of the words on the page of a book at her grade level, she was not fully comprehending what she read. Discussion of her early instruction in reading suggested that an almost total emphasis had been placed on word recognition, to the exclusion of comprehension skills.

As a program of remediation, various comprehension techniques were used that could be based on Sandy's textbooks. For example, she was given cards that contained paragraphs from texts and cards containing appropriate titles for the paragraphs. Sandy's task was to determine the general meaning of the paragraph in order to select the best title. A fade-out method was used; this activity gradually ceased to be a reading game and instead became a principle she applied to her texts. (This technique and others used with Sandy were taken from Larry A. Harris and Carl B. Smith, 1972, pp. 276–278.)

More than four months passed before Sandy ever voluntarily selected a book that she actually wanted to take home and read. Although four months seems like a long time, Sandy could not recall having willingly read anything in all of her previous junior and senior high school experience.

(6) An affectively alienated reader
Ron, age 17

Ron wasn't just a reluctant reader—he was openly defiant. The first time I met him, he slouched into the room and dropped noisily into a seat. "You the reading guy?" he demanded.

"Right," I answered.

"They made me come and see you, but I can read."

"Oh?"

"Yeah—when I feel like it."

"How come they sent you here?" I asked.

"I'm flunking all my classes."

"Why?"

"I won't read that junk."

Testing revealed that Ron was right about one thing; he could read when he wanted to, but testing didn't reveal why he was so hostile. That information came out in our informal talks. Ron's background emerged in fragments. He had been through a great deal of unpleasantness in his 17 years—a broken home, problems at school, excessive truancies, and at least two juvenile arrests. He was suspicious of everyone and hostile toward everything.

With students like Ron, a teacher can sometimes do no more than try to establish a friendship and to find some interest, some opening, where reading and learning might be introduced in a nonthreatening way. With Ron, nothing done in class ever struck a responsive note. The breakthrough involved a school talent assembly. Ron had been impressed by a magician and talked about the performance at length. When I saw Ron the next day, I said, "Remember that trick yesterday, when the magician cut the rope into three pieces, then changed them back to one rope again?" Ron nodded, and I removed a piece of rope from my pocket and did the trick for him. For the first time since I'd met him, Ron completely dropped his affectation of surly indifference as he excitedly asked how I did it. I handed him a book on magic from the school library, saying, "The answer's in here."

I won't pretend that all of Ron's reading and school problems dissolved overnight, but he did read the book on magic, plus at least one other magic book; I later saw him reading a biography of Houdini. In the short time I knew him, Ron did one school assignment as a result of his reading. When students had to give a demonstration speech in their English class, Ron performed two of his tricks.

Ron moved out of state only a few weeks after I met him, and I don't know what's happened to him—whether he came a little farther out of his shell, or whether he withdrew again. I meet pupils like Ron all the time. If their trust can be won, their imaginations sparked, and the right content supplied, the first steps toward improving their reading can be taken.

(7) A physiologically handicapped reader
Cheryl, age 14

Treating the child whose reading difficulties are caused or confounded by physiological problems is usually beyond the scope of the public school alone. In such cases the teacher's contribution is often that of observation and referral, especially in the lower grades. There are numerous ways in which physiological problems can contribute to reading difficulties. Thyroid deficiency can produce chronic fatigue that is nonconducive to reading; defective speech can inhibit a student's willingness to read in class. However, visual problems are those most frequently associated with reading. The following case describes a typical situation.

The students in Mrs. Watson's home economics class were reading from their nutrition text when Mrs. Watson thought she saw Cheryl making a face at someone. *Cheryl's the last person who should be fooling around,* Mrs. Watson thought, *she hasn't been doing well in class at all.* But then Mrs. Watson noticed that no other student was looking up; Cheryl was making a face at no one.

A few days later Mrs. Watson chanced to see Cheryl making the same face again. When she asked about it after class, Cheryl replied, "I guess

I must get tired of reading, or something like that. My eyes get tired." In addition, further observation of Cheryl indicated that she frequently slouched in her chair and read while holding the book at arm's length.

When she saw Cheryl's parents at open-house night at the school, Mrs. Watson mentioned the girl's behavior and suggested that she have her eyes checked. An examination revealed hyperopia (far sightedness). After being fitted for glasses, Cheryl was much more consistent in finishing her reading assignments and no longer made peculiar faces in classes.

(8) An educationally underdeveloped reader
Matt, age 15

Often a student's reading problem can be traced to specific factors that are the result of past poor instruction, lack of instruction, or missed instruction. Sometimes, as in Matt's case, a single factor can be the primary cause. Matt's reading scores indicated a deficiency in using affixes. As we discussed his past educational experiences, to the best of his memory, it seemed that a series of coincidences (illness, moving, etc.) had interfered with systematic instruction in using prefixes and suffixes as keys to meaning. Although lack of this ability wasn't severely hindering Matt, it was having a negative effect on his speed and power of reading. When Matt had been given instruction in affixes, he hadn't benefited much because of his lack of background.

I had Matt orally read from his general science book and underline those words he didn't know. The terminology presented many problems, but it allowed Matt to see the importance of roots and affixes. The word "epidermis," which Matt didn't know, quickly became clear to him after he was instructed in morphemic analysis (epi = on, over; derma = skin), combined with context.

Matt was given a list of morphemes common to specific content areas and encouraged to use it in connection with his textbooks. (See Burmeister, 1974, pp. 298–308, for a list of morphemes classified into content areas.) He was also shown how to study new vocabulary before reading—regardless of whether the words were introduced in prefaces, footnotes, or at the ends of chapters. This prereading study, combined with morphemic analysis, proved to be a valuable tool in improving Mike's speed and power, thus making all of his school subjects just a little easier for him.

(9) An instructionally mismatched reader
Lois, age 14

"Lois has always had trouble reading," her mother told me over the phone. "We've even paid out money for a tutor, but it didn't do any good."

I met Lois for testing and interviews and listened to her read orally.

She made numerous mistakes on her oral-reading test, which resulted in a score at the sixth-grade level. Her silent-reading score was also low, and I observed her vocalizing each word as she read.

Rather than just noting Lois's errors, I tried to discover the nature of those errors—whether there were patterns to be found in the kinds of mistakes she was making.

A procedure for classifying the kinds of miscues (differences between what the reader says and what's on the printed page) was used (Goodman and Burke, 1972). The following patterns were found: 70% of Lois's miscues evidenced a strong sound relationship to the expected word; for example, "late" for "lake." Close to 80% of the miscues had high graphic relationships; that is, they looked like the printed word, e.g., "house" for "horse." Lois was using some of the cues from the printed words, but analysis showed that she was relying too heavily on phonics or symbol-sound correspondence for the initial parts of words and was not attending carefully to cues within the words. During the early grades, she had been instructed almost exclusively in phonics. Unfortunately, a symbol-sound technique is not sufficient and was leading to more word distortion than word recognition. Moreover, attempting to sound out each letter results in too much information to remember and put together.

When shifted to syllabication as the method of analyzing new words, Lois showed a striking change in ability. At first Lois remembered few syllabication rules, because she had rarely practiced them. When she was retaught, however (on words in sentences taken from her own school books), Lois quickly recalled the principles. Using her own texts also gave Lois meaningful context in addition to syllabication strategies to use in identifying new words. Moving Lois away from a sole reliance on a phonics approach also contributed to improved speed of reading, because she did not have to take the time to sound out each letter. Also, by eliminating word distortions her comprehension improved.

I worked with Lois only once a week for two months. Her greatest improvement took place not in our sessions, but while she pursued her regular class work and pleasure reading. When I tested her again at the end of the school year, the results indicated that she was coming close to grade level. Of course, this improvement was largely through her own efforts, after the obstacle of an instructional mismatch had been removed.

Principles for individual strategies

The reading specialist must have a set of procedures and a frame of reference when diagnosing and prescribing for high school students. The reading specialist who reported the sketches above of high school readers used these procedures:

1. Reports were obtained from teachers, parents, and the students themselves about their behavior in class, attitudes toward reading and the particular content areas, and procedures used in reading their texts.

2. An interview with each student brought out the student's past reading history, present use of time, and interests. While gaining this information, the reading specialist observed and listened for possible clues to physical or physiological causes for disabilities, such as visual difficulties, and for affective and alienation responses to school, teachers, and particular content areas.

3. Observations were made of the student's reading in his or her own textbooks. Frequently, the reading specialist would test hypotheses about specific difficulties by setting up test situations. For example, procedures were used for reading science texts, identifying technical words in science or math, comprehending passages in each content area, reading orally and silently to determine word recognition and comprehension difficulties, and testing for dialect versus reading errors. Throughout these observations, the reading specialist allowed students to give their own explanations for their difficulties, attitudes, techniques, and processes used in reading. In listening, diagnosing, and prescribing, the reading specialist used imagination and ingenuity, consulting content-area specialists and professional works to get insights into diagnosis of reading problems and suggested prescriptions for improvement. A brief list of professional books for the high school reading specialist can be found in the reference section to this chapter. In addition, the reading specialist should have a professional library to consult.

4. Some problems in high school reading can be solved through interview and informal testing using the students' own texts. Other problems require use of both survey and diagnostic standardized tests. The following tests are recommended:

a) *Survey tests.* These tests, shown in Table 14.3, are useful for classifying readers into four categories of speed and power of reading.

b) *Diagnostic tests.* These batteries of tests can help determine the underlying skills and capacities of readers, particularly their difficulties in word identification. The tests are appropriate for normal readers in grades 1–8 and for students at grade levels 9–12 whose oral-reading abilities are in the grade range from 1–8.

c) *Gates-McKillop Reading Diagnostic Tests,* Grades 1–8. Published by the Bureau of Publications, Columbia University, 1962. Measures oral reading, word and phrase recognition, syllabication, letter names and sounds, visual and auditory blending, and spelling. Test time: 60 minutes. Comprehensive diagnostic test, well constructed. The oral-reading vocabulary subtest can be used as an estimate of reading expectancy. The assumption is that the reading ability of a student should equal performance in oral vocabulary.

d) *Spache Diagnostic Reading Scales,* Grades 1–8. Published by California Test Bureau/McGraw-Hill, 1963. Measures oral and silent reading, phonics, and sight-word recognition. Test time: 30 minutes. Directions for administering the tests and test-construction information are inadequate. The listening subtest provides an estimate of expectancy in comprehension. The assumption is that the students should comprehend as well through reading as they do through listening. Each measure of expectancy, however, has its own limitations (Singer, 1965).

e) *Developmental Reading Tests: Silent Reading Diagnostic Tests,* Grades 3–8. Published by Lyons and Carnahan, 1958. Measures recognition of words in isolation and in context, reversible words in context, syllabication, root words, beginning and ending sounds, word synthesis. Time: 90 minutes. This battery of silent-reading diagnostic tests can be administered to an individual or to an entire group.

f) *Reading Miscue Inventory,* Grades 1–12. Published by Macmillan, 1972. Assesses miscues and discrepancies between print and response to 1500-word selection and categorizes miscues into graphic, phonemic, and semantic classes. Measures comprehension by having reader retell a story, selected by tester, approximately one grade level above reader's ability. This inventory is not a standardized test with norms. Instead, it is a type of criterion-referenced test that is useful for determining processes of reading in word identification, particularly use of syntax, semantics, and graphophonemics in word recognition in context.

g) *Stanford-Binet Intelligence Scale* by L. M. Terman and M. A. Merrill, published by Houghton Mifflin, 1960; *Wechsler Intelligence Scale for Children* (WISC) by D. Wechsler, published by Psychological Corporation, New York, 1949. These tests of intelligence, individually administered by a certified school psychologist, are the most precise measures of general intellectual ability currently available. Although they are not infallible, they are preferable to subjective opinion and are most valid for students whose native language is English.

5. Models of reading are helpful for determining what tests to administer and how to interpret test results. Psycholinguistic, information-processing, developmental, and affective models are to be found in *Theoretical Models and Processes of Reading* (Singer and Ruddell, 1976). In general, these

models include the following determinants of speed and comprehension: visual and auditory abilities, perceptual processes, phonemics, morphemics, syntax, cognitive processes (memory and conceptualization), attitudes, and values.

In using a model, the reading specialist ascertains what determinant(s) may be involved and selects appropriate instruments for measuring them. Or, in making observations, the experienced reading specialist may mentally check these determinants while listening to a student read or explain his or her processes or problems in reading.

The high school reading specialist is also cognizant of patterns of writing and special reading requirements in the content areas that can be taught in an orientation program for incoming freshmen.

CLASSROOM STRATEGIES

High school teachers may be called content-area specialists. Their task is twofold. First, they must know the content and mode of inquiry in their content areas. For example, a content-area specialist in chemistry must know not only the properties of elements in the periodic table, but also how to determine what metals are present in a solution. Similarly, an English teacher must know not only poetry or short stories, but also how these literary works are constructed. Second, they must be able to teach students with a wide range of reading achievement how to acquire knowledge and how to inquire in each content area. As a first step in this instructional process, each content-area specialist must determine the reading ability of her or his students.

Determining reading-ability levels in specific content areas

Some standardized reading tests in content areas are available, such as the California Reading Test, Junior and Senior High Levels (McGraw-Hill, 1963). This test measures mathematics, science, social science, general knowledge, comprehension in following directions, reference skills, and interpretation of material—facts, references, organization, and sequence of events. Although the total test is reliable, its subtests are too short to be reliable. The Iowa Test of Educational Development, grades 9–12 (Science Research Associates, 1961) measures ability to interpret social studies and natural science information and uses of sources of information. This battery of tests has greater subtest reliability, but the test, like all standardized tests, probably does not have curricular validity; that is, the test does not assess instruction specifically given in any particular classroom.

To determine readability levels that are reliable and valid for a specific curriculum, a teacher must construct an informal reading inventory. This inventory can be constructed through either individual textbook assessment or multilevel textbook assessment.

Individual textbook assessment of readability According to Shepherd (1973), this type of assessment consists of three samples of 250-word passages taken from each third of the text. The instructor formulates comprehension questions on these passages, making sure to ask questions at the literal, interpretive, and evaluative levels. Students read the passages and answer comprehension questions silently; students scoring below 70% get further testing, including oral reading of passages to determine whether their relatively low comprehension scores reflect word-recognition difficulties. If not, the instructor may determine, perhaps by using a separate vocabulary test of technical and general terms used in the specific text, whether low vocabulary is a causal factor for the low comprehension.

An alternative type of comprehension test for the open-book assessment is the cloze technique, whereby every fifth word is deleted from three passages of 250 words each. These passages are also taken from each third of the book. In order to pass the test, the student must correctly fill in at least 44% of the missing words with the *exact* word that was deleted. Comprehension questions or the cloze technique can also be used with an informal reading inventory on graded passages.

Multilevel textbook assessment of readability Graded passages on the same topic are selected from several books. These books can be located by using the school catalogs. See Table 14.5 for an example of a school catalog entry. Simply select a text at each grade level on a particular subject. Then take a 100-word passage from the middle chapter of each text. Either write comprehension questions or use a cloze technique on each passage. Then, starting with passages on which the student attains more than 70% comprehension on the questions or 44% correct inserts on cloze technique, have the student proceed upward in difficulty until dropping just below these percent levels. The paragraph just before this level has been reached determines the reading level of the student in the specific content area. The scale of reading difficulty, shown in Table 14.6, can be converted into a cloze test simply by deleting every fifth word. This scale can also be used as an informal reading inventory by adding comprehension questions after each paragraph.*

* This scale is based on content in history. For constructing informal reading inventories in other fields, see the school catalogs for selecting books in particular content areas. Then select sample paragraphs from books at each grade level or every other grade level and construct five to ten comprehension questions. Try to construct not only who, what, where, when, and how types of questions, but also those at the interpretive level (why-type questions) as well as at generalization and evaluative levels.

Table 14.5. School catalog entry*

Children's catalog

Bliven, Bruce   *Author*
   The American Revolution, 1760–1783; illus. by
Albert Orbaan. Random House 1958 182p illus maps
$1.95, lib. bdg. $2.88 (5–7) ⟵   **973.3**
    1 U.S.—History—Revolution   *Grade level*
   "Landmark books"
   Here is the story of both the war and the revolution.
Here are the causes of the war and a down-to-earth picture
of colonial economics. Here are the founding fathers strug-
gling toward the agreement expressed in the Declaration of
Independence, and above all, descriptions of the battlefield
action. (Publisher)
   "This very readable account . . . may well serve as intro- *Trade journal*
ductory material for a more detailed study. . . . Events are *review of book*
viewed within the larger framework of European history.
Drawings and a section of infrequently seen photographs."
Library J

Junior high school library catalog

Phillips, Leon   *Bibliographic*
   The fantastic breed; Americans in King George's *information*
War. Doubleday 1968 213p illus $3.50   **973.2** *on book*
    1 Louisburg—Siege, 1745
   "Provoked by French-inspired Indian raids on frontier *Publisher's description*
settlements, colonial leaders, with British support, had gam- *of book*
bled on dealing the enemy a blow so devastating that they
would be compelled to cease all hostilities in the New World.
The combined British and American colonial troops were to
attack and capture the French fortress of Louisburg. . . .
[Here is the] story of this little-known campaign." Publisher's note
   Principal bibliography: p205–06. Maps on lining-papers *Information on*
                                      format of book

Senior high school library catalog

   973.3 U.S.—Revolution and   *Dewey decimal*
   confederation, 1775–1789   *subject designation*
Alden, John Richard
   The American Revolution, 1775–1783. Harper 1954
294p illus maps (The New American Nation ser) $7.95
                                        973.3

---

* These annotated references came from Children's (Shar and Fidel, 1972), Junior High
(Fidel and Bogar, 1970), and High School (Fidel and Berger, 1972) catalogs. We have added
the marginal gloss to explain the code in the references.

Table 14.5 (cont.)

1 U.S.—History—Revolution	*Subject heading*
The author presents an outline of the Revolution's background and then gives a history of the war itself. The book covers the military, political, including events in England, economic and social aspects of the period	*Brief summary of contents*
"The battle accounts are well documented and illustrated with detailed maps. They are also colorfully written." San Francisco Chronicle	*Newspaper review*
Bibliography: p269–83	

Table 14.6. Scale of reading difficulty*

Grade	Paragraph
2	*Indians Stop Dan.* "Get up," called Dan. The men got up. Then Dan said, "They need this salt in Kettle Creek. King and I will get this salt to Kettle Creek."
	"Come King," Dan said to his horse. Dan and King got ready to go. Dan got the bags of salt ready to go too. "Here we go!" Dan said. "We are on the way now. You must help me get this salt to Kettle Creek."
	Away went King and Dan. They went on and on. The wind came up. Dan did not like the wind. King did not like the wind. "I can not see far. But we must go on," said Dan. "They need this salt in Kettle Creek."
	Passage length: 118 words
	William Hurley, *Dan Frontier with the Indians,* Benefic Press, 1971, pp. 21–23.
4	The wagons carrying the emigrants and their goods were of many kinds and sizes—of all ages and in various states of repair. There were lightly built outfits from the flat farming states, huge high-sided Conestogas built for hauling freight in the Eastern mountains, and every size in between. There was even an occasional two-wheeled cart or top buggy to be seen among them. Some were drawn by strings of six or eight pairs of horses or oxen, while others were hitched to a single team.
	Passage length: 86 words
	Glen Rounds, *The Prairie Schooners,* Holiday House, 1968, p. 17.
6	In time they looked down on the Arkansas River. They had reached it at the point where the sluggish river swings north in a great bend, and lines out toward the west. A shallow stream, rarely over four feet deep and a quarter mile wide, the Arkansas flowed between low banks and over many sand bars. A few cottonwoods dotted its islands and shores. Now the men had emerged from the gentle region of the tall grass, timbered creeks, and wild flowers. They faced the Great Plains, a vast expanse of wind-whipped plain and short buffalo grass. There was no escaping the wind.

Table 14.6 (cont.)

Grade	Paragraph

Passage length: 100 words
Marian T. Place, *The First Book of the Santa Fe Trail,* Franklin Watts, 1966, p. 86.

8   Within the intimate social structure of each tribe the horse was also responsible for certain fundamental changes. The status of women improved—initially because they were relieved of the burdens they had borne on their own backs. In consequence they gained more leisure time for handicrafts and for social life. Ironically, however, among the nomadic tribes the relief women gained from traditional labors was given over to dressing, tanning, and working the buffalo hides the hunters brought in. Partly because of the hunter's need for this kind of assistance, polygamy, which had been previously practiced in a modest way in various tribes, became increasingly popular among affluent males.

Passage length: 120 words
The Old West: The Indians, © 1973 Time Inc., p. 59.

10   The Britishers dressed in the fearful costumes of their kind and were equipped with expensive sporting arms. Parkmand and Shaw wore the prairie uniforms supplied by correct outfitters and had the conventional weapons. They packed their miniature train and were off, after calling on the Kickapoo trader, in whose house Parkmand saw a loaded pistol resting on the poems of John Milton. At Fort Leavenworth, Colonel Stephen Watts Kearney of the First Dragoons (he was clearly a gentleman) had no hint of what the summer was preparing for him, talked of steeple chases and buffalo hunting, and pledged them with a bottle of Madeira

Passage length: 109 words
Bernard de Voto, *The Year of Decision,* Houghton Mifflin, 1961, p. 143.

12   Certainly the pall of impending disaster hung over the rendezvous in 1838 and 1839. Gone were the drunken shouts of the alcohol-befuddled traders, their wild revels with Indian maidens, their reckless games where a year's profits might be lost with the turn of a card. Men thought twice about risking everything when there were no beaver to replace their squandered earnings. Instead, at the 1839 rendezvous, the well-mannered trappers gathered to listen to a sermon preached by a missionary on his way west to Christianize the tribesmen of the Oregon country. "He had" wrote an observer, "quite a number of white men and more Indians to hear him. After the meeting many got drunk."

Passage length: 115 words
Ray Allen Billington, *The Far Western Frontier, 1830–1860,* Harper, 1956, p. 65.

---

* Paragraphs for this scale were selected by Michael M. Price, student enrolled in the senior author's summer-session class in Reading in the Content Areas, University of California, Riverside, 1975.

Computing readability

A useful formula for computing readability has been devised by Flesch (1946). To use this formula, do the following:

1. Take a representative sample of approximately 100 words.

2. Divide the number of words in the sample by the number of sentences. The result is the average sentence length.

3. Count the number of prefixes and suffixes, e.g., *prefixes* such as ad-, bi-, con-, dis-, en-, fore-, hypo-, intro-, mono-, ob-, peri-, sub-, tele-, un-, vice-, with-; *suffixes* such as -able, -icle, -dom, -ence, -ful, -gram, -ie, -less, -ment, -ness, -or, -scope, -tude, -ure, -vert, -wards.

4. Count the personal references: names, personal pronouns, words pertaining to humans (man, woman, child) or their relationships (mother, son, cousin).

5. Compute the readability level for the 100-word sample:
   a) Take the average sentence length
      (   ) and multiply it by (.1338)   = _____
   b) Take the number of affixes (   )
      and multiply it by (.0645)   = _____
   c) Add (a) and (b)   = _____
   d) Take the number of personal references (   )
      and multiply by (.0659)   = _____
   e) Subtract (d) from (c)   = _____
   f) Take the constant (.75)   =   .75
   g) Subtract (f) from (e)   = _____
   h) Find the readability score by entering the
      figure from (g) into the table   = _____

6. Interpret the readability score, through use of this table:

Score	Grade level
0–1	4
1–2	5
2–3	6
3–4	7–8
4–5	9–11
5–6	12–16
6 and up	College graduate

The Flesch yardstick formula has been applied to the following passage in order to show how the formula works.

READING PASSAGE ON "VIEW OF THE WORLD"

In the following passage, superscripts refer to personal reference, and circled word parts are affixes.

Each person[1] who[2] thinks about the world tends to conceive of it as a model of his[3] own outlook, shaped by his[4] training, interests, and pursuits. Shakespeare[5] views the world as a stage, a psychologist[6] thinks of it as a dynamic experimental design of nature, an executive[7] sees it as a structural organization akin to a flow chart of responsibility. Although differing philosophical perspectives influence our[8] thinking and organize our[9] perceptions of life, in any stage or age of life, the performer[10] who[11] is striving for the satisfaction of knowing he[12] is excelling is gaining self esteem[13] and the esteem of his[14] fellow man.

The Flesch yardstick formula can be applied to the reading passage above as follows:

Data on paragraph	*Computation*		
Number of words = 104	a) Average sentence length		
Number of sentences = 3	$(34.67) \times (.1338)$	=	4.79
Average sentence length = 34.67	b) Affixes $(26) \times (.0645)$	=	1.68
Affixes per hundred words = 26	c) Add (a) + (b)	=	6.47
Personal references per hundred words = 14	d) Personal references		
	$(14) \times (.0659)$	=	.92
	e) Subtract (c) − (d)	=	5.55
	f) Constant	=	.75
	g) Subtract (e) − (f)	=	4.80
	h) Readability level, find by looking up (g) in table.		
	Grade level	=	9–11

The Flesch formula requires about 60 to 90 minutes to apply. A quicker technique, requiring only a few minutes for estimating readability, is to compare a sample paragraph with a scale of paragraphs whose readability grade levels have already been computed. Such a scale was given in Table 14.6. These graded passages can be used as a "SEER" (Singer Eyeball Estimate of Readability) technique (Singer, 1975). Simply take a paragraph whose readability level you want to estimate and move it up and down until you judge that it is about equal in difficulty to the paragraph on the scale. Use such criteria as sentence length, word difficulty, writing style, and concept level for matching your paragraph to one on the scale. Then note the readability level of the paragraph on the scale. If you judge that your paragraph lies between two of the scaled paragraphs, you can assign the grade-level readability between the two paragraphs.

The scale in Table 14.6 consists of paragraphs drawn from content in history. Although this scale can be used for estimating reading in general, a scale that is specific to the content to be estimated would be preferable.

Appropriate textbook assignment   The graded reading inventory will provide the instructor with the range of reading ability of the class in the content area. The instructor can then assign students to books at the levels at which they can comprehend the contents.

Self-selection strategy

An alternative strategy (one less likely to stigmatize students) is to use the information gained for selecting a range of texts to cover the range of reading ability in the class and allow the students to select their own texts. This self-selection strategy adapts the text to the student, but does *not* upgrade the student's comprehension ability in the *particular subject area.* Other instructional techniques that include *input instruction* have to be used for this purpose. These teaching strategies will be divided into single- and multilevel strategies (Singer, 1973; Singer and Donlan, 1976). Among the single-text strategies are the following.

Directed reading activity   This strategy consists of the following steps:

1. Teach the technical vocabulary of the chapter or passage assigned. The vocabulary terms should be introduced and used in sentences. Each term should be analyzed into its prefix, root, and suffix, or into its syllables. Students can volunteer their experiences in association with the term to expand each word into a *concept,* or a term which signifies multiple attributes, as well as values for each of the attributes (Bruner, Goodnow, and Austin, 1956). Thus an apple has attributes of color, texture, size, etc., and values for each of these attributes, such as yellow to purple, soft to crunchy, and small to large.

2. Have the students formulate purposes for reading. Either the teacher can state questions for the students, or the students can construct their own questions. These questions may be stimulated by class discussion about the meaning of these terms or from the title of the selection. As students progress through the text, they should be able to formulate their own questions with greater ease and effectiveness.

The purpose of the teacher's questions is not only to focus on important aspects of the content, but also to teach the students what questions are appropriate for the content area. The students' questions not only give them a vested interest in the content and establish their purposes, but also provide a process to use throughout their reading.

3. Guide the students' reading through the beginning part of the chapter or passage. As students read a section aloud, the instructor can interject questions or elicit them. The purpose of this phase is to make sure that students are applying questioning processes to content.

4. Give time for silent reading. This stage enables students to read to answer questions with maximum attention to meaning.

5. Discussion following silent reading serves to check whether students found answers to questions or have any unanswered questions. Discussion also emphasizes transfer and application of the contents of the chapter to other situations.

The next step forward in the single-text approach gives the student more independence. This technique, widely known as a study skill, can also be used as a process for improving comprehension in reading content-area texts that do not involve suspense. The technique is called SQ3R.

SQ3R technique   An acronym for *Survey, Question, Read, Recite,* and *Review* (Robinson, 1946), the SQ3R technique is based on principles of learning. *Survey* means that the student is going to look through the entire chapter to find out how it is organized. The student will notice the topics, their sequence and relationship, and any visual aids (pictures, charts, graphs, tables, maps) which may be used in understanding the chapter. Organization facilitates comprehension (Oakan, Wiener, and Cromer, 1971; Wiener and Cromer, 1967), and visualization enhances retention (Anderson, 1974; Levin, 1972).

The second step is to formulate *questions.* Transformation of chapter and topic headings into questions will enable the reader to focus on the central points of the chapter and topics. The questioning process, however, should not end at this point, but should be continued throughout the third step (*reading*). This process makes the reader an active comprehender, one whose process of reading involves continuous questioning and searching for answers (Singer, 1973; Singer and Donlan, 1976; Singer and Rhodes, 1976).

The fourth step is *reciting.* In this step, readers systematically test themselves to determine whether they have obtained answers to their questions. If not, they engage in the fifth step, a *review* of the chapter to answer their remaining questions.

An assumption in SQ3R is that the reader is likely to know what questions to ask. A transitional step between DRA and SQ3R is the marginal gloss technique.

Marginal gloss   This technique consists of notes written by the teacher to accompany the text. Dittoed sheets with the notes and their page and line numbers can be given to students to use as they read the text. These notes can point out essential information, clarify vocabulary, and raise pertinent questions. In general, they serve as a substitute teacher reading along with the student. Difficult works frequently have marginal notes, such as those found in Charles Dickens's *Tale of Two Cities*. Marginal notes written by the instructor for less difficult texts will enhance the comprehension of all students and will help make the text fit a wider range of pupils.

Inquiry technique   A transitional technique from the single- to the multi-level text is the inquiry technique. The inquiry technique uses a single textbook (Ryan and Wheeler, 1974). The teacher leads the class to question the validity of information presented in the text. For example, a factual statement a social science class might read is that Admiral Peary was the first person to fly over the North Pole. The teacher may ask the class to determine whether this statement is correct. Before the students can make this determination, however, the teacher has to show them how to use the *Reader's Guide to Periodical Literature*. When they finally track down newspaper and magazine articles about the event, the class will discover that a controversy existed as to whether Admiral Peary did or did not fly over the North Pole, as he had claimed to have done. Then the teacher will have to teach the class to weigh the evidence and come to a decision. Perhaps the teacher can use a debate or a jury trial as a way of evaluating the evidence.

Project method   The teacher starts a unit with a classroom decorated with posters, pictures, and pamphlets about some event. In an American history class, for example, the event might be the signing of the Declaration of Independence; in a literature class, a concept such as "courage"; in a biology class, the "laws of inheritance"; in trigonometry, a spaceship's location in space in relation to the earth and moon. A creative environment is likely to arouse student curiosity so that students will have questions to raise when asked, "What would you like to know about this event?" The students' questions are then recorded on the board. Next, the class groups questions into categories. The students form groups around these categories, and each group reads in reference books to get the answers to its questions. Finally, the groups report their answers to the class. If the teacher has selected books on the topic at different levels of difficulty, students will have the opportunity to select texts at their own levels of reading ability and to use them to answer their questions.

Single- and multitext strategies will help the teacher teach content and processes to students with a wide range of reading abilities. Moreover, the teacher's use of these techniques does not stigmatize students. However, some students who are still learning to read will also need special classes for concentrated instruction in reading acquisition.

READING-ACQUISITION STRATEGIES IN THE CONTENT AREAS*

Undoubtedly specialized instruction and special classes are needed to improve the reading abilities of students who are still in the acquisition stage of reading; that is, they are still learning how to read. Although most students have mastered reading acquisition by the sixth grade (Singer, 1976), some students, particularly those whose native language is not English, may still need reading acquisition in high school. Special reading-improvement classes are necessary for these students. Other students who have mastered reading acquisition but who are below grade level in general reading achievement may also be helped in high school reading-improvement classes.

However, the effectiveness of this help is diminished if the rest of the classes in the various content areas do not adapt instruction to meet the entire range of individual differences. It's as though the special reading-improvement classes are educational "hothouses"; for one period a day students with low reading achievement are nurtured, but for the rest of the day they are in a detrimental environment. This double burden of trying to overcome both an accumulation of low reading achievement that has persisted for at least eight to nine years *and* a current environment that is still contributing to negative achievement may explain why reading-improvement classes alone do not make a significant difference in a school's reading-achievement scores (Evans, 1972).

What might help these students is not only reading-acquisition classes, but also classroom instructional strategies that will allow them to be successful in content-area instruction. But reading-acquisition classes do not have to be devoid of content-area instruction, and high school students do not have to be embarrassed by the content in acquisition classes. However, high school students in reading-acquisition classes are embarrassed by their problems in reading. This embarrassment is magnified if the instructor uses materials and methods that are appropriate for elementary school. Although the processes and procedures for learning to read are the same for all students, regardless of age, instructional techniques, tests, and topical materials suitable to more mature students can be used. For example, although all

---

* Descriptions of useful materials for use in reading laboratories and in developmental reading classes can be found in Devine (1969) and Rupley (1973).

students have to learn to identify words, high school readers at this stage of development can use word-recognition procedures on words, sentences, and passages selected from their own content-area texts.

Content-area texts (like all books) consist of some 220 basic words that account for 50 percent of all the words in the book. (For a list of Dolch sight words, see Tinker and McCullough, 1975.) These words are functional words, such as noun determiners (a, the, this, these, some), prepositions or locative words (to, for, from), and conjunctions or combining and subordinating words (and, but, while). These functional words tie the content or content-related words together (nouns, pronouns, adjectives, adverbs, and verbs). Usually all functional words are learned by 95 percent of all children by grade three. If high school readers do not know them, these words should have priority in the reading-acquisition program. However, words, particularly functional words, should not be taught in isolation. The meaning and syntactical properties of functional words require presentation in context. Hence, they should be taught, as they occur, in sentences in the content-area text. The sentences may be simplified to highlight the functional word(s) being taught. Also, the content words of the sentences should change while the functional words remain the same. For example, the functional word "to" may occur in the following sentences:

While going *to* his home, he met her.

To find interest, multiply principal by rate by time.

Content words should also be taught in sentence context. The use of sentence context will teach students not only to identify the content word, but also how to identify it by using the syntax and semantics of the sentence. For example, the context helps identify the word "constitution" in the sentence: "The people voted to change the constitution." Of course, in order for the context to work this way, the student must correctly identify the words and meanings in the preceding part of the sentence. With instructional help on this part of the sentence, however, the student could use syntax and semantics for anticipating the last word in the sentence.

In addition, the student must learn to identify word parts, such as consonants, digraphs (th, ch), blends (fr, sk), vowels, diphthongs (oi, ow), syllables, affixes (prefixes, suffixes), and roots. These word parts can be taught by grouping together words that have these parts in common and teaching the student to abstract and generalize a response to the word part. (See Singer in Singer and Ruddell, 1976; for an explanation of this instructional process, see Heilman, 1972, Chapter 7.) For example, these words may be used for teaching the initial consonant, "p": power, piston, pinion, propeller, and push.

Likewise, all word parts can be taught through this grouping strategy.

Having the student use these words in a content area and in sentence context will reinforce their meaning. (See description and use of a sentence generator in Singer and Beasley, 1970.) To select content words and their context, use the index to the text.

The student should also have opportunities to read connected discourse in which the newly acquired words are used. For this purpose, either the text in current use or passages from easier texts can be used. Easier texts can be located by using the elementary, junior high, or high school catalog, which indexes books according to content and grade level.

The combination of teaching students to identify words by selecting words from high school texts, teaching these words in context, and having students use these words in actual reading situations should result in more motivated students. Since these students will probably get further experience in using these words in content-area courses (particularly if their instructors employ learning-to-read guides for teaching technical words), they are likely to read more rapidly. Thus it is probable that this combination of techniques will accelerate their development toward mastery of reading acquisition.

In addition to reading-acquisition classes, a high school should also have orientation classes. These classes serve to introduce students to reading and learning from texts in content areas.

ORIENTATION STRATEGIES: READING AND LEARNING FROM TEXT IN CONTENT AREAS

The high school reading specialist can set up courses to teach incoming freshmen how to read and learn in each content area. These reading techniques and learning procedures can also be taught to the faculty through use of demonstrations, in-service training, and consultants.

Teaching patterns of writing in the content areas

An important element of instruction at the high school level is teaching students to respond to the different patterns of writing found in the content areas. Smith (1964b, c) has identified dominant patterns in four major content areas. Her patterns have been more fully explained and amplified in great detail in workbooks (Smith, 1964a) and in a textbook (Robinson, 1975). The highlights of these patterns are summarized below.

Social studies   Students must be able to read charts, maps, tables, graphs, and pictures. These visuals usually depict the relation between two variables, such as a rain chart that shows the amount of rainfall for each month of the year. Students need to be taught to put the data in the charts, maps, and graphs into verbal form. A questioning procedure for doing so is to (1) ask the students to state the facts, interpret them, and state the general relationship between the depicted variables, or (2) have students formulate their own questions.

Large periods of time must be viewed chronologically while concurrent series of events are organized within these blocks. For example, when discussing events chronologically in the history of the United States, the teacher would perhaps explain the succession of presidents and their impact on the country. The succession of the presidents would be the chronological pattern, and their impact would constitute a concurrent series of events.

Comparisons and contrasts of philosophies and ideologies must be made. For example, in describing political parties in the United States, the similarities and differences of opinion on federal versus local control represent a comparison-and-contrast pattern.

To apply social studies lessons to everyday activities, including television and newspaper reports, magazine stories, and even conversations, students must be able to recognize propaganda devices, which are used regularly in all forms of mass media. For example, polls may not have a representative sample, but their information is intended to promote a "bandwagon" appeal: "buy this product" or "get behind this candidate because everyone is doing so."

Mathematics Students must slowly and analytically read compact writing, in which every symbol can be of extreme importance. For example, in order to be able to apply the formula for the area of a circle, $A = \pi r^2$, the student must know that $A =$ area, π is a constant $= 22/7$, $r =$ radius, and the superscript "2" means that the radius must be squared.

Systematic procedures must be applied to problem solving. One procedure for doing so is PQ4R, where P = *preview* (read problem and understand technical terms), Q = *question* (state the direct question of the problem), and R = *read* (list all word facts in order), *recite* (without looking at the print, state the main parts and subparts of the problem), *reflect* (translate words of math facts into an equation), then solve the equation and *review* (does the solution fit the question?) (Thomas and Robinson, 1974).

Detailed explanations often require repeated reading for comprehension. Sometimes visualization or a pictorial aid may facilitate comprehension of explanations. The ability to read graphs and tables is necessary for understanding data. In order to be interpreted, the data have to be translated into words as trends and comparisons are noticed.

In doing story problems, students must recognize synonyms for technical terms and manipulate sentence syntax in written problems in order to put the information into the form of an equation. For example, in the formula for determining interest, Interest = Principal × Rate × Time, the student must recognize synonyms for principal, such as investment, loan, etc.

Science   Students must understand the importance of grouping objects into elaborate classifications, systems, and subsystems. Instruction in classifications can begin simply (e.g., earth, solar system, galaxy, universe, etc.), then proceed to more difficult scientific systems. Complex explanations of processes and detailed instructions must be read with considerable care. McAda and Hedley (1969) urge group work throughout much of the scientific process, so that many students can contribute jointly to the solving of difficult problems— just as scientists work together in research. Science patterns vary greatly; a relatively simple description of how a problem was solved might be followed by a highly detailed series of acts. The teacher may need to show the students how to set purposes for reading, as well as shift the rate and purpose as the writing patterns change. This can be done through directed reading activity. As with mathematics, special symbols must be learned. These can be introduced, like vocabulary, in context prior to lessons.

Literature   Great variation exists in patterns within the field of literature. Students should be taught to identify patterns and purposes for reading. Though both an epic and a sonnet are poems, they require very different approaches. Students can be shown how a similar idea is handled differently, depending on the medium. For example, the concept of appearance versus reality could be examined in a poem (E. A. Robinson's "Richard Cory"), a play (Durrenmatt's *The Visit*), an essay (Plato's "Allegory of the Cave"), and a short story (Poe's "The Telltale Heart"). Also, within a particular genre of literature there are numerous levels of interpretation. (See the "profundity scale" in Robinson, 1975, pp. 202–203, for an explanation of these levels.) For example, the plot of a story may be the vehicle for the *symbols,* which convey the *theme.* Directed reading activity, combined with teacher-made marginal glosses that students insert into their texts, can sensitize students to multilevels of literary meaning. It can also be helpful to take a short work (a poem), read it once for literal meaning, then go back and search for interpretations, and finally have students apply the message to their lives.

Attitudes toward study

In addition to intelligence and ability, attitudes toward school are important elements in students' achievement. To give students insight into their attitudes, administer the Carter Study Methods Inventory (Carter, 1964). (Other study tests are in Buros, 1972, and Farr, 1969.) The results of this inventory will also provide information on their ability to plan time and on mechanics of studying.

Mechanics of study

The SQ3R (Survey, Question, Read, Recite, and Review) technique for studying was devised by Francis Robinson (1946). His revised study manual is still appropriate. Since his formula first appeared, many similar formulae have been reported (see Singer and Rhodes, 1976). Although the letters in these formulae differ, they all follow the basic formula established by Robinson. Incoming freshmen should be given practice in applying the SQ3R formula to content-area material. These exercises should stress "active comprehension," i.e., having students formulate and read to answer their own questions in each content area. (For more detailed information on active comprehension, see Singer and Donlan, *Reading and Learning from Text,* in press.)

Reading instruction

Numerous manuals for teaching reading skills are available. These manuals provide exercises on vocabulary; location of main ideas; interpretation; inferences; reading of tables, charts, maps, and graphs; evaluating propaganda; locating sources of information; using a table of contents and index; following directions; determining cause and effect; skimming; and flexibility in rate of reading. (For a review of materials in teaching comprehension, see Devine, 1969; for an annotated list of resources, see Seligson, 1964.)

Reading laboratories: procedure

A useful procedure for use in a reading laboratory is construction of a diagnostic and prescriptive index. Survey and diagnostic test variables should be placed on one side of the list and materials for developing these variables placed across the top of the list. This list can be constructed by using the test variables in whatever test is administered for survey and diagnostic purposes. The material for developing these variables can be gleaned from those given in Devine (1969) and Seligson (1964).

A chart or checklist should also be kept for each student enrolled in the lab. The chart should have the student's name on one side of the list and the skills across the top of the list. The chart can be used for communicating needed skills to the student and can also serve as a summary of progress. As a student progresses in acquiring a skill, the level of progress can be noted on a chart.

Motivational techniques

Progress charts that place "learning under the control of students" are highly motivating (Singer and Beasley, 1970). These progress charts are cumulative.

The reader determines his or her own rate of progress by deciding how many pages per session to read or how many words per session to learn. An example of such a cumulative chart is given in Fig. 14.1. The pages read each session are added to the previous total to find cumulative pages read. The curve on this chart cannot go down. It can only stay at the same level or go up. Most students make it rise.

To facilitate students' reading, teach them new words in advance of their reading. Teach them to pronounce the words, to use them in sentence context, to syllabify the words, and to learn the meanings of their roots and affixes. The same root word may occur in each content area. For example, "duc," meaning "to lead," can be found in English (introduction), social studies (production), science (conductor), and mathematics (deductive). (An excellent list of morphemes—affixes and roots—can be found in Burmeister, 1974, pp. 299–308.) A set of words, on individual cards, should be kept by the student.

Words in content areas can be readily identified through use of the index of each high school textbook. By arranging the index numerically according to page number, references to the meaning and sentence usage of terms used in the content areas can be facilitated. Students can be taught to use their re-organized textbook indexes to improve their vocabularies in the reading laboratory or in their orientation program, and this practice may transfer to their reading and learning from texts in their content areas.

Thus orientation and reading laboratory classes can teach students how to learn from texts in their content areas and how to improve their reading and study skills. If all students in a high school have such instruction as freshmen, some reading and learning problems can be prevented, and students enrolled in such classes are not likely to be stigmatized. The total reading and achievement of the school could be enhanced by this omnibus high school program.

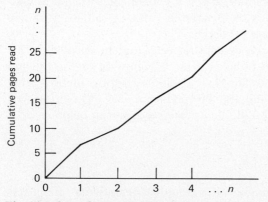

Fig. 14.1. Cumulative progress chart.

SUMMARY

Almost all students in the 14- to 17-year-old age group now tend to remain in high school to graduation. Consequently, the high school has a student body with a range of reading ability that spans 10 to 12 years, from an average of grade 5 to college graduate. This range of individual differences in reading abilities cannot be solved by a remedial reading program alone. Instead, an omnibus program consisting of individual, classroom, and orientation strategies must be devised.

A high school reading specialist can conduct courses in reading acquisition, using content-area materials, diagnose and prescribe for the school and for individual students, consult with classroom teachers on strategies for handling individual differences in the classroom, and conduct orientation courses in reading and learning from texts in the content areas. This school-wide approach to the problem of individual differences should help the school overcome its difficulties and provide equality of educational opportunity for all students.

REFERENCES

Anderson, Richard C. "Concretization and Sentence Learning," *Journal of Educational Psychology* **66** (1974): 179–183.

Bond, Guy L., and Miles A. Tinker *Reading Difficulties: Their Diagnosis and Correction,* 2d ed., New York: Appleton-Century-Crofts, 1957.

Bruner, Jerome, J. J. Goodnow, and G. A. Austin *A Study of Thinking,* New York: Wiley, 1956.

Burmeister, Lou E. *Reading Strategies for Secondary Teachers,* Reading, Mass.: Addison-Wesley, 1974.

Buros, Oscar K. *Seventh Mental Measurements Yearbook,* Highland Park, N.J.: Gryphon Press, 1972.

Carter, Harold D. *California Study Methods Survey,* Monterey: California Test Bureau/McGraw-Hill, 1964.

Caswell, Hollis S., and A. Wellesley Foshay *Education in the Elementary School,* 2d ed., New York: American Book Co., 1950.

Cook, Walter W. "The Function of Measurement in the Facilitation of Learning," in E. F. Lindquist, ed., *Educational Measurement,* Washington, D.C.: American Council on Education, 1951.

Devine, Thomas "What Does Research in Reading Reveal About Materials for Teaching Reading?" *English Journal* **58** (Sept. 1969): 847–857.

Emery, Raymond, and Margaret Houshower *High Interest–Easy Reading for Junior and Senior High School Students,* Champaign, Ill.: National Council of Teachers of English, 1965.

Evans, Howard M. "Remedial Reading in Secondary Schools—Still a Matter of Faith," *Journal of Reading* **16** (1972): 111–114.

Farr, Roger *Reading: What Can Be Measured?* Newark, Del.: International Reading Association, 1969.

Fay, Leo, and Lee Ann Jared *Reading in the Content Fields,* Newark, Del.: International Reading Association, 1975.

Fidel, Estelle A., and Toby M. Berger, eds. *Senior High School Library Catalog*, 10th ed. (annual supplements), New York: H. W. Wilson, 1972.

Fidel, Estelle A., and Gary L. Bogart, eds. *Junior High School Library Catalog*, 2d ed., annual supplements, New York: H. W. Wilson, 1970.

Flesch, Rudolf *The Art of Plain Talk*, New York: Harper, 1946.

Gates, Arthur I., and Walter H. MacGinitie *Gates-MacGinitie Reading Tests*, Survey F, New York: Columbia University Press, 1972.

Gates, Arthur I., and Anne S. McKillop *Gates-McKillop Reading Diagnostic Tests*, New York: Teachers College Press, Columbia University, 1962.

Goodman, Yetta M., and Carolyn L. Burke *Reading Miscue Inventory*, New York: Macmillan, 1972.

Hafner, Lawrence E., and Hayden B. Jolly *Patterns of Teaching Reading in the Elementary School*, New York: Macmillan, 1972, pp. 55–88.

Harris, Albert J. *How to Increase Reading Ability*, 5th ed., New York: McKay, 1970.

Harris, Larry A., and Carl B. Smith *Reading Instruction Through Diagnostic Teaching*, New York: Holt, Rinehart and Winston, 1972.

Heilman, Arthur *Principles and Practices of Teaching Reading*, Columbus, Ohio: Merrill, 1972.

Herber, Harold L. "Reading in Content Areas: A District Develops its Own Personnel," *Journal of Reading* 13 (1970a): 587–592.

Herber, Harold L. *Teaching Reading in Content Areas*, Englewood Cliffs, N.J.: Prentice-Hall, 1970b.

Hill, Walter "Characteristics of Secondary Reading: 1940–1970," in Frank P. Greene, ed., *National Reading Conference 20th Yearbook*, 1971, pp. 20–29.

Holmes, Jack A., and Harry Singer "Speed and Power of Reading in High School," *Cooperative Research Monograph No. 14*, Washington, D.C.: U.S. Government Printing Office, Supt. of Documents Catalog No. F55230: 30016, 1966.

Jencks, Christopher S. "Effects of High Schools on their Students," *Harvard Educational Review* 45 (August 1975): 273–324.

Karlin, Robert "What Does Research in Reading Reveal about Reading and the High School Student?" *English Journal* 58 (1969): 386–395.

Levin, Joel "Comprehending What We Read: An Outsider Looks In," *Journal of Reading Behavior* 4 (Fall 1972): 18–27.

McAda, Harleen W., and Carolyn Neal Hedley "Reading and the New Science," *Science Education* 53 (March 1969): 151–153.

Mavrogenes, Nancy A., Carol K. Winkley, Earl Hanson, and Richard T. Vacca Concise Guide to Standardized Secondary and College Reading Tests," *Journal of Reading* 18 (1974): 12–22.

Oakan, R., M. Wiener, and W. Cromer "Identification, Organization, and Comprehension for Good and Poor Readers," *Journal of Educational Psychology* 62 (1971): 71–78.

Otto, Wayne, and Richard J. Smith "Junior and Senior High School Teachers' Attitudes toward Teaching Reading in the Content Areas," in G. B. Schick and M. May, eds., *National Reading Conference 18th Yearbook*, 1969, pp. 49–54.

Reid, Virginia M., ed. *Reading Ladders for Human Relations*, 5th ed., Washington, D.C.: American Council on Education, 1972.

Robinson, Francis P. *Effective Study*, New York: Harper, 1946.

Robinson, H. Alan *Teaching Reading and Study Strategies: The Content Areas*, Boston: Allyn and Bacon, 1975.

Rupley, W. H. "ERIC/RCS: Secondary Reading Materials," *Journal of Reading* 17 (Dec. 1973): 252–254.

Russell, David H. "Reading Research that Makes a Difference," *Elementary English* **38** (1961): 74–78.

Ryan, Frank, and R. Wheeler "Truth-Loving Mind Is a Sleuth-Loving Mind," *Instructor* (1974): 84, 136.

Schleich, Miriam "Groundwork for Better Reading in the Content Areas, *Journal of Reading* **15** (1971): 119–126.

Seligson, Yemena "Resources for Reading Teachers," *Journal of Education* **146** (April 1964): 31–74.

Shepard, David *Comprehensive High School Methods,* Columbus, Ohio: Merrill, 1973.

Shor, Rachel, and Estelle A. Fidel, eds. *The Children's Catalog,* New York: H. Wilson, 1972.

Singer, Harry "IQ Is and Is Not Related to Reading," in S. Wanat, ed., *Intelligence and Reading,* Newark, Del.: International Reading Association, 1976 (in press). Also in ERIC, ED 088 004, CS 000 925, May 1973. EDRS Price MF $0.75, HC $1.85.

Singer, Harry "The SEER Technique: A Non-computational Procedure for Quickly Estimating Readability Level," *Journal of Reading Behavior* **7** (Fall 1975): 255–267.

Singer, Harry *Preparing Content Reading Specialists for the Junior High School Level,* Washington, D.C.: U.S. Office of Education, 1973.

Singer, Harry "Factors Involved in General Reading Ability and Reading in the Content Areas," in G. B. Schick and M. M. May, eds., *National Reading Conference 19th Yearbook,* 1970, pp. 295–305.

Singer, Harry "Validity of the Durrell-Sullivan Reading Capacity Test," *Educational and Psychological Measurement* **25** (1965): 479–491.

Singer, Harry, and Sherrel Beasley "Motivating a Disabled Reader," in Malcolm P. Douglas, ed., *Claremont Reading Conference Yearbook,* 1970, pp. 141–160.

Singer, Harry, and Dan Donlan *Reading and Learning from Texts* (in press).

Singer, Harry, and Irving B. Hendrick "Total School Integration: An Experiment in Social Reconstruction," *Phi Delta Kappan* **49** (Nov. 1967): 143–147.

Singer, Harry, and Alan Rhodes "Learning from Text: Theories, Strategies, and Research at the High School Level," *National Reading Conference Yearbook,* 1976, in press.

Singer, Harry, and Robert B. Ruddell, eds. *Theoretical Models and Processes of Reading,* 2d ed., Newark, Del.: International Reading Association, 1976.

Smith, Nila Banton *Be a Better Reader,* Englewood Cliffs, N.J.: Prentice-Hall, 1964a.

Smith, Nila Banton "Patterns of Writing in Different Subject Areas: Part I," *Journal of Reading* **8** (1964b): 31–37.

Smith, Nila Banton "Patterns of Writing in Different Subject Areas: Part II," *Journal of Reading* **8** (1964c): 97–102.

Spache, George *Toward Better Reading,* Champaign, Ill.: Garrard, 1963, p. 94.

Strang, Ruth *Exploration in Reading Patterns,* Chicago: University of Chicago Press, 1942.

Strang, Ruth *Problems in the Improvement of Reading in High School and College,* Lancaster, Penn.: Science Press, 1938.

Strang, Ruth, Constance McCullough, and Arthur Traxler *The Improvement of Reading,* 4th ed., New York: McGraw-Hill, 1967.

Strang, Ruth, Constance McCullough, and Arthur Traxler *The Improvement of Reading,* New York: McGraw-Hill, 1946.

Thomas, Ellen Lamar, and H. Alan Robinson *Improving Reading in Every Class,* abridged ed., Boston: Allyn and Bacon, 1974.

Tiegs, E. W., and W. W. Clark *California Reading Test: Advanced,* Monterey: California Test Bureau, 1963.

Tinker, Miles A., and Constance McCullough *Teaching Elementary Reading,* 4th ed., Englewood Cliffs, N.J.: Prentice-Hall, 1975.

Tyack, David B. *Turning Points in American Educational History,* Waltham, Mass.: Blaisdell/Ginn, 1967, pp. 360–361.

Wiener, M., and W. Cromer "Reading and Reading Difficulty: A Conceptual Analysis," *Harvard Educational Review* 37 (1967): 620–643.

Chapter 15

ADULT BASIC EDUCATION

BURTON W. KREITLOW • *University of Wisconsin*

Literacy programs throughout the world have been designed to increase the level of literacy for adults who cannot read or write their native or national language. Objectives of such programs looked toward the development of a desire for literacy among the illiterate and the provision of the resources to help them become literate.

Literacy is a vital element in the economic, political, and social development in any cultural group or country. It is essential for personal satisfaction, enrichment, and performance in most developed countries and for nation building in those less developed.

In colonial America, literacy programs emphasized learning to read the Bible. In the late nineteenth and early twentieth centuries, the emphasis was on Americanization. Today the emphasis has changed to reflect the social-economic-cultural setting of the times. Literacy programs are now called Adult Basic Education.

Adult Basic Education (ABE) in the United States is a program for adults who have not reached a level of literacy commensurate with the demands of modern life. The program is for those who need the academic skills missed in school or whose limited skills have deteriorated. People in ABE programs need the coping skills essential for physical, emotional, and intellectual survival. Some need career information and skill building to move them from the ranks of the unemployed or to give them the potential for another step up the career ladder. Some need to gain the emotional security to deal more effectively with the job level they achieved from hard work and long tenure.

In general, Adult Basic Education is for those who left school before completing grade 8, who dropped out of high school after having been promoted year after year for attendance alone, or who are blessed with knowledge of a non-English first language but are disadvantaged in not knowing English. Programs for the latter group are often called ESL (English as a Second Language) rather than ABE (Adult Basic Education).

It would be well to remember that we are all illiterate in some things. The ABE program is for those whose illiteracy is in the basic tools for learning and for coping. It is difficult for people in this group to learn by their own efforts, as do teachers and others who have the skills with which to learn.

THE LITERACY GAP

Any perspective of reading problems in the United States cannot overlook the 54,000,000 adults 16 years of age or older *who are not in school* and *who have never finished grade 12.* A viewer of reading problems has cause to wonder why there are more illiterates in the world in 1976 than at any earlier period of history.

Illiteracy is the world's greatest overall reading problem.* Until all of the correlates of reading disability are caught and corrected in the early years of schooling, it will continue to be so in the United States. Also, many early school leavers are the product of poor teaching or of inadequate assessment of early reading problems. As adults they are still turned off by classrooms, books, and teachers. Whereas children are often partially disabled readers by reason of physiological, neuropsychological, or emotional disorders, adults may retain the original disorders and in addition be subjected to the trauma of being illiterate in a society where economic survival depends on literacy.

Literacy and illiteracy defined

"A person is literate who can, with understanding, both read and write a short, simple statement on his everyday life" was a definition proposed by UNESCO's Expert Committee on the Standardization of Educational Statistics in 1951 (UNESCO, 1965, p. 7). In 1962 another functional definition was proposed: "A person is literate when he has acquired the essential knowl-

---

* The best sources on illiteracy in other countries are in publications of the United Nations (UNESCO). Examples are: *World Literacy in Mid Century: A Statistical Study* (1957); *Statistics of Illiteracy* (1965); *World Conference of Ministers of Education on the Eradication of Illiteracy: Final Report* (1965); *Bulletin of the International Bureau of Education* (appears quarterly).

For the best summary data on illiteracy in the United States and by states, see the annual reports of the National Advisory Council on Adult Education (NACAE), Washington, D.C.

edge and skills which enable him to engage in all those activities in which literacy is required for effective functioning in his group and community, and whose attainment in reading, writing and arithmetic make it possible for him to continue to use these skills towards his own and his community's development."

The United States Office of Education has used grade equivalencies ranging from grade 4 as late as 1961 to grade 8 in 1975 as the upper grade level of illiteracy. The "right to read" movement has decided that literacy assessments should be made independent of grade equivalents. In the 1974 amendment to the Adult Education Act, Adult Basic Education was defined without grade-level designation and in functional terms:

> The term "adult basic education" means adult education for adults whose inability to speak, read or write the English language constitutes a substantial impairment of their ability to get or retain employment commensurate with their real ability, which is designed to help eliminate such inability and raise the level of education of such individuals with a view of making them less likely to become dependent on others, to improving their ability to benefit from occupational training and otherwise increasing their opportunities for more productive and profitable employment, and to make them better able to meet their adult responsibility.*

Another type of literacy definition is that of O'Neil (1970), who writes: "Being able to read means that you can follow words across a page, getting generally what's superficially there. Being literate means you can bring your knowledge and your experience to bear on what passes before you. Let us call the latter proper literacy, the former improper." (p. 262)

Social factors suppressing literacy

A teacher concerned about improving the level of literacy in the United States needs to recognize those social barriers that work against such improvement. Variations in social class, in cultural heritage, and in first-learned language stem from and lead to variations in individual and family goals.

Most teachers find it easier and far more comfortable to work with children from middle-class families than with those from the lower class. The teachers themselves tend to come from the middle class and thus find

---

* I apologize for using a 98-word sentence in a book on reading whose readers are aware of the concept of readability.

that their own life goals and those of their students and the students' parents are congruent. A middle-class teacher finds it all too easy to overlook a small cluster of youngsters who come from the inner city, who have different language and speech patterns, who wear nonconforming clothes, and who have had to "fight" for their personal dignity and are still willing to do so.

Research relating class to verbal behavior of children has been studied extensively. The influence of social class on learning verbal behavior in general and on learning in particular has been well documented. Davis (1962) saw this relationship as "the pivotal meaning of social classes" which defines and systematizes different learning environments for children in different classes.

Lower-class children incorporate a greater need for direct and immediate satisfactions into their behavior patterns. They also learn how to communicate within their own family in ways that may not seem appropriate to the teachers. In the school situation their home language may fail them, and they will be failed by the school.

The Spanish-speaking youngster, whether native or foreign-born, cannot be expected to progress at the same rate as children who know only English when that is the language of instruction. If their problems are ignored, the logical outcome will be nonpromotion, dropout, and illiteracy.

Curriculum and instructional materials developed by and used from the stance of either male or female teacher has the potential of leading one-half of the students out of the classroom in either body or spirit or both. Differences in rates of physical and intellectual development, in sex-role acculturation, and in learning goals beg for sufficient flexibility in teaching to accommodate both male and female. To the millions of low literates in the United States who never reached or completed high school should be added other millions who were in school without attention and millions more whose attitude toward learning when they finished high school (considered literate by definition) was such that they refused to keep up with the changes about them. These adults are in fact no longer able to bring their knowledge and experience to bear on what passes before them.

Teachers of low-literate adults, even more than teachers of elementary or secondary school children, need to be sensitive to the diversity in attitudes, behavior patterns, and culture-related ability among their students. Experienced ABE teachers who have had elementary teaching experience report that there are more variations in ability, attitudes, and interests in adult students than in children. They admit to a higher clustering of the nonacademically oriented, but claim that the range of abilities and interests is greater. The ABE teacher needs to understand and respond to the individual regardless of his or her subculture, be able to diagnose need, propose learning experiences, and lead the learner to early success.

THE PSYCHOLOGY OF ADULTS

Long-standing myths have been barriers to the establishment of sound instructional programs for the low-literate adult. The greatest of all myths is one reinforced in 1928 by Thorndike's cross-sectional research, which concluded that the peak of learning is reached at age 22 and declines thereafter. At the time adult educators felt good about the finding, since earlier students of learning believed that the peak of intellectual development is reached at age 16 or 18.

It was not until the mid-1930s that the first cracks appeared in Thorndike's findings and in those of Conrad and Jones, Miles, and of Wechsler, whose data revealed findings similar to Thorndike's. Iriving Lorge not only questioned the cross-sectional design of their age-related research on adult intelligence, but also raised questions about the validity of their measure. In the process of his own investigations, he proved quite sufficiently that what Thorndike and others had been measuring was ability to handle stress in a timed, speed-related, child-type exercise. He agreed that older people do not respond as quickly. In his studies, responses to tests that required speed continued to show a decline with age; tests of learning power with no linked speed variable showed no decline.

Facts do not support the "peak at 22" myth, and the facts are overwhelming. It was the longitudinal studies that put the myth to rest. One of the first was the Owens and Charles report from the University of Iowa. A group of old Army-Alpha tests from World War I were about to be thrown away in 1949, but instead this team located many of the earlier test takers (as freshman male students in 1919), gave the test to them again in 1950, and compared the results. The researchers repeated this test in 1960. The results astounded those who still believed the old myth. They found no overall decline in the test results. There was evidence that on verbal tests, the performance was better than when the men had been tested earlier. In the numerical components, there was some decline.

Other longitudinal tests followed and verified the Owens and Charles research. Social-generational factors *do* lead to different scores on cross-sectional studies, as reported by Baltes, Schai, and Nardi (1971). In their research design, they were able to examine cross-sectional and longitudinal data simultaneously, showing the potential misinformation in cross-sectional data dealing with learning throughout the life span.

Attitudes of adults are a product of their experience from whatever culture base they come. Adult Basic Education enrollees are more often than not from either a community or family-level subculture that did not stress the values in education. It is the attitude built from this base that ABE teachers must recognize. In local recruitment and in communicating with students who take the bold and brave step of enrolling in a program, it is essential to treat them as adults and with a mature understanding of differences.

PROGRAM DEVELOPMENT

The ABE thrust

Adult Basic Education is more than reading, but the ability to teach adults to read is the most important ingredient in the teacher's credentials. Being able to teach first graders to read a simple story or fifth graders to read with greater comprehension is no guarantee that adults can be taught reading as effectively.

In response to needs of low-literate disadvantaged adults, the largest target group of ABE students, three key program objectives have emerged. They are the development of:

1. *Academic skills,* including reading, writing, and mathematics.
2. *Coping skills,* including those essential to survival on a limited budget, such as comparison shopping, job hunting, and health maintenance.
3. *Career orientation skills,* including occupational knowledge, knowledge of one's own skills and abilities, and sources of employment.

The objectives generally lead to an integrated curriculum that requires a great deal of flexibility on the part of the teacher. Program-development processes in Adult Basic Education have consistently led to strong ties between the academic and the coping segments and with a somewhat less firm tie to careers. On occasion, administrators and teachers have failed to plan programs; instead, they have lifted pieces of other plans and "layed them on" the ABE participants. These so-called programs have been short-lived. The voluntary nature of participation in adult programs leads to "drop in," "test the water," and if it's not right, "drop out." Unless the needs of the potential learner are not considered in planning the program, "dropout" is the result.

Involvement of the learner in planning ABE programs

The Tyler rationale for curriculum development (program planning) identified the learner as one of the sources of curriculum objectives. Other sources are the expert (specialist) and the nature of the society in which a person lives.

Perhaps in no other adult education program is the need for involvement of learners more important to continuing participation than in ABE.

For many in ABE, much of their early education failed to interest them or even give them hope for the future. Since learners come to ABE after much inner conflict as to whether it will be worth their time, their needs should be assessed by going directly to them. The program can be theirs only if they help in the planning. This may be direct involvement in the program-planning process or the knowledge that their peers are involved in the planning.

In observing curriculum planning in ABE programs in Indiana, consultants (Kreitlow, 1972, pp. 72, 73) reported the following:

No evidence of student involvement. Teacher is in charge.

Very little client involvement seen, but the director advises teachers to build around client questions and problems.

Some students (4–6) want to go above their heads, teachers let them for awhile. Better too high than too low. If students really want to try something which the teacher feels is too hard, she will work with them until *they* decide it's too tough. She doesn't set limits for them. The student discovers and sets his own. Good input!

Students have been asked what their goals are—one man (born and educated in India) needs to be able to read, write, and speak English better. Three or four students are referrals from CAP (Community Action Program) and their goal is to improve their chances for employment. These student goals are known to the teacher—she takes it from there.

Much reliance on student interest via highly individualized program (maybe to a fault).

Two adult students want more high school credit for individual work in the Learning Lab. This would increase the incentive to work for a high school diploma, since it would allow them to work out a more flexible schedule (they both work at a steel company). They believe 16 credits for high school equivalency (out of 32 needed) should be available from work in the Lab.

Yes, clients are involved in the planning. Interviews with individual students are made on entering the Learning Lab, and there are ongoing group discussions of areas of interest.

Students frequently indicate willingness to learn particular aspects of a subject area. General planning of subjects is left to the instructor.

Students express their needs in a particular subject. There was definite consciousness on the part of the clients regarding their needs to help their children.

The variations noted in the observations above were from very little to too much student involvement. In comparing programs, it was clear that in those with adult student input into program development, the attendance in ABE classes was more regular and the students were less likely to drop out before completing the planned program of work.

The motivations and incentives for a low literate to begin participation either have to be strong or the steps for entering the program have to be easy. Holding an ABE class in an elementary or secondary school building would be too formidable a barrier for some. Enrollment in a Pittsburgh program quadrupled after the program was moved from the fourth to the first floor. An adult, aware of the limitations his or her low literacy carries, often needs the helping hand of an indigenous recruiter or of someone already in the class in order to take that first step. One of the most effective ways of making that step easy is for program leaders to make sure that low literates know that it is their program. It can be their program only if they are both part of the original planning (if beginning a new program) or responsible for input into ongoing programs. This participant involvement can be as limited as an informal conference with a recruiter or counselor or as extensive as participation on a community adult program planning committee. At whatever level, participation must be meaningful to both parties—the learner and the program planner. A program planner who "uses" potential learners' participation to manipulate them into participating and then forgets to use their contribution will see the program ignored.

Although many potential ABE students are not very sophisticated in describing their needs and goals, the program planner must keep in mind how important those goals are to the learners. A program to which the new learner can relate on the first day or evening of attendance is essential. The low literate is very alert to techniques of manipulation, and if a teacher's activities are manipulations rather than a sincere desire to help, it will be known soon enough.

The societal base for program development

Federal legislation that came to grips with the need for ABE programs in the United States was a long time in coming. Major changes in society and social thinking during mid-century made possible the Adult Education Act of 1965. An awareness of the need for higher literacy in the United States finally percolated through the system so that a program for increasing literacy became a priority of Congress and the president. In the movement to legislative and executive recognition, leaders for the program by-passed many who neither recognized the need nor approved of the legislation. Some of these people were in educational systems and were to stand as barriers to early ABE program development and execution in local communities. Some of those people are still around.

To build an ABE curriculum without considering the social base of the learner would be disastrous. An ABE curriculum designed for migrant farm workers must have certain facilities and characteristics that distinguish it from one designed for unemployed auto workers. A "drop in" learning center in the downtown of a city needs a curriculum that can respond to at least several clusters of adults whose social base varies. Elementary teachers have found that it is a mistake to use an elementary school curriculum that treats all children as if they had the same background. ABE teachers have learned that it is a disaster to deal with adults in this way.

The person in charge of ABE program development at the classroom, school, or state level needs to develop means by which data on the clients' social setting can be used in programming. Among the sources of data are community surveys, summaries of the most recent census data in each tract, results of conferences with local businesses, political and educational leaders, results of inquiries with social welfare agencies and those churches with a social concern, and the most recent published reports on social change as it affects lower economic groups.

Once data are available, they must be integrated with the other sources of objectives. The means by which this is done are varied. For some teachers, integration is a very individual task; for others, it is part of the extended program-planning process that heavily involves the potential participants and committees representing the staff and administration. Integration of social data can be formal or informal, but in ABE the learners must see how the finished program ties to the society that they experience. Unless they see this tie, the program will not hold its new learners. The program needs to relate to both the learners' recognized needs and their societal base.

The expert's role in planning ABE programs

The ABE curriculum requires the best thinking and suggestions of many experts. The reading specialist is one of these experts, as are the mathematics specialist and persons specializing in language arts and the social sciences. Specialists in the academic subjects can contribute greatly to the program. They can aid in identifying the key ingredients for beginning reading, the approach to the concept of fractions, the most useful content for use in developing the skill of writing literate sentences, etc.

But there is other content for the ABE curriculum, and there are other experts. If one of the major problems of the low literate is how to cope effectively with the larger society, experts on coping-skill content may be equally important as reading specialists. What real-life problems does the low literate face? Recent research by Northcutt (1975) in selected areas of human need suggests that over one-fourth of the population is "functionally incompetent" in the areas of consumer economics, government and law, problem solving, and computation. In other words, over one-fourth cannot cope. This lack of coping skills is clearly associated with inadequate income, eight or fewer years of schooling, and unemployment or low job status. These and other such evidences on coping deficiencies demonstrate some of the content essential to any ABE program.

Behind much of the effort in American literacy-raising programs is the belief that the literate person will be more likely to be gainfully employed and move from lower- to higher-status jobs. This may be due to the middle-class orientation of those who promote the program and their generally positive belief in the value of education and of work.

A direct tie to the career ladder has often been overlooked in ABE program building. More likely than not, the tie of ABE to a career goal has been more belief than plan. Just because the census data show a remarkably high correlation between years of schooling and income, there is no guarantee that a man with less than eight years of schooling (mean 1972 income = $5235) who takes an ABE class and then prepares for and passes the GED examination will double his salary (mean 1972 income for men with 12 years of schooling = $10,433). These data can be quite devastating to any ABE program when a man believes that his income will double and then finds that it does not.

The dangers of generalizing from census mean income data related to years of schooling must be recognized by ABE program planners. More than any other factor, this danger should provide pressure for the integration of career understanding and vocational-orientation data with the social setting and learner need as programs are developed. There is potential for increased income following completion of ABE and GED programs, but it is unlikely to occur if the completion of the ABE program and the building of sufficient "test wiseness" to pass the GED are not accompanied by a person's ability to cope with the environment and an improved understanding of oneself and new skills in relation to a career.

An integrated program

The ABE program is not something that can be handed down and a demand made that it be followed by everyone in the system. Rather, the program should be a policy guide to the individual teacher working with individual adults. The learning center must have a rich variety of resources. The program should be flexible enough to meet the needs of the problem learner and the adult who was "turned off" by early schooling and who "dropped out" with or without legal sanction. Many of these problems may have been curriculum (program) based, with everyone jumping through the same little hoops. The key to any ABE program is the classroom teacher and aides who pick and choose from among material resources and processes that are meaningful to an individual or to a homogeneous group. The program for the low literate needs structure, but that structure needs to develop and grow as program administrators, teachers, and learners fashion it together.

The integrated program is one that provides a balance among academic, coping, and career-development goals as they affect the individual learner. One can't expect the new adult student to do this balancing alone, but he or she does recognize it when a program responds to all three. An interview with a student in an Indiana prison demonstrates how one new learner perceived the program in academic, coping, and career-related terms (Kreitlow, 1972, pp. 212–215):

Consultant: I want to have you repeat for me some of our conversation about your experience. I am going to have it typed off, in order to show what one man has experienced here.

You went to school here, but you never went to school before?

Student: Yeh, I never went to school on the street.

Consultant: If I remember correctly, you said that when you came in here you could just write your name.

Student: Yeh, my sister helped me, you know, to learn to write my name and tell time.

Consultant: Right.

Student: I could tell what time it is, but I couldn't read.

Consultant: And you were working for auto repair?

Student: Yeh, I was working for _____'s Body Shop.

Consultant: Now, just what can you read today?

Student: Oh, I can read my own mail.

Consultant: How long have you been to class?

Student: In school . . . I'm in here all day.

Consultant: You've been in this class . . .

Student: About ten months.

Consultant: In that time you've learned to read?

Student: Yes, sir!

Consultant: And you now know how to write?

Student: Yeh, I write my own letters. I write my wife about three letters a week, and my sister too. And I read all my own letters.

Consultant: Can you read the newspaper?

Student: Yeh, part of it.

Consultant: Suppose you tell me what parts you like to read?

Student: I read the funny papers, and I try to pick up a little of what's going on.

Consultant: Of course, you're not all that far along are you? You're in, what is it . . . the second, Mr. _____'s class?

Student: Yeh.

Consultant: How do you feel about class? Is it interesting to work all day long?

Student: It is to me.

Consultant: You enjoy it and you learn arithmetic too?

Student: Yeh.

Consultant: You haven't had any numbers before?

Student: No.

Consultant: Except the numbers of the clock?

Student: Yeh.

Consultant: Could you read a bill when it was written out?

Student: No.

Consultant: So this is really changing your life?

Student: Yeh, it's helped me a whole lot.

Consultant: Tell me, we spoke about the other men in the prison, and I asked you if you thought other men could benefit from going here to school; you said you thought there were a lot of men who couldn't read.

Student: **Oh yeh . . . at first, I thought I was the only one who couldn't read. When I was going to work I saw people who was going down the street like this and then I said to myself, they know that I can't read. I thought I was the only one but after I found out, a lot of people can't read. You can't tell by looking at them. But I had a feeling, I'm the only one.**

Consultant: Some people pull off pretty good the fact that they can't read and you don't know it until something happens and you discover they don't know it.

Student: Yeh.

Consultant: Do you think that men don't come up here because they don't know that they can, or just that they don't have the feeling that they can do it?

Student: You can't tell. I couldn't tell.

Consultant: You didn't believe you could do it?

Student: No.

Consultant: How did you get into this class?

Student: I talked to Mr. _____ and I met another guy and **he said, "Take a crack at it."**

Consultant: You decided to take a crack at it and found that you could. That's great.

Student: **I learned something new every day. The more I pick them words up, the more I want to. I got a lot of books in my cell and I read 'um and pick up what I can.**

Consultant: How about use of Television-TV? or films? Do they show films often?

Student: Yeh, they show films often, but I don't like to watch 'em . . . I rather work in books.

Consultant: You prefer to work in books. That is interesting. How about TV?

Student: We have TV out in the field house.

Consultant: So it's for recreation?

Student: Yeh, sometimes I go, but I usually stay in the cell. When the rest of 'em are gone the place is quiet and I can concentrate. That's what I need. That'll help me meet the Board . . . and when I get out.

Consultant: Yes, that'll help you.

Student: You see, like I was telling you, when I get out my boss's got a job for me and I can use this in my job . . . I'll be able to do a lot more for him.

Consultant: What's this paper you've brought? Today's work?

Student: Yeh, some of the words I've been writing.

Consultant: Can you read this to me?

> Student: Yeh ... I wrote it down there. (He read off perfectly—and then told how he would write plurals of some irregular forms.)
>
> Consultant: It's hard to believe you never went to school, isn't it?
>
> Student: **Yeh, it sure makes me feel good. I wish everybody could know what good it does him to read and write. I didn't know how well I was doing until one day I showed Mr. _____ ... then I wrote to my boss, sort of afraid I didn't write too well. He wrote back, "That's a very good letter!"**

The inmate's responses to questioning illustrated academic, coping, and career needs: *academic,* "I couldn't read"; *coping,* "That'll help me meet the board ..."; *career,* "I can use this in my job." The inmate's description shows that he did recognize these three areas in the program as it was organized for him.

The ABE program and institutional philosophy

It is important that the ABE program conform to the goals and philosophy of its supporting institution. A public school that emphasizes an academic tradition and that values efficient means for reaching predefined ends would approve of a tightly structured ABE program. Such a school would be suspicious of a program with guidelines that emphasized the role of individual learners' contributing to the curriculum.

A program left largely unplanned until a dialogue is established between teachers and learner, as proposed by Paulo Freiere (1970), would likely be shunned by most ABE programs in the schools. Such a program may be accepted heartily by planners in a Community Action Program, however, in which a low literate's power to control his or her own destiny is of high priority in the program.

There needs to be a reasonable fit between institutional philosophy and the program process. The needs of the economically disadvantaged and low literates became so severe in the United States that programs organized to respond to these needs were more flexible than were the usual programs of the educational institutions. The public schools looked to their most creative and innovative teachers and supervisors to design the programs. As a result, learning laboratories and resource centers are now considered essential, teaching machines and programed instruction are available in most, and a one-to-one relationship between teacher and learner is more possible than in elementary and secondary schools, where the teacher-pupil ratio is higher.

The format of an ABE program will vary according to the process used to determine needs. The educational institution must be ready to accept the variations that involvement in planning will produce. Without this acceptance, client involvement in the planning process is futile. Some adult education agencies would prefer to view program development as book selection by an authoritarian teacher or administrator. Under this type of planning, the content is directly controlled to fit the philosophy of the agency. There is no solid research evidence to show that one approach is superior to the other.

Adult performance level

The most extensive effort to develop a set of guidelines and specific objectives for ABE programs on the national level was made in the Adult Performance Level project at the University of Texas (Northcutt, 1975). Many of the previously mentioned guides to program development were used in arriving at a curriculum model. This project had as its objectives: (1) the specification of the competencies an adult needs in order to achieve economic and educational success in modern society, and (2) the development of devices to assess those competencies.

In arriving at the competencies, the project staff sought input from most of the sources suggested earlier in this chapter. For example, the staff carefully reviewed past behavioral and social research about undereducated and underemployed adults, conducted extensive surveys of agencies and foundations in an effort to distinguish successful from unsuccessful adults, conferred with specialists in both the public and private sectors, and interviewed many undereducated and unemployed persons. Although an examination of society and social-change phenomena were not direct aspects of the staff's formulation, these phenomena were given significant weight in the findings obtained from the other sources. Following the data gathering and identification of needed adult competencies, the project staff chose to eliminate the words "literacy" and "illiteracy" from their reports and to use the term "functional competency" instead. Thus the model developed to describe curriculum or program needs was based on "adult functional competency."

The reading teacher should not be alarmed in thinking that ABE programs based on such a model will eliminate reading from the curriculum. On the contrary, the opportunity for a functional use of reading as part of the program is essential. What the model does do is demonstrate how academic skills are functionally integrated with coping skills and career-building concepts.

An advantage of such a model is the ease with which a classroom teacher can use it as a guide in making a clear tie-in between academic skill development and the knowledge areas of importance to a disadvantaged adult.

Figure 15.1 shows the functional competency model as developed in the

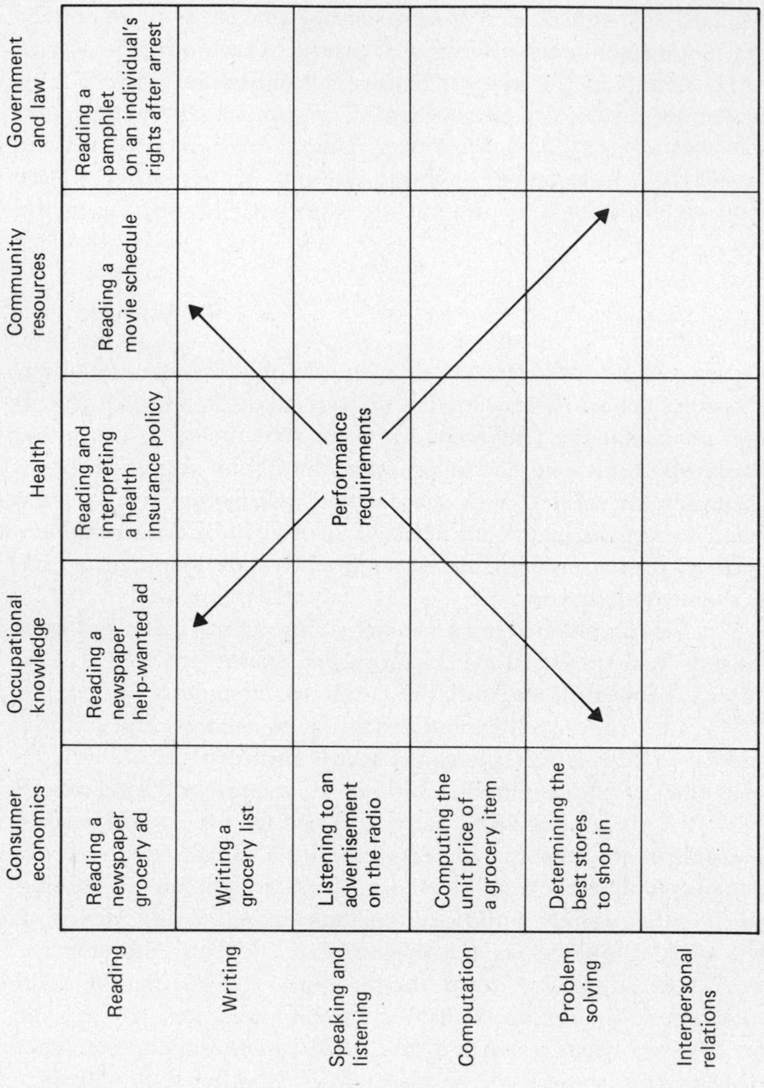
Consumer economics
Occupational knowledge
Health
Community resources
Government and law
Reading
Writing
Speaking and listening
Computation
Problem solving
Interpersonal relations
Reading a newspaper grocery ad
Reading a newspaper help-wanted ad
Reading and interpreting a health insurance policy
Reading a movie schedule
Reading a pamphlet on an individual's rights after arrest
Writing a grocery list
Listening to an advertisement on the radio
Computing the unit price of a grocery item
Determining the best stores to shop in
Performance requirements

Fig. 15.1. The APL literacy model.

project. The horizontal axis identifies the general areas of need, or "general knowledge areas," that were identified from the many resources examined and interviews and discussions held: (1) consumer economics, (2) occupational or occupationally related knowledge, (3) community resources, (4) health, and (5) government and law. Although there are other general knowledge areas, the project team judged these five to be the most critical.

The vertical axis identifies the four primary skills that are believed to account for the vast majority of requirements placed on adults in the United States today. These skills are in the areas of: (1) communication (reading, writing, speaking, and listening), (2) computation, (3) problem solving, and (4) interpersonal relations.

Using the APL model shown in Fig. 15.1, it was possible for the APL project staff to identify a number of important competencies in each cell, write behavioral objectives related to that competency, and develop an APL curriculum module for any of the objectives. This APL module included a statement of the objective, a discussion of the learning outcome expected, a matrix of the skills needed in each task, a matrix outlining the problem-solving level of each task, a series of tasks identifying teaching/learning activities and materials, and lists of teachers' resources. In developing examples of curriculum modules, the project staff chose materials and used resources that an adult would normally encounter in daily life, such as newspaper ads, tapes of radio and TV commercials, flyers, catalogs, etc.

In reporting on the project, the staff noted that the level of competency was associated with income, education, and employment status. Data on these three factors were used to describe three performance levels: APL 1, APL 2, and APL 3. These levels are described in some detail by Northcutt (1975).

1. *"APL 1"—adults who function with difficulty.* APL 1's are those adults whose mastery of competency objectives is associated with: *inadequate income* (poverty level or less), *inadequate education* (eight years or less of school), and *unemployment or occupations of low job status.*

2. *"APL 2"—functional adults.* APL 2's are those adults whose mastery of competency objectives is associated with: *income of more than poverty level* but no discretionary income, *education of nine to eleven* years of school, and occupations falling in *menial job* status range.

3. *"APL 3"—proficient adults.* APL 3's are those adults whose mastery of competency objectives is associated with: *high levels of income* or varying amounts of discretionary income, *high levels of education* (high school completion or more), and *high levels of job status.*

Those persons classified as APL 1 are, by and large, "functionally incompetent"—adults who function with difficulty; APL 2's are competent—adults who function at a minimum level; and APL 3's are proficient in that their mastery of competency objectives is associated with the highest levels of income, job status, and education.

On a survey designed to be representative nationally, it is possible to estimate the proportion of American adults comprising each of the APL levels. The project did this through a subcontract with the Opinion Research

Corporation and reported in 1975 (Northcutt, 1975). In addition to overall data on the specific knowledge and skill areas, selected demographic data were also described and categorized by APL competency levels. A summary from one of the project reports follows.

Competency levels by knowledge area and skills. The percentages of the adult population which are in APL levels 1, 2 or 3 as determined by performance on those indicators in the survey which measure knowledge and skills are presented in the following table.

Areas	APL competency levels 1	2	3
Occupational Knowledge	19.1	31.9	49.0
Consumer Economics	29.4	33.0	37.6
Government and Law	25.8	26.2	48.0
Health	21.3	30.3	48.3
Community Resources	22.6	26.0	51.4
Reading	21.7	32.2	46.1
Problem Solving	28.0	23.4	48.5
Computation	32.9	26.3	40.8
Writing	16.4	25.5	58.1
Overall Competency Levels	19.7	33.9	46.3

In terms of the general knowledge areas, the greatest area of difficulty appears to be Consumer Economics. Almost 30% of the population falls into the lowest level (APL 1), while one-third of the population is categorized as APL 2. Translated into population figures, some 34.7 million adult Americans function with difficulty and an additional 39 million are functional (but not proficient) in coping with basic requirements that are related to Consumer Economics.

The highest proportion of proficient persons (most able to cope) is found in relation to Community Resources. Over half of the U.S. population falls into APL level 3. This is followed by Occupational Knowledge; again, almost half of the population is estimated to be proficient in dealing with occupationally-related tasks. Although the least proportion of persons in comparison to all areas are in level 1 of Occupational Knowledge, this still indicates that about one of every five adults in the U.S. function with difficulty or are unable to perform correctly on occupationally related performance indicators.

A greater proportion of people is unable to perform basic computations than the other skills. Approximately one-third of the population, or 39 million adults, functions with difficulty, and a little over one-fourth, or 29.5 million adults, is functional but not proficient in task performance on items requiring mathematical manipulation. The area of greatest competency in comparison with other skills is in writing. However, even though almost three-fifths of the population performed adequately on tasks requiring writing skills, 16% of the adults in the U.S., or, some 18.9 million persons, are unable to cope successfully.

Competency levels by demographic groupings. The purpose for selecting certain demographic groupings and comparing the results within a group is to discover trends which might arise. As seen in the definitions given earlier for the APL three competency levels, "success" was an important variable in the study. In general, the three success indices (level of education, family income and job status) demonstrate a positive relationship with performance. The percent of the population estimated to be in APL levels 1, 2, and 3 for each reporting group of relevant demographic variables as indicated by task performance is presented in the following table.

| | *APL competency levels* | | |
Demographic variables	1	2	3
Education:			
0–3 years	85%	10%	6%
4–5	84	16	0
6–7	49	37	14
8–11	18	55	27
High school completed	11	37	52
Some college	9	27	64
College graduate plus	2	17	80
Family Income:			
under $5000	40%	39%	21%
$5000–$6999	20	44	36
$7000–$9999	24	39	37
$10,000–$14,999	14	34	52
$15,000 plus	8	26	66
Job Status:			
Unskilled	30%	38%	32%
Semi-skilled	29	42	29
Skilled	24	33	43
Clerical-Sales	8	38	54
Professional-Managerial	11	28	61
Age:			
18–29	16%	35%	49%
30–39	11	29	60

Demographic variables	APL competency levels		
	1	2	3
40–49	19	32	49
50–59	28	37	35
60–65	35	40	24
Sex:			
Male	17%	31%	52%
Female	23	35	42
Ethnicity:			
White	16%	34%	50%
Black	44	39	17
Spanish-surname	56	26	18
Other	26	41	33
Occupational Status:			
Employed	15%	28%	57%
Unemployed	36	30	34
Housewives	27	38	35
Number in Household:			
1 person	21%	23%	56%
2–3	20	35	45
4–5	19	31	50
6–7	21	33	46
8 plus	43	22	35
Region:			
Northeast	16%	36%	48%
North Central	15	42	43
South	25	37	38
West	15	35	50
Metropolitan Areas:			
1 million plus	21%	39%	40%
under 1 million	15	38	47
Suburb	21	32	47
Urban	14	29	57

In relation to the "success" variables, for level of education the percentage of APL 1's rises steadily from about 2% for college graduates to about 85% for adults with less than 4 years of formal schooling. For family income, the percentage of functionally incompetent persons rises from about 8% for incomes of $15,000 or greater to 40% for those under

$5000 a year. For occupation of chief wage earner, the percentage of APL 1's rises from about 11% for the professional and managerial category to approximately 30% for the unskilled.

There is a generally negative relationship between age and performance. Although the youngest group (18–29) does not have the lowest level of functionally incompetent adults, still the general trend is that the older the individual, the more likely that he/she is incompetent. It appears that males and females perform about the same; although there are minor differences with males estimated to have a greater percentage of APL 3's than females. As for ethnic groups, it appears that there are great differences between Whites and all other minority groups. While 16% of the Whites are estimated to be functionally incompetent, about 44% of the Black and 56% of the Spanish-surname groups are estimated to be so. Here, as with other variables that have been discussed, the differences are probably due to the relatively lower levels of income, education, job status, and job opportunity found among minority groups in this country.

The employed show a smaller percentage of APL 1's (15%) than did housewives (27%) who, in turn, show a smaller percentage than did the unemployed (36%). Here, again, the differences in the "success" levels (i.e., amount of income, etc.) of especially the employed and unemployed may be used to explain the variations.

With regard to the number of people in the household, the only apparent difference in percentage of APL 1's occurred in households where more than 7 people lived. While for most household populations, the percentage of functional incompetents is about 20%, for the eight or greater group, the percentage rises to 43%.

The demographic comparison of regions of the U.S. indicates that while the Northeast, North Central and Western parts of the U.S. have about the same percentage of APL 1's, 2's, and 3's, the South has more APL 1's and less APL 3's. While all other regions of the country are estimated to have about 16% functionally incompetent adults, approximately 25% in the South are predicted to be APL's. Thus, a greater percentage of adults in the South appear to be in need of educational assistance than other parts of the country.

Rural areas have the greatest estimated percentage of APL 1's (27%) with cities over one million and suburbs slightly less (about 21%), and cities under one million and other urban areas having the least percentage of APL 1's.*

---

* N. Northcutt, *Adult Functional Competency: A Summary,* Austin: The University of Texas, Adult Performance Level Project, 1975. Reprinted by permission.

These data clearly indicate the large numbers of adults in the United States whose competency falls far short of mastery of very simple skills. The data show how closely related the lack of mastery is to limited formal education, to lower job status, and to lower family income. In addition, the adults who function with difficulty are shown to be a greater proportion of the population in rural areas and in the South.

The APL project provides the ABE classroom teacher with a wealth of data about low literates and their characteristics. These data can be used as a guide if verified in terms of the community situation and the agency in which one works.

In program development, teachers need all the help they can get. ABE calls for great individualization in planning and execution. Many low literates suffer from just that flaw in their earlier education; teachers had limited time for individualization of instruction and even less for planning. ABE teachers need all the help they can get from books, curriculum guides, resource centers, and understanding and knowledgeable administrators.

THE LEARNER IN THE ABE PROGRAM

By now you should be aware of some of the characteristics of the learner in an ABE program. You may even wonder how it is possible for programs to attract one million low literates each year. It isn't easy, and the drop-out rate is often over 50 percent.

A safe environment

One of the primary ingredients of a sound ABE program is an environment that gives the new enrollee some sense of security. Although physical safety may be a part of this, psychic security is the greatest need. A person who has had so much experience at losing doesn't want to take a chance at losing again. The ease of physical entry, the interior decor, and the friendly faces of staff and other students should all be inviting. Potential learners for ABE programs don't line up at the school house door waiting to get in. If by some miracle they do get to the door and have to wait, it is unlikely that they will wait long.

The potential for a "drop-in" is almost totally eliminated in ABE when classes and the learning labs are housed in elementary and secondary schools. To get potential learners in requires planning, work, overcoming personal and community barriers, and also overcoming the low literate adult's negative image of both self and schools.

To put even five percent of a community's potential learners into a program is a creditable achievement. A history of failure in school, past and present prejudice against the disadvantaged low-literate poor (a self-concept little understood and long ignored by middle-class teachers), and the uncomfortableness of gambling on a strange situation—all build a high wall between student and classroom. Only a few have penetrated or climbed over that wall.

ABE directors and teachers often forget, or never knew, how physically exhausting it is to work eight hours a day at an unskilled job with little hope of advancement. Nor do they understand how emotionally exhausting it is for a mother on ADC to get through another day. ABE classes are not very high on the priority list of choices for use of available time.

A low literate's physical, emotional, and intellectual margin can be very limited. It should be easy for new learners to enter the program. They need an understanding of their problem by the staff and an opportunity to be with old friends or make new ones. They need the security of knowing that it is their decision to stay or leave as they wish. The ABE program should be a place for learning in an atmosphere of freedom and trust. When this occurs the program is like a second family to the learners. In superior programs there are numerous instances of both husband and wife participating. Often one will start and if the program is "safe," the other will come. Likewise, a young adult may start and if "safe," parents will enroll.

The need for counseling

There are only a few professional counselors in any adult education program. This is also true in the special programs for low-literate adults. Yet in ABE the need for perceptive and skilled counselors is essential. The special characteristics of ABE learners call for the best the field of counseling has to offer.

Counseling is part of a system of guidance designed to help individuals realize their full potential. Poor counseling or no counseling in the elementary grades and in high school may be part of the reason for low literacy among adults. No one stood between the potential dropout and inconsiderate demands of school systems bent on uniformity of objectives. In some systems, Carnegie Units were more sacred than human needs. Without counseling, many of today's low literates were virtually programed to drop out, to build a negative self-image in relation to learning, and to see school personnel as the "enemy."

Counselors are needed to help the institution adjust to the student as much as to help the student adjust to the institution. When school counselors are not assigned to adult counseling in the ABE program, that role should be carried out by someone else—perhaps the program director, but more likely the teacher or a paraprofessional.

If the classroom teachers wish to transfer the counseling role to system counselors, it is important that these counselors understand the needs and characteristics of the ABE student. In many instances it would be better for the program to have limited counseling by the teacher who understands the student's problem than to have a great deal of counseling by a counselor who treats the ABE student as a hopeless failure, who administers a battery of tests, and who has no perception of the social and economic survival problems the student faces each day.

Short-term achievement, long-term goals

Learning to read, passing the GED examination, and learning to keep the accounts as a newly elected treasurer for a small local church are rather long-term goals for the low literate. Recognizing the letters in one's own name, being able to find one's home town on a map, and being able to add a four-column, four-row series of expenses are short-term objectives.

The person entering an ABE program at Level I in reading and mathematics (zero to about grade four)* may have high hopes on long-term goals, but must have the satisfaction that comes with achieving something. ABE teachers have a very special responsibility with Level I students—to provide for recognized achievements each time a student attends a class or a learning center. Short-term achievements are important for Level II (grades four to six) students as well as for Level III (grades six to eight). It is considerably easier to provide experiences that give achievement to those who can already do some of their own decoding, can add and subtract, can listen to and discuss the news of the day, and can handle an oral conversation with a reasonable level of thought and understanding.

Open enrollment and alternative routes

Two aspects of ABE programs need to be especially flexible—the enrollment procedure and the learning modes. When a potential learner for an ABE program, contacted by a teacher, volunteer, recruiter, or an ABE student, asks, "When can I begin?" the answer must be, "Right away." Suggestions that the recruit wait until next semester, next month, or even next week should be avoided. When a low literate is ready to begin, begin. Very often these early beginnings can build that rapport that makes it possible at a later date to move to selective groupings, to change sections, or even to changes in the day or evening of the week that the learner attends. In beginning new ABE programs, the sponsoring agency needs to be ready to forego all general policies that guide the more standard, middle-class adult offerings that may

---

* ABE levels should not be related directly to elementary grade levels, but clues to these levels in the academic areas are helpful. The teacher needs to keep in mind that adult's general knowledge and experience base far surpass children's, and in some areas, the teacher's.

require eight, ten, or twelve students to start a class. In ABE it is essential to start—even with but one student—and build from there.

Just as ABE enrollment and numbers of students in a program require flexibility, so does the learning program itself. Simply remembering that the ABE student likely "failed" in the old system or that the old system "failed" the individual should be enough to open up the ABE program to flexibility. This does not mean a lack of academic discipline, but rather making the most positive use of the discipline of education. It is here that knowledge of the learner, methods and techniques of teaching, and the objectives of the learning program can be integrated into a positive achievement.

PROGRAM RESOURCES

An effective ABE program properly orchestrates the resources at the disposal of program personnel. An effective program is the result of the correct mix of human, physical, organizational, and financial resources. A breakdown in any one of these resource areas will damage the entire program.

Human resources

The primary human resources in a program are the administrators, teachers, teacher aides, and others with special responsibilities, e.g., recruiters and counselors. When ABE began from almost ground zero in 1965, it was often necessary to select administrators and teachers to start the programs and to organize in-service programs to improve them on the job. By 1976 on-the-job improvement was of continuing importance, but in ten years a sufficient number of academic programs for ABE staff had been developed in colleges and universities to provide a great deal of preservice training. During this ten-year period federal funds stimulated an effort to upgrade those selected to organize and staff ABE programs. Since much of ABE began with part-time administrators and teachers, there was a great turnover of staff and a continuing need for in-service programs. Some administrators and teachers were more concerned about the extra pay from "moonlighting" than about the disadvantaged students. Such personnel either left the program early, thus requiring the search for new part-time employees, or they became very committed to the program after recognizing the contributions it could make in the lives of the low literates.

Although administrators were sometimes able to find teaching aides with professional qualifications, most aides were selected for their basic understanding of the poor and the low literate. After the program had developed, some aides were those who had successfully completed work in ABE and had gone on to the GED program. Whether aides were professionally trained or not, it was believed important to provide special in-service programs for them, and this was done on the local, state, and regional levels.

Counselors for many ABE programs were borrowed part-time from elementary or secondary schools. Though professionals prepared for counseling, they often had no understanding of, nor much sympathy for, the special group of learners in ABE. As did some teachers and administrators in the public elementary and secondary schools, they too looked at the low literate as one of their failures. This attitude has made it essential to choose part-time counselors carefully and insofar as possible to provide in-service training for them.

Physical resources

In the first years of ABE programs, the most typical physical facility was a classroom—most often in an elementary or secondary school, sometimes in a church or in a public building (village hall or library), and occasionally in a commercial building or factory. But it was a classroom that administrators and teachers looked for. This has changed. Although the basic shell of the physical resource may be the same (the floor, four walls, and a ceiling), the resources in that shell have changed from chairs and desks to tables and carrels. Instead of closets to hold books, there is now open shelving to display instructional materials and equipment. Every effort has been made to eliminate the traditional classroom atmosphere. The result of this move has led to the change from classrooms to learning centers (often called learning laboratories or resource centers). Today when administrators or teachers look for the physical resources to house a new ABE class, they determine whether or not the resource can be made into a learning center.

Although physical resources are still largely in schools, the advent of the learning-center concept has resulted in a trend toward the use of off-street rented buildings in urban areas of high illiteracy, so as to make "walk-in" recruiting possible. In addition, mobile learning centers have been developed for rural areas. This has meant changing a bus or mobile home into a place for learning.

The move from classroom to learning center has been correlated with a move from limited numbers and variety of learning tools to a rich array of such resources. The classroom with a teacher and several sets of books and a few workbooks has given way to an individualized instructional system that still has the teacher and the books, but also has a multitude of commercially and locally prepared materials. Some are programed, some are self-instructional, and some use a multimedia system. There are language masters, tape and cassette recorders, record players, video tape recorders and playback systems, autotutors, various reading and math systems, film strips, and more. The concept of the learning center is most conducive to building a learning environment that is a far cry from the barren room and sterile learning program that often led today's low literate out of school at an early age.

Organizational resources

Adult Basic Education has been greatly aided by various government agencies and related institutions that recognize the need and cooperate with the program. The leadership given to ABE by the Office of Education (USOE) and its regional offices could well be a model for other segments of the educational enterprise. Funding of special staff-development projects, flexibility in programing, and coordination of in-service education at a regional level have all been part of that leadership thrust. State departments of education and local districts had to gamble in developing their first programs. Many of these gambles were innovative—such as the first learning centers—and they became models for others.

In some states, colleges and universities were willing to accept much of the responsibility for organizing and carrying through special in-service programs in everything from teaching reading to adults to evaluating the improvement in coping skills in new adult learners. Other government agencies cooperated with local school districts and the states in serving the new ABE learner. Where the Cooperative Extension Service of the United States Department of Agriculture had concerned agents, there were efforts to bring health and nutrition information into ABE programs. Social welfare services aided in recruiting students. Community action progams volunteered the use of their buildings for learning centers. In addition, many private organizations, such as churches, fraternal organizations, and service clubs, aided in recruiting, supplying materials, and in some instances donating physical facilities.

Financial resources

It is unlikely that ABE would have grown as much as it has without the initial financial stimulation provided by the federal government. Low literacy is a national problem, and substantial support should come from the national level. It is also a state problem, and each year this has become more clearly recognized. Over the last ten years there has been an increasing outlay of funds for ABE in state budgets. The same is true for local school districts which recognize that low literacy is their problem too. This combination of federal, state, and local financial resources for ABE should continue until the illiteracy problem is solved.

Reducing illiteracy to the point where only the uneducatable fall into that category is a reasonable goal for any country. That certain other countries have surpassed the United States in meeting this goal should be and is an embarrassment. The framework for federal, state, and local cooperation to meet this goal is sound, and if pursued diligently the goal will be met.

Reading specialists may well find this a cause to which they wish to dedicate their time and expertise.

REFERENCES

Baltes, P. B., K. W. Schai, and H. H. Nardi "Age and Experimental Mortality in a Seven-Year Longitudinal Study of Cognitive Behavior," *Developmental Psychology* 5 (1971): 18–26.

Davis, A. *Social Class Influences Upon Learning,* Cambridge, Mass.: Harvard University Press, 1962.

Freiere, P. *Pedagogy of the Oppressed,* New York: Herder and Herder, 1970.

Kreitlow, B. *Adult Basic Education—An Improvement Evaluation,* Indianapolis: Indiana State Department of Public Instruction, 1972.

Northcutt, N. *Adult Functional Competency: A Summary,* Austin: University of Texas, 1975.

O'Neil, W. "Properly Literate," *Harvard Educational Review* 40 (1970): 260–263.

UNESCO *Literacy as a Factor in Development,* Paris: UNESCO, Minedlit, 3, 1965.

Chapter 16

MEDIA IN READING INSTRUCTION

SHIRLEY C. FELDMANN • *The City College, City University of New York*

Although media materials have long been used in classroom reading programs, they have played a relatively minor role, e.g., a slide series or set of records used to supplement the major reading lesson. Their potential as a major source for direct reading learning remained untapped until the 1960s, when more significant change was seen in reading practices and materials than had occurred in the entire period since 1900. One major factor in this change was the explosion of educational technology, which provided a variety of inexpensive equipment for individual use. As a result, production of multimedia materials for school use has increased, with filmstrips, tapes, television, 8-mm film loops, cassettes, etc., inundating the educational market. Such media materials have become so educationally "desirable" that even the most traditional reading programs now include some media materials in their total packages.

In addition to the increased availability of media materials and the production of inexpensive, easily operated equipment, a major shift has also occurred in educational thinking. Educators have begun to seek reading methods and materials which can meet the needs of individual children with special learning characteristics. Such concerns have resulted in the construction of varied instructional programs and materials for use with either individuals or small groups and which permit many levels of instruction to operate simultaneously in the same classroom. As the quality of such materials has begun to improve, the advantages of a media approach have become more evident to educators. In addition to facilitating an individualized learning approach, such materials also provide a broad base for learning by including many vicarious experiences from outside the classroom walls. The use of motion, color, music, and drama to focus on ideas or events gives to learning sensory dimensions not possible through books or conversation. Media materials bring both variety of experience and the possibility of many approaches to learning the needed reading skills and competences.

Today the variety of materials and programs available on the educational market seems unlimited. Multimedia kits, tape programs, and filmstrip series are available to function as either supplements to reading programs or programs in themselves. The overhead projector, tape recorder, TV set, and filmstrip projector are so familiar to teachers today that curriculum use of media materials is not likely to be disputed. The larger questions concern, however, their value in the learning process and managing equipment and programs within the classroom itself.

INFLUENCE OF CULTURAL MEDIA ON CHILDREN

It seems curious that educators have not adopted a media approach more readily, considering the vast influence the media have had on children's learning and experiences outside of the school. Television programing has been a primary source of learning and entertainment during the last 30 years, yet it was only in the 1960s that serious thought was given to using television educationally within schools. Psychologists claim that large numbers of children spend more hours watching television each week than they spend in school. Apparently television affords them a more interesting variety of entertainment and information than they have ever experienced in school. Perhaps today's children are astute in their preference for television, for they are no doubt better informed and educated about many aspects of life than were children of previous generations.

Television, of course, is not the only popular medium of education for children. The easy accessibility to and relatively low cost of media such as records, radio, films, and tape recorders have facilitated widespread transmission of a pop culture, with a tendency for "instant" coverage of events, fads, or ideas, no matter what their ultimate importance. Children of today seem accustomed to a media-dominated world that bombards them continually with messages they receive through various sensory channels. Scholastic achievement seems to play no role in this media world, so even the poor reader has access to this communication network. Paradoxically, this child may be considered well "educated" in his or her own world, even though considered an academic failure in school.

Two characteristics of the child's media culture seem to affect school learning, and both may tend to widen the gap between the poor reader's interest in his or her own world and in the traditional curriculum of the school. First, since commercial media need to hold the attention of the listener or viewer in order to overcome the lure of competing media, considerable time and money are spent in providing interesting and polished performances. As a result, commercial media are doubtless more attractive and sophisticated than most school curricula could ever be. School programs have not been able to match the lively and attractive materials produced by many commercial media.

Second, little is expected of the viewer or listener while partaking of the media. The relationship is a passive one, requiring no feedback or response of any kind from the viewer. One merely expects to be entertained without any individual effort. This is in sharp contrast to school, where active participation in learning is often required. Thus school programs, having less interesting materials and yet requiring active participation in learning, offer little competition to the highly sophisticated media materials from the child's world. It is not hard to understand why many children who are having trouble with school learning may prefer to be part of the less demanding media culture than to attempt to ameliorate their failures in school.

USE OF MEDIA MATERIAL WITH PROBLEM READERS

As the poor reader grows older, his or her values and interests from the outside world may begin to conflict with those of the school. Finding the outside culture more comfortable than that of the school, the poor reader's already weakened motivation to learn in school may increase, thus widening the gap between the two worlds. One possible way to bridge such a gap is to bring the media culture of television and tapes with which the learner is already familiar into the classroom learning situation. There are several advantages to this approach.

First, use of a variety of media is often highly motivating to the poor reader, whose previous failure in learning, usually over an extended period, often results in a conviction of inability to learn or of being "slow." Although this conviction can be manifested in several ways, it most often surfaces as decreased motivation in the reading-learning situation. The reader is likely to show apathy or distaste for traditional materials and methods, since such have not worked in previous learning situations. Media materials such as filmstrips, 8-mm loops, tapes, and cassettes represent a fresh start. Not only do they seem to be less schoollike, but they are also familiar media from the child's outside world and thus are less threatening.

Media materials also have special characteristics that may both attract the learner and enhance the learning process. For example, color seems inherently appealing, and it can also be used to highlight features requiring extra attention in the learning sequence, such as beginning digraphs or punctuation marks. Music has long been used in commercial media to provide underlying rhythm, bridges for action, or dramatization of mood. Such functions could be exploited in educational films and tapes. For example, music could aid in learning names or rules, as alphabet songs have shown for so long. It could provide emphasis for pronunciation of multisyllable words or teach intonation of sentences. Visual animation can show word parts joining, sentences becoming transposed, or other word/sentence relationships impossible to portray in static materials. Dramatic rendering of stories or poetry by public figures or actors may provide a clearer meaning than when read by peers. Some media forms, such as tapes and filmstrips, can be stopped or rerun at any particular point and thus are advantageous for repetitious presentation of skills, if needed. Such materials also have the capability of building in repetition, with slight variations each time to insure practice without boredom.

Probably a most important advantage is that media materials can provide the problem reader with individualized instruction for a minimum of effort. For the reader who learns better visually, film loops or filmstrips will give practice in word-analysis skills. The reader needing more language experiences may benefit from taped stories. The teacher may assign a supplementary videotape to several children to reinforce the reading skills presented to the larger reading group earlier in the day. Media materials may provide the repetitious practice needed by one child, thus freeing the teacher to introduce new concepts or to read with that child. Since poor readers often seem to need twice as much time and effort to master simple skills in reading, well-planned media activities or programs may allow for those extra opportunities without taking the teacher away from the rest of the class.

Despite the strong arguments favoring the use of media materials, there are some possible disadvantages which, although not inherent in such materials, could distract the poor reader from the intended learning. It is possible that extended use of varied materials and media could fragment the learning experiences if a well-articulated program has not been outlined. Also, the attractions of the hardware and resultant mechanical operations may distract some children from attending to the concepts that are the focus of the materials. For other children, the entertainment value of some materials may overwhelm the intended learning goals. These are common problems for poor readers, however, as such children may resist learning in many ways until they are convinced that they *can* learn. The teacher must be alert to any distracting characteristics in materials and instead attempt to present the skills more clearly and with proper pacing and balancing between attractiveness and learning potential. Although this is a large order for any teacher, well-designed media materials may help to meet that challenge.

DESCRIPTION OF MEDIA MATERIALS

Media materials may be divided into three general groups. These groups may overlap, but each seems to have dominant features: visual materials, auditory materials, and multimedia materials, or those combining auditory and visual modes.

Visual materials

Visual media, in the form of filmstrips and slides, have been familiar tools in the classroom, but until inexpensive versions of the hardware were made available in the recent decade, they had little potential for flexible use. In the past, visual materials served primarily as enrichment activities for the language-arts curriculum. Slides or filmstrips were typically viewed by the whole class, with images projected on a large screen hung in front of the darkened classroom. With the recent introduction of small desk models of filmstrip projectors, 8-mm film-loop projectors, and slide and transparency equipment, there has been a shift of emphasis from whole-group presentation to use with individuals or small groups. Now the filmstrip projector is more often used at a table in a corner of the room, and the visual images are projected on a small table screen or into a shadow box. Thus the class is freed from a whole-group activity, and the teacher is no longer involved in management of the lesson. Such individual use also allows for a wider range of possible goals for the visual lessons themselves. Visual materials can be used as needed for direct teaching, for reinforcement of skills, for checking concepts, for enrichment, or for pleasure.

Although many visual materials are available, they are somewhat limited because they lack an auditory component. Although some materials, such as 8-mm film loops, do include limited animation, most merely project still images or print onto a screen. However, a major attraction of visual materials may be their color; it is often used in filmstrips to highlight concepts or skills, such as pointing out the existence of prefixes or long vowels. For some poor readers, visual materials have inherent difficulties. If they are to be used independently, directions for their use must be presented through a visual mode. The poor reader who cannot use print very well to decode messages thus requires either a very lucid pictorial explanation or carefully controlled text and vocabulary. Thus for some readers, visual materials have the same disadvantages as do books, unless the materials have been carefully chosen and monitored by the teacher.

Other visual materials seem better suited to the problem reader. Filmstrips presenting stories or folktales in pictures, film loops dealing with a single picturable reading concept, such as sequence, may be attractive and useful. Such materials may be more appropriate as supplementary reinforcement materials than as primary skills-instruction materials, because of the difficulties poor readers have in comprehending new ideas from visual-only materials.

Visual materials lend themselves easily to small-group use. When a particular reading group needs practice with compound words, the students can work on their assignment together by viewing a filmstrip. Another group, preparing to write a story based on a folktale, may review the story first on a film loop. A transparency may be used to help two learners to review sight words before they read a story in their basal readers. Photographs can be taken of an individual project or a class experience and then made into slides for a class presentation. For problem readers who have not fully grasped the relationship between stories and printed materials, a familiar story viewed on a filmstrip may aid them in reading the story more easily when they later encounter it in a book. All such activities may be more valuable than dozens of workbook pages in terms of motivation and learner involvement in the media lessons.

Available materials

1. Controlled Reading Program

    EDL/McGraw-Hill
    Hightstown, N.J. 08520

    Filmstrips include skills of concentration, observation, and logical reasoning—for intermediate-level readers.

2. Craig Reading Skills Program

    Craig Education
    921 W. Artesia Blvd.
    Compton, Cal. 90220

    Slides present context, root words, and dictionary skills—for readers above fourth-grade level.

3. Early Reading Recognition Skills
    I can Read Signs

    Miller-Brady Productions, Inc.
    342 Madison Ave.
    New York, N.Y. 10017

    Color filmstrips present phonic skills in the first set and familiar sight words in the second—for beginning readers.

4. Holt/Ealing Reading Skills Series I and II

    Holt, Rinehart and Winston, Inc.
    383 Madison Ave.
    New York, N.Y. 10017

    Eight-mm color loops of four minutes each include various vowel sounds —for elementary-level readers.

5. Weston Woods Filmstrips

Weston Woods Studio
Weston, Conn. 06880

Color filmstrips depict familiar stories and folktales—for beginning readers.

6. Words and Sounds Series—Sets II, III, IV

McGraw-Hill Films
1221 Avenue of the Americas
New York, N.Y. 10021

Color filmstrips include consonant and vowel sounds, as well as teachers' guide—for elementary-level readers.

Auditory materials

The teaching-learning functions of records, tapes, and cassettes have also been greatly expanded in recent years. Records, once the province of music and dramatic productions, now provide phonics programs and vocabulary-building programs as well. The size and weight of the record player once was a formidable factor for classroom use, but today's small, plastic portable units can be easily handled by the youngest student. Records, although now less bulky and nonbreakable, are still somewhat inflexible in terms of re-playing a particular portion of the recording. As a result, tapes seem to be more suitable for many learning programs today.

Tapes and cassettes (self-contained tape packages) have almost unlimited potential for classroom use. The development of inexpensive, durable tape recorders with fair auditory fidelity has encouraged the widespread use by students of all ages, from nursery through adult. Although combined audio-visual materials have even greater learning potential, there are many practical uses for audio tapes in classroom reading programs. Many skills programs are now available on tapes, and the tape recorder is useful as a recording device for a wide range of classroom skill lessons and activities.

Class-made tapes may serve as substitute teachers in many instances, as the recorded voice can present almost any directed lesson that the teacher has planned. In reading programs, recorded materials may provide practice or reinforcement of skills. Stories may be taped ahead of time by a skilled reader and used in a variety of ways—as a comprehension passage, as a monitor to or as an accuracy check after the reader has finished reading. The student may then tape an oral production of the text as a sample to be compared later with oral reading or to be submitted to the teacher for evaluation. Comprehension questions about passages the students will read silently may be taped for individual or small-group use. When a group is discussing the meaning of a story or poem, a taping of the session may prove useful for later review by group members.

Taped evaluations of a student's production of word-analysis skills or of oral reading may be useful to the teacher. The teacher's recorded voice can also serve as a model for reading a story a less able reader is studying.

Tapes are easy to make. With some effort to keep background noises at a minimum, one can quickly make fairly accurate reproductions. Since tapes can also be erased and reused, their use-value in relation to the initial cost is high. Considering all of the available media materials, tapes are probably the easiest to make and to use in a variety of learning situations. That advantage, combined with the fascination that many people, including teachers, have for hearing their own voices reproduced, easily make tapes the most popular media material in schools today.

Available materials

1. Building Verbal Power I
   Comprehension Through Listening

   Miller-Brody Productions, Inc.
   342 Madison Ave.
   New York, N.Y. 10017

   Records with teachers' manuals: Set I includes language and vocabulary skills for oral and receptive language; Set II presents exercises for selective and analytic listening—for elementary- and intermediate-level readers.

2. Challenge

   Teaching Technology Corp.
   7471 Greenbush Ave.
   North Hollywood, Cal. 91609

   One hundred forty kits containing cassette lessons, reinforcement lessons, and teachers' guide which cover word-attack skills, phrase accuracy, sentence meaning, and vocabularly development—for grades 1–6.

3. Creature Teachers, Space Talk, Ears, Base, Reach

   Economy Company
   P.O. Box 25308
   Oklahoma City, Oklahoma 73125

   Five kits containing pace tapes and student activity books which cover word perception, auditory perception and comprehension, word structure, and comprehension—for beginning- to intermediate-level readers.

4. How to Read in the Content Areas

   Learning Arts
   P.O. Box 917
   Wichita, Kansas 67201

   Cassettes and student material dealing with content-area reading—for intermediate-level readers.

5. Individualized Cassette Learning Packages

   Media Materials, Inc.
   Baltimore, Maryland 21202

   One hundred seventy-five cassette lessons, student response booklets, and library cataloging kit include phonic skills, structural analysis, vocabulary, comprehension, and study skills—for grades K–9.

6. Language Builders

   Milton Bradley Co.
   Educational Division
   Springfield, Mass. 01101

   Contain lesson tapes, manipulatives, activity cards, and response sheets. Four builders kits contain language and vocabulary skills for intermediate-level readers. Five programs include vowel and consonant sounds, language patterns, vocabulary development, and study skills—for elementary- and intermediate-level readers.

7. Phonic Skill Texts/Skill Tapes

   Charles Merrill Publishing Co.
   1300 Alum Creek Drive
   Columbus, Ohio 43216

   Tapes are correlated with workbook series and include sounds of words, structure of words, and understanding of words—for elementary-level readers.

8. Plus Ten Vocabulary Booster

   Webster Division, McGraw-Hill
   1221 Avenue of the Americas
   New York, N.Y. 10020

   Ninety tapes, readers' and teachers' workbook covering vocabulary and comprehension skills needed in content areas—for intermediate level readers.

9. Point 31

   Readers Digest Services, Inc.
   Educational Division
   Pleasantville, N.Y. 10570

Audio lessons, decode books, and teachers' guide provide nonreaders with word patterns. Audio lessons, activity books, magazine, readers', and teachers' guide contain phonic and comprehension skills—for the elementary-level reader.

Multimedia materials

Multimedia reading materials, in which auditory and visual presentations are combined in various ways, are now available and already in use in many classrooms. Such programs or kits may consist of tapes and slides packaged with workbooks, the latter to be used as independent work following the audio-visual presentations. Other programs combine tapes and filmstrips, coordinated to give a sight-sound presentation. Films, videotapes, or television presentations combine visual animation with audio presentation and may include practice materials as well. Computer-assisted instruction may use any of the above forms and has an additional advantage of providing feedback to a student's individual responses. Such programs, however, are not often found in school systems, since they require expensive computer equipment. Often multimedia programs include traditional materials, such as books, workbooks, and games, all of which are organized into one instructional package.

Multimedia programs, whether simple or elaborate, have the potential of providing fresh and stimulating material to students in novel ways that could help to circumvent existing learning difficulties. Only a few such programs have met that challenge to date.

"The Electric Company," an innovative television series, has been a leader in experimenting with novel forms for learning reading skills and concepts. Research conducted by the show's producer, Children's Television Workshop, shows that sight and sound combinations are more attractive to the learner if the concept being taught has a clear focus and is not cluttered by details, such as other action in the frame, irrelevant sounds, or color emphasizing lesser details. The process of blending sounds seems to be enhanced when the presentation shows the letters visually moving toward each other from the lips of silhouettes as the words are blended together auditorially. It was also found that music can be used to underline the rhythm of sentences and that songs can teach rules, such as the rule of the silent *e*. Animation can help to focus on addition or deletion of word endings or on the substitution of words. Animation can also be used to emphasize a left-to-right presentation, by having objects or letters move emphatically across the screen. Such preliminary findings are indicative of the potential of multimedia techniques in teaching.

Multimedia materials can be used in unlimited ways. Although some existing programs are designed as total reading programs and others as supplementary to basal reading programs, the teacher will most likely use only parts of any program for the poor reader, whose skill needs may not parallel any particular program. The design and purposes of any given materials must be considered when choosing materials for the poor reader. Some programs present new lessons in such a way that the learner cannot use them without teacher introduction. Some students may not be able to handle workbook materials independently; others may need visual stimuli to keep their attention on the materials. Some children benefit from repetitious work on skills, whereas others need continual variation in the same presentation. Therefore, the variety of multimedia materials at hand needs to be large enough to enable the teacher to choose a lesson with the appropriate learning modes and content for a particular reader.

In some instances it may be desirable to set up a learning center in the classroom to make efficient use of multimedia programs. There children can work on the lessons designated for them with a minimum of interference from other classroom activities. On the other hand, if television programs are to be a part of the learning center, the TV set can be moved there so that it will not interfere with other class activities. A daily assignment sheet prominently displayed will help to regulate the traffic in the area and to reduce confusion about who is to use what equipment.

It is unlikely that teachers will design or construct complete multimedia programs for their own use, because of the complexity of materials and equipment needed. Follow-up activities stemming from commercial programs can be easily undertaken. For example, children may want to write another chapter for a story seen on television or to produce additional games for practicing skills presented on a film. The teacher can list related activities on cards kept with a particular multimedia program to provide extended practice and/or application of skills and concepts. Although most multimedia materials are sold as programs, they are not necessarily appropriate for all learning purposes; thus addition or modification may make them more useful for individual students.

Available materials

1. Critical Reading and Listening Skills Program
   Guided Reading Program

   Instructional/Communications Technology, Inc.
   Huntington, N.Y. 11743

   Filmstrips, audio cassettes, study guides, spivet masters, and teachers' guide include vocabulary, comprehension, and listening skills—for elementary- and intermediate-level readers.

2. Learning with Laughter

Scott Education Division
Holyoke, Mass. 01040

Fifty-four kits containing sound filmstrips, posters, and manipulatives present alphabet, phonic skills, inflectional endings, and high-frequency words—for the beginning reader.

3. LEIR (Language Experience in Reading), Levels II and III

Encyclopaedia Britannica Educational Corp.
525 N. Michigan Ave.
Chicago, Ill. 60611

Filmstrips, records, activity books, ditto masters, resource cards, and guides present comprehension, word-recognition, and study skills—for the elementary-level reader.

4. Read On! Series I and II

ACI Films
35 West 45th Street
New York, N.Y. 10036

Color-sound films, six to nine minutes long, include basic reading and writing concepts and vocabulary—for the beginning reader.

5. Score Reading Improvement Series—Sports

Scott Education Division
Holyoke, Mass. 01040

Fifteen color-sound filmstrips and story and game books with a read-along tape include phonics skills, word-analysis skills, and comprehension—for the intermediate-level reader.

6. Reading with a Purpose

Coronet Films
65 East South Water St.
Chicago, Ill. 60601

A sound-film demonstrating a specific skill—for intermediate-level readers. This is one of a series presenting comprehension and study skills.

7. Scribner/Miller-Brody Filmstrip and Listening Cassette Library

Miller-Brody Productions, Inc.
342 Madison Ave.
New York, N.Y. 10017

Seventeen color filmstrips, cassettes, paperback books, and teachers' notes present award-winning books for comprehension and pleasure reading—for elementary- and intermediate-level readers.

8. The Electric Company

   Children's Television Workshop
   1 Lincoln Plaza
   New York, N.Y. 10023

   Half-hour television programs, shown daily on educational television channels, present beginning word-analysis skills, comprehension, and the process of reading—for the beginning reader in the 7–10 age group. Teachers' guides available.

9. The Sesame Street/Electric Company Reading Kits
   Prereading and Sentence Comprehension

   Addison-Wesley Publishing Co.
   Menlo Park, Cal. 94025

   Filmstrips, audio cassettes, activity books, games, comic books, mini-books, and teachers' resource book contain auditory- and visual-perception skills and coding in the first kit and comprehension skills in the second kit—for the beginning reader through grade 3.

10. Wordcraft I

    Communicard
    Box 541
    Wilton, Conn. 06897

    Filmstrips, cassettes, and student manual present rapid vocabulary building within the context of stories—for the intermediate-level reader.

USING MEDIA IN THE CLASSROOM

The advantages of using media materials in the classroom are often overshadowed by the problems related to selection and classroom management. Some initial planning about both selection and management will ensure later efficient use with the children for whom they are intended.

As with any reading materials, careful selection of media materials will help to stimulate the interests of the learner as well as to provide appropriate experiences for skill development. In addition to some knowledge of the characteristics of such materials, the teacher needs to preview the actual materials before making a final selection. Many professional journals offer monthly reviews. Journals such as *Instructor, Reading Teaching,* and *Elementary English* include good descriptive information and authoritative reviews. Curriculum libraries of nearby colleges or public libraries often have such materials for examination. Also, professional organizations or schools frequently invite publishers to demonstrate their new materials, which permits teachers to look over new materials before purchase. Before acquiring any materials, one should consider their purpose, intended audience, format and content, and ease of use.

In evaluating *purpose,* a first question is whether the materials can provide the experience or practice that is desired for the learner. In addition, such materials should correlate with other learning materials already in use; that is, if a learner has been working on outlining in a content area but still needs additional practice, the proposed materials should give that additional practice.

The teacher can also discern what advantages the media material may have over other classroom materials. For example, is introduction of a film projector worthwhile, or could paper-and-pencil materials be as easily substituted? The teacher can calculate any possible negative side effects from use of a media program, such as boredom from listening to too long a tape or confusion from a skill practice that contradicts a process already established in other skills work.

Good media materials should also show the poor reader how to learn as well as provide specific skills. Often skill information is too limited and fragmented for poor readers to understand the learning process itself. Thus practice is needed in developing techniques for getting meaning from print in an efficient and intelligent way. No materials are perfect, of course, but the clarity of purpose should be a major consideration in judging the merits of any media materials.

In judging the *intended audience* for any set of materials, the teacher should examine the content not only for reading levels and skill content, but also for their interest levels. Stories intended for ten-year-olds do not necessarily interest the adolescent, nor will simple, pictorial explanations hold the attention of a sixth grader. Style, format, pacing, size of materials— all may be important factors in determining the intended audience. Materials should be capable of stimulating a child's interest and yet look as if they can be handled easily. Motivational factors are crucial in inducing poor readers to try again, so careful evaluation of materials may pay high dividends later.

The *content and format* of media materials also need careful examination. One efficient way is to work through the materials as any learner would, noting strengths and weaknesses in the process. Some useful questions are:

1. Is the task to be done explained clearly enough so that the learner can complete it?

2. Does the presentation of the concepts or skills give enough examples and practice so that a slow learner can master it?

3. Is there enough program flexibility that a child who masters a concept can skip the next 20 examples?

4. Are the concepts or skills presented accurately, e.g., do all short *a* words used as examples have short *a* sounds?

5. Would it be possible to alter the pace of the lesson for learners with different styles, or is the presentation locked into a fixed time organization?

6. Could any lesson be broken into smaller parts or be shortened if necessary?

A last, but nonetheless important, set of questions focuses on the *ease of use* of media materials by both the learner and teacher. Many good materials are unused in the classroom because they were poorly packaged or had unintelligible instructions. In examining a set of materials, the teacher might check the following:

1. Can the materials be used independently by the learner after the initial teacher introduction and explanation?

2. Are the materials durable; will they hold up under continual handling?

3. Can the materials be stored together in identifiable closed containers?

4. Does the teacher's guide go beyond general instructions; will it be helpful when specific questions arise?

5. Will materials repay in learning the time needed to organize and maintain them in the classroom?

Management procedures are equally important for optimum use of media materials. When the materials are received in the classroom, their management routines should be worked out before they are used. First, the teacher should define the intended purposes for the materials, deciding how they will be coordinated with the present reading program in the classroom. If the media materials are to function coequally as primary learning materials, along with books and workbooks, they should be readily accessible to the children in a central part of the classroom. If media materials are to be used as supplementary materials, they can be placed in a less accessible part of the room where small groups of children may use them independently. If they are to be used individually, work space for several children is needed apart from the general work areas of the classroom. If the teacher plans to distribute and control the materials, they should be placed conveniently close by. If the children are to have access to media materials on their own, the storage-space requirements are different. Clear identification of the program components and easily followed retrieval procedures should be set up to avoid later confusion. Clearly, the teacher's decisions in relating the media materials to the major reading curriculum are key factors in managing the materials.

When television programs are planned for classroom viewing, their possible educational purposes should be delineated before the TV set is placed in the room. If the teacher plans to have the class view programs together, all of the students should be able to see the screen easily, without having to crowd too closely around it. On the other hand, if the programs are to be viewed by small groups or by individuals, the set can be placed in a recess of the room, with a rug in front of it.

In many classrooms, especially those tending toward informal or individualized instruction, skills or media centers have been established where the students have access to the equipment and media materials, so arranged to minimize distractions from the rest of the classroom. A similar center, even though a small area, can be set up in many classrooms to house the tape recorders and other hardware, as well as the media materials. A table, a few chairs or carrels, and some storage space are the minimum requirements. If, instead, the teacher plans to use the hardware and materials in various places in the classroom, a portable center can be set up on a rolling cart, complete with cords, earphones, and storage places for films and other materials. The major goal with any plan is easy accessibility of the equipment and materials and convenient routines for use and storage of materials. Obviously, if at the end of the day equipment and materials are scattered around the room, waiting to be boxed and stored by the teacher, media materials will soon find their way to the back closet shelves.

One way to avoid confusion is to provide a specific storage place for each set of materials and piece of equipment. A written or pictorial label identical for both the unit and the storage space will increase the likelihood that they will be stored properly. If such labels seem too complicated for young or poor readers, color coding of materials by content, reading level, or storage spot should work. Almost any space can be used—shelves, a closet, or a carton. Every piece of material should have a clearly designated place, so that all users can take responsibility for their own use of materials. When introducing the materials, the teacher should plan to demonstrate the storage system and to go over the routines expected of the users. Initially, it may be helpful to have a student monitor to supervise, but eventually the procedures should be manageable by the users themselves.

If the equipment itself seems complicated to operate, a large card outlining pertinent instructions, using both diagrams and simple sentences, can be permanently attached to each piece. One possibility is to train several students as technicians; these students would operate the equipment at first and would also be responsible for training additional children later. Another alternative is to appoint monitors to operate the equipment for everyone; these jobs would be rotated as other children became interested. In general, children seem to have less trouble managing technical equipment than do teachers. Thus after initial training, the children have few problems in maintaining the equipment.

Advance planning of groupings for children using media materials also contributes to better use. In the crowded space of a typical classroom, facilities can be easily overloaded at any given time. In determining the purpose of a given activity, the teacher also decides the size of the group to be working with the materials or equipment. Sometimes the nature of the equipment is a determining factor. A desk-model filmstrip projector may be viewed easily by only a few children; the number of earphones or the size of the tape may limit the number using an audio unit. Sequential use of materials by children or rotation of materials among different groups requires considerable advance planning as well as a clear explanation to the users of how the plan is to work.

In many schools the media equipment and materials are concentrated in a central learning-resource center, with the capability of providing a wider range of materials and services to the entire school. Although such an arrangement does not preclude location of tape recorders and filmstrips in the classroom, it does mean that the majority of media materials will be located in and borrowed from the media center. A major advantage to the classroom teacher is the assistance provided by the center's staff in locating specific materials, demonstrating the use of new materials, constructing materials for a specific need, or assisting students who use the center during school time. Students needing extra practice in reading skills often are assigned work time in the center and are supervised by staff there. The reading teacher in the school also may work in the center with remedial groups. Time may also be reserved both for teachers to familiarize themselves with media materials and for children seeking special help with an independent project.

If instruction or practice is carried out in the media center, coordination of learning activities between the center supervisor and the classroom teacher is essential. Too often the student receiving instruction in two places is placed on parallel tracks of skill learning which may be confusing or even conflicting. Therefore, the classroom teacher, who has primary responsibility for each student's reading goals, will need to review and help plan the work done with center personnel to make sure it correlates with curriculum goals.

Coordination of media work with classroom curriculum is, of course, important, no matter where such materials are housed. As discussed earlier, previewing materials for their potential use is an important step in choosing relevant materials. With so many media materials available, time taken to review them is often wasted unless some record system is worked out to keep them straight. One suggestion is to catalog all the media programs and materials by subject. Materials dealing with similar skills can be grouped on the same card. An example of a subject card follows.

BEGINNING CONSONANT BLENDS

1. Smith tape no. 6: practice in identifying and saying blends; for groups or individuals; 15 minutes.

2. Jones filmstrip no. 23: introduces blends; practice in substitution in words; individual or group practice; 4 minutes.

3. Transparency: practice in supplying correct blend in context; child writes answers; individual; about 6 minutes.

Although such cataloging systems may take time to develop, their value is inestimable for maintaining an individualized approach for poor readers. Recently developed media programs provide correlation charts listing specific pages in various basal reading systems which deal with the similar skills activities in the media materials. Such charts are particularly helpful in coordinating primary work and skills practice for the problem reader.

EVALUATING MATERIALS AND STUDENT PROGRESS

An integral part of all individualized instruction, including media programs, is evaluation of the effectiveness of the materials. In terms of the learning goals set by the authors of the materials, it is important to know how students have performed. Since educational materials are rarely field-tested extensively before publication, any claims about their teaching effectiveness should not be taken too seriously without further evaluation. Classroom teachers themselves, who are in daily contact with children, sometimes overestimate (or underestimate) the potential of materials for particular learners. Even if materials have been carefully reviewed initially, they need to be reevaluated after use. Even materials that may seem quite adequate must pass the final test: Do students learn the reading skills claimed, and do the materials accomplish such in a satisfactory way?

An excellent way to evaluate materials is to observe children using them on a daily basis. Practical information on several levels is gained from observation, such as whether the students could handle the materials and equipment easily without adult intervention, or whether the materials held up physically through the first few months of use.

In addition, the teacher can observe whether the format was attractive enough so that the children wanted to use the materials again after the first few trials. Were the audio aspects clear and the visual aspects uncluttered so that the intended messages could be received without strain? In listening to a tape, the teacher can discern whether the content and enunciation of the directions were clear and useable. Were the directions repeated when complex messages were given? Similarly, activity books can be inspected for readability level.

One important aspect of evaluating the format and structure of the materials is the pacing of the lesson. For example, could the pace be adjusted for the slow learner? What provisions are made for the student who did not understand the first presentation of a concept? Is the amount of practice available for specific skills adequate before a new skill is introduced? Could the child be overwhelmed by too much material or bored by too little?

A check of the reading level at various points in the materials will determine whether that level was maintained. Another consideration is any provision for the student's knowledge of the correctness of his or her response. Is there opportunity for the student to amend a response after the feedback? All of the above lead back to the central question: Do the materials seem to help the student learn or reinforce the appropriate skills? Media materials should be judged primarily on their specific effectiveness for selected learning situations; therefore, their worth is relative to the purposes for which they were chosen. Few materials will, of course, meet all of the criteria discussed above; if, however, media materials seem to be aiding a poor reader to learn, weaknesses in subsidiary areas may not be so important.

Learners themselves may enjoy commenting on materials and often give valuable information about their instructional value. Although the younger child may merely give a nonverbal opinion by choosing to work with one set of materials instead of another, older students often give accurate statements about the worth of materials they have used. A student may comment on the value of the practice session, on the clarity of the presentation, or on his or her understanding of the purpose for the work.

Evaluation of student achievement is, of course, another way to determine the educational worth of media materials. In addition to traditional achievement or criterion-referenced test results, there are informal ways to assess student achievement. A teacher can judge how far a learner has come in skill learning after using the materials. The amount of skill generalization, i.e., application of skills in new but similar situations, can also be observed. The child too can evaluate amount of learning, perhaps noting any improvement, mastery of the skills in that area, or the need for more work in that area.

MAKING ONE'S OWN MEDIA MATERIALS

Often commercial media materials are too costly or are unavailable to the classroom teacher. Sometimes those materials that are available are not appropriate for the poor reader or are not likely to be attractive or motivating for that child. Often a teacher can construct a limited number of media materials or programs. Although such an endeavor requires time and a long-term commitment, especially when assembling a workable collection, the investment may be wise for particular learning situations. The poor reader is often highly motivated when involved in creating his or her own learning materials; even when the child no longer needs such materials, they will still be useful to other struggling learners.

Only a few suggestions are offered here for class-made materials, since creative teachers can undoubtedly think of more varied activities. For the beginning teacher, audio tapes are simple to make and can be erased when no longer needed. Such tapes can be used for directions for activities, spelling tests, assignments for written activities, stories and poetry for listening, test items, and so forth. All can be taped in advance for later classroom use by the teacher, by one child, or by a group. When directed activities are taped, space can be left on the tape for a response activity, e.g., a set of questions, with space left after each question for the child's answers. Also, a feedback tape can be prepared for the student or group to listen to after they have responded to the original activity. Tapes can also be prepared to go with silent visual materials, such as slides, pictures, and filmstrips. Although synchronization between auditory and visual media may not be as smooth as in commercial media, it usually is adequate for classroom use.

Visual media, such as filmstrips, slides, 8-mm loops, and transparencies, require considerably more skill in preparation to be attractive to users, but often they can be prepared by more able students for the others. Although the contents of student-prepared materials often reflect the children's own interests in exploring their world rather than specific reading skill practice, such materials will nonetheless have high interest value in reading situations.

Teachers with sound movie cameras or videotape equipment have an even wider range of content to explore, but must spend more time in planning and executing such a production. For example, a student-planned and produced version of a Letterman adventure from "The Electric Company" may help to focus attention on reading-oriented materials more than merely viewing the TV show would. Children, especially problem readers, can derive much pleasure from recreating media experiences they have enjoyed, and the gain in sense of achievement in the recreation process may be worth much in their learning endeavors. Therefore, audiovisual productions may best be handled by class members, with the teacher acting as consultant, to give them experience with planning and creation of the materials. Even if the resultant media materials are not of the highest quality, the experiences generated may have produced positive learning accruals for the children involved. The time and effort needed for flawless productions are usually not justified in terms of the learning goals for classroom productions. Although commercial materials may meet technical standards more easily, the interests and learning needs of the students are more important than the quality of their media productions.

In summary, media materials have the potential to be exciting and attractive modes of learning for problem readers. With some attention to the management of media materials in the classroom, the teacher can use them flexibly and imaginatively to provide successful reading experiences for diverse learning needs.

Chapter 17

ORGANIZING THE READING PROGRAM

ROBERT T. RUDE · *Rhode Island College*

A reduction in the large number of students who exhibit reading problems requires a coordinated instructional effort on the part of the entire educational community. Although it is easy to verbalize this commitment, the implementation of such an effort is a slow and often arduous undertaking. The fact is, however, that unless an interdisciplinary approach to the problem is undertaken, improvement in reading ability will not be as rapid as it might be. The successful implementation of the interdisciplinary model discussed in Chapter 8 depends on the orchestrated efforts of groups of classroom teachers, reading specialists, specialized personnel, support staff, and school administrators. Accordingly, this chapter will describe the implications of and procedures for implementing a broad attack on the reading problems of students.

A PROPOSED ORGANIZATIONAL MODEL: INTERFACE BETWEEN THE SCHOOL READING PROGRAM AND THE INTERDISCIPLINARY MODEL

Increasingly, educators are receiving more specialized training in learning how to deal with the learning problems of students. Although specialization permits the educator to be better prepared to contend with difficulties encountered by pupils, there is the danger that communication breakdowns between the various specialists may result. A lack of communication among members of the interdisciplinary team could result in impeding the progress of a student who might otherwise be reading better had greater team interaction existed. One of the crucial factors in the smooth operation of the interdisciplinary team is an understanding of each member's role.

Role of the classroom teacher

The most important factor in any educational program is the classroom teacher. At times, however, we seem to forget that fact. Instead, we are led to believe that the more instructional materials we have at our disposal, the more effective we will be in our teaching efforts. This belief is perpetuated by publishers who are quick to flood the market with "innovative" programs and gimmicks and by college professors who emphasize materials instead of challenging students to think critically about their performance as teachers of reading. Although good instructional materials are essential to the teaching of reading, materials are only means to an end rather than ends in themselves. Both teachers and professors often forget that fact. What, then, is the role of the classroom teacher on the interdisciplinary team?

Perhaps more than any other team member, the classroom teacher is in the key position of effecting more change with the problem reader than any other individual. It is the teacher's job to identify initially the student with reading problems. In many school systems, identification is accomplished by administering a standardized, norm-referenced reading test. Students who score poorly on the test are potential candidates for a more thorough reading diagnosis. In addition to norm-referenced reading tests, more and more teachers are utilizing criterion-referenced assessment procedures in their classrooms. Results from these instruments, when used in conjunction with norm-referenced tests, can provide the teacher with information about the student's specific reading skill development and overall reading ability.

Students who score poorly on both types of tests should have their intellectual ability assessed by an appropriate member of the team, since this can help the teacher and other team members in determining whether the child needs adapted or corrective instruction within the classroom or should receive intensive remedial assistance—perhaps outside the classroom, if necessary—from the reading specialist (Otto and Smith, 1970).

Following the diagnosis, classroom teachers have the responsibility to focus their instruction in areas where the student has performed poorly. This is where "the rubber meets the road," so to speak. Unless the classroom teacher can effectively implement an instructional program in line with the needs of the student, there is small chance that the child will be effectively assisted in overcoming his or her reading problem.

It is also the responsibility of the classroom teacher to monitor the progress of the student throughout the school year. Not only must teachers focus their instruction on areas where skills have been found lacking, but they must also check to see that the skills taught are being applied in reading-required situations. This may mean contacting parents or other teachers to acquaint them with the instructional efforts that have transpired and making them aware that newly acquired reading skills should be applied in situations outside of the classroom teacher's immediate control. Additionally, the classroom teacher has the responsibility of keeping the rest of the interdisciplinary team informed of the classroom progress of students who have been diagnosed by the team.

Role of the reading specialist

The reading specialist, another key member of the team, cooperates and works closely with the classroom teacher as well as coordinates other efforts of the team. Since they have received intensive training in the teaching of reading, reading specialists are in the unique position of being able to articulate the concerns of the classroom teacher to other specialists on the team. Moreover, there may be times when they are asked to interpret data from other specialists into pedagogical implications for the classroom teacher. In a very real sense, the reading specialist is a vital person on the team.

In some instances, school systems cannot afford the luxury of employing reading specialists. In such cases, a classroom teacher who has received additional training in the area of teaching reading may be asked to become a team member and to provide a practitioner's insight into the causes of a student's learning disability. In either case, whether the individual is called a reading specialist or is a classroom teacher with training in reading, the person must be well read in the professional literature of the field and must be able to communicate effectively with other team members.

Most reading specialists are expected to demonstrate expertise in both teaching effectiveness and in the role of consultant. As a teacher, the reading specialist is asked to work primarily with remedial cases whose reading disabilities are so severe that they must receive intensive, one-to-one or small-group tutoring outside of the classroom setting. An example of such a situation would be when the severity of a case requires the use of behavior-modification techniques; because of excessive demands on teacher time, the treatment could not be implemented in the regular classroom. The specialist may also be asked to work for short periods of time with learners who need corrective teaching—readers who can benefit from short-term, highly focused instruction to help them overcome gaps in skill development.

Reading specialists are often called on to perform consultant duties as well. They may, for example, be required to conduct more extensive testing of a student than the classroom teacher can be expected to perform. Once the testing has been completed, they will need to interpret the test results to the student's classroom teachers. In addition to matters related to testing, the reading specialist may be asked to demonstrate or explain new instructional materials or techniques to the teachers in a school or system. Hence, they must keep abreast of new developments in the field and be able to identify programs that have demonstrated effectiveness. Similarly, they may be asked to interpret current research in the field of education and describe its classroom implications. Along these lines, they will be in a position to act as a liaison between the classroom teacher and the school administrator. In this capacity, they may be asked to do such things as assume the responsibility for implementing an effective reading program and periodically reporting its impact to the school principal.

Role of specialized personnel

Specialized personnel are generally considered to be those professionals who work within the school system but have demonstrated expertise in specified areas, e.g., the school psychologist, the school social worker, the guidance counselor, the speech therapist, and the school librarian. The roles of the school psychologist and school social worker have already been described in Chapter 8. These other individuals also have important functions within the reading program.

School districts often employ the services of guidance counselors. Although their duties vary widely from system to system, some of the services they may be called on to perform include developing a school- or system-wide testing program, administering and interpreting personality tests or inventories, and providing an information service for vocational-educational planning. It is only logical, therefore, that guidance counselors be considered as part of the interdisciplinary team. Working closely with the classroom teacher, counselors can provide additional insights into a student's behavior which may eventually result in improved reading achievement.

More and more schools are now able to provide the services of a speech therapist for their students. Since there is a close relationship between language and reading, it is only right that an amicable relationship exist between the classroom teacher and the speech therapist. Moreover, logic would seem to indicate that if both the classroom teacher and the speech therapist were focusing their instructional efforts in the same area for a particular child (e.g., auditory discrimination exercises), the student's progress would be greater than if close coordination between the two teachers did not exist. Since most speech therapists have been trained to administer tests of auditory acuity and discrimination, classroom teachers should not hesitate to refer students who are suspected of having a hearing deficiency. Another area in which the speech therapist can play a vital role relates to the use of non-standard dialects in the school setting. Classroom teachers often raise questions related to correct use of instructional materials in the area of phonics and the "mismatch" between responses called for in the material and the responses given by students. Speech therapists should be able to help teachers resolve questions concerning cultural and regional dialects and their relationships to reading instruction. (See also Chapter 7.)

Finally, a sometimes overlooked person in the specialized personnel category is the school librarian. Good librarians are an integral part of an effective reading program. An uncooperative school librarian can hamper the best instructional efforts of the classroom teacher and the reading specialist. A sympathetic, supportive librarian, on the other hand, can play a vital role in helping to reduce the incidence of reading problems within a school. Good librarians realize that some students are not interested in what is perceived as "good literature." Instead, these students need to be shown that books can be resource tools. Books can provide answers to sought-after questions as well as being informative in a more general way. Too often, librarians try, albeit inadvertently, to project middle-class ideals on students who reject those values.

Role of support staff

Again, the roles of the support staff—the psychiatrist, the pediatrician, and the pediatric neurologist—were delineated in detail in Chapters 5, 6, and 8. At this point, it is sufficient to say that the reading specialist should recommend that support staff be brought into the picture whenever necessary. These individuals have received extensive, thorough training in their respective fields, and their expertise should be sought when needed. Reading specialists have been trained as educators. They would do well to remember that point and tread cautiously in fields outside their domain. Likewise, the support personnel have not been trained as educators and should therefore be cautious about offering remedies for complex educational problems.

Role of the school administrators

Broadly speaking, the term "school administrators" includes the superintendent of schools and his or her assistants, the director of instruction, the school principal, and perhaps the system's reading consultant. In a very practical sense, it is the school principal and the reading consultant who determine the thrust and ultimately the success of the school reading program. Many reading specialists who have worked in two or more schools within a school system can testify to the fact that the school principal is, to a large degree, responsible for the success of all instructional programs. There are several reasons for this.

First, the school principal is responsible for the allocation of funds to ensure that a sound instructional program takes place. For example, without administrative financial support, tests, test manuals, and scoring services usually cannot be acquired. Even if they can be purchased, the program will be meaningless if the administrator is opposed to the testing program or even nonsupportive. In addition to financial support for the testing program, the reading program needs a variety of instructional materials to help achieve its program objectives. Again, the school principal is responsible for seeing that these monies are wisely invested in materials that have demonstrated effectiveness and will be frequently used. A third responsibility of the school administrator is to be active in supporting staff-development efforts. More will be said about this later in the chapter. Here, however, it is important to note that there are many things an administrator can do to upgrade faculty efforts. Coordinating locally sponsored in-service efforts, contacting college administrators to have off-campus-conducted college courses held in the school, and gaining consultant assistance from state departments of public education are but three resources that can contribute to further staff-development efforts.

ASSESSING THE READING PROGRAM

Good instructional programs have a broad, well-conceived assessment program at their foundation. Although some educators feel that assessment programs are a luxury that can be overlooked, they should instead be viewed as an integral part of any reading program. This is especially true in this age of accountability and tight financial resources. Increasingly, concerned taxpayers are demanding to see educational results as an end product of their tax dollars. The writing is clearly on the wall. Educators at all levels must take the initiative and demonstrate their effectiveness in dealing with students. A formal assessment program can be an important step in that direction.

Guidelines for assessment

Assessment of reading ability has typically implied the "once-a-year standardized testing ritual" and has been a relatively common practice since the 1930s and 1940s. The procedures are well known: group-administered achievement tests are given (usually in April or May), scored, and entered in each child's cumulative record folder, seldom to be used again. Although standardized achievement tests can play an important role in the overall evaluation program, they certainly must be seen as only a partial solution to the assessment issue. The following suggestions are offered for those charged with the task of establishing a meaningful approach to assessment.

First, determine your program skills and objectives. In other words, what types of behaviors are expected of the students as they proceed through the reading program? Will they be expected to be fluent "decoders" in the broadest meaning of the term: possess a sight vocabulary, know basic structural-analysis skills, and be able to apply phonic generalization? Will comprehension skills be stressed heavily? If so, which specific subskills—main idea, detail, sequence, or context clues? What about study skills? Will students be taught how to read maps, graphs, and tables? Will reference skills be included in the school's instructional program? Once skills can be agreed on, program objectives can be articulated and, if desired, written in behavioral terms.

Following the identification of skills and objectives, tests can be chosen to measure the objectives. As straightforward as this may seem, it is disconcerting to see how many teachers and administrators continue to use assessment devices that are not in line with the realities of classroom instruction. If you are not going to expend the time and effort to teach study skills, for example, why try to assess that ability? Such efforts will only lead to frustration and anxiety. Instead, assess only what you plan to teach! Obviously, then, you will need to spend considerable time determining what you should be teaching and how you are going to assess those learned behaviors. But this is time well spent.

Some additional points concerning assessment should also be made. For one thing, do only enough testing to permit you to accomplish what you need to accomplish. As a rule, too little testing is done in most schools, but too much testing can also prove disastrous. What good are test data if they become overwhelming and unmanageable? Next, be cautious when selecting tests. Make sure that they are valid and have demonstrated reliability. Tests that yield inaccurate scores only serve to frustrate teachers, not help them. When selecting tests, make sure that they can be easily administered (preferably group-administrable) and readily scored. Again, classroom teachers quickly become frustrated when tests are difficult to administer and hard to score. An additional factor to be considered is the cost of the tests. Even though school budgets are tight, however, do not make the mistake of being "penny-wise and pound-foolish" by selecting a cheaper, inferior assessment tool that fails to do the job it was intended to do.

Available assessment procedures

The reading specialist, along with other members of the interdisciplinary team, should be involved in planning how the reading program will be evaluated. In some instances, people outside the interdisciplinary team may be included when the reading program is evaluated. Representative teachers, parents, central office personnel, college or university consultants, and representatives from outside evaluation teams, for example, may assist in conducting the reading-program evaluation. The evaluation procedures used in assessing the effectiveness of the program can range in breadth from simply administering standardized reading tests to more meaningful, comprehensive evaluation plans.

A thorough evaluation should include the use of standardized (norm-referenced) as well as objective-based (criterion-referenced) tests designed to assess students' decoding, comprehension, and study-skill abilities. Norm-referenced tests have been designed to allow the educator to compare the performance of his or her students with the performance of a larger, nation-wide sample. Tests such as the *Gates-MacGinitie Reading Tests* (Gates-MacGinitie, 1965), *California Reading Tests* (Tiegs and Clark, 1957), and the *Stanford Reading Tests* (Kelley *et al.*, 1966) are examples of instruments which permit the teacher to make this kind of comparison. Results on these instruments are usually reported as Z scores, T scores, stanines, or percentiles.

Criterion-referenced tests, or "skill tests," permit the teacher to compare each student's performance to a predetermined criterion or "mastery level." Examples of objective-based reading systems that rely heavily on criterion-referenced tests are the *Croft Inservice Reading Program* (Cooper and McGuire, 1970), the *Prescriptive Reading Inventory* (CTB/McGraw-Hill, 1972), and the *Wisconsin Design for Reading Skill Development* (Otto and Askov, 1973). In each of these programs, reading skills have been identified, behavioral objectives have been stated for each skill, and criterion-referenced tests have been designed to assess students' mastery of the stated skills.

Additionally, appropriate management techniques have been developed for each system to enable the classroom teacher to provide focused instruction to only those students who need work in specific skills. Readers interested in learning how criterion-referenced assessment can further be used as a supplement to norm-referenced assessment are encouraged to reflect on Millman's article entitled "Criterion Referenced Measurement: An Alternative" (Millman, 1972). Comparisons of some of the currently available objective-based reading systems have also been done by Thompson and Dziuban (1973) and Rude (1974).

In addition to utilizing standardized and criterion-referenced tests, instruments measuring a child's attitude toward reading should also be used. Askov (1974), for one, has developed such an instrument. Other techniques and instruments attempting to measure students' attitudes should not be overlooked, either. Additionally, the teacher who collects periodic work samples from students can assist in evaluating the program. Informal reading inventories, interest inventories, and student interviews can add considerable insights into the effectiveness of the teaching of reading. Moreover, questionnaires completed by parents can also prove valuable. Finally, if at all possible, the teachers of reading might be evaluated. Although this suggestion may be controversial, it seems only right that the teacher's understanding of content and correct utilization of instructional materials—to mention only two factors—be considered in the evaluation scheme.

Whatever assessment procedures are chosen, it is important to see the evaluation as continuous, ongoing, and in line with predetermined objectives. These conditions permit monitoring of the instructional program and should result in improved performance on the part of students.

The evaluators

Recently, much has been written about the concept of accountability. With the price of education continuing to sky-rocket, more and more parents are expecting to see tangible results as an end product of their tax dollars. It behooves educators, then, to take the initiative and to demonstrate to their boards of education and school committees that they too are interested in the performance of their students. Accountability should imply that each *teacher* is able to demonstrate that his or her students are progressing toward predetermined, explicated goals. If norm-referenced or criterion-referenced test scores play a part in these goals, then so be it. The message is clear. Know where you are going, how you will get there, and when you have reached your goal. Teachers must be first and foremost accountable to *themselves;* they must, in a very real sense, be their own evaluators.

The second phase of evaluation must be the responsibility of the school administrators. School principals are responsible for seeing that the goals of each teacher's reading program are in line with the overall goals of the school. Occasionally, the school principal may assign this responsibility to the reading specialist, who in turn is directly accountable to that administrator. In small school districts, the principals may report directly to the superintendent of schools. In larger districts, one or more assistants may be the liaison between the principal and the superintendent. In either case, however, the superintendent is directly accountable to the board of education, whose members are usually elected by the district's constituents. In theory, the ultimate evaluators are the parents. Most parents, however, are unable to articulate precisely how the reading program should be evaluated. Parents can describe in general terms, however, what they feel the program should accomplish. By working closely with parents and the boards of education, teachers and administrators have a unique opportunity to clearly describe their program objectives and assume the responsibility of evaluating their programs. Unless they seize this opportunity, the practice of hiring outside, independent evaluation agencies to monitor the achievement of students will increase.

REMEDIAL TEACHING IN THE TOTAL READING PROGRAM

Traditionally, efforts to reduce the high incidence of reading disability have been the primary responsibility of the school reading specialist. At first glance, this appears to be sound educational practice, since the reading specialist has usually received extensive training in the area of reading diagnosis and treatment. Closer examination of this practice, however, usually finds little, if any, correlation between the instructional effort of the specialist and the classroom teacher.

Traditional treatment procedure

The traditional treatment methodology employed at the elementary school level is usually as follows. First, the reading specialist questions classroom teachers early in the school year to determine if they have students who may be candidates for more extensive instruction, usually individual or small group tutoring. Tutoring of each child is then scheduled for 45- to 60-minute blocks two or three times per week. Thus the reading specialist sees a typical student between one and a half and three hours per week and has a class load between 30 and 60 students in any one week. Students who are accepted for remedial help receive this concentrated instruction outside of their regular classroom setting.

This plan is commendable in that students receive focused instruction by someone with special skills in the area of reading education, but the plan suffers from several serious drawbacks. First, unless the reading specialists employ extensive screening procedures in selecting candidates for their programs, teachers may refer children who have severe emotional, not reading, difficulties. Additionally, students of limited intellectual ability are often referred for further help in reading. Although these students may indeed have limited reading ability, their problem may be a lack of general learning ability in all areas, not solely reading. To state it another way, these students are probably working at their expectancy level, which, because of their limited intellectual ability, falls below that of most children in the classroom. These students do not need remedial help, but instead can benefit from intensive sequential instruction (at a slower pace) in their regular classroom. A final overriding shortcoming of this traditional effort to improve reading instruction at the elementary school level is that there is usually little relationship between the instructional efforts of the reading specialist and the classroom teachers. The expectancy of the classroom teachers is that students with reading problems will be helped by receiving individual attention from the reading specialist. The specialist, on the other hand, realizes that only limited progress can be made by seeing students for such brief periods, usually less than one-tenth of the student's total in-school time.

The plight of the secondary school reading specialists has been even more dismal. Often these reading specialists are former English teachers who have been given new assignments—to teach reading—without having received the much-needed additional training in order to help them cope with problem readers. Their usual charge, issued from the administration, is to make every secondary teacher a teacher of reading. Needless to say, there is small chance of achieving this goal. Content-area teachers who teach math, science, or social studies see little need for becoming "teachers of reading." Instead, they reason that it would be much easier for them if the newly appointed reading teacher could assume the responsibility of working with *all* students at a particular grade level and thereby totally eliminate the reading problems at the secondary level.

The futility of this approach soon becomes apparent. First, the reading specialist cannot effectively individualize instruction for classes of 25 or more students of widely differing abilities. Second, students with long-standing reading problems are not going to be significantly helped in one or two years. Third, not all secondary students need intensive instruction in reading; many of them are already mature, adult readers. Finally, just as in the case of the elementary school reading specialist, there is minimal carry-over between the efforts of the reading specialist and the teaching practices of the content-area teachers.

Proposed treatment procedure

Traditional approaches designed to alleviate reading disabilities have not been as effective as they might have been. Clearly, a more comprehensive approach to working with students with reading problems is in order. Accordingly, a proposed elementary and secondary model will be described.

The new role of the elementary school reading specialist is to serve more as a consultant than as a teacher. Although a portion of the specialist's duties entails working with students with genuinely severe reading difficulties, the majority of the specialist's time must be spent working intimately with classroom teachers, trying to up-grade efforts to individualize instruction, on a daily basis, in the classroom. This requires that the specialist work hand in hand with classroom teachers *in their classrooms* instead of working solely in a remedial reading room "down the hall." In addition to working in the classroom setting with teachers, the reading specialist is called on to conduct demonstration lessons with students, thereby providing a model for classroom teachers to replicate. Moreover, along these same lines, the specialist should be capable of acquainting staff personnel with new materials which can facilitate the individualization of instruction. Another function the reading specialist performs is that of prescribing instructional materials or techniques which classroom teachers can use with students whose learning disabilities have been diagnosed. This requires that the specialist know what materials are available within the building or district and have an efficient manner of cataloging these materials, so that items needed for use by the classroom teachers can be retrieved quickly.

The role of the elementary school reading specialist should evolve, then, from that of a teacher who works exclusively with students with reading difficulties to that of a combination teacher-consultant. This more comprehensive role necessitates a well-trained individual, one who can work effectively with students as well as with teachers.

The role of the secondary school reading specialist also must change. In many ways, this new role description will closely parallel that of the elementary school reading specialist. The secondary reading specialist must, for example, begin to work closely with content-area teachers. That is not to say that they will no longer work with students, however. Instead of working with classes of between 15 and 30 students, though, they must work toward reducing the number of cases they are expected to service. As was true at the elementary school level, the secondary reading specialist must begin to function increasingly as a teacher-consultant. Although students with legitimate, severe reading difficulties will receive the specialist's help, the person identified as the reading specialist must begin to provide possible alternatives to the one-textbook-for-all-students philosophy adopted by many content teachers. Unless this happens, there is little hope that students with reading disabilities will be able to function effectively in the secondary school curriculum.

The reading specialist needs to convince content-area teachers that they need not all become "teachers of reading." Instead, specialists should better utilize their time and efforts by demonstrating how multiple texts of varying difficulty might be used by the content-area teachers. Or, they may acquaint individuals on the staff with procedures related to how to teach their students effective and efficient study techniques. The point is, the specialist, through his or her understanding of reading skills, should attempt to make the content-area teachers even more effective teachers of content, not teachers of reading. Whereas the elementary school reading specialist's efforts center on the development of basic skills, the secondary reading specialist's job is less skills-oriented and more attitude-oriented. Elementary reading specialists must do a better job of ensuring that students know *how* to read; secondary reading specialists must see to it that students *want* to continue to read.

IMPLEMENTATION OF THE MODEL

To effectively implement the proposed organization, a number of internal as well as external resources can be utilized. Internal resources refer to those services available from within the school system. External resources, an often overlooked aspect of education, can provide needed assistance, both financial and professional, from outside the school district.

Internal resources

Administrative support is the first prerequisite for implementation of the interdisciplinary model. Since in many instances the request for a change in the reading specialist's role description must be initiated from the reading specialist, a detailed description of the duties and responsibilities of that role should be drafted and presented to the appropriate administrator—usually the director of instruction, an assistant superintendent, or the superintendent of schools. In all likelihood, one of these administrators will discuss the implications of the new role with the school principals affected.

In addition to the spiritual support needed from the school administrators, any additional financial support needed will have to be reckoned with. The specialist may, for example, need to purchase professional reading texts and "idea books" that can be loaned to teachers, thereby providing them with added insights into the teaching of specific skills. Or, additional assessment or instructional materials may need to be procured if increased individualization of instruction within classrooms is to transpire. If demonstration lessons are to be an integral part of the staff-development efforts, the specialist should consider the feasibility of videotaping the lessons, so that they can be used when needed. Efforts such as these necessitate that monies be set aside for the purchase of equipment or materials. Another factor to be considered is the need to hire outside consultants and determine the duties they would be asked to perform.

The successful implementation of any educational program depends on the support of the teaching staff. Although total staff support should be the ultimate goal of the reading specialist, the fact is that few programs receive such widespread backing. The specialist should realize that there always will be individuals who are reluctant to support change from the status quo. In the long run, the reading specialist is better off not spending undue amounts of time and energy trying to win the approval of those teachers unwilling to support new programs. Instead, this time can be more profitably spent working with those who hold a positive attitude toward change. Nonsupporters should not be "written off," however. The task of implementing the model will be strenuous enough, though, without trying to convince those who have no intention, at least presently, of being convinced.

To a large degree, staff support will be directly related to the openness of communication among members of the professional staff. Because communication is essential among members of the interdisciplinary team, the reading specialist must ensure that members have a close working relationship. This can happen if the model is implemented carefully and methodically. Ideally, implementation should parallel the reading specialist's staff-development efforts. In this manner, teachers and administrators can better see the interrelationship between the two efforts.

Continuous staff development should be the goal of every reading specialist. If children with reading difficulties are to be truly helped, the majority of the remediation effort *must* come from classroom teachers. It does little good to send disabled readers out of the classroom and to the reading specialist when the students return one hour later and are faced with reading materials at their frustrational level for the remainder of the day. If readers are to be helped, they must be helped primarily by the individual who has the most contact with them during their school hours—the classroom teacher.

Since the onus of responsibility for helping students with reading difficulties falls on the classroom teacher, extensive efforts to improve the quality of reading instruction must be teacher-directed and must come about through focused, staff-development efforts. In-service efforts will be described in detail in the following chapter, but several recommendations are offered here to the specialist who is planning staff-development efforts for the first time or for the experienced reading specialist who is attempting to improve his or her in-service programs in reading.

First, conduct a thorough needs assessment and determine what teachers in the system want to know. Next, work only with those teachers and administrators who want to be helped. Don't try to accomplish too much in a short period of time. It is better to move slowly and make sure that concepts, techniques, and materials are thoroughly understood than to frustrate teachers by presenting "too much, too fast." This is especially true when explaining the operation of the interdisciplinary model to in-service participants. Finally, involve the teachers and other specialists in the planning and implementation of the model. Through involvement, they will feel more committed to the idea of an interdisciplinary approach.

External resources

Effective implementation of the interdisciplinary model will, to a large degree, be based on the degree of acceptance from the noneducational community. Specifically, the program should have the active support of parents whose children will benefit from the program. Opportunities, then, should be provided to make parents aware of the proposed program. This can occur through the local parent-teacher organization. The reading specialist should work closely with the school administration in planning meetings during which various members of the interdisciplinary team have an opportunity to explain their specific roles on the team. Parents would then be given an opportunity to question team members, thereby clarifying any misconceptions they might have about the function of the team. Another means by which to inform the community is by speaking at meetings of local civic groups. The superintendent or a designated representative could do much along these lines to enlist the moral support of influential community leaders. In a similar vein, a well-written news release explaining the approach would do much to win parental and community support for implementation of the program.

Often public school officials know what needs to be done, but lack the financial resources to accomplish the task. This may be the case with efforts to implement the interdisciplinary model. School personnel should look into the procurement of funds from outside the usual property tax budget. One idea would be to explore the feasibility of obtaining additional monies from the United States Office of Education. Often funds are available from Right-to-Read efforts or under one or more of the various title programs, the most recent being Title VII, the National Reading Improvement Program. Also, grants of a less substantial nature are frequently available from local state departments of public instruction. In many states, consultants from the state agency are available to help draft specific proposals to request funds for noteworthy projects. A final avenue of outside funding is private companies or foundations. The reading specialist who is persistent enough to inquire into the availability of funds and who is willing to work with the individual within the system who is responsible for drafting proposals and coordinating grant efforts will often be rewarded.

Most public school systems are already aware of the services that can be obtained from local colleges and universities. Although the primary services applicable to the interdisciplinary model would be consultive in nature, many other services can be used to improve the overall nature of the instructional program in reading. Most colleges and universities are able to assign professors to teach graduate-level courses on-site in the local school system. In some instances, tailor-made graduate courses can be designed cooperatively by the school system reading specialist and the university professor. Such courses have a twofold payoff. First, they allow the expressed needs of the teachers to be met; second, they provide an opportunity for the reading specialist to follow up on course content when working with classroom teachers throughout the duration of the course. One warning needs to be made when considering utilizing the services of professors of higher education, though. Alone, they should not be expected to change overnight conditions which have existed in school systems for years or possibly decades. Changes in public education must come from within the system, not from outside. The local reading specialist must assume a large degree of the responsibility for bringing about that change. Professors can provide technical and consulting services, but their impact on changing a system in which they are tangentially involved can only be minimal.

Often smaller school districts are unable to financially support the full-time positions of members of the interdisciplinary team, such as speech therapists, psychologists, psychiatrists, social workers, psychometrists, or guidance counselors. If this is the case, the reading specialist, along with other school administrators, should investigate services that can be obtained from outside educational agencies. Two such agencies are the Cooperative Educational Service Agencies (CESA) in Wisconsin and the Board of Cooperative Educational Services (BOCES) in New York State. These programs provide itinerant specialized personnel to two or more school districts on a shared-time basis. Additionally, these agencies are able to provide additional supportive services, such as testing assistance, computer services, or regional libraries of instructional materials. For the reading specialist who is interested in implementing the interdisciplinary model in a small or medium-sized school district, a CESA or BOCES agency might be able to provide the additional professional services. One other final source of assistance may be available—community mental health centers. In Rhode Island, for example, county mental health clinics are able to provide the services of social workers, registered nurses, child psychiatrists, psychologists, and psychiatric nurses. The reading specialist who works for a school system with limited financial resources would do well to inquire into the feasibility of seeking additional aid from these outside agencies.

SUMMARY

The effective treatment of students with reading disabilities can no longer be thought of as the sole responsibility of the reading specialist. The effective remediation of a child's problem can occur only if an extensive and ongoing diagnosis takes place. A thorough diagnosis is best conducted by involving a variety of highly skilled professionals—the classroom teacher, the reading specialist, specialized personnel, support staff, and the school administrators. This contemporary approach permits a more accurate and insightful diagnosis to occur and thus increases the chances of alleviating the student's reading problem.

A key component in organizing an effective reading program is to establish a comprehensive assessment program. Such a program permits individuals with potentially severe reading problems to be identified early and also serves as a vehicle for implementing a personal accountability system for each teacher within the system.

Along with implementation of the interdisciplinary model, reading specialists need to adapt to a new role. No longer can they be isolated from the day-to-day instructional activities of the classroom teacher. Instead, they must assume a more direct leadership role in the school and serve in a consultive capacity, working closely with teachers on the improvement of classroom instruction. To accomplish this goal, they need administrative, financial, and staff support. In addition to internal support, the external support of the community, local colleges and universities, and outside educational agencies can be brought to bear on the problem. Through this cooperative effort, the role of the reading specialist can be expanded to provide maximum services to the widest population of administrators, teachers, and students, thereby making significant improvements in the quality of reading instruction in the public schools.

REFERENCES

Askov, E. *Primary Pupil Reading Attitude Inventory,* Dubuque, Iowa: Kendall/ Hunt, 1973.

CTB/McGraw-Hill *Prescriptive Reading Inventory,* Monterey, Calif.: CTB/McGraw-Hill, 1972.

Cooper, J. L., and M. L. McGuire *The Croft Inservice Reading Program,* New London, Conn.: Croft Educational Services, 1970.

Gates, A., and W. H. MacGinitie *Gates-MacGinitie Reading Tests,* New York: Teachers College Press, 1965.

Hill, W. "Testing for Reading Evaluation," in W. E. Blanton, R. Farr, and J. J. Tuinman, *Measuring Reading Performance,* Newark, Del.: International Reading Association, 1974.

Kelley, T. L., et al. *Stanford Achievement Test: Reading Tests,* New York: Harcourt Brace Jovanovich, 1966.

Millman, J. "Criterion Referenced Measurement: An Alternative," *The Reading Teacher* 26, 3 (December 1972): 278–281.

Otto, W., and E. Askov *The Wisconsin Design for Reading Skill Development,* Minneapolis: National Computer Systems, 1973.

Otto, W., and R. J. Smith *Administering the School Reading Program,* Boston: Houghton Mifflin, 1970.

Rude, R. T. "Objective-Based Reading Systems: An Evaluation," *The Reading Teacher* 28, 2 (November 1974): 169–175.

Thompson, R. A., and C. D. Dziuban "Criterion Referenced Reading Tests in Perspective," *The Reading Teacher* 27, 3 (December 1973): 292–294.

Tiegs, E. W., and W. W. Clark *California Reading Test,* Monterey, Calif.: CTB/ McGraw-Hill, 1957.

Chapter 18

IMPROVING THE TEACHING OF READING THROUGH IN-SERVICE

LAWRENCE G. ERICKSON • *West Virginia University—Morgantown*

An observation made by many teachers is: "I learned more about teaching during my first year than in any education class." What seems to happen is that the demands of the classroom provide a setting for teacher training that no college classroom or student-teaching experience can duplicate. The first-hand, practical experiences of dealing with pupils, a principal, a curriculum, parents, and other teachers provide a proving ground where ideas and plans on paper are forced into action on a daily basis. The continual and rapid cycle of setting instructional objectives, planning activities, and assessing outcomes in order to determine success or failure creates a dynamic learning situation. What follows is an attempt to suggest that the school is an optimal place to improve teacher competencies.

This chapter is based on the assumption that the potential of the school as a teacher-training facility has not been realized. The overall intent is to point out how in-service education can take advantage of the school as a setting where teachers can learn to improve reading instruction. The basic process of in-service is discussed first. The major focus is on the practical aspects of in-service as it relates to reading instruction. Specific in-service *formats* and *strategies* for implementing reading in-service programs are discussed. The last part of the chapter contains *examples* of in-service programs designed to help teachers and other staff members meet the needs of disabled readers.

THE IN-SERVICE PROCESS

The training potential of the school has not been fully realized because in-service education has not always been meaningful and worthwhile for teachers. Serious mistakes are made when the genuine needs of the instructional staff are overlooked, when in-service efforts are short-ranged, or when programs are more responsive to administrative than to instructional needs. Such mistakes can be corrected if steps are taken to: (1) identify the crucial in-service needs, (2) determine worthwhile goals, (3) establish specific in-service objectives, and (4) follow up and evaluate the results of the in-service effort.

Identify needs

In order to be worthwhile and meaningful, reading in-service must be based on the needs of the participants. This means that staff members must be actively involved in attempts to direct the in-service activities toward the reading needs that exist and that need attention. Actively involving participants and determining specific needs is no easy task. Even interest surveys do not always tap genuine teacher concerns, and individual teacher needs can easily be ignored because of the great variations within a school group. It is imperative that school leaders stimulate interest and assist school personnel to recognize crucial needs that exist in three key areas: reading programs, pupil reading performance, and staff performance related to reading instruction.

Reading program needs   Profitable in-service efforts can focus on the needs that exist in total school reading programs. A good strategy for determining the reading needs of the total school is to involve the principal and teachers in seeking answers to questions such as the ones that follow. A series of faculty meetings or small-group discussions devoted to these issues could reveal worthwhile in-service needs.

1. Is there a sequential program aimed at the development of basic reading skills for each student through grade six?
2. Are teachers using a variety of diagnostic measures to determine each student's reading level and specific reading skill needs?
3. Is there an overall school program of planned opportunities for functional and recreational reading?
4. Are there ample opportunities for students to carry out meaningful speaking and writing activities pertaining to reading experiences?
5. Is there a schoolwide emphasis on self-directed, guided silent reading?
6. Is the librarian considered to be part of the classroom reading program?
7. Is oral round-robin reading being deemphasized except for diagnostic and audience or entertainment purposes?

Another technique for determining school program needs is to use a questionnaire that provides a series of choices to which the staff can respond. For example, in a large school the following items could reveal overall preferences of the faculty:

Which of the following in-service topics would be most beneficial for improving our school reading program?

_____ Developing overall school reading objectives.

_____ Assessing techniques for determining specific reading needs of students.

_____ Teaching ideas and materials for disabled readers.

_____ Improving reading in content areas (science, math, social studies, etc.).

_____ Grouping students for reading instruction.

_____ Improving the teaching of word-attack skills.

_____ Improving the teaching of comprehension.

_____ Combining reading, writing, and speaking.

_____ Improving the use of the school library.

A committee could compile the results and report them to the faculty. Consensus could be reached at a faculty meeting and an overall school in-service program developed.

Ample opportunity by the total faculty to determine the school reading needs can have electrifying results when common interests and goals are agreed on. Too often, teachers work alone and receive little stimulating feedback. The common goals that teachers and administrators jointly determine can provide the impetus for the development of productive reading in-service that improves school reading programs.

Pupil reading needs   Focused attention on student performance in reading can reveal additional instructional needs. Certainly standardized test scores are one source for locating general strengths and weaknesses. For example, one school district observed that at the sixth-grade level the average word-attack scores for the district were much higher than the average reading comprehension scores. Further observation and discussion revealed that the junior high school teachers felt that students *could* read, that is, they had the decoding skills, but that they had little interest or motivation to *want* to read. This concern was the source for a long-range in-service effort that focused on improving reading comprehension and increasing the student's desire to read.

Another technique for assessing student reading performance is to have teachers ask students the following questions:

1. Are you interpreting difficult words accurately by using the context in which the words appear?
2. In a situation that demands oral reading, do you indicate your ability to convey meaning by supplying the appropriate intonation to the written words?
3. Are you able to read for a purpose by predicting outcomes, adjusting reading rates, formulating questions to be answered, etc.?
4. Do you have a flexible reading rate that varies according to different purposes and materials?
5. Are you able to outline a reading assignment, recall a sequence presented in print, summarize a paragraph, etc.?
6. Are you applying skills learned in developmental reading instruction to functional and recreational reading experiences?
7. Are you able to reflect and then intelligently discuss a reading selection?

At grade-level meetings, teachers should share the answers to these questions, identify common pupil reading needs, and begin to focus on in-service strategies designed to meet those common needs.

Staff needs Reading in-service efforts that are intended to improve staff performance must be based on accurate, specific, and observable staff behavior. One such needs-assessment technique is to ask school personnel involved with reading instruction to respond to a series of statements in this manner: To what extent *should* this be happening, and to what extent *is* it actually happening? The procedure is as follows:

Directions: Respond to the following items by indicating which of the following choices apply to each statement. Write the value (?, 1, 4, etc.) in both columns.

(?) *Do not know* the extent to which the condition exists in my school.

(0) Condition does *not* or should not exist *at all* in my school.

(1) Condition should or does exist *to a slight extent.*

(2) Condition should or does exist *to a moderate extent.*

(3) Condition should or does exist *to a fairly large extent.*

(4) Condition should or does exist *to a very large extent.*

Sample item: A wide variety of reading materials is available for efficient use by all classroom teachers.

	Should exist	*Actually exists*
	4	1

Sample assessment items:

1. In my classroom I use an informal reading inventory or some other diagnostic technique, such as the Spache Diagnostic Scales, to measure the appropriate level of instruction for each child.   _____   _____

2. Special assistance is provided outside the classroom for students in special need of reading help.   _____   _____

3. Students are assigned to small skill groups for short-term (three weeks or less) instruction in skills they have not yet mastered.   _____   _____

Another form of staff self-assessment is to ask teachers to rate their relative confidence in specific areas related to teaching reading. This self-report format can reveal areas of strength as well as areas of in-service need. An example of this format follows:

1. Motivating students:
   a) Creating and maintaining children's interest in reading.
      No confidence 1 2 3 4 5 6 7 Total confidence
   b) Integrating reading into both school-oriented and nonschool-oriented activities of children.
      No confidence 1 2 3 4 5 6 7 Total confidence

2. Diagnosing reading problems:
   a) Selecting an evaluation instrument to determine individual problem areas.
      No confidence 1 2 3 4 5 6 7 Total confidence
   b) Determining the proper instructional level for individual students.
      No confidence 1 2 3 4 5 6 7 Total confidence

3. Prescribing and implementing solutions to reading problems:
   a) Knowing of available alternative teaching methods.
      No confidence 1 2 3 4 5 6 7 Total confidence
   b) Choosing materials and methods appropriate for a given reading problem.
      No confidence 1 2 3 4 5 6 7 Total confidence
   c) Evaluating the level of mastery of specific reading skills.
      No confidence 1 2 3 4 5 6 7 Total confidence

This type of self-reporting can reveal accurate and specific strengths and weaknesses in staff behavior. Also, by using an assessment instrument like the ones previously described, the participants may feel more involved and committed to changing their own behavior. However, a self-assessment may overlook some crucial and hard-to-admit-to faults, especially if the performance of the supervisor or principal appears to be an area of weakness. One strategy for dealing with this problem is to involve an outside agent who is somewhat free of local school politics. Someone who is "temporary and powerless" can play a key role in determining the specific strengths and weaknesses that exist in the area of staff behavior as it relates to reading. For example, a respected reading specialist from another school district may assist in determining the strong and weak points in the behavior of teachers, principals, and local reading specialists. Or, a team of reading specialists from a local college or university could observe staff behavior over a period of time and present a report of their findings to the entire staff.

Changing staff behavior is no easy task. Forces within the schools tend to counteract in-service efforts to improve staff performance in reading. Unless staff performance in reading is accurately, specifically, and fairly assessed, in-service efforts will not have much effect. Identifying staff strengths and weaknesses deserves at least as much, if not more, attention than any other aspect of the needs-assessment portion of the in-service process. The entire process of improving reading instruction through in-service is based on the identification of need. Leadership and careful planning are necessary to accomplish this first step. The next step is to establish worthwhile, realistic goals and objectives.

Establish goals and objectives

All educators are somewhat guilty of not paying enough attention to outcomes. For example, teachers often focus *first on activities,* and later, when asked, "What are the objectives of these activities?" they will reply, "Oh, they were reading maps!" or "Phonics skills, yes, you know, like auditory and visual discrimination!" When pressed to supply details about which specific map skills or which phonic-analysis skills were focused on, the teacher may blurt out, "Well, if you were a teacher, you'd know!" In much the same manner and for the same reasons, many in-service efforts have also been no more than a collection of activities with little regard for improved instruction. Little effort, if any, is spent trying to decide exactly what is to be accomplished. It is no wonder that reading in-service efforts have been ineffective!

In order to move toward the overall goal of a specific in-service training experience, one must have specific objectives to guide the selection of activities that will enable the participants to reach their goals. Unfortunately, it is not unusual to find the in-service activity as the goal! That is, the goal of the in-service program appears to be no more than to have an in-service activity.

To overcome this problem it is a good idea to state objectives in behavioral, or performance, terms. That is, try to write the in-service objectives in words that describe what the participants should be able to do after completing the in-service. The big advantage to this step is that behavioral objectives will increase the chances of selecting worthwhile in-service activities. It is imperative to select activities that not only are meaningful to the participants, but also match the need and the overall goals of the in-service. Another reason for performance objectives is that they facilitate attempts to measure whether or not the activity did indeed help the participants reach the goal. For example, look at the following initial in-service plan. A second version of this plan indicates an attempt to clarify the goal, the objectives, and the activities. You can judge for yourself which plan is better.

INITIAL VERSION OF AN IN-SERVICE ON DIAGNOSING STUDENT READING NEEDS

Need: The teachers at Valley School have indicated a strong desire to learn about and implement techniques for diagnosing student reading needs.

Goal: Diagnosing student reading needs. (Comment: How can this be stated to more clearly designate a goal to be reached by the participants?)

Objectives/Activities: (Comment: Why do you think these have been combined? Are they behavioral?)

1. Given the article "Developing Reading Maturity in the Elementary School" by Smith, each participant will read and discuss the eight questions raised in the article.

2. Each participant will administer a criterion-referenced word-attack test to a student group.

3. Each participant will examine the variety of diagnostic tools available as listed in the booklet *Diagnosis of Reading Difficulties.*

4. The participants will examine the cloze procedure as outlined in *Diagnosis of Reading Difficulties.*

5. The participants will examine cumulative records and interpret the information on file for a student, using the information on stanines and percentiles in the booklet *Diagnosis of Reading Difficulties.*

Evaluation: Using a scale developed from the eight questions in the article "Developing Reading Maturity in the Elementary School," each participant will assess the current reading program at Valley School. After administering the diagnostic word-analysis test, each participant will record the data obtained on a class record sheet. Each participant will also administer at least one informal reading inventory and determine the instructional, frustrational, and optimal reading levels of a student. The participants will take a cloze test and decide individually if they will use it in their classroom. Finally, each participant will prepare a diagnostic summary sheet on one student.

REVISED VERSION OF THE VALLEY SCHOOL READING IN-SERVICE

Need: At a series of faculty meetings, the principal and teachers have reached a consensus that it would be very worthwhile to learn about and implement practical techniques for diagnosing specific student reading needs.

Goal: The staff will diagnose student reading needs, using a variety of group and individual measuring devices.

Specific Objectives/Activities/Evaluation:

1. The staff will be able to describe the characteristics of mature readers as outlined by Smith. At the first session the participants will read and discuss the article "Developing Reading Maturity in the Elementary School." Following a discussion of the article, the teachers will help develop a questionnaire based on the eight questions Smith calls "characteristics of mature readers." The teachers will then use the questionnaire to evaluate their classroom reading programs. The rationale for this step is that in order to deal with the reading needs of elementary students, it is necessary and most helpful to compare the *actual* reading behaviors in the school with some statements describing the *ideal* reading behaviors the staff hopes students will achieve.

2. The staff will be able to describe and evaluate the most effective use of a variety of reading diagnostic tools. At the second session, the participants will receive a copy of the handbook *Diagnosis of Reading Difficulties,* prepared by the school district reading specialists. It describes a variety of diagnostic procedures, including criterion-referenced tests, informal reading inventories, vocabulary tests, and the cloze procedure. The in-service leader will use the booklet to familiarize the participants with the best uses of the tests. The participants will work in small groups, sharing their reactions to the tests. This will be followed by a total group discussion to clarify and summarize points made in the booklet as well as pertinent issues raised by the group.

3. The staff will become familiar with and use a cloze test, a criterion-referenced test, and an informal reading inventory. At the third session, participants will receive copies of the criterion-referenced test as well as directions for constructing an IRI and a cloze test. The participants will work together by grade levels and plan specific uses for these assessment measures. Each teacher will administer the cloze test and the criterion-referenced test to a group of students and an IRI to selected individual students.

4. Using the booklet *Diagnosis of Reading Difficulties,* and with the assistance of the in-service leaders, each teacher will use the reading test results

and the cumulative records to prepare a report of the reading needs of groups and selected individuals at Valley School.

5. The participants will meet in appropriate grade-level groups to share results and begin to plan specific instruction based on the report of reading needs. (*Comment:* Although this portion of the in-service appears to go beyond the stated goal of the in-service, it seems rather incomplete to assess specific needs and not plan instruction to get at those needs.) Of course, the final evaluation of the in-service would depend on the ability of the staff to: (1) state the characteristics of mature readers, (2) identify the specific strengths and needs of groups and individual students, and (3) plan instruction based on those strengths and weaknesses.

After reading these two versions, do you see some advantages to writing specific behavioral objectives? For example, compare the first objective in the two versions. In the former, the participants were to "read and discuss" eight questions; in the revised version, they were to "describe the characteristics of good readers as outlined by Smith." Do you agree that the revised version describes a more specific behavior? Do you see how specific objectives force in-service planners to consider outcomes and to predict behaviors that will result in relevant learning for the participants? Writing specific objectives based on the needs of the participants is crucial to planning workable and effective in-service activities and facilitates the next step in the process, the selection of activities for the in-service participants.

Select activities

At this point in the process, there is a strong temptation to select activities on the basis of their past success, their entertainment value, or some factor other than how well they match the objectives determined prior to the in-service. The point, of course, is that activities in and of themselves are neither good nor bad; their success rests not on their current popularity, but rather on the extent to which they help achieve a specific objective as well as attain the overall goal. Matching activities and objectives is no easy task, because the kinds of possible activities are controlled by the characteristics of the participants and the availability of time and resources. For example, it is of little value to present oversimplified information to a group of teachers with a highly sophisticated level of competence. Nor would it be worthwhile to plan a series of lectures or demonstrations without a budget to adequately pay the expenses or honorarium of a distinguished authority. Similarly, it is foolish to expect teachers to fully understand a complex individualized reading management system in a one-hour session after school. Given the restrictions of time, resources, and the type of audience, what are some guidelines for selecting activities to match objectives?

First, consider the goals and objectives of the in-service. Do they all seem to suggest that information-providing activities will suffice, or do they point toward activities designed to effect significant changes in staff attitudes and instructional practices? If information is called for, lectures, observations, demonstrations, and audiovisual presentations will probably do the job. But if new behaviors and attitude changes are required, activities such as large- and small-group discussions, buzz sessions, brainstorming, role playing, and guided practice sessions are needed. Thus the relationship between the specific goals and objectives and the actual activities that the participants engage in will determine the success or failure of the program. Because activity selection is most crucial, the following questions may serve as guidelines for matching activities with objectives:

1. What is each activity supposed to accomplish in light of the overall goal and the specific in-service objective?
2. When has the activity been successful in the past? What conditions attributed to its success?
3. When has the activity been unsuccessful? What conditions attributed to its failure? What were the undesirable outcomes?
4. How can the activity be modified to fit a specific situation?

In addition to the process of matching activities to goals and objectives, there are the more mundane but equally crucial realities of time, personnel, and budget. Districtwide *in-service days* are a sound idea, provided they do not deteriorate into record-keeping days, staff visits to the "model" school and a buffet luncheon at a fancy eatery, or a presentation by a reading authority at a districtwide meeting where more consideration is given to making sure that everyone attends than to any preplanning or follow-up activity. To better utilize such resources as released time, personnel, and money, individual schools or clusters of schools should seek to match needs with objectives. For example, districtwide in-service days could be handled on an individual school basis, *provided that each school has an in-service plan*. Requiring schools to plan in-service in the spring for the coming year could help reverse the all too common practice of determining time first and then figuring out what to do. It also has the added positive condition of placing the responsibility on the school staff for determining needs, planning activities, and then considering the time needed to meet the objectives. The point is, *time* must be considered in the light of the overall goals, objectives, and specific activities required to meet the goals. Finally, what kinds of changes are to be realized as a result of the in-service? If the objectives call for informational activities, perhaps shorter, one-session time slots will do the job. But if significant behavior changes and attitude shifts are to be realized, longer individual time slots may have to be made available over a two- or even three-year period.

In addition to time factors, the success or failure of many activities is often determined by the personnel available to lead the activities. Again, take a look at the objectives and the participants. Will the participants need an overall theoretical understanding, or can that be omitted for more practical ideas? Is there a person who can do both? Is there an "outsider" who can communicate with the participants? Is there an experienced classroom teacher who can demonstrate a technique? Are there local teachers willing to share instructional alternatives they have devised? Very often teachers have the answers to other teachers' questions, and in-service activities that allow the sharing of such ideas can be very successful. On the other hand, maybe the solution to problems with a school's reading curriculum can be found by bringing in an outside expert. This temporary and powerless "expert" may be unencumbered by local school district political intrigue and may trod on touchy areas that would otherwise go unexplored because of their sensitive nature.

Of course, the ability to select personnel is directly related to in-service budget considerations. There is no getting around the fact that unless in-service activities are supported by funds, there will be less than satisfactory success. Along with time considerations, in-service planning must include budgeting money for cost of materials, equipment purchase and maintenance, facility rental, clerical supplies, consultant fees, and even compensation for participants. Finally, even though funds are not limitless, there is little reason to expect something for nothing. Those charged with planning in-service activities must give serious consideration to the realistic money demands incurred by meaningful activities. To omit financial needs may limit the alternatives to the point where it might be better to not try anything!

Selecting activities, the most crucial part of the process, requires that in-service planners have more than their share of ESP. Paying keen attention to the needs of the participants, as well as to the objectives flowing out of those needs, will help in selecting activities that will not only be acceptable to the participants, but will also result in improved reading instruction.

Evaluate results

It is sad but true that most in-service efforts are rarely followed up in any fashion to see if the expenditure of time, money, and effort resulted in any payoff. There is little doubt that the one-shot, released-time syndrome characteristic of in-service programing hinders any worthwhile evaluation. That is why basing programs on demonstrated needs, establishing goals, stating objectives, and selecting activities that will move participants toward the goals is needed if there is to be any accounting for time, money, and effort. There is little doubt that accounting for in-service efforts is greatly enhanced when specific objectives are employed as criteria for judging the relative success or failure of a program.

For example, in the Valley School plan described earlier, the objective was for the staff to diagnose student reading needs with a variety of group and individual measuring devices. Assessing this in-service program would involve looking at the teachers' reports of the reading needs of groups and individuals based on the results of such activities as the cloze test, criterion-referenced test, and the informal reading inventory. Of course, there are other ways to measure outcomes: paper-and-pencil tests to get at facts and concepts, samples of products produced during the in-service to reveal progress toward a goal, and observation of school and classroom performance to find out whether or not teachers are using the diagnostic techniques in their classrooms.

Measuring outcomes is also useful because goals are not always achieved. Evaluation gives in-service leaders and staff members a method for determining a number of things. Maybe additional information, more time, or a different activity will help meet the goal. Or, perhaps the goal needs to be modified if it appears to be irrelevant or unrealistic because of time factors, resource limitations, or the changing needs of the participants.

A final point on evaluation needs to be made. Because almost all school districts conduct some type of in-service program, it makes good sense to find out what works and what fails. Why keep repeating the same mistakes over and over? Maybe the reason that most in-service time is viewed as "something we *have* to do" rather than "something we *want* to do" is because very little effort has gone into measuring outcomes. As a result, the same mistakes are made over and over again; thus mediocre in-service activities are the rule rather than the exception.

Summary

The in-service process involves the following steps:

1. *Identifying needs.* Determine the problems that need attention by examining the school reading program, the students' reading performance, and the instructional staff's performance.
2. *Establish goals.* Since it is likely that a number of needs exist, have the participants reach consensus about working on a specific problem together.
3. *State objectives.* Look ahead and state specific objectives that describe the in-service goal in terms of what the participants will do as a result of the in-service.

4. *Select activities.* In matching the objectives with appropriate activities, consider the characteristics of the participants, the available in-service personnel, time, and money.

5. *Evaluate results.* Use a variety of techniques (paper-and-pencil tests, work samples, and performance observation) to determine whether the objectives and the goals were attained.

IN-SERVICE FORMATS

This section describes some of the formats, or basic activities, that comprise in-service programs. As you read about each activity, think about the ways you could modify or combine activities to carefully construct a program that not only matches the objectives, but that also fits the leaders, participants, and the available time and resources. The basic formats are: lectures, group discussions, demonstrations and observations, buzz sessions, brainstorming, group interviews, role playing, and contracts.

Lecture

If the objectives call for providing a one-way, controlled flow of information that is efficient and straightforward, a lecture is probably a good activity. Basic facts, examples, and directions for future activities can be presented very effectively in a lecture format. For example, an explanation of an informal reading inventory is probably necessary when beginning an in-service program that will eventually require teachers to design, administer, and interpret the test. On the other hand, if the in-service is attempting to move teachers toward more individualized reading instruction, a single lecture by a dynamic authority may begin, but certainly will not complete, the process. In other words, save lectures for controlling input of information, initiating sessions, clarifying and sustaining key concepts, and reviewing and summarizing portions of a program.

Group interview

When there is a need to share a number of viewpoints in a structured manner, a group interview may be quite effective. Two examples of this activity are:

1. Interview a group of people who are thoroughly familiar with a reading program that is being considered by the audience.

2. Follow a presentation about criterion-referenced reading management with buzz groups. The purpose of the buzz groups would be to raise questions about the apparent strengths and weaknesses of the program.

In order to share its results, each group would appoint a reporter, who would respond to a series of questions posed by the interviewer. The success of such a reporting session is enhanced by minimizing repetitive comments.

This type of activity is an efficient way to share expert opinion or small-group ideas with a larger audience.

Group discussion

It is often disheartening to find that even though many school activities involve problem-solving committees, relatively few group participants, including many educational leaders, exhibit the group interaction skills necessary for successful, worthwhile group discussions.

Some crucial points to remember when using group discussions as in-service activities are listed below:

1. Try to make sure that the participants have both a real interest in and information about the topic.

2. Try to get the group to reach consensus on what is the problem or topic for discussion. Many group discussions flounder because the participants have a variety of concerns. For example, some people will offer statements that are solutions to problems outside of the main topic; others will remain unclear about what the topic for discussion really is. Take definite steps to get the group to reach consensus, by writing down the main objective of the discussion and displaying it for all to see.

3. Group discussions are sometimes facilitated by projecting a timetable for carrying out activities, keeping a record of the group decisions, and by following up group discussions with a brief written report.

4. Groups should be limited in size. A range of six to twenty members is an optimal group size, because problem-solving groups need to be large enough to accomplish their objectives yet small enough to provide considerable personal interaction. In groups with more than 20 members, it is a good idea to subdivide the group. The conclusions reached by each smaller unit would then be shared with the total group.

5. Superficial characteristics, such as eagerness to lead or affability, can be misleading. Training and experience with group interaction skills should be an essential requisite for good group leadership.

6. Do not assume that getting a group of people together to discuss a problem will automatically result in a solution. There must be a need, an agreed-on objective, careful preplanning, and usually some written report or follow-up activity.

Demonstrations and observations

Two preferred activities are demonstrations and observations. However, there are two problems with these approaches. First, teachers have a tendency to reject some modeling behavior; second, some teachers often misperceive the key behaviors of the model. In order to eliminate such potential problems, the audience should be prompted to focus intently on the crucial behavior being demonstrated. Also, keep in mind that there is a tendency for some teachers to reject some modeling behavior because they are aware of an array of alternatives and often react by thinking, "That isn't what I would say!" For these reasons, demonstrations and observations should focus on rather specific behavior, followed immediately by communication between the audience and the model. Another caution to keep in mind is that observing in schools is often less than ideal because of the unpredictability of everyday classroom life and the lack of preplanning between the school and the visitors. However, if there is a need to see a specific technique in a live situation, the following guidelines should help maximize the effectiveness of these activities:

1. When planning a demonstration or an observation, select a specific objective and determine if the activity will indeed match the objective. Don't assume that an expert authority or a model school has exactly what is needed.

2. Avoid lengthy introductions and move rather quickly into the demonstration. Allow plenty of time *afterwards* for a complete discussion.

3. If possible, limit one-shot observations and demonstrations to somewhat general objectives. Although difficult to manage, try to observe a specific activity repeatedly or over a period of time under varying conditions. This will allow the observers to catch more details.

Buzz sessions

In buzz sessions, small groups meet briefly (15 to 45 minutes) to discuss specific topics. The intent is to stimulate verbal interaction. The purpose of buzz groups is to identify points of agreement and conflict, which should increase interest in the topic and even obtain commitment to attempt changes. Some necessary procedures are as follows:

1. Buzz sessions need leaders who can encourage full discussion and recorders who are able to sort ideas and synthesize them for feedback to the total group.

2. Round tables or circles of chairs facilitate discussion. Also, groups should be separated somewhat from other groups to minimize noise interference.

3. Buzz sessions should be used only after attempts have been made to interest people and provide them with information about the topic.

4. In order for buzz groups to work, people must have definite feelings and opinions to express, there must be more than one solution available, or there must be a need to react to an "apparent" solution.

A buzz-session activity in an in-service program is appropriate when the objective is, for example, to have intermediate-grade teachers alter their content-area reading activities to account for students with reading disabilities. For example, after making the point that poor readers often cannot read science or social studies selections, buzz groups would be formed to seek solutions to the problem.

Buzz sessions are especially useful in school in-service efforts because they are active, highly flexible, easy to use, and suited to situations in which small groups of teachers need to generate and share alternatives.

Brainstorming

If there is a need to generate many ideas, solutions, problems, and issues, brainstorming is a good activity. However, it is imperative that special care be taken by in-service leaders to see that the correct "climate" for brainstorming exists. Criticism, analysis, and discussion of emerging ideas must be avoided. If participants have not brainstormed extensively, one way to help ensure that ideas do not get edited immediately is to post the following rules for all to see:

1. We want a maximum number of ideas that are related to the topic.
2. You can modify, adapt, or express one idea as another.
3. Try to express all ideas as clearly and concisely as possible.
4. No one should discuss or criticize anyone's contributions until all of the ideas have been generated by the small group.

Of course, small groups facilitate brainstorming. But even 75 people can brainstorm at the same time, provided that three or more leaders can take ideas at the same time and capture them on the chalkboard, overhead projector, or large sheets of paper.

A sound practice is to establish a time limit and terminate the session when interest wanes. Brainstorming should be followed by a group discussion or buzz sessions in order to analyze, criticize, edit, and suggest ways to implement the ideas.

There is no need to brainstorm when there are no real issues or if the participants believe that their ideas will not be used. But if fresh ideas are needed, brainstorm!

In addition to the previously mentioned small-group activities, there are times when there is an urgent need for in-service activities that focus rather sharply on personal attitudes, feelings, and behaviors. There is ample evidence to support the notion that significant behavior changes occur for very personal and intimate reasons. Two activities intended to deal with this issue are role playing and contracts.

Role playing

When there is a need for spontaneous oral interaction, role playing may enable participants to act and feel as though they were in the real situation. Role playing is enhanced when there is genuine rapport among the participants. The usual procedure is to identify a situation, assign roles, play out the scene, and stop at an appropriate time. Leaders of role-playing activities should take steps to ensure that participants feel comfortable with their roles. This means that role playing should focus on a specific problem, and explicit role assignments should be made so that participants will know what is to be expected of them. Also, participants must be cautioned to stick to the assigned roles and to stop *playing* before overinvolvement causes someone embarrassment.

Some good follow-up activities include seeking reactions from the audience and the role players and switching roles. For example, groups of ten to fifteen teachers, administrators, and supervisiors could observe two actors, discuss the play or have buzz sessions to react, and also have a chance to role play.

One in-service activity is to have a teacher play a principal or supervisor role while the supervisor or principal acts as the teacher. Have the teacher/actor seek the principal's approval to try a different grouping plan or some new materials for disabled readers. Another variation is to have the supervisor/principal actor try to convince the person playing the teacher to implement a different grouping plan or new reading activities designed to meet the needs of disabled readers. As you can see, the variations of roles and situtions are flexible and are especially suitable when in-service objectives call for participants to *feel* the need for change.

Contracts

When participants seem to be ready to implement strategies gleaned from recent in-service experiences, a good plan is for teachers, principals, and supervisors to reach consensus in the form of a contract. The agreement should predict specific pupil and teacher behaviors and contain a time line and an evaluation plan. A contract should state that the teacher will be responsible for pupil attainment of selected, specific reading objectives.

In order for this to happen, a number of basic steps must be followed. First, it is imperative that everyone understands that the teacher's job is to *produce learning* and that the administrator's job is to *help the teacher* achieve that end. Next, the teacher and the administrator should jointly describe, define, and agree on what is to be taught and when, how, and to whom it will be taught. The contract must also state what student performance behavior will be accepted as evidence that the teacher did indeed produce learning.

An example of an instructional contract in reading is the following hypothetical plan. Assume that Valley School has recently completed an inservice program to implement a reading-management system that contains specific reading objectives, criterion-referenced tests for measuring the objectives, and teaching activities that match the objectives. These components provide basic information for the contract. That is, when students respond to the criterion-referenced test, any specific objectives the students have not mastered become a source for what is specified in the contract. In the contract the teacher and the administrator should state the objectives that the children will learn in a specified period of time. The teacher must have every assurance that the children should be able to achieve the selected objectives. The contract should also specify how the administrator will support instruction with supervision, materials, time, space, equipment, and even additional help, such as an aide or volunteer. The key to the contract plan is that the reading-management system, which states specific instructional objectives in reading, allows the teacher and administrator to *agree in advance* on what will be accepted as evidence that the teacher has been successful.

In this type of individualized in-service activity, the teacher does not have to choose objectives that are too difficult or that have already been mastered. Also, the individual characteristics of students should be considered when predicting future achievement. Finally, it is a good idea to make it possible to revise the contract by altering objectives when initial instruction reveals new information about the students.

Summary

Because selecting activities that match in-service objectives is a most crucial task, in-service leaders are advised to: (1) become familiar with a range of alternatives by examining all of the activities that have been described, and (2) select, combine, and adapt these basic formats in order to meet both the objectives of the program and the educational, social, and emotional needs of the participants.

IMPLEMENTATION STRATEGIES

If, up to this point, you see some sense to the in-service process and the basic activities, but still feel that there is more to consider, you're absolutely right! Preplanning considerations and strategies for involving personnel need further elaboration.

Preplanning

A basic error in in-service planning is to omit considering all of the crucial school components that must be adjusted in order to improve reading instruction. In-service programs should not focus solely on teacher behavior. Other issues that must be considered are the principal's expectations for teachers, money for different tests and materials, a new time schedule, a new record-keeping system, a different report card, increased planning time, as well as different supply, equipment, and space needs. In addition to these obvious factors there are often many formal and informal rules and policies that may have to be adjusted in order to support the staff during the early and difficult stages encountered when new instructional practices are initiated.

If all of these components are to be considered in the preplanning stages, it is obvious that the planning group must include someone in the school who carries enough weight to make changes in policies and current practices. Who will that be?

Extensive in-service experience in large and small, rural and urban, and elementary and secondary schools reveals the local school principal to be a key person. Principals are crucial to preplanning; indeed, some of the most successful reading in-service programs have been directed by well-informed principals. It is not imperative that principals train teachers themselves. Obviously, many principals lack the time and expertise to do so, but they must be actively involved because they can help point out changes that will have to be made before the objectives of the in-service can be reached.

In many schools there are other influential staff members who must be involved besides the principal. In any case, it is useful to develop a checklist of questions that will help determine whether or not all of the important components of the total school have been considered. Some of the questions might be:

1. Has the *need* for in-service been clearly demonstrated?
   a) Is there information available which accurately describes ways in which the needs of disabled readers are or are not being met by the current program?

b) Are there data on pupil reading performance, including norm-referenced and/or criterion-referenced test results and teachers' anecdotal comments?

c) Is there evidence that teachers need and want help in meeting the needs of disabled readers?

d) Is there research or personal testimony available that supports the need to change current practices?

2. Have *factors outside of reading instruction* been considered?

a) Do any existing policies and procedures inhibit attaining the objectives of the program?

b) What other in-service programs are currently being carried out or planned?

c) Are curriculum changes, such as new textbooks in science, mathematics, or social studies, being contemplated?

3. Have *personnel factors* been considered?

a) Can significant changes in key staff assignments, such as transfer, retirement, or new duties, be foreseen?

b) Is there written commitment or other evidence of support from the key administrators, supervisors, and central office reading people?

c) Have key people been selected to coordinate, lead, or act as local consultants?

d) Is there a need for social activities during or following workshop sessions?

4. Has a detailed *budget* been determined?

a) Are funds available for rewarding participants, paying consultant fees, buying refreshments, materials, clerical supplies, equipment, and finally, renting facilities?

b) Is money available for continuing consultant help, new material and equipment, and other long-range needs?

5. Has a *time line* been planned?

a) Has adequate time been allowed for all crucial aspects of the in-service to be fully developed?

b) Have definite dates been established and agreed on by all leaders, participants, and support staff?

c) Are facilities and equipment available on the dates they are needed?

6. Have *communications* been planned to inform other people both inside and outside the organization?

a) How will the changes affect students' and parents' roles?

b) Will the changes affect the duties and responsibilities of maintenance and purchasing procedures?

c) Will the changes affect the roles and responsibilities of special education teachers, school psychologists, guidance counselors, and art, music, and physical education teachers?

7. Have facility needs been checked?

a) Will remodeling of the present facilities be needed?

b) Should additional or new facilities be planned?

c) Will special equipment or furnishings be necessary to meet the in-service objectives?

This list is only a beginning, but it does demonstrate the need to consider reading in-service as part of a larger environment. It should be obvious that improving one portion of an instructional plan requires an accounting of many factors that may need adjustment before changes can be made.

Involving personnel

In the preceding discussion there was a plea to give principals a leadership role in the preplanning phase. This section will outline steps for obtaining the involvement and commitment of not only principals and teachers, but also central office administrators, supervisors, and reading specialists.

Strategy one   Because the pupils, teachers, principal, and the parents are the primary sources of reading-instructional needs, the *single school* should be considered the optimum unit for improving reading instruction. To approach in-service on a systemwide basis is to ignore the different needs that exist among and within schools. To approach in-service on a teacher-by-teacher basis is to ignore factors that can be changed only when groups of teachers, along with the principal and other staff members, support one another in seeking changes. In-service education arising out of the demands placed on teachers by the problems confronting them on a daily basis taps a most powerful source of motivation for change—the daily grind!

Strategy two   In order to involve local school personnel, each school needs an active group of staff representatives who meet each week to deal with the problems that everyone says they have. It is not uncommon to find everyone busy running the school, but no one trying to deal with the problems that are heatedly discussed in the teachers' lounge! Each school should have an *in-service committee* or an instructional-improvement committee of representative teachers who meet regularly with the principal to seek ways of improving instruction. This group should deal with such questions as: Who are the disabled readers? What are we doing in our classrooms to help them? What expectancies do we have for them? Do we assess their performance, teach them what they need, and determine whether or not they are making any progress? How do we help disabled readers in science, mathematics, and social studies?

This group should play a major role in determining local school policies, planning the local curriculum to fit the local students' needs, and in general act as the "conscience of the school" by continually focusing on student needs.

Strategy three   Some schools have found it most valuable to have a *reading resource teacher* who is easily accessible to all teachers and the principal. Rather than teaching disabled readers, the reading resource teacher helps the teachers and the principal meet the needs of disabled readers. This plan works well at both the elementary and secondary levels, provided that the person interacts regularly and cooperatively with the staff. In order to obtain such a person, a classroom teacher who has good rapport with the staff and who has some reading expertise might serve in this capacity. In order to free this person to help with reading instruction, hire a substitute for a half day or a full day each week. To maintain continuity, try to use the same substitute each week. In this way the resource teacher is free to confer, plan, coordinate, locate reading material, test children, and help keep an eye on reading instruction. Of course, this is just one example. The strategy is to have a *person* who is accepted by the teachers and principal and who can devote regular efforts toward the reading needs that exist within a given school.

Strategy four   In each school the principal, each grade-level or teaching unit, and each teacher should be responsible for *written goal statements* about the reading needs that exist. The in-service committee, the reading resource teacher (if there is one), and the principal should develop these statements together. The process of reaching consensus on common needs and goals is no easy task and involves considerable leadership skill by the principal. In many cases principals have relied on consultants to help schools complete this task.

The process of preparing statements might work like this. In March or April the teachers and their representatives or team leaders meet and list the reading instructional needs from their viewpoint. At the same time the principal and the reading resource teacher should draft their version of the reading needs. At a series of meetings in April or May the total staff should reach consensus on some goals designed to meet the needs everyone says they have. Usually, the wide range of needs that this process generates makes it imperative to narrow the problems to four or five that deserve attention and that have a good chance for solution.

This process allows the entire staff to focus on the needs that exist in the context of a given school. This kind of planning should not only help teachers feel involved and committed to improved instruction, but also commit the principal to the same goals. Also, by starting the process in the spring and framing common goals early enough, the entire staff can get a head start on future changes.

Strategy five   The first four steps may be only a paper exercise unless the principal takes the school goals to his or her immediate superior and tries to mesh them with the district goals. At this stage a good plan is to form a triad of the principal, the principal's superior, and curriculum staff members who have some reading expertise. For example, if one of the goals is to improve the reading achievement of disabled readers, a reading specialist must check to see that the plan has realistic goals, appropriate reading activities, and valid tests of reading achievement. The principal's "boss" must be included in order to secure a commitment from the central administration for time, funds, expert advice, and overall support for improving instruction. This is crucial, because many instructional improvements are hindered by decisions made at rather high levels in school systems. The intent of this strategy is to create an administrative process whereby the principal, the central office administrator, and the curriculum expert all agree to work together to attain common and realistic goals which are based on school needs.

Summary

Implementing in-service activities requires extensive preplanning and administrative policies which allow teachers, principals, administrators, and curriculum experts to agree on common needs and goals. All of these strategies go together to make a delivery system for in-service education which takes advantage of the school as an ideal setting for improving teacher competencies.

EXAMPLES OF READING IN-SERVICE PROGRAMS

This section will describe examples of reading in-service programs that represent much of what has been presented so far in this chapter. The examples are school-based rather than districtwide, because in-service activities tailored to the immediate needs of students, teachers, principals, and parents have the most potential for improving instruction. In considering these examples, it is important to keep in mind that they are *examples* rather than models to be copied without regard for local conditions. Second, they cover more than what is often expected when discussing disabled readers. This is intentional. Too often, reading in-service programs have implied separate instruction in separate places for disabled readers. It makes good sense to keep instruction for disabled readers closely related to the regular curriculum, because often the most meaningful instruction is that related directly to the objectives of the content areas.

Example 1: Setting appropriate objectives for junior high readers

Need   At a series of faculty meetings the staff decided that there was a great need to help disabled readers better comprehend social studies, science, home economics, mathematics, and other content material.

Goal   To set realistic reading instructional objectives for disabled readers.

Objective   Working together, the teachers, principal, and district reading specialist will design a social studies unit on West Virginia history that contains objectives, activities, and evaluation items for disabled readers.

Activities   In March a series of bimonthly early dismissal times will be arranged by the principal. At the first meeting the reading specialist will present a plan for teachers to follow when attempting to adjust instruction to meet individual differences. A portion of the presentation could contain the following information, adapted from Duffy (1974).

1. Differentiating instruction can be facilitated when teachers attempt to answer these questions:
   a) "How can student *objectives* be adjusted to compensate for decoding deficiencies?
   b) How can learning *activities* be adjusted to compensate for decoding deficiencies?
   c) How can student *evaluations* be adjusted to compensate for decoding deficiencies?"*
2. Planning differentiated instruction involves completing Table 18.1.* Teachers should identify the student's strengths and weaknesses and fill in the spaces with details of how objectives, activities, and evaluations will be adjusted to ensure learning.

---

* Gerald G. Duffy and George B. Sherman, "Improving Achievement through Differentiated Instruction," in Gerald G. Duffy, ed., *Reading in the Middle School*, Newark, Del.: IRA, 1974, p. 123. Reprinted with permission of Gerald G. Duffy and the International Reading Association.

Table 18.1. Planning for differentiated instruction

Unit plan	Student differences			
	Decoding	Experience	Interest	Thinking
Student objectives				
Learning activities				
Evaluations				

3. The leader should provide the teachers and principal with examples of how to differentiate for disabled readers in social studies by using West Virginia history objectives as a starting point.

4. The leader should present some strategies for intraclass grouping, independent activities, and ways to make use of volunteers, paraprofessionals, and student tutors.

During this initial presentation, the leader should anticipate a thorough discussion and even heated exchange about teachers' attitudes toward setting different objectives for different students. Some teachers may argue that because there is one text to be used with all students, there is little chance to allow for different objectives, activities, and evaluations. Other teachers will be concerned about managing small groups and independent activities within a classroom.

It is important to deal with these concerns, because differentiated instruction works only for teachers who accept individual differences as part of teaching junior high students. Since there is a good chance that there will be some indecision in accepting this plan, the leader should say something like: "You say that you are concerned about disabled readers and you have asked me to show you some ways to help them. I believe that you do want to help these kids. The plan I have presented seems to be one reasonable way to get at your concern. I guess the question boils down to whether you really *want* to do something. If you do, let's start now; if not, let's go home!" Regardless of how it is said, the point is to get commitment from the group to begin working on a plan. Reluctance to accept differentiated instruction may be further reduced by pointing out that the in-service objective calls for the total staff to collectively develop a social studies unit on a familiar topic. The assumption is that this *group approach* will afford more security and motivation than if individual teachers were to tackle differentiated instruction alone.

A good way to end this initial presentation is to have the participants agree to take on specific tasks. For example, small subgroups should tentatively agree to: (1) collect a variety of reading materials on West Virginia history; (2) write objectives that reflect the range of reading abilities present in the eighth grade; (3) design and match both reading and nonreading activities to the objectives; (4) design a variety of evaluation activities that would check on the objectives but not penalize disabled readers; and (5) look into possible ways to use peer tutors, small-group instruction within classrooms, independent learning activities, new time schedules, and parents and volunteers from the community.

At the second session, the subgroups should project time lines for completing their activities in time to implement differentiated instruction in September. Specific assignments should also be finalized at this session. For example, the social studies teachers, the librarian, and a group of teachers should collect materials; the reading consultant should help other teachers write objectives, design activities, and consider evaluation. Finally, the principal and a committee of teachers should tackle the time schedule, grouping plans, and tutoring possibilities.

At the third and fourth sessions in April, the group should review the objectives and activities and examine the materials. If an adopted text contains valuable information on West Virginia history, portions may be tape recorded so that students with the most severe reading problems can listen. Another alternative is to find easier material that presents the same concepts and matches the reading skill of the disabled reader. Because this may not always be possible, some teachers should try to rewrite some key portions of the basic text. Reading-study guides should also be prepared to assist students in focusing on key concepts and vocabulary items. Teachers who are gathering materials should try to provide resources, e.g., filmstrips, magazines, newspaper articles, pictures, and other materials, which may be easier to understand. One benefit of the staff's doing these activities together with the principal is that they should be comfortable altering objectives and activities. The staff should realize that they are not watering down the objectives as much as they are altering *how* the student obtains the necessary information. Finally, in order to assess disabled readers on West Virginia history concepts, all tests should be based only on the materials that these students used to learn West Virginia history. Another idea is to use oral tests with students who would be completely frustrated by written examinations.

Evaluation   In September the social studies teachers should be ready to implement a carefully thought-out plan that includes differentiated objectives, activities, and evaluations. There should also be some plans for grouping within a given section. If possible, a new time schedule, peer tutors, and teacher aides should be available. The social studies teacher should try the plan in one or more sections and report successes and failures to the staff at least every two weeks. It is most crucial to demonstrate support for the teacher even when failures are reported, because no new plan such as this one will ever be free of problems. Teachers should have the opportunity to discuss problems openly with assurances of administrative and peer support. The report sessions should generate new alternatives for future individualization rather than deal only with immediate past failures.

If at all possible, the plan should be followed for as long as it takes to obtain relative success. In any event, the decision to continue or abandon the plan should be made by the teachers who have worked closely with the plan, for they have the most intimate knowledge of its relative merits.

Example 2: Scheduling time for helping disabled readers

Need The teachers have expressed concern that they cannot find time to help disabled readers.

Goal To discuss alternatives and to plan definite times for a "special-help period."

Objective The teachers, principal, and some parents will meet to arrange a definite special-help time for students in grades 1–3 who need individual attention in reading.

Activities At the first session, the group should focus on the crucial points of concern that teachers have, as well as the concerns of the principal and the parents. For example, the principal may point out that children need immediate help on the same day that they have difficulty with a skill or concept. The teachers may also point out how difficult it is to do this in a typical busy classroom. It will help to present specific facts about the school time schedule, each teacher's daily class schedule, the lunch hour, the number of students who usually need help, as well as the parents' concern about the lunch hour and the length of the school day. Keeping facts like these in mind will help the group focus on the prime issue, which seems to be *time*.

Assuming that the problem is finding time to give individual help, a good activity would be to brainstorm some alternatives in small groups. After reviewing the rules for brainstorming (see the previous discussion of this activity), allow the groups of teachers and parents about 20 minutes to generate some alternatives. Then share the information by writing down ideas on large sheets of paper for everyone to see, take a short refreshment break, and evaluate the alternatives that are posted. Some of the possible points of consensus that might emerge are the following.

1. A daily 30-minute special-help period is desirable.
2. Each teacher should try to arrange his or her own daily schedule to include a 30-minute special-help period.
3. The school should arrange a 30-minute special-help period, such as an arranged dismissal time, so that all primary-grade teachers could have a chance to work with individual children while the other children are dismissed for lunch.

Let's assume that the group stopped at this point and arranged a future meeting. During this interval the teachers and the principal should try to work out some detailed alternatives which fit the three points of consensus. For example, if everyone agreed that each teacher should plan a 30-minute special-help period, the following ideas are pertinent.

1. A daily 30-minute independent work period requires a lot of planning in order to ensure that every student has some meaningful work to do.
2. Spend some time during the school day teaching students what to do during this time. Don't expect students to know how to work independently. Don't give up after a few days of less than satisfactory results.
3. Provide a list of activities that are appropriate for this time. Put the list on a large poster for everyone to refer to.
4. Give the students a chance to experience success and praise for working alone. Teach them some signals that will tell them when they can come to you for help and when they should not interrupt you.
5. Use this time to work with individual children who need immediate help with skills.

However, if the school dismissal times can be altered, an even better plan may be to arrange a schedule that allows teachers to keep students who need special help. For example, it might be possible to start school 15 minutes earlier and dismiss classes 15 minutes earlier at lunchtime. Thus the primary grades might be dismissed at 11:15 A.M. so that the next 30 minutes could be used for a special-help period. Children not needing such help would go home or to the lunch room. The others would stay until 11:45 A.M., yet still have time to go home for lunch or to eat at school.

This schedule allows the teacher to devote full attention to disabled readers while avoiding the management problem of having all the children in the room. The problem, however, is to arrange the time to suit the parents, the noon hour, the food service personnel, the crossing guards, and everything else affected by school schedules.

Evaluation The objective will be met if a special-help period is arranged that meets everyone's needs. It is a good idea to keep track of who has been helped during this time as well as what teachers and parents think about the plan. Periodic discussions should be held to see if modifications are called for because of unforeseen problems.

SUMMARY

Improved instruction for disabled readers can result from in-service programs directed toward student and staff reading needs that have been identified at the school and classroom level. Worthwhile in-service planning starts with those needs, establishes goals and objectives, selects activities, and evaluates results. Because it is crucial to match activities to the objectives in order to get at the instructional needs, it is a good idea to know how to use lectures, interviews, discussions, demonstrations, observations, buzz sessions, brainstorming, role playing, and contracts.

Also, preplanning is necessary in order to consider all of the factors that may work to enhance or inhibit changes. In addition, in-service leaders must know some strategies for increasing teacher and administrator commitment to change.

Finally, the two examples presented of in-service programs illustrate that reading in-service should take full advantage of the school as an optimal training ground for improving the teaching of reading.

REFERENCE

Duffy, Gerald G., and George B. Sherman "Improving Achievement Through Differentiated Instruction," in Gerald G. Duffy, ed., *Reading in the Middle School,* Newark, Del.: International Reading Association, 1974.

Biographies

Daniel A. Briggs holds undergraduate and master's degrees from SUNY at Albany and received his Ph.D. in reading from Syracuse University in 1958. For eight years he was Director of the Reading Center at Glassboro State College in Glassboro, New Jersey, for two years Director of the Reading Center at Oakland Schools in Pontiac, Michigan, and for eight years was Reading Coordinator for the Schenectady, New York, City School District. Dr. Briggs is now a member of the teacher education faculty at Russell Sage College, Troy, New York.

While in New Jersey, Dr. Briggs was a member of the Executive Board of the New Jersey Reading Association and was president of that group in 1964–65. He has served on the New York State Reading Association Board since 1971 and was chairman of the group's annual conference from 1971 to 1974. As a member of the Reading Examinations Committee of the Division of Teacher Education and Certification of the New York State Education Department, Dr. Briggs is working with the committee to establish exams to be used as one method of obtaining certification in reading. As Chairman of the Commissioner's Committee on Reading Certification, Dr. Briggs has been actively promoting statewide and national certification for reading teachers.

Florence C. Coulter holds B.S. and M.S. degrees from Glassboro State and an Ed.D. from the University of Pennsylvania. She has directed a reading internship program at Oakland Schools Intermediate District, Reading and Language Center in Pontiac, Michigan, for nine years. Prior to that she taught primary grades and remedial reading. She has been a visiting lecturer in reading diagnosis and remediation at the University of Michigan and the

University of Detroit. She also has been a program participant at conferences of the Michigan Reading Association and the International Reading Association.

Doris R. Entwisle holds a joint appointment as Professor of Social Relations and Engineering Science at The Johns Hopkins University, where she also received her Ph.D. in 1960. Her major areas of research interest include socialization of language and other cognitive behaviors, development of expectations in children, and methodological problems in social-psychological research. Professor Entwisle is the author of *Auto-Primer in Computer Programming* and *Word Associations of Young Children* and is a coauthor with W. H. Huggins of *Introductory Systems and Design* and *Iconic Communication: An Annotated Bibliography*.

Lawrence G. Erickson, Associate Professor of Reading at West Virginia University in Morgantown, received a Ph.D. in reading from the University of Wisconsin in 1972. He has taught elementary school and was an elementary principal for six years. He has also been a reading consultant. Currently he teaches graduate reading courses, conducts research, directs reading in-service programs, and trains school personnel to carry out school-based and district-wide in-service efforts in reading. He has published research articles and co-authored with Wayne Otto the IRA monograph *Inservice Education To Improve Reading Instruction*.

Shirley C. Feldmann is Professor of Education at the School of Education at the City College, CUNY, where she is head of the reading programs. Her research studies have been concerned with the reading acquisition of urban children. She has long been consultant for Children's Television Workshop, where she helped to plan "The Electric Company" and now advises on educational products and publications related to "Sesame Street" and "The Electric Company." She has a Ph.D. in educational psychology from Columbia University.

Gerald G. Freeman has been the Director of the Oakland Schools Speech and Hearing Clinic, Pontiac, Michigan, for 18 years. A graduate of the University of Michigan, he is a Fellow of The American Speech and Hearing Association, in which he has served on numerous committees and as Vice-President for Clinical Affairs. Dr. Freeman has been a visiting faculty member on the staff of seven universities. The author of several articles on the management of children with speech and language problems, he currently is editor of the journal *Language, Speech and Hearing Services in Schools*.

Burton W. Kreitlow, Professor of Continuing and Vocational Education at the University of Wisconsin, received his Ph.D. from the University of Minnesota. Since 1949 he has been Professor of Continuing Education at the University of Wisconsin—Madison. Previously he was an elementary teacher and county extension agent in Minnesota. His extensive research has been on school district organization, curriculum needs for graduate programs in adult education, and teaching improvement in adult basic education. His consulting and research have taken him to the Soviet Union, Nigeria, Taiwan, and England. More than 100 graduate students have completed work in adult education under his direction.

Peter P. Medrano received his M.D. in 1960 and did residency work in general and child psychiatry. In addition to his private practice, Dr. Medrano has served as a consulting psychiatrist to the Oakland and West Bloomfield, Michigan, Schools and as Chief, Preadolescent Service, Fairlawn Center, Pontiac, Michigan. He is currently a consulting psychiatrist at the Whaley Children's Center, Flint, Michigan, and is Director of Children's Services, Oakland County Community Health Board, Pontiac, Michigan.

Wayne Otto received his B.S., M.S., and Ph.D. from the University of Wisconsin. Formerly a public school teacher and professor at the University of Oregon and the University of Georgia, Dr. Otto is now Professor of Curriculum and Instruction and Associate Director of the Wisconsin Research and Development Center, University of Wisconsin—Madison. He is Executive Editor of the *Journal of Educational Research*, coauthor of *Corrective and Remedial Teaching*, principal investigator for the *Wisconsin Design for Reading Skill Development*, and author of research reports and instructional materials related to both developmental and corrective/remedial teaching.

Mark N. Ozer, M.D., is currently Associate Professor of Child Health and Development at the George Washington School of Medicine. His training in neurology emphasized the function of the brain rather than merely its structure. A postdoctoral fellowship at the Washington School of Psychiatry during 1964–65 related the behavior of brain-injured patients to the social context of the examination itself. He began to integrate principles of operant conditioning so as to study how one may change behavior during the examination. Since then, in daily work with children with learning and behavior problems, Dr. Ozer has developed assessment procedures that are themselves treatment programs in miniature and thus illustrate the process of child development one is trying to enhance. Ideas from cybernetics, general systems theory, and humanistic psychology have become increasingly influential in his work. He has also developed systems for the delivery of such approaches involving school and health personnel.

Charles W. Peters is a secondary reading consultant for Oakland Schools, Pontiac, Michigan, where he provides in-service training and program development for administrators and teachers in the more than 125 junior and senior high schools that make up the 28 school districts he serves. Since Dr.

Peters completed his Ph.D. at the University of Wisconsin—Madison in 1973, he has received the Outstanding Dissertation of the Year Award presented by the International Reading Association, taught at several universities and colleges, and published several articles in professional journals. He is currently serving as editorial consultant for two journals—the *Journal of Educational Research* and *The Epistle*.

Nathaniel A. Peters is Assistant Director of the Pontiac, Michigan, Oakland Schools Reading and Language Center, which provides consulting, clinical, and professional development training to 28 school districts in suburban Detroit. Dr. Peters earned his Ph.D. at the University of Wisconsin—Madison, his M.A. at Columbia University, and his B.A. at the University of Kansas. He is a school psychologist and is an active member of many professional organizations (American Psychological Association, Association for Children with Learning Disabilities, Council of Exceptional Children, and the International Reading Association). He has taught at the University of Wisconsin—Madison and is an adjunct instructor at Marygrove College, Detroit. He has published several articles in professional journals.

Alan Rhodes holds an M.A. in English from Arizona State University and is completing a Ph.D. in education, specializing in educational psychology and reading, at the University of California, Riverside. He has taught English and reading in public high schools for ten years. In 1973–74 he served as consultant to a Scripps College/National Endowment for the Humanities project for the development of programs for gifted high school students. He has written for the *Journal of Reading* and the *Yearbook of the National Reading Conference* (with Harry Singer). He is also interested in creative writing, and his stories and poems have appeared in several quarterly magazines.

Robert T. Rude has been an elementary school teacher, a remedial reading teacher, and a reading consultant. He presently teaches undergraduate and graduate courses at Rhode Island College, Providence, Rhode Island. He has published in professional journals and currently serves as a consulting editor to the *Journal of Educational Research*.

S. Jay Samuels received his doctorate in educational psychology and has done postdoctoral work in experimental child psychology. He taught grades two through six for ten years before coming to the University of Minnesota, where he is the Director of the Minnesota Reading Research Project and is studying how children become fluent readers. Dr. Samuels is a Fellow in the American Psychological Association and has been chairman of the Studies and Research Committee of the International Reading Association. In addition to his journal contributions, he is coediting *Perception and Comprehension in Reading* and editing *Research Implications for Reading*. He is a consulting editor for the *Journal of Educational Psychology* and the *Journal of Educational Research.*

Paul Satz obtained his Ph.D. in the Department of Clinical Psychology, University of Kentucky, in 1963. His clinical training was obtained at South Florida State Hospital, Hollywood, Florida; Speech Clinic, University of Kentucky; U.S. Public Health Hospital, Lexington, Kentucky; and at the following V.A. Hospitals: Lexington, Kentucky; Coral Gables, Florida; and Cincinnati, Ohio. After completing an NIMH postdoctoral fellowship, he joined the faculty in the Department of Clinical Psychology at the University of Florida in 1964. At present he is Professor of Psychology and Clinical Psychology and Director of the Neuropsychology Laboratory at the University of Florida.

Harry Singer received his Ph.D. from the University of California at Berkeley in 1960. After establishing the Reading and Study Skills Center at the University of Arizona, Tucson, in 1961–62, Dr. Singer was called back to the University of California at Riverside, where he had been a Lecturer in Educational Psychology in 1960–61. He is now Professor of Education, Chairman of the Reading and Language Development Committee, and Director of the Reading Specialist Program. In 1975–76, Dr. Singer provided in-service training to the faculty at Ontario High School, Ontario, California. Among his publications are *Speed and Power of Reading in High School* (with J. A. Holmes), *Preparing Content Reading Specialists for the Junior High School,* and *Theoretical Models and Processes of Reading* (with R. B. Ruddell).

Index

451